ART IN A CITY

BY THE SAME AUTHOR

The Theatre of Bertolt Brecht

and *Popski*. A Life of Vladimir Peniakoff DSO., MC

ART IN A CITY

John Willett

Liverpool University Press
and the Bluecoat

Published 2007 by
Liverpool University Press
4 Cambridge Street
Liverpool L69 7ZU
and
the Bluecoat
School Lane
Liverpool L1 3BX

First published by Methuen, 1967

British Library Cataloguing-in-Publication data
A British Library CIP record is available

ISBN 978-1-84631-082-9 paper

Project funded by the European Regional Development Fund, Arts Council England, Department for Culture Media and Sport and the Liverpool Culture Company. Working together for European Capital of Culture 2008.

Typeset by Koinonia
Printed and bound in the European Union by Biddles Ltd, King's Lynn

CONTENTS

INTRODUCTION
'Art in a city is not a static affair'

Much heralded as a seminal study of visual art's relationship to place, *Art in a City*'s impact has been felt widely beyond Liverpool, the city that it takes as its subject. Now, forty years after the book first appeared, I am delighted to introduce this re-publication of the study that the then Bluecoat Society of Arts commissioned from John Willett in 1962. There are several reasons why its reappearance is so timely.

First, as a piece of research about the history and development of the visual arts in Liverpool, it remains a key text, and – long out of print – has become increasingly difficult to track down. More than a conventional art history, Willett's identification of visual art's interaction with the worlds of poetry and music, for instance, was the first articulation of an interdisciplinary aspect to Liverpool culture and as such makes the book of value historically in this broader sphere. Secondly, it remains an instructive study concerning art and public, a book that was among the first to look seriously and in depth at art and society and whose historical significance deserves wider recognition for the agenda it set out. Thirdly, Willett's analysis of the particular character of Liverpool's culture, and his indication of what might be possible for the visual arts in particular to achieve, provide lessons for a city that finds itself at the start of the twenty-first century – as it did in the 1960s when the spotlight fell on it in the wake of the Beatles' phenomenal global success – with its cultural offer again being scrutinised. This time it is positioning itself as an international cultural destination, engaging with questions about the role of art in the process of economic regeneration, while the European Capital of Culture status bestowed upon the city for 2008 has in particular brought such concerns into sharp focus.

Art in a City contains recommendations that, while specific to an earlier age and a particular context, nonetheless offer an interesting blueprint for Liverpool's cultural aspirations that is worth revisiting, even if only to see how the cultural landscape has changed. The new socially accountable, instrumental role, for instance, that government-driven agendas are challenging the arts to adopt is a world away from art's earlier focus on aesthetic purpose, which Willett espoused and the Arts Council's founding 'arm's length' principle helped ensure. Yet the individual artist's relevance and responsibility to society was something that the writer was passionate about too. And as his quote taken for the title of this introduction says, art – like the city itself – does not stand still, and he would doubtless have been delighted to see the debate about the role of art in a transforming urban landscape once again occupying centre stage in Liverpool.

Bemoaning the lack of a sociology of the arts, Willett proposed his study as an attempt to show that a 'quite low-level investigation, based on the experience of a single English city, can not only be reasonably constructive but also might suggest conclusions of wider scope'. *Art in a City* exceeded these modest claims and remains the definitive survey of how art developed in Liverpool from the early nineteenth century to the 1960s. It is also a pioneering piece of research into art and its public, its findings here being of interest and value well beyond a purely local context. Even if the language we use to talk about art and audiences has changed, the relationships that Willett highlighted are still largely pertinent, not least the one between how art is made and how it is received, which he saw as inseparable: 'today nobody can view art as consumption or production alone'.

The sizeable gap identified by Willett between art and everyday life defined the problem to be addressed in the study, which in focusing on questions of taste, the education of the eye, and art's relationship to civic society and popular culture, set down a challenge for artists, arts venues, educators, social scientists, planners, policymakers, politicians – those who should be concerned with, and whom Willett saw as having the capacity for, making the arts more relevant to society. In *Art, Space and the City* Malcolm Miles cites *Art in a City* as the first attempt to interrogate public art, a term then still in its infancy, and its reception. The debate that Willett was instrumental in initiating 'opened up questions which it could not at the time answer',[1] and the study remained isolated within the literature on public art for almost thirty years, until publication in 1995 of Sara Selwood's *The Benefits of Public Art*.[2]

How then did *Art in a City* come about? The Calouste Gulbenkian Foundation had been established in 1956 as an enlightened trust that was to have a significant impact on the country's cultural map, its funds acting as a catalyst on arts, education and social welfare agendas. The Bluecoat Society of Art's relationship with the Foundation began in 1957 when it received funds to support young artists to work or study. Feeling, however, that the Society's efforts to stimulate the arts locally were getting nowhere and that nothing lasting was being achieved with the Gulbenkian grant, Nicholas Horsfield, an artist not at the time connected to Bluecoat, urged action. When invited to join the Society's working party he, together with

[1] Malcolm Miles, Art, *Space and the City*, Routledge, 1997, pp. 91–92.

[2] Sara Selwood, *The Benefits of Public Art*, commissioned by the Policy Studies Institute, Routledge, 1995.

the Director of the Walker Art Gallery, Hugh Scrutton, proposed the name of John Willett, assistant editor of the *Times Literary Supplement*, to undertake a study into the state of the visual arts in the city and make proposals for the future. Willett, known as the translator and scholar widely credited with bringing Bertolt Brecht to the English-speaking world, may not have appeared an obvious choice to investigate the prospects for contemporary art in a provincial English city. But Horsfield's hunch paid off, and the resulting report far exceeded expectations, becoming 'obligatory reading for anyone taking up an appointment in the region'.[3]

Commissioned in autumn 1962 to carry out the study, Willett began research early in the following year, intending it to take three months. It actually took till 1965, finally being published as a book by Methuen on behalf of the Bluecoat in 1967. In an interim report in the Liverpool *Daily Post* he outlined the scope of his research, which included questions such as why Liverpool no longer supported its artists as it had in the nineteenth century, why there was not a more flourishing art market, and how Liverpool rated as a centre for the arts. Subsequent features in the same newspaper provided glimpses of what would be in the book, as Willett articulated his main themes. These were very much informed by the city's post-war redevelopment context and coincided with Liverpool Corporation's recognition that wartime dereliction, still a visible scar on the city, offered unique prospects for physical and spiritual renaissance. Willett considered the plans drawn up in the first half of the 1960s by Shankland and Bor to redevelop the city centre as reversing the downward trend, 'post war lethargy turned into a source of strength'.

Seeing opportunities to integrate public art on a large scale into this process of regeneration, Willett analysed why public art works invariably failed: it was because of their conformity with prevailing good taste standards, their irrelevance to their setting and to their public, and their reliance on second-rate artists. Liverpool should learn from the model of European cities such as Rotterdam where works by major international figures such as Gabo and Zadkine had become emblematic of a rejuvenated city, while at the same time too much mediocre art commissioned for unremarkable buildings provided a lesson in what not to do. Liverpool had the material for a renaissance and its art could catch the public eye if artists and planners were brought together to work creatively. The city should have the ambition as well to attract international artists to teach, as Augustus John had done, in the city. And Willett saw signs of growing confidence in the city's arts institutions, the Walker Art Gallery for instance transforming itself, through the John Moores painting

[3] Nicholas Horsfield, catalogue to his exhibition at the Walker Art Gallery, 1997, pp. 43–44.

prize, into one of the finest galleries outside London, this prize becoming for young artists 'nearly as stimulating as those (biennials) of Venice, San Paolo and Paris, and in a way more accessible'.

In Liverpool Willett found a stronger and more active visual arts infrastructure than most English cities could boast, though one he felt not sufficiently appreciated by the city itself. Despite this he detected in Liverpudlians a generosity of spirit, an individuality that was 'congenial to our age', and an independence that, combined with civic determination for the visual arts, could create something distinctive. Something important could emerge if the city struck out on its own: a new look and new life for the city centre, a revival of Merseyside art resistant to London fashions, 'even perhaps a less artificial relationship between art and the rest of life'. Willett set out his recommendations in the book's final chapter, a plan of campaign that encompassed art in the public sphere, the teaching of art and its dissemination, and how it might be integrated into the life of the city. He saw no reason why Liverpool should not succeed in asserting herself visually as she had already done in music and sport.

On its publication, *Art in a City* received generally very favourable reviews. David Piper in the *Guardian* pointed out that, though published when Liverpool had attained a degree of fashionability with Merseybeat, football and Edward Lucie-Smith's anthology of the Liverpool poets, this 'idealistic and commonsensical report' had been commissioned *before* the city attained this credibility. With its posing of fundamental questions rarely asked about the motives of local patronage, and as a challenging first step towards discovering what art does socially for and to people, the book should be 'compulsory reading for all members of municipal art committees at least' and should be followed by a whole series of related studies across the country.[4] The *Scotsman* hailed the book as being 'as important as anything by Lewis Mumford or Herbert Read, and a good deal less idealistic'.[5] The *Times Literary Supplement* recognised Willett's achievement in pointing to a more imaginative future for the UK's large towns, a future informed by artists: 'It is a book like *Art in a City* that will create the artistic millennium this implies, if anything can, for it is well informed about the past, critical of the present, and hopeful of the future'.[6] The *Daily Telegraph* commented on the frankness of the report and noted, long before the rhetoric surrounding arts-led regeneration became so familiar, that 'an attractive place is likely to become more prosperous than a dreary one'.[7] The journal of the British

[4] David Piper, 'Art and its environment', *The Guardian*, 26 May 1967.

[5] Robert Nye, *The Scotsman*, 1967.

[6] *Times Literary Supplement* review, 17 August 1967.

[7] F. J. Salfeld, 'Renaissance in Liverpool', *Daily Telegraph*, 11 May 1967.

Sociological Association, *Sociology*, welcomed the book but felt that its survey – rudimentary compared to today's professional arts market research standards – on the public interest in art could have gone a lot further and been one of the publication's most valuable features.[8] And the book continues to be referenced. As recently as this year, David Briers writing in *Art Monthly* regarded the book as 'a thoughtful, thorough and outward-looking analysis' of Liverpool's visual arts, one that revealed a rich tradition of experimentalism informing, and stretching back long before, the decade of *Art in a City*'s publication.[9]

An exhibition, *Art in a City: The Liverpool Look*, was arranged by Willett at London's ICA in the summer of 1967, exploring the same themes as the recently published book and consisting of a mixture of paintings from Liverpool historic collections, contemporary works from the city's artists, documentation of the two cathedrals still being constructed, public art designs, 'indigenous' art from school children, amateur artists and hospital patients, a section on Liverpool poetry and happenings, and documentary photographs of the city. The exhibition provided a framework for a discussion series about city planning and art, patronage and the provinces, and possibilities for cities to express themselves through art.

The book's critical reception and subsequent function as a catalyst for debate about the role of art within changing cities reflects Willett's achievement in producing a study about a particular place that at the same time provided a template for wider discourse about art and society. But how was the book received in Liverpool at the time, and what immediate impact did it have on the city's cultural life? On receipt of Willett's report in 1965 the Bluecoat Society of Arts' response was positive, and despite disagreement with some of its more controversial findings, it was convinced that it should be published as a book, since its message was of significance for the whole of Liverpool and ought to 'inspire action in other cities'.[10] For the Bluecoat the report prompted its own actions: it set up an exhibitions committee, later enlarging the gallery and appointing a full-time director. This more formalised arrangement led to a continuous exhibitions programme, and laid the foundations for the Bluecoat to become a regionally, and ultimately nationally, recognised gallery over the next two decades. There were plans for a picture loan scheme in collaboration with the Liverpool Academy, and ideas to develop the Bluecoat Arts Forum bulletin into a more comprehensive visual arts publication.

[8] Brian Elliot, review in *Sociology: the Journal of the British Sociological Association*, 2.2, May 1968, p. 254.
[9] David Briers, review of the exhibition, *Centre of the Creative Universe* at Tate Liverpool, *Art Monthly* 306, May 2007, pp. 25–27.
[10] Bluecoat Society of Arts minutes of committee meeting, 30 December 1965.

To put Willett's ideas to the test in this wider environment, towards the end of 1967 the Bluecoat set up a 'Willett Working Party' chaired by Robert Gardner-Medwin, Professor of Architecture at Liverpool University. It consisted of representatives of relevant departments from the City Council, artists, academics, arts organisations and others involved in the teaching of arts. Its purpose was to drive forward the book's recommendations and implement its ten-point plan for the visual arts in the city. The Bluecoat also invited Willett to put forward his wider recommendations in a public meeting. These included a call for a city art adviser, free of City Council control, to guard against mediocrity in public art commissioning. The city planning officer's response, however, was that such control could not be relinquished – who otherwise would be the guardians of public taste? It was a response at once rebuffed by artist and poet Adrian Henri who pointed, as an example of local authority lack of vision, to recent council redevelopments in Toxteth. Here fine architecture had been demolished, bringing the spectre of homogenisation to an area whose special character had been instrumental in attracting and nurturing a vibrant artistic community, Liverpool's own bohemia.[11]

Needless to say, a Corporation-funded art adviser never materialised, and hopes for a dynamic public art programme to enliven a revitalised city centre faded as the decade approached its end. The city's reconstruction lacked the grand urban designs that seemed to offer so much during the optimism of the early 1960s, which in the following decades evaporated altogether as the city experienced a spiral of economic decline. A proposed design fellowship for the city did not materialise either, despite encouraging noises from the Granada Foundation, and other recommendations were not taken up. In retrospect it would seem that the city was not ready to embrace Willett's bold vision. Instead of the local authority taking on a more strategic and proactive role in cultural development, art education and art in the public realm, it fell to the new Merseyside Arts Association, mainly using regional funds devolved from the Arts Council of Great Britain, to at least provide modest support to enable the city's arts infrastructure to grow. And Willett's vision for art to move closer to and engage with the life of the city found an echo elsewhere, within the emerging community arts movement where initiatives such as the Great George's Community Project (the Blackie) sought a different, more grassroots engagement with local people, without compromising its commitment to working with artists of the avant-garde.

While *Art in a City*'s plan of action was not taken up wholesale at the time by those in a position to effect real change, in the years that followed

[11] Adrian Henri quoted in *Liverpool Echo*, 25 November 1967.

the book's publication much of what Willett advocated started to become a reality. His diagnosis of art in Liverpool was necessarily of its time; however, many of his ideas were eventually taken up, and it is no exaggeration to say that his vision for an art integrated into the urban environment is now being realised, and that art has become more commonly accepted as part of the fabric of daily life, with more people in the city than ever taking part in arts activities and Liverpool's pioneering approaches to innovative arts participation attracting attention nationally and internationally. When one looks at Antony Gormley's 'iron men' installation *Another Place* on Crosby beach, Richard Wilson's ingenious architectural intervention *Turning the Place Over* cut into the side of a building in Moorfields, or other ambitious, temporary public art works that have become such an important feature of the Liverpool Biennial, Willett was right to foresee that the city could be as bold and as adventurous as other cities who expressed their confidence through world-class public art. In this respect Willett pointed the way.

This prescience is reflected most notably in Liverpool's current infrastructure of visual arts venues and organisations, widely considered unparalleled outside London. Willett's belief that the city had the potential to take its place as an international centre for the contemporary arts was echoed in decisions such as the one to locate Tate's Northern gallery at Albert Dock in 1988, contributing to the regeneration of this area in the process. The establishment of the aforementioned Liverpool Biennial in 1999, the UK's largest visual arts festival, and the meteoric rise of FACT as a leading centre for artists working in moving image, are further examples of the confidence and international ambition of the visual arts in the city. The transformation of the Bluecoat Society of Arts, commissioners of the study in 1962, into a truly integrated arts space where art can be experienced from production to consumption emphasises Willett's belief in the organisation's catalytic role in the city's cultural life, building on a history as the UK's oldest arts centre. The Bluecoat is now about to reopen its doors following a major capital development of its building, designed by Biq Architecten from Rotterdam, one of the cities whose renaissance Willett points to in *Art in a City* for the lessons, good and bad, it can teach about the place of art in rejuvenating a city.

The huge regeneration developments currently being undertaken around the Bluecoat and elsewhere in the city appear as the most visible sign of an upturn in Liverpool's fortunes, a reflection of the feeling that the city has now, finally, turned the corner. The redevelopment plans of the 1960s, like others during that decade which promised to transform the UK's cities, failed. But whether this new optimism is unfounded or not, and whether the economic recovery turns out to be but a mirage, what is undeniable is the renaissance in creativity that the city is experiencing, which will be most visible to the outside world during European Capital of Culture in 2008. It is appropriate that the reappearance of *Art in a City* has come about as a direct result of this designation, its publication made possible with support from Liverpool Culture Company, following the initial enthusiasm of Robyn Archer, who regarded John Willett as her mentor and the book as her main introduction to the city. With Liverpool again resurgent, there is a parallel today with the opportunities that Willett envisaged for the visual arts not only to contribute to but to influence the urban regeneration process and to play a part in the daily life of the city and its inhabitants. A companion volume to *Art in a City* will be published in 2008, revisiting the book's themes from the perspective of what has changed in the visual arts in Liverpool in the forty years since its publication, including the extent to which the type of opportunities so imaginatively set out by Willett are being seized.

In conclusion, I should like to thank all those who have helped make possible this publication, a collaboration between the Bluecoat and Liverpool University Press. Robin Bloxsidge in particular at LUP has been instrumental in bringing the project to fruition and Jackie Malcolm at Liverpool Culture Company has been supportive throughout. I particularly want to thank John's widow, Ann Willett, for giving permission to reprint the text, and Sophie Wallace who carried out valuable research for this introduction. Finally on a personal note, this seems an appropriate occasion to express my gratitude to Nicholas Horsfield, who, having taught me at Liverpool Art School, was enormously helpful when I started work at Bluecoat. It was he who earlier had also been instrumental in getting the same organisation to invite John Willett to carry out this study. Sadly both men, who were lifelong friends to each other, are no longer alive and so are unable to see *Art in a City* in circulation again. I am sure, however, that they would both be delighted that the book still has the capacity to stimulate, enlighten and provoke, just as it did when it first appeared.

Bryan Biggs
Artistic Director, the Bluecoat
June 2007

LIST OF ILLUSTRATIONS

Art in a City was first published in 1967 and many images were uncredited or inadequately credited. Every effort has been made to identify the holders of copyright material included in this book and it is noted below where this has been possible. Liverpool University Press would be pleased to hear from copyright holders not identified below in order to give them recognition in corrected future editions of this book.

ACKNOWLEDGMENTS

This book was developed from a report to the Bluecoat Society of Arts, originally presented in autumn 1965 and commissioned thanks to a grant from the Calouste Gulbenkian Foundation. Opinions expressed in it are my own. I am very grateful to both bodies for making its publication possible. The Chairman and Committee of the Bluecoat Society have been helpful, informative, hospitable and patient over a long period. More than anything I hope that it proves of real value to them and to their city.

The city authorities were of the utmost help. Among those who gave me their time were the Lord Mayor (Alderman David J. Lewis), the Town Clerk, the City Architect, the City Planning Officer and the Planning Consultant (both of whom supplied me generously with any material I asked for), the Director of Education and his Art and Crafts Adviser, the City Librarian and the City Public Relations Officer. Alderman H. Macdonald Steward of the Planning Committee and Councillors Shaw, Bessell and Heffer of the (then) Arts Sub-Committee all saw me. The Director of the Walker Art Gallery, his Deputy and his staff co-operated in a great number of ways; my job would have been very much harder without them. The Principal of the College of Art and the heads of the Department of Printing and the Schools of Graphic Design and Teacher Training gave me every facility.

The gallery kindly submitted my questionnaire to its visitors, as did Littlewood's Mail Order Stores to its staff, and Gateacre Comprehensive School to its staff and pupils. I am grateful to all those who answered it so carefully, to Susan Beckett, Paul Eachus, L. M. Green, Susan R. Hasleton and Suzanne Stuart of the College of Art who helped with the interviewing, and to Mr Ainsworth, Mr Baillie, Mr Ellison, Mr Howey, Mr Maskell and Mr Panther on whom I first tested the questions.

Colonel Vere E. Cotton gave me much information from his long experience and lent me valuable papers. Brian Patten, Roger McGough and Adrian Henri generously allowed me to reprint their poems. Dr Joan Evans in London gave me an advance view of her most interesting book on *The Conways*. The editor of the *Liverpool Post* printed three articles in which I aired some of the book's ideas. Mr Bor, Mr Scrutton, Mr Norman, Professor Quentin Bell, Roderick Bisson, John Rees-Jones, Mr Patchin, Sir Emrys Williams and (of the artists) Messrs Horsfield, Ballard, Dooley, Henri, MacKarell and Jardine were kind enough to check relevant sections of the typescript, and a number of amendments of fact are due to them. Sources of photographs have been given separately on page xiii, but I would like here to thank Jürgen Seuss, G. C. Macpherson, Robin Riley, Quentin Hughes, Ralph Fastnedge, Richard Huws, L. Ruscoe, Mr David Wood of Pilkingtons and Roderick Bisson and the Sandon Studios Society for the trouble they took to make prints available.

In a long series of visits to Liverpool so many other people also saw me that I can only try to list them, hoping that omissions will be put down to incompetence rather than ingratitude: Michael Argles (Institute of Education), C. B. Barber (W. R. Jacob and Co.), Leslie Blond, F. C. Boydell, the Headmaster of Breckfield SMS and Messrs Allan, McConkey and Moffat of his staff, Robert Buckley (Stanley Park SMS), Denis Chapman, James Cliffe, Patrick Cohen, Mr Colley of the College of Technology, J. L. Crockatt (Johnson Brothers), Norman Cullen, Mr Davey of J. Davey and Sons, John Eames, the late John Edkins, R. L. Ellis (Dunlops), K. H. Evans, Mrs Featherstone, A. W. Fraser (Rainhill Hospital), Professor and Mrs Fröhlich, the art staff of Gateacre CS (G. C. Drewitt and Messrs Jamieson, Jones, Lewis and Mrs Rooke), E. Gledhill (Kirkby College of Further Education), Mr Godwin of British-American Tobacco, Eric Goldrein, John Gorman, J. A. Haddy (College of Building), the late Neville Hill, Harry Hoodless (Laird School of Art, Birkenhead), C. D. Humphries (Medici Society), the Rev. J. Keir Murren, Dr T. Kelly (University Extra-Mural Department), P. L. Kemp (University Assistant Registrar), G. R. Kennerley, Norman Kingham, Frank Lambert, Sean Leak (St Martin's SMS), the Rev. W. Lockett, R. S. McArthur (Bootle School of Art), W. S. MacCunn, D. M. M'Farquhar (Art High School), the Very Rev. Mgr. McKenna, Dr R. F. McMahon (College of Technology), the Headmaster of Maghull GS, John Metcalfe (Goodlass Wall), G. Moyes (Birkenhead College of Technology), Mr Naylor of Winwick Hospital, the Headmistress of New Heys High School and Miss Monks and Miss Thearle of her staff, Miss M. W. Odell (Mabel Fletcher Technical College), Morton Oliphant, the late S. Pater (Weightman and Bullen), E. C. Roberts (College of Technology), Eric Rowan, John Roxburgh, the Deputy Headmaster of Ruffwood CS, D. R. Scarland (Bluecoat School), E. R. Scott (Lever Brothers), A. Shand (Evans Medical), Professor Lord Simey, Rodger Smith, W. H. Smith's Liverpool Manager, G. J. Stephens (British-American Tobacco), W. L. Stevenson

(Littlewoods), Mrs and Miss Sutcliffe, George Thomas, Sam Walsh, Mr and Mrs Colin Wilson and Professor H. Myles Wright. I would also like to thank Mr and Mrs Roy Burlend for making the visits in question so agreeable, often at very short notice.

Elsewhere I saw the Musée Royale des Beaux-Arts in Antwerp, the Arts Council, Centre 42, the Civic Trust, the Council of Industrial Design, Alexander Dunbar (North East Association for the Arts), Granada Television, the Hochschule für Bildende Kunst in Hamburg, Astrid Kirchherr, the LCC, Peter Markmann, the Rotterdam City Council (Afd. Kunstzaken), the Royal College of Art (Industrial Design Department) and Mr Sheridan Russell. Others who gave information by letter or telephone included Thomas Agnew and Sons Ltd., the Town Clerk of Antwerp, the Automatic Telephone and Electric Co. Ltd., Sir Gerald Barry, the BBC (Liverpool), the Belgian Ministry of Education, the West Berlin Senator for Bau-und Wohnungswesen, Birkenhead Hospital Management Committee, Blackburn's (Liverpool) Ltd., Arthur Blenkinsop MP, Bootle Technical College, the Mayor of Boston, the Boston Museum of Fine Arts, BICC Further Education Centre, P. J. Broomhall and Partners, Richard Buckle, John M. Caven (Boots), Mrs Joan B. Clarke, Clatterbridge Hospital, the Conway Librarian (Courtauld Institute), William Crawford and Sons Ltd., S. J. Cross (Norwich), the Cunard Steam-Ship Co. Ltd., Deva Hospital Management Committee, Stanley Dumbell, Elder Dempster Lines Ltd., the Estates Officer of Liverpool University, the Ford Motor Co. Ltd., the Town Clerk of Genoa, Alfred Holt Ltd., John A. Hunter Ltd., ICI Paints Division, the International Association of Plastic Arts, Lamport and Holt Line, George Henry Lee and Co. Ltd., the secretary of Littlewoods' Sculptural Design Competition, Liverpool and District Fazackerley Group of Hospitals Management Committee, Liverpool Chamber of Commerce, Liverpool College of Commerce, Liverpool Region Children's Hospital Management Committee, Liverpool Regional Hospital Board, the London Group, London Press Exchange, Market Investigations Ltd., the Mayor and Prefect of Marseilles, Canon Martineau, Mass Observation, N. K. Michael, Ambassador Bowling, the National Gallery, North Liverpool Hospital Management Committee, the North Western Gas Board (Mersey Group), North Wirral Hospital Management Committee, Old Swan Technical College, Owen Owen Ltd., Eduardo Paolozzi, Pilkington Brothers Ltd., Queens Drive Evening Institute, Rainhill Hospital Management Committee, the Royal Academy, the Royal Institute of British Architects, the Royal Society of British Artists, Shaw Street Evening Institute, Sir Alfred Shennan and Partners, South Liverpool Hospital Management Committee, the Tate

Gallery, Mrs Thompson, Peter Walker (Warrington) Ltd, Wallasey Technical College, Walton Technical College, Widnes College of Further Education, Winwick and Newchurch Hospital Management Committee, Andrew McLaren Young, Philip N. Youtz. The getting of information from abroad would have been much harder without the help of HM consular representatives in Antwerp, Boston, Gdynia, Genoa, Marseilles and Rotterdam. I am only sorry that the efforts of Mr D. S. Clarke of the British Council were in vain.

I would like to thank the Bluecoat Society's secretaries, Mr and Mrs Van Mullem, for their many kindnesses, as well as Mrs Cowin and Mrs Ashcroft for help with paperwork. Perhaps my main personal debt is to those who asked me to do the job and to my editor and employers who allowed me to spend so much time on it. Place and people have made it, in all sorts of ways, an unforgettable experience.

1 : PROBLEM AND PLACE

Art and society: over the past hundred years or so these words have become inseparables, till today their coupling produces an automatic yawn. They are as much of a pair as oil and vinegar, or chalk and cheese; like them they owe their association in our minds largely to the fact that they don't mix. Whose fault this is is open to endless debate: you can blame the present-day artists for talking an unduly private language, or the public for making too little effort to understand them, or the critics and educationalists for failing to reconcile the two groups, or the private or public patron for refusing to support the artists in the meantime or for backing the wrong ones. You can shrug your shoulders and say that the discrepancy is natural to an aimless, fragmented, alienated or godless social system: that it is just a symptom of larger human disasters. The fact itself remains a commonplace: art is cut off from our society by a sizeable gap.

It is remarkable how few constructive ideas this has led to. One would-be scoutmaster after another has rubbed the two terms vigorously together in the hope of producing sparks, but so far there have been clouds of smoke and remarkably little fire. The one or two instances this century where a coherent doctrine of art and society has emerged have been the work of politicians or at best political theorists, who felt entitled to impose their views on the world of art and, as it were, declare the gap closed by decree. Such remedies however are not just superficial and deceptive; they actually make any lasting reconciliation the more remote by discrediting the very word 'society' in the ears of the more independent-minded artists and critics. Except in the field of architecture, with its more obvious social relevance, there is now no vision of the relationship between the two concepts which could act as a stimulus to the visual arts. Though plenty of artists are worried or dissatisfied at their apparent incompatibility there is no inspiring alternative to work for.

But suppose we were to start at the other end. Suppose that instead of theorising from the highest artistic and social principles we were to take a close look, somewhere near ground level, at the situation of the visual arts in a particular community: might this not lead to fresh conclusions, not so much about the ideal relationship in theory but about the network of actual relationships on the ground? Might it not suggest ways in which they could be improved? At least the experiment ought to be worth trying. And yet oddly enough this is just what is never done. In no country is there more than the first rudiments of a sociology of the arts: a tradition of inquiry into all those outside factors – psychological, economic, social, administrative, ideological – on which the practice of art at any given time and place depends. Instead we treat works of art as god-given pieces of inspiration, finding it unnecessary to ask exactly what they do to people, or who paid for them and from what motive, or quite simply how they came to be there. Our instinct is to regard such questions as sacrilege. Our mistake is to feel that wrapping up art in a woolly cocoon of words must enhance it: that analysis can only destroy.

The report which follows is an attempt to show that a quite low-level investigation, based on the experience of a single English city, can not only be reasonably constructive but also suggest conclusions of wider scope. It sets out to see what tasks and possibilities exist for the visual arts in the city; how they have been fulfilled in the past and what the tradition is; how the various sections of a community appear to support art or reject it, together with their apparent tastes and motives; what the resources in local talent are, both actual and potential; and what policy the public authority follows in its schools and galleries. From all this flows a set of specific proposals designed to set the visual arts in a new framework: that of a modern community's interests, plans and needs. Where most proposals for the visual arts, in this country at least, amount to a demand for more of everything – more exhibitions, more artists, more prizes, more pictures for the public collections, more art history, more arts centres, more committees and above all more money – these aim rather to establish a relationship on new lines.

The community under discussion is the city of Liverpool, which not only contains perhaps the best municipal art gallery in England but has long harboured an active body of professional artists. In 1962 the Bluecoat Society of Arts there (a body described in Chapters 2 and 3) decided that its attempts to encourage painting and sculpture locally were not producing results, and that its policy in these matters needed rethinking. Accordingly it looked for an independent outsider who would make a general survey of the visual arts in Liverpool: of needs, demands, openings, and the individuals and institutions available to fulfil them. A Londoner himself, the author is glad that the choice fell on him. Quite apart from the sheer interest of the problem and the sometimes rather unfamiliar directions in which it led, it is difficult to have much to do with Liverpool without developing a special affection for the place. A special affection, because it also embraces exasperation and

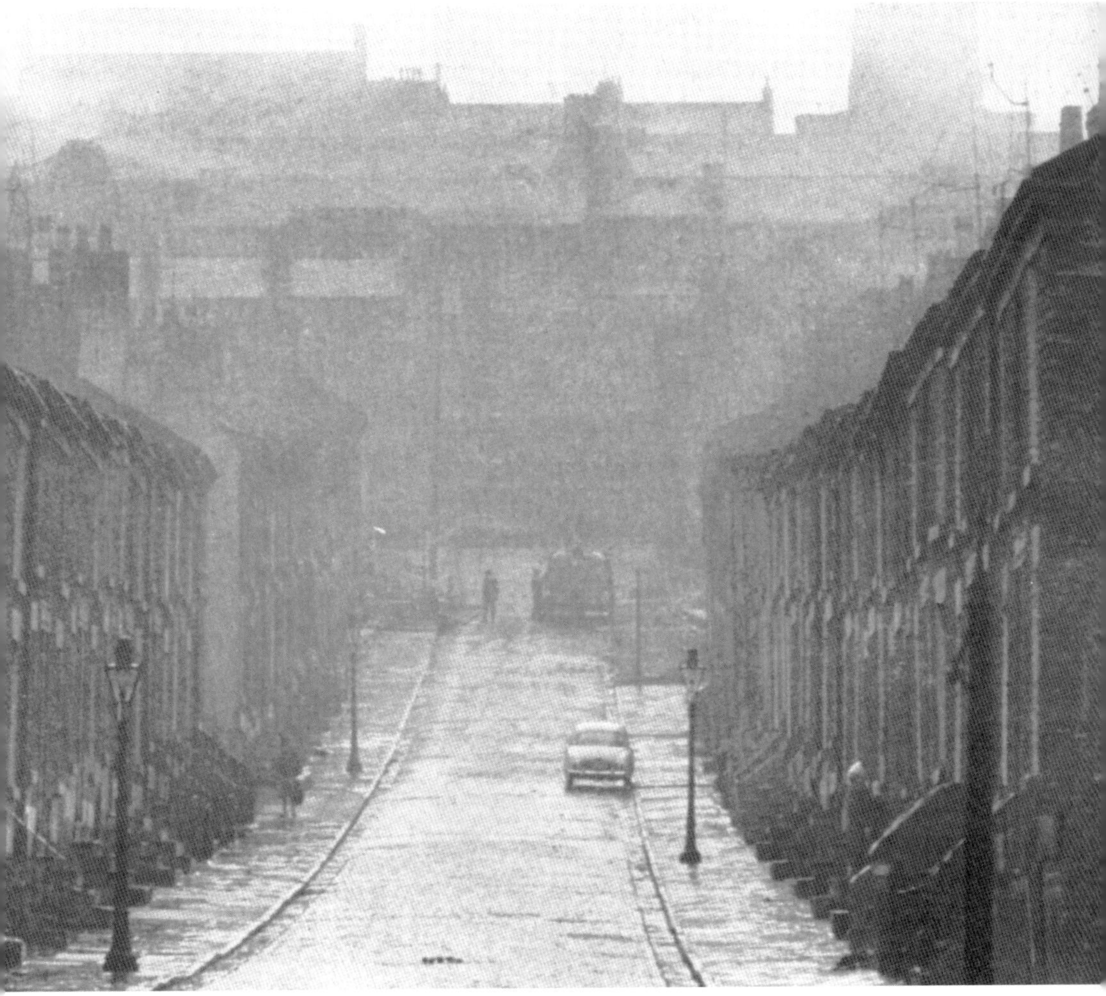

1 Liverpool 1965. Looking eastwards towards the ridge that forms the city's spine

regret at the conditions in which many of its inhabitants have had to live.

There is nowhere like Liverpool, and as it is the background to everything that follows we had best start with an account of its particular characteristics and of the situation in which it now finds itself, at least as far as seems relevant to this report. Like Antwerp, Rotterdam and Bremen (with which more detailed comparisons will be made in Chapter 8) it is a great port of about three-quarters of a million inhabitants, with all the openness and curiosity that this implies. But these three-quarters of a million are an unusually mixed lot, and Liverpool's peculiar scurrying liveliness may well be due to the fact that its inhabitants are tugged in a number of directions.

They represent many races: the Irish – for this is still the cheapest crossing to England from Dublin – the Welsh whose hills one can (with luck) see in the distance, the native English of course, the West Indians and – more noticeable than their actual numbers would suggest – a small but centrally-located colony of Chinese. They are of mixed religion, with Catholic and Protestant more or less balancing one another, though the old fierce hostility has now given way to a keen mutual awareness. Politically they have been unable to relax into the common post-war stupor, for since 1945 power in the city council has passed from Labour to Conservative and back again, and the regular dismissal of the vanquished party's aldermen makes for an unusually quick turnover in municipal life. All this combines to give the Liverpool character its very individual stamp.

One sees it immediately in the children. It is hardly possible to imagine a stronger contrast than that between the children of Hamburg, neatly tucked into their hats, coats and gloves, with their well-ordered ways, their satchels tightly strapped on their backs, and the swarming Liverpool kids, off like small rodents on their own private or collective affairs, remote from grown-up control. Right in the middle of the town you see these anarchic apparitions,

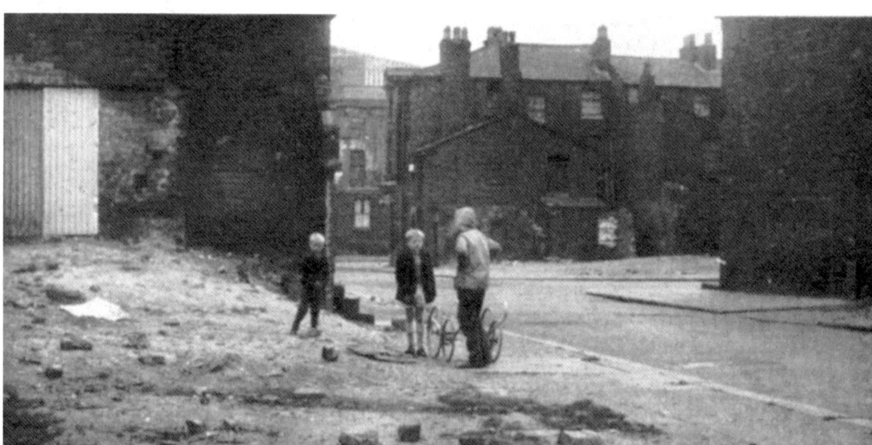

2 Liverpool 7. Children on a derelict site close to the University

exceedingly startling to the unprepared visitor, but at the same time suggesting a certain profound freedom in which exceptional qualities might be developed. Something of the same outward abandon is visible in their elders, as they convert the main shopping streets into virtual pedestrian precincts on a Saturday afternoon, contemptuously ignoring the power and dignity of the motor-car. It is not surprising that they should as a community be at once open- and independent-minded, quite willing to be influenced by the best Dutch and Viennese models in their prewar housing policy, for instance, or to introduce a French system of prefabricated housing now, yet always loath to be in any way linked with Manchester, only 36 miles away.

Physically the centre of the city is dominated by a long ridge about 150 feet high running parallel to the river Mersey and the 6 miles of docks that line it. On this stand the two cathedrals and the university, and between and around them what used before the middle of the last century to be the elegant residential area: square-cut terraces of dull red brick, interestingly greyed by the old local practice of mixing cinders in the mortar, and sometimes bearing in handsome cast-iron lettering the great Liverpool names of the period; Canning and Huskisson Streets for instance record the city's two most famous early nineteenth-century MPs. Across the edge of this area runs

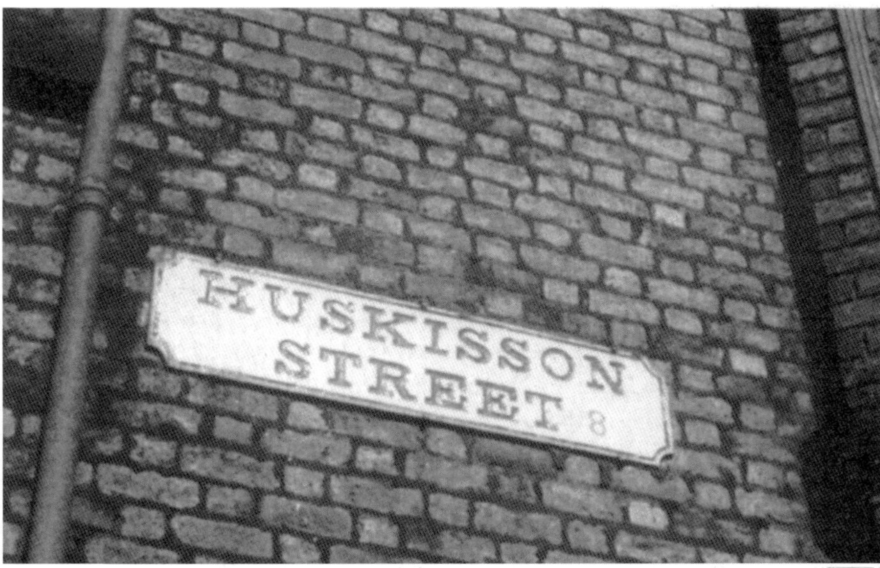

3 Liverpool 8. Cast-iron; red brick; black mortar; great nineteenth-century names

the deep cutting of the old Liverpool and Manchester Railway, blasted in the solid red sandstone of which Giles Gilbert Scott built his cathedral, but walled off and invisible from above. The docks, though some of the older among them are unforgettably impressive, like the wholly enclosed early nineteenth-century Albert Dock with its arcaded warehouses, are similarly

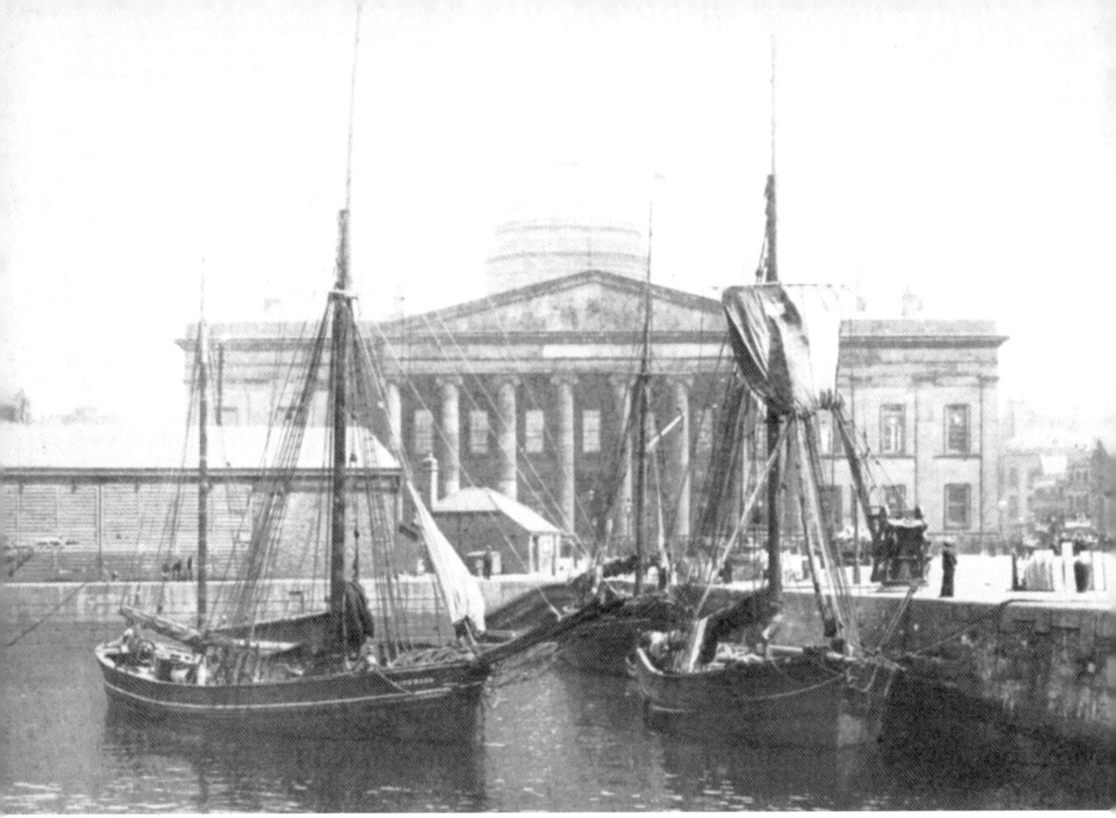

4 The Customs House (1828) by John Foster, Junior, the best-known Liverpool architect of the early Industrial Revolution. Gibson's statue of Huskisson (see illustration 23) originally stood in front of the building, which was destroyed in the Second World War

shut off from view; the splendid vistas down to the river with its shipping which might be expected from the tilt of the land just don't exist. It is one of the great town-planning mistakes of Liverpool that except for the misleadingly-called Pier Head in the middle, with its messy-looking landing-stages, and the Dingle in the south where the ridge actually seems to hang right over the docks, all that can be seen of the waterfront is a high wall with heavy gates in it. As the late City Planning Officer said, Liverpool seems to turn its back on the sea.

Its buildings bear witness to the Industrial Revolution, to the days when, well ahead of the rest of the world, steam brought it prosperity. The tall warehouses with their narrow recesses for hoists set back in the brick facades, the factories and workshops crowding in towards the city centre, the great black commercial buildings, the unmistakeable pubs built by Walker's of Warrington, with a certain comforting opulence, in the domesticated Art Nouveau of the end of the century; these, interwoven with late Georgian back streets containing many small classical details, are the characteristic architecture of the place. Unlike so much of the rest of Lancashire, or indeed

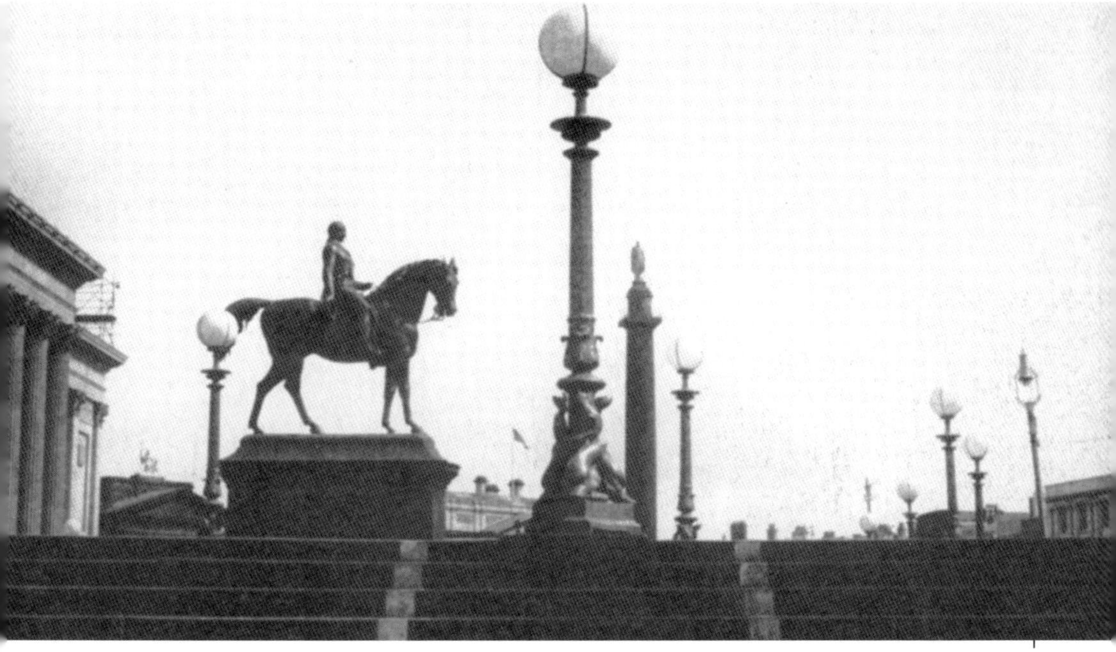

5 The nineteenth-century presence. In front of the St George's Hall portico, with the Prince Consort on horseback, Wellington on his column (right, centre) and (in the distance half-left) the symbolical figure of Commerce on the Walker Art Gallery

of all Victorian England from the Houses of Parliament down, it is not Gothic. It was one of the points of insistence of the leaders of the Liverpool Royal Institution, which dominated the city's artistic and intellectual life after the Napoleonic wars, that a classical revival was the proper architectural expression for a booming mercantile community; and the building of St George's Hall in the 1840s meant that the formal core of the city – library, museum, art gallery, county sessions court and college of technology spreading along the slope to one side of the great public hall – is in a grandly classical style. Even later the dislike of Gothic persisted, most notably when the late Sir Charles Reilly came to be Professor of Architecture at the beginning of this century. The Anglican cathedral constitutes a single massive exception. Otherwise the buildings of central Liverpool seem, consciously or not, to reflect its early leaders' feeling that the Industrial Revolution was a second Renaissance.

At present this is scarcely appreciated except by architectural enthusiasts, for the change in the city's fortunes has been too overwhelming for most of its inhabitants to see the nineteenth-century legacy as anything but a terrible and cramping handicap. As England began to lose her position as the world's leading manufacturer to Germany and the United States – this was something that Conway, the first Liverpool Professor of Fine Art, already saw to be happening at the turn of the century[1] – and far more so after the 1914–18 war, Liverpool became one of the most vulnerable communities in our whole precarious economy. Nobody can forget the unemployment of the 1930s,

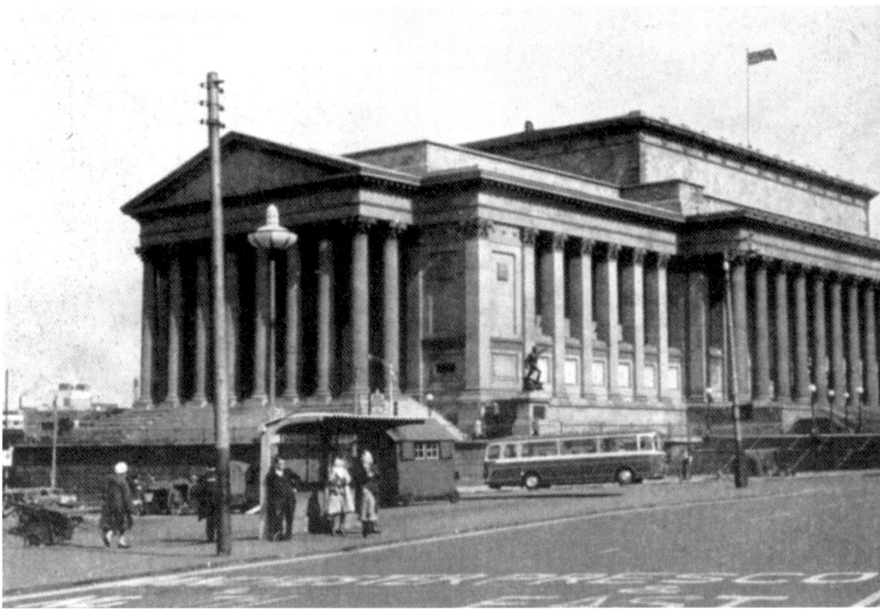

6 St George's Hall in 1965. The abominably-designed bus shelter and the fancy lamp standard have since been removed, but there are new and disfiguring signs on gantries over the street

and even today the visitor continually sees, as he does not in London or in comparable foreign ports, the symptoms of a population living close to the margin: too many poorly dressed children and old people; wretched shops in the poorer districts; dockers and labourers who show few outward marks of the social changes of the last twenty years. Today the wealthier citizens have moved away from the city centre, leaving the once elegant terraces to be invaded by a different kind of tenant, Irish, Chinese, coloured, with their children and their clubs and their various street debris. Rateable values have fallen; trees can no longer be planted in public places because of the general destructiveness; people who would once have supported intelligent evening

[1] See his *The Domain of Art;* John Murray, 1901, pp. 85–6.

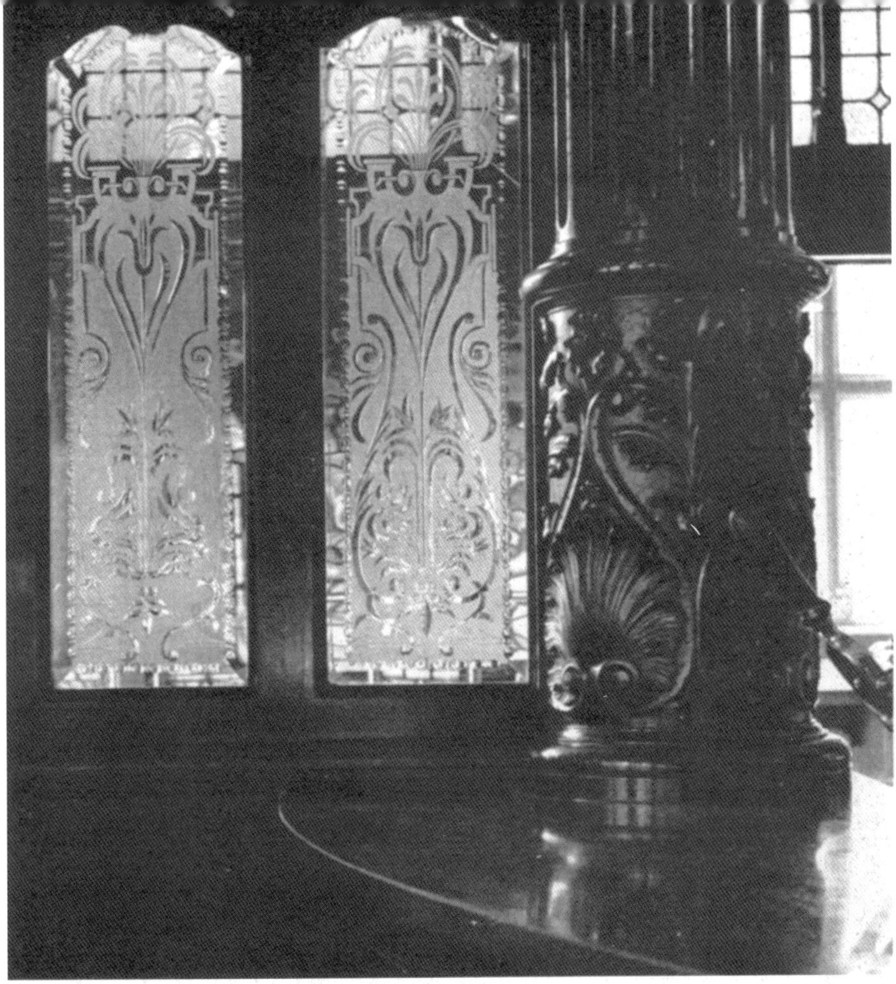

7 & 8 Apogee of the Liverpool public house. *Above:* In the Philharmonic Hotel, built between 1898 and 1900 with the co-operation of members of the University Appeal Arts department. *Below:* The Crown Hotel in Lime Street, before its defacement by advertising signs. Both these houses belong to Walker's, the firm that gave the city its art gallery.

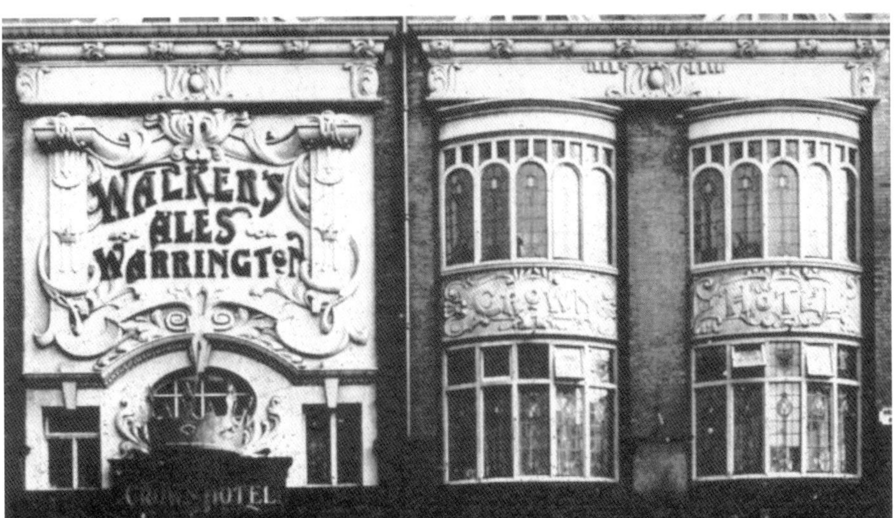

entertainment and served in local government have in many cases gone to live outside. Even the University is dead at weekends or after working hours.

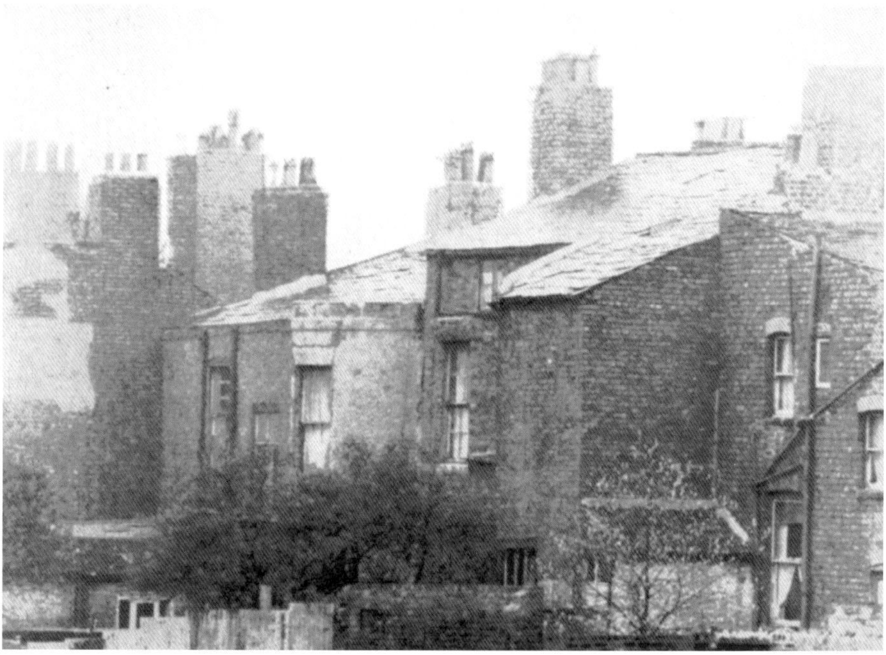

9 The darker side of a heritage: some of the housing

A recent attempt to keep the senior common room bar open in the evenings drew only two visitors in an entire term.

What so often impresses people about the physical make-up of Liverpool is neither the dingy grandeur of its buildings nor their special power to express its history, but above all the dirt, the poverty and the slums, now seen as a legacy of the 'Victorian' age, even though they are quite equally the result of our own century's inability to cope. These slums run mainly north and south behind the docks, starting almost from the centre of the town; even inland it is not until one reaches the new suburbs built in the 1930s that there are well-planned residential districts other than a few shabby areas of former grandeur. The problem has become overwhelming. In 1963 there were 27,000 dwellings that had been condemned and ought to be demolished and a further 61,000 that had been declared due (which means overdue) for major repair; thus, with an average of 3.32 persons per dwelling in the city as a whole, it could be said that roughly 300,000 of Liverpool's population were living in conditions officially recognized as intolerable. No city council since 1939 has come near to solving this. And even the areas of new housing are hardly attractive by the standards of, say, Bremen or Rotterdam. Kirkby, the brand-new suburb outside the city boundaries to the north-east, is the most commonly criticised for its poor amenities and lack of social coherence; but

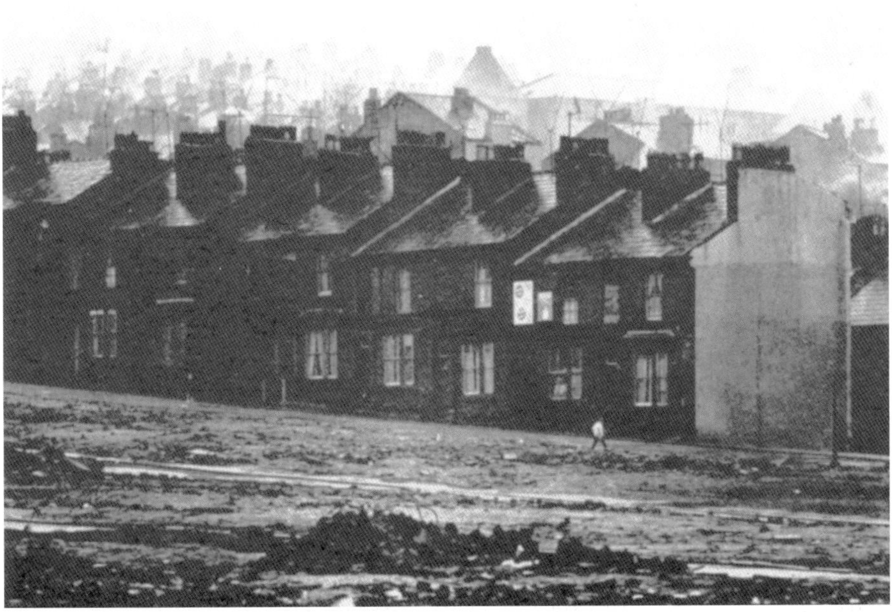

10 In the slum belt

Kirkby is still running in, as it were, and seems on every count preferable to the barrack-like district of Speke, built in sub-Georgian style and laid out with grisly symmetry in a treeless waste at the southern tip of the city[1].

It is this burden of poverty and bad planning that has largely decided Merseyside's reputation, not only with the outside world – which is bad enough, as it makes it difficult to attract fresh talent and fresh resources – but, more demoralisingly, with many of its own inhabitants. And yet in spite of every temptation to defeatism there has traditionally been a certain boldness about many of the city's ideas. 'If a thing's big', said Ben Shaw, who was Labour's chairman of the council's Arts Sub-Committee till 1965, 'it'll get big support. If it's little we'll just dodder around.' Two cathedrals are now going up in Liverpool: Scott's Anglican one, started some sixty years ago and still slowly going forward, and Frederick Gibberd's revolutionary Catholic structure, founded on the huge crypt that remains from Lutyens's original plan. The Mersey Tunnel was another great communal effort (which is now being repeated with a second tunnel half a mile further north), while the resources put into the Royal Liverpool Philharmonic Orchestra, the Walker Art Gallery or the two great football teams, Liverpool and Everton, would seem remarkable even in a much more prosperous society. There is a largeness of spirit here which contrasts unexpectedly with the various symptoms of decline.

Partly this is due to the strong tradition of independence and local pride among the heads of the older Liverpool businesses, which such newcomers

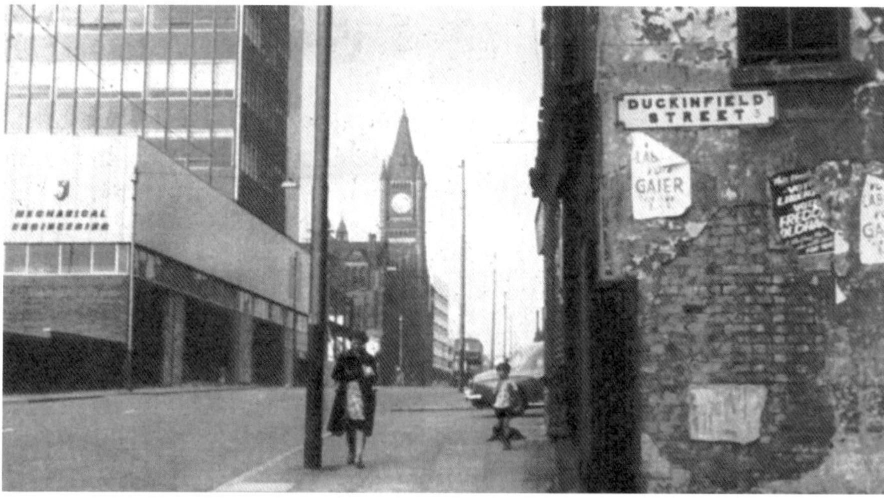

11 Liverpool University in its setting, showing the original red stone building by Alfred Waterhouse. In size and seniority it is the fifth English university

as the football pools have tried to emulate. Local government itself may have been weakened by the drift away from the old residential areas, and by the fact that retired people of real ability tend to settle elsewhere; but there is an enlightened Establishment, however small, which has something like a nineteenth century sense of duty. The urge to self-government remains strong, and both this and the sense that Commerce must be the chief cultural patron in the industrial age have long determined the city's attitude to the arts. Wherever these are accepted as a credit to the community and an essential part of its equipment they are generously supported. As will presently be seen, the Art Gallery now not only has one of the biggest annual purchase grants from the rates allowed to any English provincial gallery, but also gets larger sums from local industry and trade than probably any gallery outside the United States.

Under these contradictory impulses there have in the recent history of the town been waves of hope and deep troughs of apathy. There was a remarkable period of reconstruction in the 1930s, when the garden-city-like suburbs were built, with well-lit double carriageway roads running through them: a development that was far ahead of what most English municipalities, including the London County Council, were doing at that time. Then came the war, and with it the destruction of a great part of central Liverpool. For nearly twenty years the opportunity which this presented for a radical replanning of the city was not taken. Planning, as in so many English towns even today, was one of the subsidiary responsibilities of the City Engineer, and the 1947 city plan was hardly a document to fire the imagination. Nor was it put into effect. Two of the principal shopping streets were rebuilt by private enterprise on the old alignments, partly as a result of the well-intentioned views of the late Sir Alfred Shennan, chairman of the city's Post-War Redevelopment Committee and himself the architect of Littlewood's Spinney House, the Pearl Assurance in Lord Street and one or two others of the more deplorable of the new buildings. But where the great bulk of the bombed area was concerned nothing was done at all. No great city outside England, and few inside, have been so slow to set themselves straight after the war, and for a long while the effect on the citizens was, to say the least of it, disheartening. Decline breeds decline. If the centre of a city is allowed to run down the rate income from it drops accordingly; the authorities become less and less able to pay for remedial measures; the richer inhabitants drift off, taking many of the frills of life with them; the attraction offered to new industries and new immigrants grows steadily less. Once this process begins it is difficult to see how it can ever be reversed.

It was against this background that the present inquiry was commissioned, and the past history of the city, from the heady optimism of the post-Napoleonic era to the disillusionments of the 1950s, will be seen to underly much of the eight chapters that follow, as well as some of the positive proposals put forward in the tenth. But cities are always on the move, particularly such mercurial communities as this one, and from the very start of the undertaking Liverpool has been rising on another great wave which has not only made its name known throughout the world but taken it a good way towards permanent recovery. The public symptoms of this new Merseyside renaissance hardly need reciting: on record and as performers the Beatles were the great world-beaters of 1964; Liverpool won the Association Football Cup in 1965 and the League championship in 1966; Everton won the Cup in 1966; Ken Dodd was the top British entertainer of 1965; Liverpool poets and novelists are beginning to become known, notably with Sean Hignett's *A Picture to Hang on the Wall*, published in autumn 1966; the new Roman Catholic cathedral is about to be consecrated now. At the same time however, though much less conspicuously, a major planning operation has been started which looks like taking Liverpool purposefully and efficiently into the

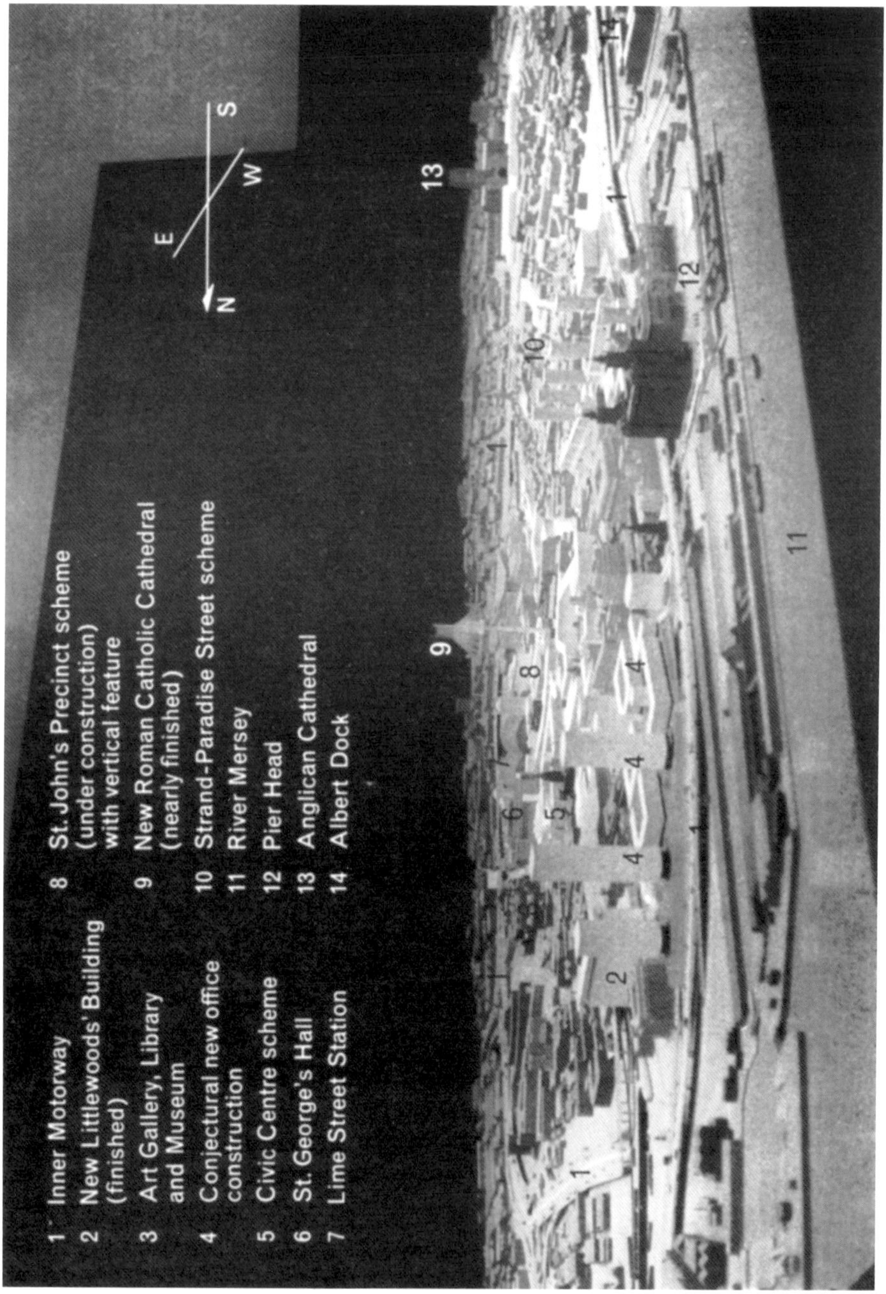

12 A new plan for Liverpool. Model showing the city centre, as planned for the corporation by Graeme Shankland and Walter Bor. From the permanent planning exhibit in the Walker Art Gallery

twenty-first century. The result is that there is not only a real spirit of revival in the city but also a new framework, new tasks, new opportunities for the visual artist. It is difficult for the printed word to keep pace with any situation which is developing quite so quickly. The reader must none the less try to bear in mind the probable or projected future. It belongs to the background quite as much as does the Liverpool we know.

What the city did, on the initiative of the former chairman of the Special Redevelopment (1961–2) and Planning Committees (from 1962 to 1963) Harold Macdonald Steward MP, was to appoint two of the leading architect-planners from the London County Council: first Graeme Shankland, who was brought in early 1962 as a consultant to replan the central area, then Walter Bor, who became the first City Planning Officer at the end of the same year, and set up a permanent City Planning Department. These two and their respective teams have worked very closely together and produced a succession of radical reports, proposing a whole new shape for the city; both parties in the Council have backed them, and important parts of the ensuing plan are already being executed or passing through the legislative stage. It really is as if the downward trend were being reversed and Liverpool's long postwar lethargy turned into a source of strength. As the 1965 City Centre Plan puts it, the derelict or underdeveloped areas are so extensive and the proportion of municipally-owned land so high as to

> present redevelopment opportunities unequalled by any other major city in this country and few in the world. Large areas of comprehensive development are therefore feasible and they, in turn, make the creation of a new and attractive urban environment an early possibility in several parts of the city centre.[1]

This could no doubt have been said at any time since the war. The difference now is that action is being taken.

The first outlines of a new city are there for all to study, and they, together with the calibre of the men responsible and their evident power to work as a team, give hope of a transformation such as no other town in England has yet undergone. Its scope is best conveyed by the map overleaf. In the centre three stages are already under way: the remodelling of the Pier Head area, the building of a new seventeen-storey headquarters for Littlewoods' Mail Order Stores and a new St Paul's Square adjoining it, and the construction by developers of a highly original complex of shops, market, car park and hotel straddling the site of the old St John's Market just below

[1] City and County Borough of Liverpool: *Liverpool City Centre Plan*. Liverpool 1965, p. 2. This impressive document follows on the Planning Consultant's eleven reports and is the work of a joint City Centre Planning Group directed by the two planners. There is an account of it by Walter Bor in *The London Magazine;* July 1966, p. 81ff.

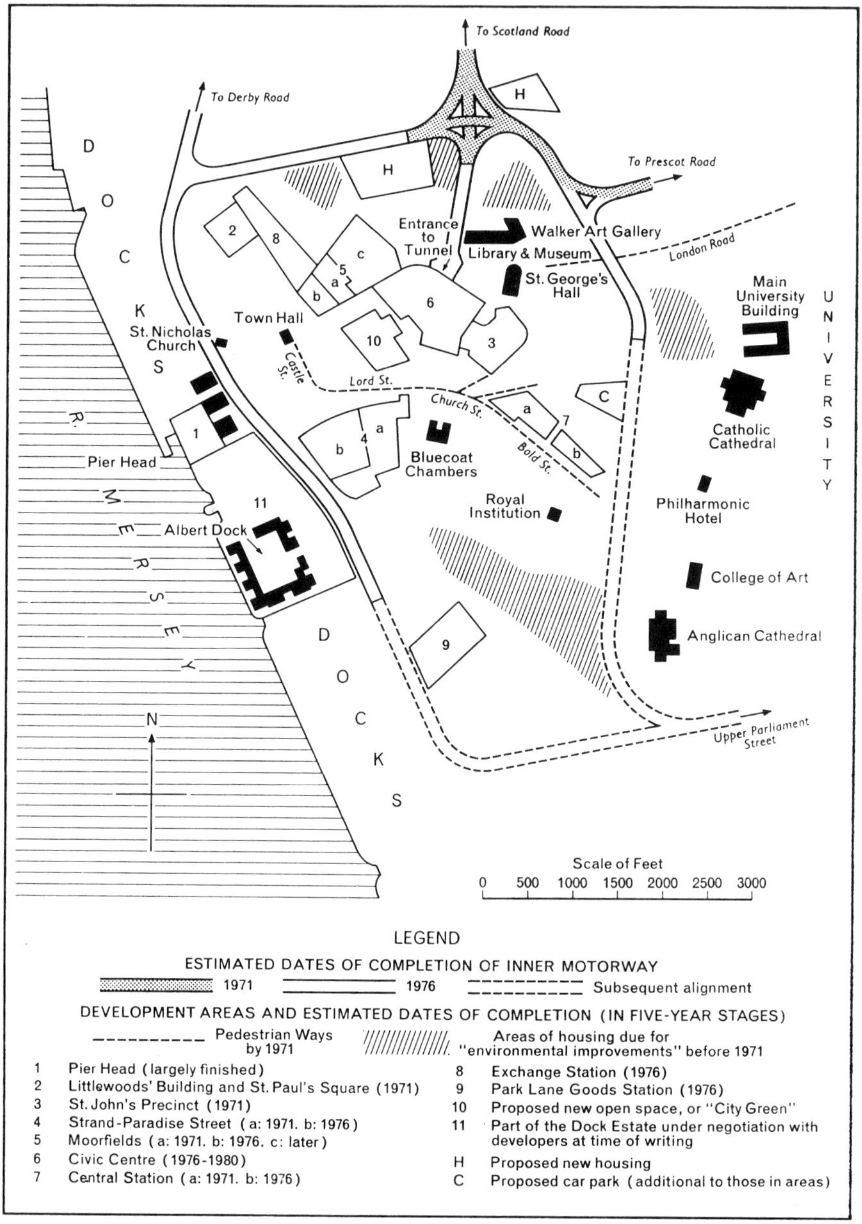

The reconstruction of the city centre. The map above shows the probable stages of construction of the inner motorway and of the principal redevelopment areas. (*Top right*) clearing the way for the first of these, the St John's Precinct scheme (a photograph taken in 1965). It is no 3 on the map. Beneath is a model of the same project, backed by a perspective drawing of the view from the north (curved) end of St George's Hall towards the proposed new civic centre (no 6 on the map) and the Mersey Tunnel entrance. (*Bottom right*) two of the towers in the second major development area, the Strand-Paradise Street scheme (no 4 on the map), by two firms of Liverpool architects: Kingham Knight Associates and Hall, O'Donahue, Wilson

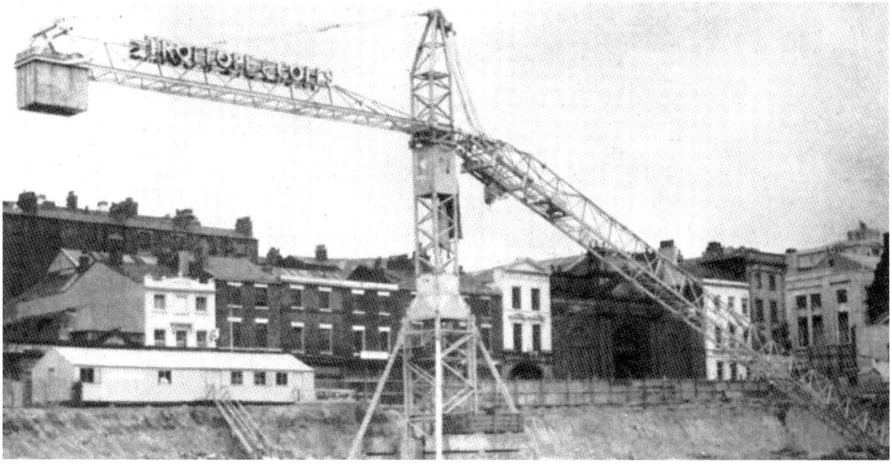

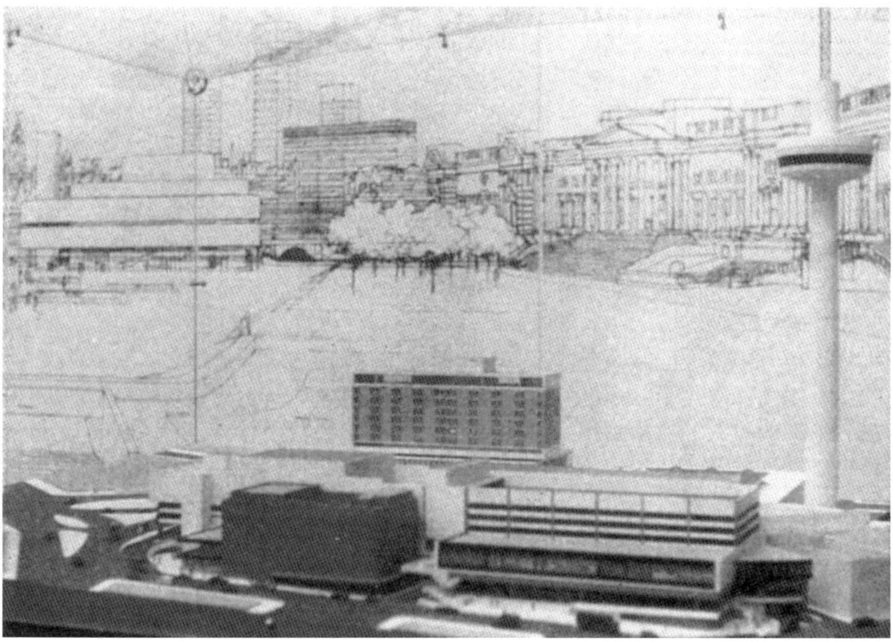

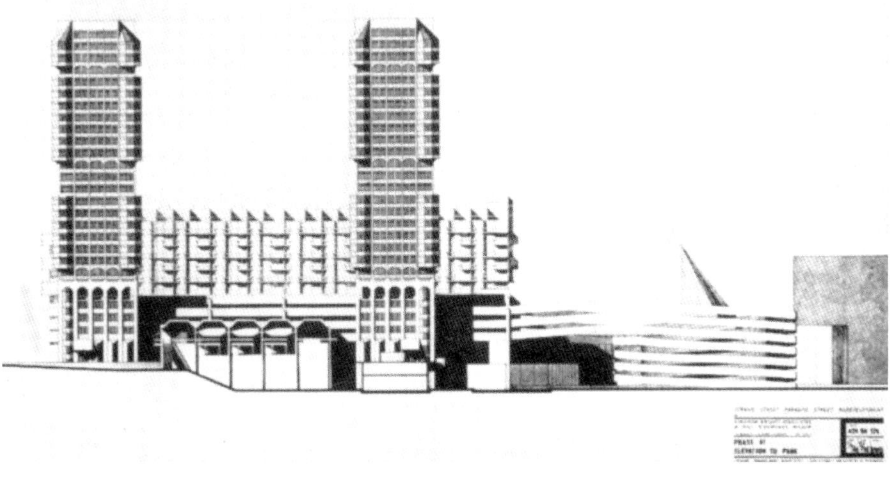
PHASE
ELEVATION TO PARK

Lime Street. Architects are now working on a rather larger scheme towards the docks, including the five tall towers of flats seen in the model; at the time of writing the council were still negotiating with developers. Beyond this there is (now that Parliament has given its approval) to be an inner motorway circling the centre; a clear segregation of motorway from local traffic, and the establishment of some wholly pedestrian streets; the redevelopment of another large area (Moorfields) on the north side of Dale Street; finally the resiting of the municipal offices and the law courts in a brilliantly-conceived civic centre, masking the Mersey Tunnel entrance and decking over the necropolis-like gardens that at present link it to St George's Hall. The council proposes to build this itself, and it could well become one of the most handsome of Europe's great squares, with the hall itself restored to useful life as a place for national conferences.

In the 'inner residential area' backing the docks and surrounding the centre 50,000 dwellings are to be cleared by 1985, together with all obsolete school buildings. Fringing this area on the east is to be a new north-south motorway bypassing the centre to link eventually with a third Mersey crossing. A new South Lancashire motorway link is to be brought into the city during the same period, joining the inner motorway close to the Anglican cathedral. The aim in all residential areas of the city, as now envisaged, will be to win back pedestrian space from the present street network, to establish a pattern of new parks (10 acres or so, not more than half a mile apart; there will even be new green spaces in the city centre), and to build up District Centres akin to the centres of small towns. In addition the plan calls for four new parks of 200 acres or more on the edges of the city. These are only the guiding lines laid down in the Interim Planning Policy Statement of March 1965; the whole programme which this document sketches is hardly expected to take less than fifty years.

There are also other elements in the picture, particularly a new scheme to use the oldest part of the Dock Estate, some 50 acres centring on Albert Dock, as a vast office centre. The Dock Estate has hitherto been outside the planners' province, and the Dock Board's negotiations with the prospective developers were independently conducted, with the result that the project greatly alters the carefully calculated balances of the plan as a whole, both by crowding the area and by its short-sighted demand that the noble Albert Dock warehouses – one of the city's great historical and architectural assets – should be pulled down. The Ministry of Housing still has to see and rule on the developers' plan, but with these extremely serious reservations (which the local politicians of both parties unfortunately seem keen to waive) the planners are enthusiastic about the scheme in principle, and they also support the other independent plans being worked out for the University and the area round it along the central section of the ridge. This is not only where the Regional College of Art, the Philharmonic Hall and the University Schools of Architecture and Civic Design are situated but also where a number of artists still choose to live. A scheme is at present being examined for the rehabilitation of the early nineteenth-century terraces there as part of a wider experiment in 'urban renewal' sponsored by the Royal Institute of British Architects. The University itself is being developed by a variety of different architects, including some of the best now working in this country, under the general supervision of Myles Wright, the Civic Design (i.e. Town-planning) Professor. And it is worth bearing in mind that a great many eyes are very

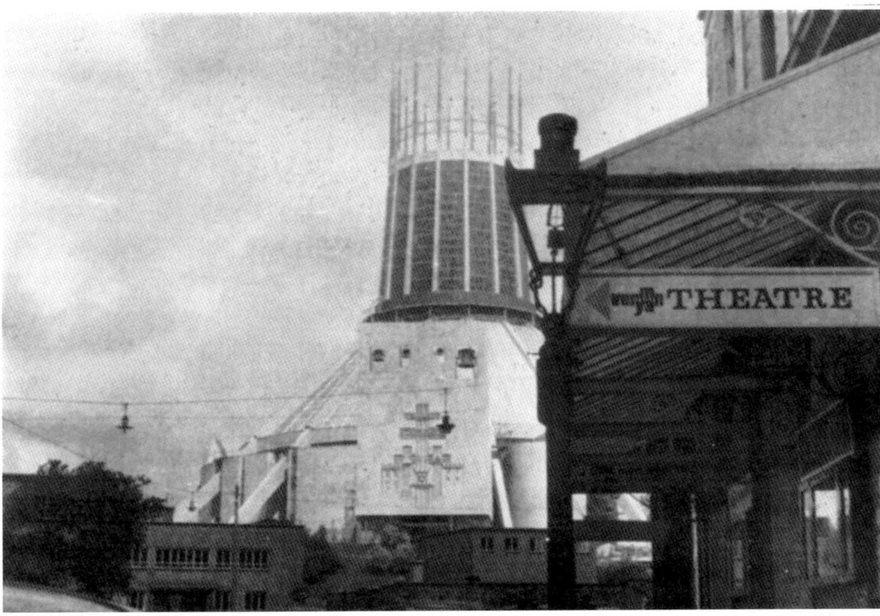

17 The new Roman Catholic cathedral seen from Hope Street (December 1965). Right: the Hope Hall, now the Everyman Theatre

soon likely to be turned on Liverpool (just as they are at present turned on Coventry) with the completion and consecration of the new cathedral, right beside the present university area.

Perhaps the case chosen is hardly typical, for both the strongly individual character of Liverpool and the ambitious scale of its plans are remarkable by any standard. But, quite apart from the fact that without such character and such ambitions no inquiry would have been set on foot in the first place, they are still important, if less conspicuous, considerations in the life of any city

Art in a city is not a static affair, concerned only with permanent treasures kept under glass or in air-conditioned rooms; even a museum is likely to be evolving all the time, subtly changing its relationships both with the community that pays for it and with the outside world of art. In other places it might be easy to forget this. The local roots of the arts might be too difficult to spot, or at least to distinguish from those in other parts of England; the future might seem like a hazy and haphazard extension of the past, a matter for pure speculation. In Liverpool they are obvious and urgent.

The chapters that follow are designed to do two things. They are on the one hand a study of the specific situation in Liverpool, as seen between 1963 and 1966 (the date of my last revisions), with certain recommendations for that city which I hope may influence future action there. At the same time they are meant to illuminate the whole relationship between the visual arts and the modern community, in a way which will be helpful outside the area specifically dealt with. This wider setting of the problem is discussed in Chapters 8 and 9, the former giving some account of social-artistic developments in Britain since the Second World War, as well as certain analogous exmples from the Continent, while the latter sketches the background of theoretical debate from the early nineteenth century onward, before focusing yet again on the local scene. These chapters are by no means intended to be skipped by readers concerned with Liverpool's situation, for it seems important that those locally responsible should realize what can be and has been done already, and what ground has already been argued over, to what effect. The tenth chapter however, is an unashamedly parochial one, apart from its ending, and the unconcerned reader has every justification for skimming it quickly. From his point of view what matters here is less the exact detail of the measures recommended than the drawing up of a plan of campaign which can be seen as a whole and will dovetail with the city's reconstruction plans.

I hope that the book points the way to this, though I hope also that it does not overlap too much with the planning documents or with other relevant publications. Liverpool has been the subject of a good deal of outside interest since the Beatles rose to fame, and much else has been written about the city lately, from fan magazines upwards; it may be noticed that photographs by one of the authors of *Beat in Liverpool*,[1] a remarkable study produced by three young Germans and published in Frankfurt, have appeared on previous pages. One such book, Quentin Hughes's *Seaport*,[2] is of the

[1] Jürgen Seuss, Gerold Dommermuth and Hans Maier: *Beat in Liverpool;* Europäische Verlagsanstalt, Frankfurt, 1965.

[2] *Seaport. Architecture and Townscape in Liverpool;* Lund Humphries, London, 1964.

first importance, both for its revelation of Liverpool's very original architectural character, together with the reasons for it, and for its use as a reminder of what in the city is worth preserving. Here again I have tried not to overlap, though I have reproduced one or two photographs from Dr Hughes's collection; readers who feel interested enough in the place to turn to his book will find their reading of the present work greatly enriched. My object where Liverpool's own future is concerned is to supplement *Seaport* and the plans in such a way that all three contribute to the same end: a singularly interesting and enjoyable city. Whether this is so will depend on the action taken. But it should be remembered that everything that follows has likewise got a practical purpose, being written with an eye to that future even where it plunges back into the past.

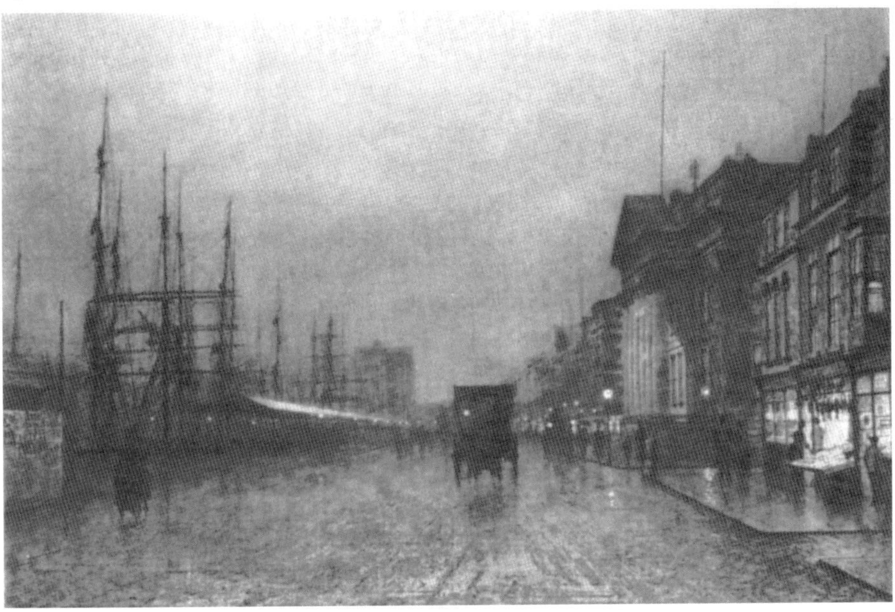

18 Genius loci. Atkinson Grimshaw (1836-1893): *The Customs House, Liverpool (looking north). Private Collection*

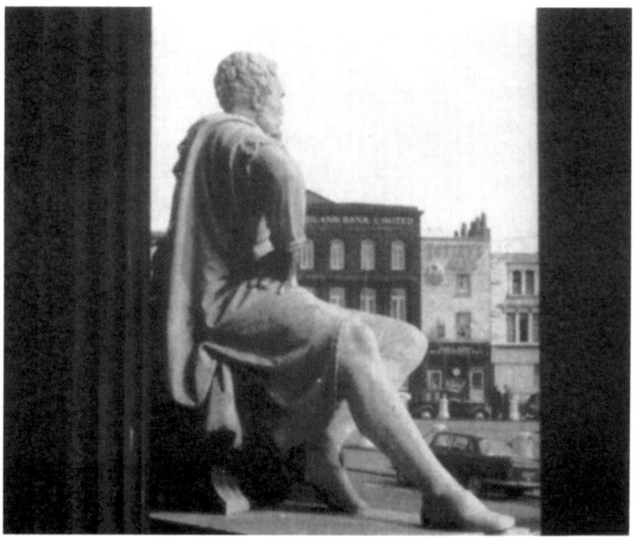

19 Michelangelo looking out from the porch of the Walker Art Gallery. (St George's Hall is off the picture to the right)

2 : VIEWS OF THE PAST

Liverpool has a long tradition in the visual arts, and for the best part of two hundred years the city has been the centre for some of our most important provincial exhibitions. It still attracts young artists from all parts of the country by this very fact, though the relative cheapness of living and lodging there is another obvious inducement. In such surroundings the past is much more in evidence than in corresponding ports on the continent, or even in other big British towns. Prosperity came earlier, with its solid monuments in the way of industrial and public buildings; poverty followed quicker, so that there were fewer of those inessential changes of fashion (in shopfronts, signs, offices, public houses) which so drastically transform the urban face. Today the nineteenth century still lies all around the artist: in the facade of the Walker Art Gallery for instance, with Raphael and Michelangelo[1] forbiddingly enthroned either side of the portico and the substantial figure of Commerce on top. None of the major art institutions is less than fifty years old.

Yet something has vanished, as we shall see if we go back over the history of these institutions and the tradition which they represent. For the leading citizens of Liverpool in the nineteenth century were conscious of art as an embodiment and an advancement of their society's aims in a way that is no longer fashionable, and as the century progressed they wanted its benefits to be more and more widely diffused. It was these feelings that provided the motive power of the city's artistic life. Probably it was not so spontaneous a life as now, and none of the artists could be called distinctively Liverpudlian in style, but at least it arose in response to a real demand. Today the most gifted of the local artists remain largely unknown and unbought; the demand is a national and not a specifically local one; and it is for art teachers or art gossip rather than for works of art. The notion that art itself could have a relevance to the community's hopes and ideals, to its work and its leisure, seems to have gone with the Victorian age.

[1] By the sculptor John Warrington Wood, 1839–86, a native of Warrington who studied and worked in Rome.

The rise of art in the city is linked with the figure of William Roscoe (1753–1831), poet, antiquarian, amateur painter, lawyer, biographer of Lorenzo de Medici, self-made merchant banker and Whig MP for Liverpool in 1806–7. Roscoe is now perhaps known primarily for the splendid collection of Primitives which he made and which are now the outstanding feature of the Walker Art Gallery. He bought these, as a former member of the gallery staff has shown,[1] for their historical significance and as curiosities rather than because they were what he liked most; he was an Italophile somewhat of the cast of Samuel Rogers, though one who never left England. He was also a good friend and patron to Fuseli from the 1780s onwards, hanging his dining-room at Allerton Hall (where he moved in 1799) with that painter's works.[2] Fuseli indeed called him 'the man nearest my heart'. In many ways he was pompous and humourless, yet both his sympathies and his interests were ahead of his times; he was opposed to the war with revolutionary France, for instance, and fought long and hard for the abolition of the slave trade on which so many Liverpool fortunes depended. Brougham judged him to be 'in some respects one of the most remarkable persons that have of late years appeared in either the political or the literary world'.[3] Art to Roscoe, and apparently to his friends too, was at once a symbol and a tool for the free, progressive commercial society that they believed in. And it was in this spirit that the forerunners of the present-day College of Art and Liverpool Academy were formed.

Such sentiments were characteristically expressed in the opening of Roscoe's inaugural ode read to the local Society for the Encouragement of Designing, Drawing and Painting on 17 December 1773:

From climes where Slavery's iron chain
Has bound to earth the soaring mind,
Where GRECIA mourns her blasted plain
To want and indolence resigned;
From fair ITALIA'S once-loved shore,
(The land of Freedom now no more)
Disdainful of each former seat,

[1] Michael Compton: 'William Roscoe and Early Collectors of Italian Primitives' in *Liverpool Bulletin*, no. 9, 1960–1.

[2] See Hugh Macandrew: 'Henry Fuseli and William Roscoe' in *Liverpool Bulletin*. Vol. 8, 1959–60. This article is largely based on 113 letters from Fuseli to Roscoe now in the Liverpool Libraries, and includes particulars of twenty-seven pictures belonging to Roscoe and other Liverpool collectors.

[3] *Speeches of Henry Lord Brougham;* A. & C. Black, Edinburgh, 1838. Vol. 1, p. 467, in the (retrospective) introduction to his 'Speech at the Liverpool Election 1812'.

The ARTS, a lovely train, retreat:
Still prospering under FREEDOM'S eye,
With her they bloom, with her they fly;
And when the Power transferred her smile
To ALBION'S ever-grateful isle,
The lovely fugitives forgot to roam,
But raised their altars here, and fixed their happier home.

The society thus celebrated was the second of the eventual Liverpool Academy's precursors, the first having been formed at the same premises (30 John Street) in 1769, only a year after the foundation of the Royal Academy in London. In 1774 the society held the first art exhibition ever to be staged in the provinces,[1] a largely amateur affair which included works by Roscoe himself (an ink drawing called *The Mother*, after a French engraving) and his brother-in-law Daniel Daulby. It quickly petered out however, and was again re-founded in 1783, as the Society for Promoting the Arts in Liverpool, which for the first time began to include the work of metropolitan artists in its shows: Paul Sandby and Wright of Derby in 1784; Reynolds, Gainsborough, Fuseli and others in 1787. Its classes were meant to appeal to a wide public. 'It is the aim of the present times,' said the catalogue of the 1784 exhibition,[2] 'to unite beauty with utility; and even the Mechanic who would wish to arrive at eminence, ought not only to cultivate his taste, but to acquire . . . practical knowledge of the art of design. . . .'

Like its predecessors, this attempt failed, and the Liverpool Academy of Arts as we now know it was only founded in 1810. It quickly became incorporated in a larger literary, artistic and scientific body, the Liverpool Royal Institution, with Roscoe, the Liverpool banker B. A. Heywood and Dr T. S. Traill (subsequently Professor of Forensic Medicine at Edinburgh and editor of the eighth edition of the Encyclopedia Britannica) as moving spirits; this had a 'spacious and elegant exhibition room for the use of the members of the Liverpool Academy'[3] and a School of Design 'for instruction in Drawing, as subservient to Professions, Mechanical Employments, or the Study of the Fine Arts.'[4] Apparently the £1,600 bequeathed to the Academy by Henry Blundell of Ince, together with £200 accumulated interest, was

[1] According to the catalogue of the Liverpool Academy of Art's 150th Anniversary Exhibition, Walker Art Gallery Liverpool, 1960.

[2] Reprinted in Joseph Mayer: *Roscoe and the Influence of his Writing on the Fine Arts;* T. Brakell, Liverpool, 1853, p. 12.

[3] *Resolutions, Reports and Bye-Laws of the Liverpool Royal Institution, March 1814–March 1822*; Liverpool, 1822. Report of the Committee 17 July 1817, p. 15.

[4] Ibid. p. 25.

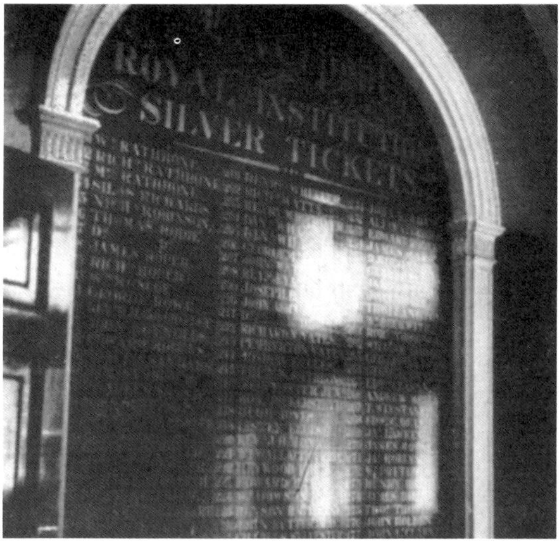

20 Names of early members of the Liverpool Royal Institution, founded in 1814, from the board in its entrance hall. Among those shown here are William Rathbone, William Roscoe, R. V. Yates, John Foster Junior, Andrew Melly and T. Winstanley

handed over to the trustees of this Institution on condition that the Academy should be permanently housed by it.[1] In 1817 the combined bodies moved into the square brick building in Colquitt Street which is still known as the Royal Institution (today it is an adult education centre under the wing of the University Extra-Mural Department and the Academy has no accommodation of its own). Roscoe spoke protractedly at the opening ceremony, giving his own picture of the 'union of the pursuits of literature with the affairs of the world', and preaching the need for a flourishing artistic life as at once obligatory for a self-respecting mercantile community and a welcome means of improvement for the working class. He quoted the Italian states and the Hanseatic towns as proof that 'in every nation where commerce has been cultivated upon great and enlightened principles, a considerable proficiency has always been made in liberal studies and pursuits'. This was no argument for a policy of subsidy however, for 'There is not a greater error, than to think that the arts can subsist upon the generosity of the public' except possibly in their very earliest stages. It was just a matter of intelligent self-interest, where pleasure and utility must necessarily coincide. 'If you will protect the arts, the arts will, and ought to remunerate you.'[2]

[1] According to E. R. Dibdin's paper on Liverpool Art History in the *Transactions of the National Association for the Advancement of Art; Liverpool Meeting 1888;* London, 1888, p. 314. He says that 'this right exists to the present day'.

[2] William Roscoe: *On the Origin and Vicissitudes of Literature, Science and Art, and their Influence on the present State of Society.* A Discourse delivered on the opening of the Liverpool Royal Institution, 25 November 1817. Liverpool. Printed by Harris and Co. And sold by Cadell and Davis, London, 1817.

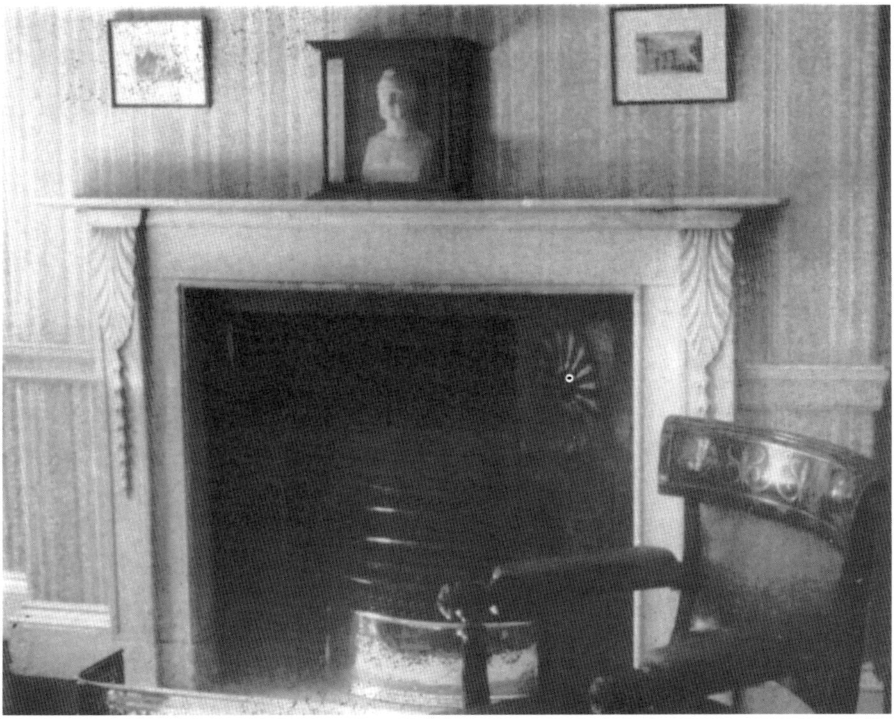

21 Director's room at the Royal Institution, with original furniture and bust of William Roscoe, its moving spirit

Views of this kind are to be found in a number of the speeches which Traill and Heywood delivered to the Royal Institution in the 1820s, when the Academy was holding exhibitions nearly every year and the Corporation itself began to give prizes for works of art. It was a moment when peace (and commerce) were being re-established after the Napoleonic wars, and there was something of a local artistic boom. In 1819 the Institution formed the nucleus of its own collection when a group of members presented some thirty-five of Roscoe's pictures which he had sold to help stave off his impending bankruptcy (a quarter of a century later when it opened its own art gallery across Colquitt Street another eighty had been added, mostly through Roscoe's dealer and friend Winstanley). In 1823 Romney's son John presented a group of eighteen cartoons by his father. The outstanding local artist of the time was certainly the sculptor John Gibson (1790–1866, elected RA in 1838), who after 1817 lived in Rome, where Roscoe and Fuseli had put him in touch with Canova; his last work before leaving Liverpool was a mantelpiece for Sir John Gladstone, the future Prime Minister's father.[1] There were however other worthy professionals of less distinction, in men like Samuel Williamson, Charles Towne, Thomas Hargreaves and the head of the School of Design, Alexander Mosses. In 1829 Dr Traill re-

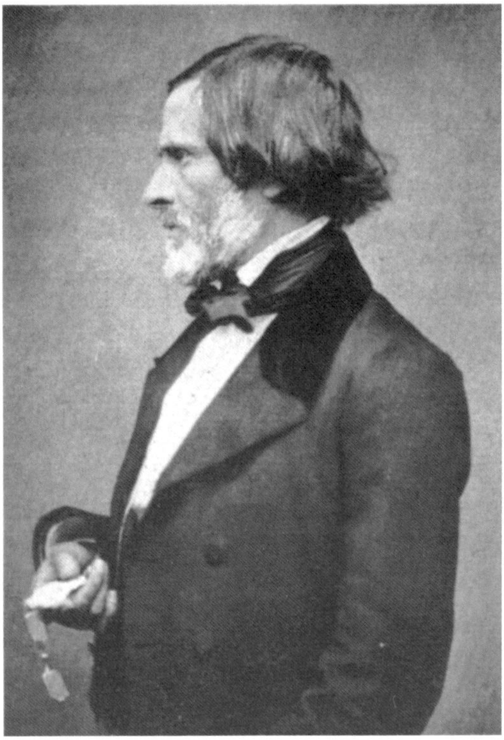

22 The sculptor John Gibson RA (1790-1866), the first eminent Liverpool artist

ported that sales from the last Academy exhibition had totalled £846: 'a decisive proof of an increasing love for the fine arts among our opulent merchants'. Like Roscoe he believed that commerce largely accounted for the cultural achievements of Florence, Genoa and Venice, and he hoped that Liverpool too might now commission works of art for public buildings and churches.[2]

Heywood died in 1828, on the eve of the first Reform Act, Roscoe in 1831. Traill left Liverpool a year or two later, having practised there for about

[1] Gibson left his fortune and a large number of his works to the Royal Academy, which still has some eighty of his sculptures (mostly in the vaults or in the Keeper's House) and some bound volumes of drawings. Among the subjects Venus, Psyche, Cupid, etc, tend to predominate, with Sappho and Queen Victoria also prominent. His portrait by Landseer hangs in the Academy's general assembly room.

[2] *See his Address delivered in February* 1829 *at the General Meeting of the Members of the Liverpool Royal Institution;* Harris and Co, 1829, pp. 20–1. Roscoe had written to much the same effect to Fuseli in 1803, in a letter quoted on p. 50 of Mr Macandrew's article.

thirty years. By then the Academy had become strongly enough established to make it largely independent of the Institution; in 1830 the Corporation began giving it an annual grant of £200, and in 1831 it moved to its own

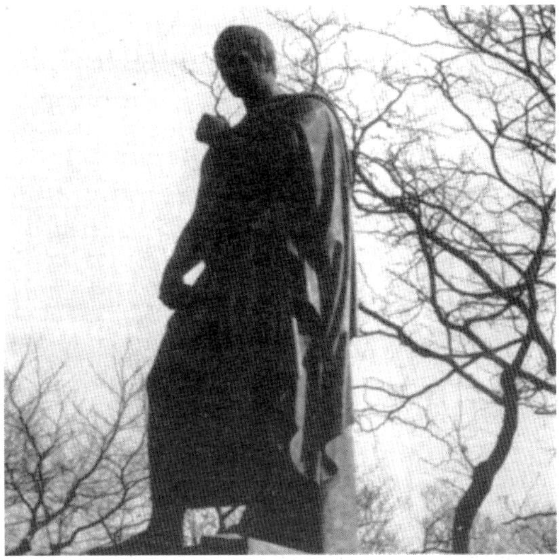

23 Gibson's statue of Huskisson (MP for Liverpool from 1823 till his death at the opening of the Liverpool and Manchester Railway in 1830). Formerly on the Customs House site and now, rather inappropriately, in an area of late nineteenth-century development on Prince's Avenue

rooms in Post Office Place, leaving the School of Design where it was. The same group of enthusiasts had meantime made the first moves towards a more widely-based form of adult education, inspired partly by Birkbeck's original London Mechanics' Institute of 1824 and partly, it seems, by the recommendations of M. M. Noah, Sheriff of New York.[1] Originally set up privately in 1821, an Apprentices' and Mechanics' Library, with Roscoe's son as its treasurer, was officially adopted by the town after a public meeting in January 1824 and soon had over 800 readers; according to Brougham's 'Practical Observations upon the Education of the People' it was modelled on the Philadelphia Library Company founded by Franklin a century earlier.[2] The same month Heywood was telling Institution members that Dr Traill (who had been a fellow student of Brougham's at Edinburgh) was involved in 'the meetings of a Mechanics' Institute'; in June 1825 he presided over the foundation of the Liverpool Mechanics' School of Arts from which the present College of Art was to grow. This new body had Huskisson as its first president and Heywood and Sir John Gladstone[3] as chief supporters; its original motto 'Knowledge is power' somewhat alarmed the less enlightened

[1] According to an article in *Kaleidoscope*, Liverpool, 3 February 1824, Vol. IV, p. 255.
[2] *Speeches of Henry Lord Brougham*, Vol. III, p. 140.
[3] President of the Institution in 1828 and 1829. Among the other Liverpool families whose names recur in the list of presidents were the Rathbones, Heyworths and Holts.

members of the Corporation. 'If you go on,' they are supposed to have said, 'in instructing the working classes, they will be so much enlightened that they will be treading on the heels of their superiors.'[1] A painting at the school showed Britannicus crowning Mechanicus. Alas, it seems not to have survived.

During the great reforming decade which followed the new school was put firmly on its feet. In 1832–3 it was reorganized as the Liverpool Mechanics'

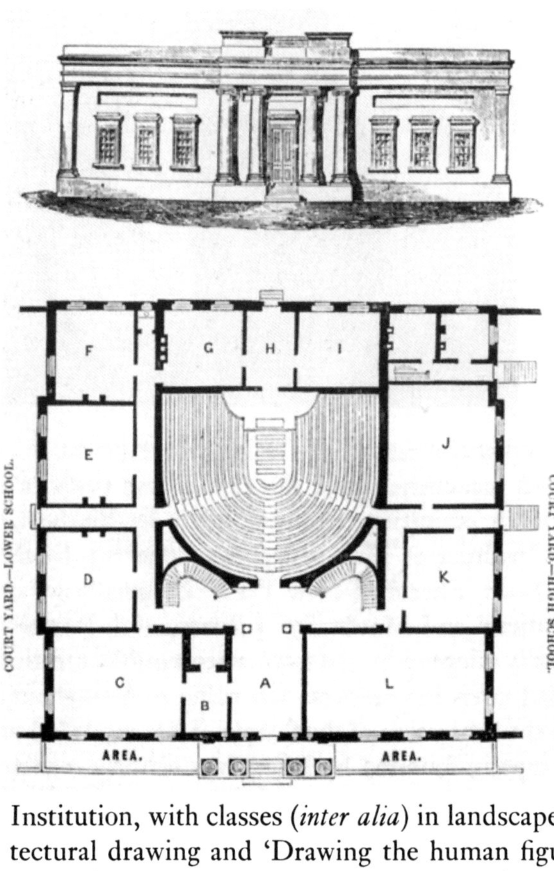

24 The Liverpool Mechanics' Institution. The new building of 1837, still existing as the nucleus of the Liverpool Institute School, a well-known boys' day school in Mount Street, next to the present College of Art

Institution, with classes (*inter alia*) in landscape, mechanical drawing, architectural drawing and 'Drawing the human figure, Ornamental Design and Modelling'; membership rose from 232 before the reorganization to 1,010 in September 1832. In 1835, the year of the Municipal Reform Act, when there were only two Tory members left on the City Council, Brougham came over from Manchester – his first experience of railway locomotion – to lay the foundation stone of its new building. Brougham had been co-founder with

[1] See the Mayor's tribute to Dr Traill in the Report of the Liverpool Mechanics' Institution, 15 March, 1836, p. 21. At a soirée in February 1844, Dickens spoke of it ironically as 'an unpopular, dangerous, irreligious and revolutionary establishment'.

Birkbeck of the original Mechanics' Institute in London, and for many years had been associated with Liverpool; he was its counsel in 1808 and stood for Parliament unsuccessfully there against Canning in 1812. 'Today,' he told his listeners at the ceremony, ' . . . all agree in favour of Popular Education' (Cheers).[1] The finished building, to J. A. Picton's design, was opened two years later by another Liberal educationist, Thomas Wyse, a Catholic who was member for Waterford from 1835 to 1847. He called for 'a national school system like a national system of justice, of defence, of protection for our sick and poor . . .'; no class should be cut off from it. For in both France and England education acted as a barrier to crime; it built up the middle class, which is 'essentially the life-principle of society'.[2] Wyse himself was another interesting figure, though largely forgotten today. A governor of the National Gallery and a member of the 1841 Royal Commission on the decoration of the Houses of Parliament, he was also an early advocate of public art galleries, libraries and museums. He was (disastrously) married to Lucien Bonaparte's third daughter Letitia, whose tutor had been a pupil of David; he knew Canova and Thorwaldsen in Rome, yet regarded the classical languages as a luxury and recommended the teaching of music, psychology, history and civics instead.[3]

This was the building where Benjamin Robert Haydon, the great anti-Royal-Academician, came to lecture on a number of occasions between 1836 and 1840, once to an audience he estimated at 1,500. In those days he was the chief propagandist for a national system of art schools, for art professorships in the universities and for the public employment of painters on large decorative tasks. He was also a very strong influence on one member of the building committee, the Liverpool Radical MP William Ewart,[4] who had been chairman of the Select Committee on Arts and Manufactures of 1835–6 which paved the way for the Government Schools of Design, and later

[1] *A Full Report of the Speeches delivered by Lord Brougham and Vaux at Liverpool on Monday, 20 July 1835; on laying the first stone of the new Mechanics' Institution, and at the dinner given to his Lordship at the Amphitheatre, James Brancker, Esq, in the Chair.* Liverpool: printed and published by Egerton Smith and Co; Lord-Street, 1835. The speeches can also be found in Vol. III of the *Speeches of Henry Lord Brougham* already quoted.

[2] *Prospectus of the Course of Instruction, Terms and Regulations of the Schools attached to the Liverpool Mechanics' Institution, with a speech by Thomas Wyse, Esq, MP, Chairman of the late Parliamentary Education Committee, delivered at the opening of the New Mechanics' Institution, 15 September 1837;* D. Marples and Co, Lord-Street, Liverpool, 1837.

[3] See Dr J. J. Auchtermuchty: *Sir Thomas Wyse 1791–1862;* P. S. King & Son, Ltd, London, 1939. His own book *Education Reform* was published in 1834. On losing his seat he became British Minister in Athens till his death.

[4] Son of the Liverpool merchant of the same name, after whom Sir John Gladstone, a close friend, called his own son. William Ewart Gladstone followed the second William Ewart to Eton and Christ Church, but the two men seem to have had nothing else in common. None the less Gladstone gave Ewart's portrait by Mosses to the city after his death in 1869.

sponsored the Museums Act of 1845 and the Public Libraries Act of 1850: the two great milestones in the history of official British policy towards the arts. Haydon found the new structure 'a magnificent establishment' and the people lively but rough.

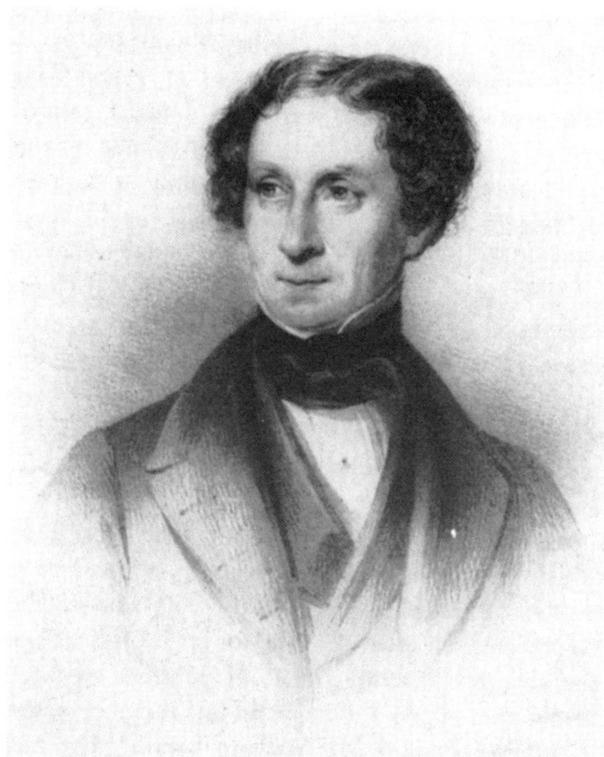

25 William Ewart (1798-1869), MP for Liverpool from 1830-1837, and Chairman of the Select Committee on Arts and Manufactures to which we owe our art school system

> The room is too large. You feel pained to fill it. There are too many boys belonging to the schools, and the savage brutality behind is dreadful. No attention or common civility.[1]

In September 1837, through the agency of a Mr Lowndes (with some help from Winstanley) he was commissioned to paint *Christ Blessing the Little Children* for the Asylum of the Blind – a work which had been taken down by 1852[2] and has now vanished – while most of 1839 was spent painting the Wellington portraits now in St George's Hall. 'Liverpool,' he said flatter-

[1] Tom Taylor (editor): *Life of Benjamin Robert Haydon;* Second Edition, London, 1853, Vol. III, p. 99.

[2] Ibid. Footnote to p. 72. The Asylum was where the police headquarters now is in Hardman Street, opposite the Philharmonic Hall.

ingly in one of his lectures there,[1] 'is the only distinguished town since the Reformation which has had the moral courage to employ native historical painters, on the true, thoroughbred principles of patronage, which produced such glorious results in Italy and Greece.' Other cities would surely follow her example, with excellent effects on the country's wealth, taste and manufactures. And this he saw as fulfilling the ambitions of Roscoe, whose 'literature and his love of art have cast a halo round the name of Liverpool, which is felt in conjunction with its commercial power, in every part of the world....'

In March 1842 the secretary reported that the Institution had 3,767 members. By then it seems to have been divided into two boys' schools

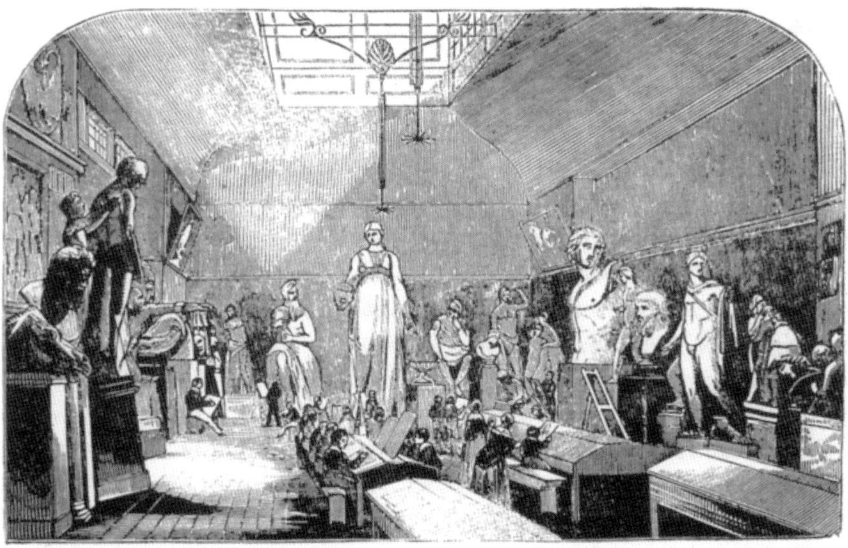

THE SCULPTURE GALLERY AND DRAWING-SCHOOL, LIVERPOOL MECHANICS' INSTITUTION.

26 A wood-engraving from *The Illustrated London News* of 2 March 1844, showing what eventually became the College of Art

(High School and Lower School), and an evening school with some twenty-five departments. The attendance at the evening art classes, which had a staff of eight teachers under W. J. Bishop, was over 400; there were also drawing classes in the High School under Charles Barber, a friend of David Cox and president of the Liverpool Academy for 1841–2 and 1847–53. 'At the last exhibition of the Liverpool Academy there were eight paintings by teachers in this Institution, and twenty-one by artists who were formerly pupils within its walls.' Nearly 100,000 visitors (or about double the attendance at the most successful exhibition of our own time, that of Van Gogh

[1] B. R. Haydon: *Lectures on Painting and Design*. London 1846, Vol. II, Lecture X, pp. 115–17.

at the Walker Gallery in 1955) saw an exhibition in the first half of 1840 which had been arranged to raise funds. Here there was sculpture by Gibson and Deare; drawings by the topographical artist W. G. Herdman (another teacher in the evening classes), whose *Pictorial Relics of Ancient Liverpool* was published in 1843; paintings or copies of paintings by various famous names; scientific apparatus, daguerreotypes, and a cap, gloves and shoes worn by Byron in Greece. *The Congress of Science*, an anonymous poem written for the occasion,[1] finishes on a familiar note of cultural optimism:

> Thus forward proceeding, transcendent you'll shine,
> And, trimming the bright lamp of freedom divine,
> Diffuse, while your standard of freedom's unfurled,
> LIGHT, LIBERTY, HAPPINESS over the world.

This whole association of flourishing commerce, radical politics and the neo-classical style in art determined the artistic and intellectual climate of Liverpool in the first half of the century, and it was splendidly commemorated in the building of St George's Hall in the middle of the city. The foundation stone had been hopefully laid in 1837, a year after the building of the new railway terminus the other side of Lime Street; in 1839 and 1840 competitions for its actual design were won by the twenty-five-year-old architect Harvey Lonsdale Elmes; in 1842 work began and in 1854 the hall was opened, after Elmes had prematurely died and C. R. Cockerell had been brought in to finish the work. It was Cockerell who called on the services of the greatest of English classical sculptors, Alfred Stevens, who had worked for him on the doors of the London Geological Museum in Jermyn Street and had already visited Liverpool in 1847 to decorate three rooms for the Blundell family at Deysbrook House, West Derby. The sculpture for the pediment, based on an original design of 1843 by Cockerell which Elmes had seen and admired in the Royal Academy, was actually carried out by W. G. Nicholl, who was also responsible for the four lions in front of the hall, but Stevens saw the half-finished group in Nicholl's studio and suggested changes; its subject, characteristically, was described as 'Commerce and the Arts bearing tribute to Britannia', etc., etc.,[2] though whether that was what

[1] *The Congress of Science; A tributary lay on the exhibition at the Liverpool Mechanics' Institute. MDCCCXL.* Printed by D. Marples, Lord-Street, Liverpool 1840. The figures of attendance come from the Institution's annual report of 1842.

[2] See the anonymous notes appended to Stevens's lithograph of the pediment in the Victoria and Albert Museum, also Robert Pepys Cockerell's paper to the Liverpool Architectural Society, printed in *The Architectural Review*, London, October 1902 (especially pp. 139–41). There is an account of the building in Quentin Hughes's *Seaport*; Lund Humphries, London, 1964, pp. 96–104.

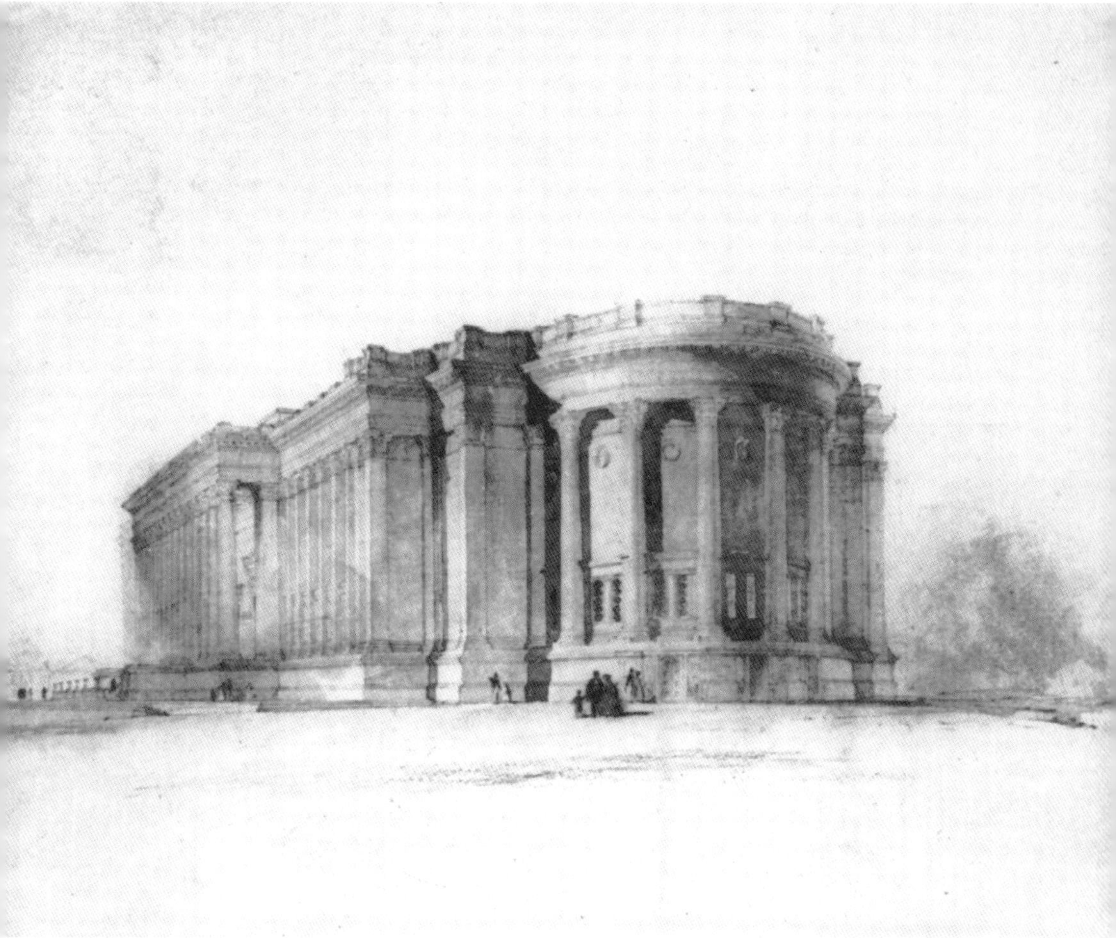

27 Harvey Lonsdale Elmes: perspective drawing of St George's Hall from the north end. (RIBA drawings collection)

Cockerell originally had in mind seems doubtful. The interior pavement was apparently Stevens's own. This pavement is now normally kept covered over, while the sculpture has been taken down as dangerously liable to crumble and is since reported to have been broken up for builders' rubble.[1] The main part of the building, the Great Hall and the beautiful smaller concert hall, are now hardly used. The citizens, alas, seem not to appreciate what a marvellous monument this is to the liveliest period of their history.

[1] This was established by Stanley Ashworth in a thesis essay at the Liverpool College of Art. The decision was taken by the City Engineer's department, unknown to the staff of the Walker Art Gallery, who at the time of Mr Ashworth's enquiries still believed that the sculptures were among those stored in the basement of the hall.

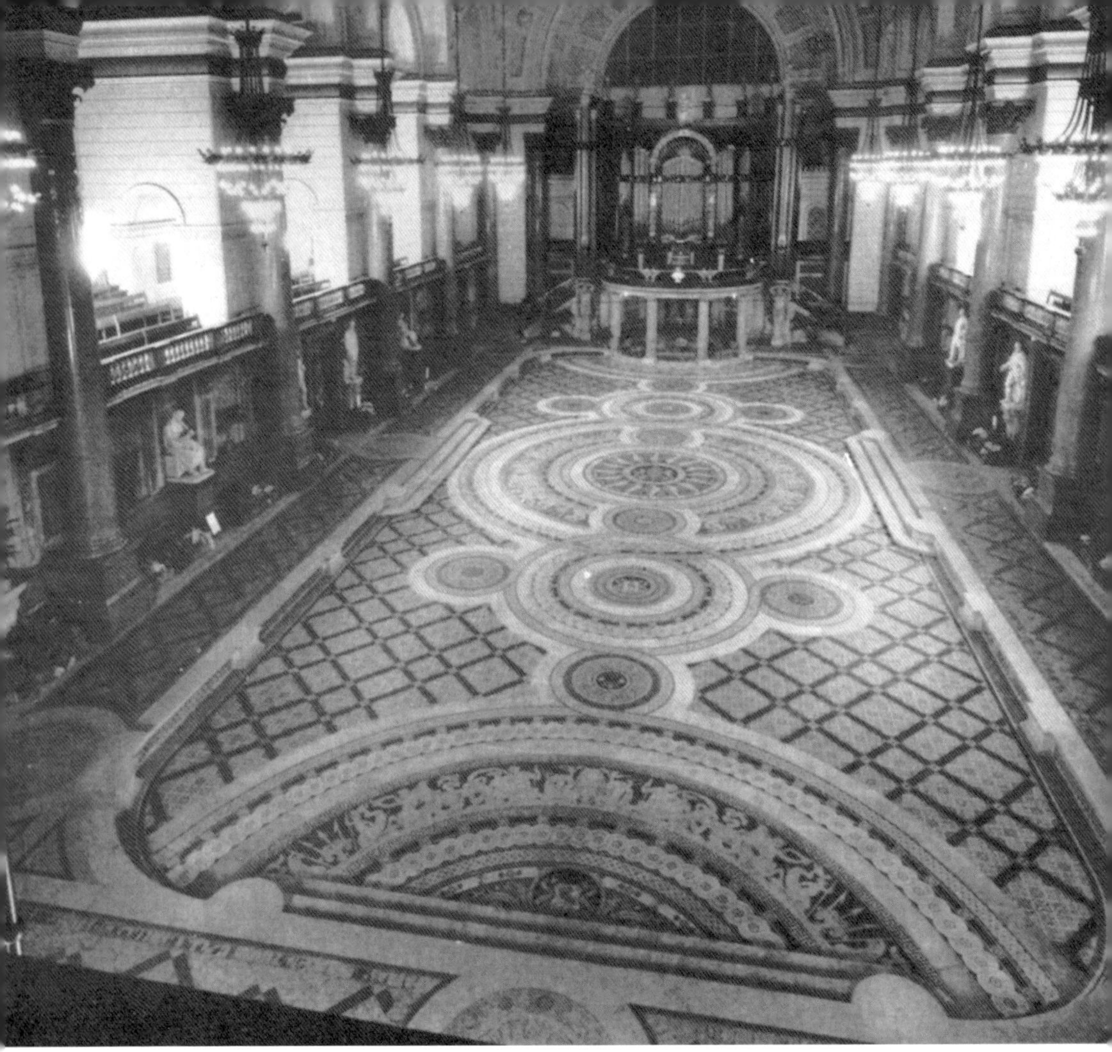

28 Alfred Stevens: Mosaic pavement inside St George's Hall. (This is normally kept boarded over)

Since the building of St Paul's no British city has had such an expressive and grandly conceived central feature.

During the 1840s a decline set in. The Royal Institution had passed its peak; the chief pioneers of Liverpool culture were dead or departed; the reformers had lost control of the City Council in 1841. The Mechanics' Institution ran into financial difficulties and in 1851 had its art department reorganized on Government School of Design lines; Bishop went over to the new Collegiate Institution in Shaw Street, Everton in 1842 and remained art master there till the eighties; John Finnie became head of the reformed School of

Design in 1855 and stayed for forty-two years. However, the young artists who had been trained in Liverpool under the older optimistic regime were now beginning to enter the Liverpool Academy, and it was they who around the middle of the century brought a genuine if controversial distinction to Liverpool art. William Huggins became an associate of the academy in 1847 at twenty-seven, W. L. Windus the same year at twenty-five, his brother-in-law Robert Tonge in 1850 at twenty-seven, James Campbell in 1854 at twenty-nine, A. W. Hunt in 1854 at twenty-four. The example of such promising painters, plus the institution of a £50 annual award out of the Corporation's grant, now encouraged some of the most interesting artists in the country to exhibit there: Millais from 1846, Holman Hunt from 1847, Ford Madox Brown from 1848. The second of these came to Liverpool in 1856 and found the Academy 'a homely company' dominated by the merchant John Miller, one of the chief patrons of the Pre-Raphaelites. He went out to Miller's house on Everton Brow, where he found the paintings stacked several deep against the walls, and concluded that Miller was more interested in owning than in looking at them. At that time the merchant was

> a hearty septuagenarian of fresh complexion and boyish temperament, with a cheery word for everybody on the way. His home was superintended by his daughters, who seated themselves to preside over high tea.[1]

One of these daughters married that shadowy figure P. P. Marshall, who for a time was William Morris's partner. Miller was also a good friend to Windus, whose *Burd Helen* in the 1856 Royal Academy caught Rossetti's attention and then Ruskin's, and was perhaps the best picture to come out of Liverpool in the nineteenth century.

But such developments were no longer in line with the tastes and interests of the city fathers. In 1851 the Academy, largely under Windus's influence, began giving its annual award to the Pre-Raphaelite exhibitors, whom it thus decided to honour well in advance of London. The controversy aroused by this far-sighted policy came to a head in 1857, when the prize went to Millais's *The Blind Girl*. W. G. Herdman, then a man of fifty-two, was expelled from the Academy for the protests which he made in the local press, and took a number of other artists with him to form a new Liverpool Society of Fine

[1] Quoted in *John Lea, Citizen and Art Lover*. A sketch by Frank Elias. Philip, Son and Nephew, Liverpool 1928, p. 16. Miller was followed by George Rae of Birkenhead, who bought Madox Brown's *English Autumn Afternoon* (now in Birmingham City Art Gallery) in 1861 and 'became an ardent collector of the later and lusher Rossetti's portraits'. See Mary Bennett: 'The Pre-Raphaelites and the Liverpool Prize' in *Apollo*, London, December 1962, p. 750. The third great local collector of these artists was F. R. Leyland (see pp. 44–6 below), who knew Miller but started collecting slightly later.

Arts. This body had the local Establishment behind it; it was backed by both mayor and bishop, and had the Earl of Sefton as its president.[1] At its first exhibition in 1858 the prize money added up to £200; in 1860 over £4,000 worth of pictures was sold. Worse still for the Academy, the Corporation in 1859 stopped the annual £200 subsidy which it had paid towards the rent of the Post Office Place exhibition room. At A. W. Hunt's request Ruskin wrote a stirring letter of support, which was partly reprinted in the weekly *Liverpool Albion* of 11 January, 1858, calling the Academy's policy 'the first instance on record of the entirely just and beneficial working of academical system'.[2] But by 1861 they were £600 in debt.[3]

There followed a brief period of artistic competition: on the one hand the Pre-Raphaelites, with Miller helping organize their show at Russell Place in London in 1857 and such local artists as Windus, Williamson, Campbell and the Dublin-born William Davis all coming under their influence; on the other, the introduction of foreign painters, notably from Düsseldorf and Brussels, into the rival society's shows.[4] This pace could not be kept up, and in 1861 the council of the new society, again with the mayor's approval, was calling for a fusion of the two bodies. Nothing occurred, so that two years later there was no exhibition by either; the giving of prizes stopped. There were a few makeshift exhibitions by the Academy later in the 1860s, then from 1867 to 1897 there were again none at all. In effect the Academy was defunct, though Ruskin's prophecy proved to be right enough:

[1] The Earls of Sefton and Derby are the two great Liverpool aristocrats, whose estates abut against the city even today. Aintree Racecourse is on land sold by Lord Sefton to Mrs Topham.

[2] *The Works of John Ruskin*. Edited by E. T. Cook and Alexander Wedderburn. George Allen, London, 1904, Vol. XIV, p. 327. The *Albion* appeared between 1827 and 1887.

[3] The prize-winning pictures in the critical years were as follows:

1851 W. Holman Hunt. *Valentine rescuing Sylvia* (Birmingham City Art Gallery). E. R. Dibdin, writing on 26 May 1910 about the Academy centenary, said that this award decided Hunt not to abandon painting.

1852 Millais. *The Huguenot* (private collector, New York)

1853 Holman Hunt. *Claudio and Isabella* (Tate Gallery).

1854 Mark Anthony. *Nature's Mirror* (With Hunt's *The Light of the World* as runner-up).

1855 Augustus Egg. *Life and Death of Buckingham* (Millais's *The Rescue* as runner-up).

1856 Ford Madox Brown. *Jesus Washing Peter's Feet* (Tate Gallery).

1857 Millais. *The Blind Girl* (City of Birmingham Art Gallery). At the time the picture was in Miller's collection.

1858 Ford Madox Brown. *Chaucer reading the Legend of Coustance* (Sydney). Renamed *Chaucer at the Court of King Edward III*. Another version, now in the Tate Gallery, belonged to F. R. Leyland.

1859 William Dyce. *The Good Shepherd*.

[4] In 1860 the exhibitors included Koekkoek, O. Achenbach, Louis and Eugene Verboeckhoven and others; in 1861 several more, plus the interesting French industrial painter Bonhommé who showed *Interior of a Coal Mine* (No. 666) and *Open-Air working of Lapis Calaminaris in the Vieille Montagne, Rhenish Prussia* (No. 755). There were also some Brussels exhibitors in 1859.

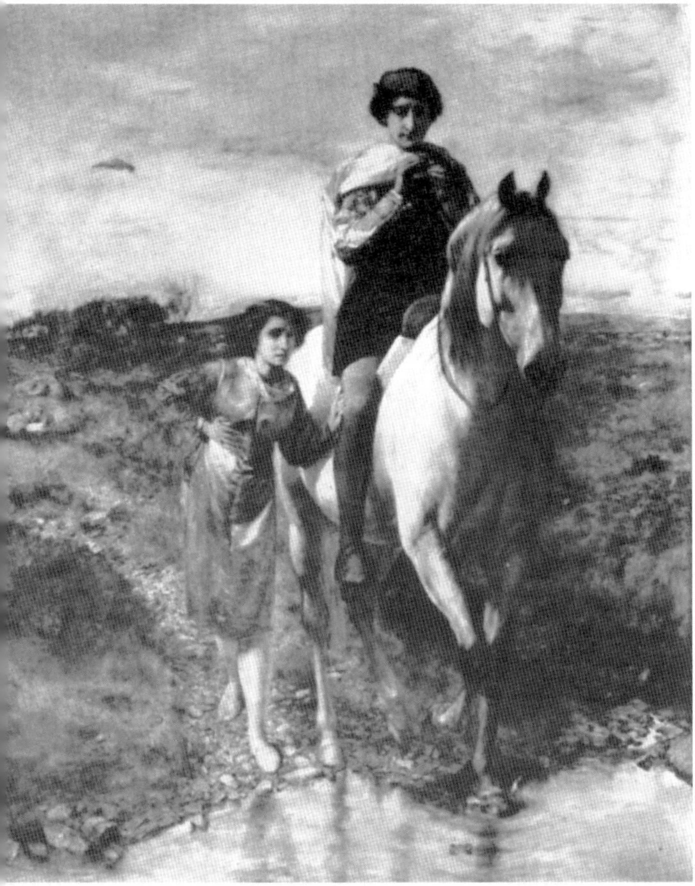

29 The most famous nineteenth-century Liverpool painting: W. L. Windus's *Burd Helen*, which was shown in the 1856 Royal Academy, admired by Ruskin and owned for a time by F. R. Leyland. It is now in the Walker Art Gallery

> Let the Academy be broken up on the quarrel; let the Liverpool people buy whatever rubbish they have a mind to; and when they see, as in time they will, that it *is* rubbish, and find, as find they will, every Pre-Raphaelite picture gradually advance in influence and in value, you will be acknowledged to have borne a witness all the more noble and useful, because it seemed to end in discomfiture; though it will *not* end in discomfiture.[1]

Unhappily Windus, the one really notable painter to come out of so much friction, who, given a different temperament, might have been stimulated to great things by it, seems to have been totally discouraged[2] and to have painted nothing to speak of between 1862 and his death in 1907. 1862 was the year when he left Liverpool, having lost his wife after only four years of marriage: a tragic figure in the history of Liverpool art.

[1] *The Works of John Ruskin*. Vol. XIV, p. 328.

[2] He had also apparently fallen from Ruskin's favour. Ruskin's account of his 1857 Royal Academy picture *Too Late* was one of the harshest he ever wrote.

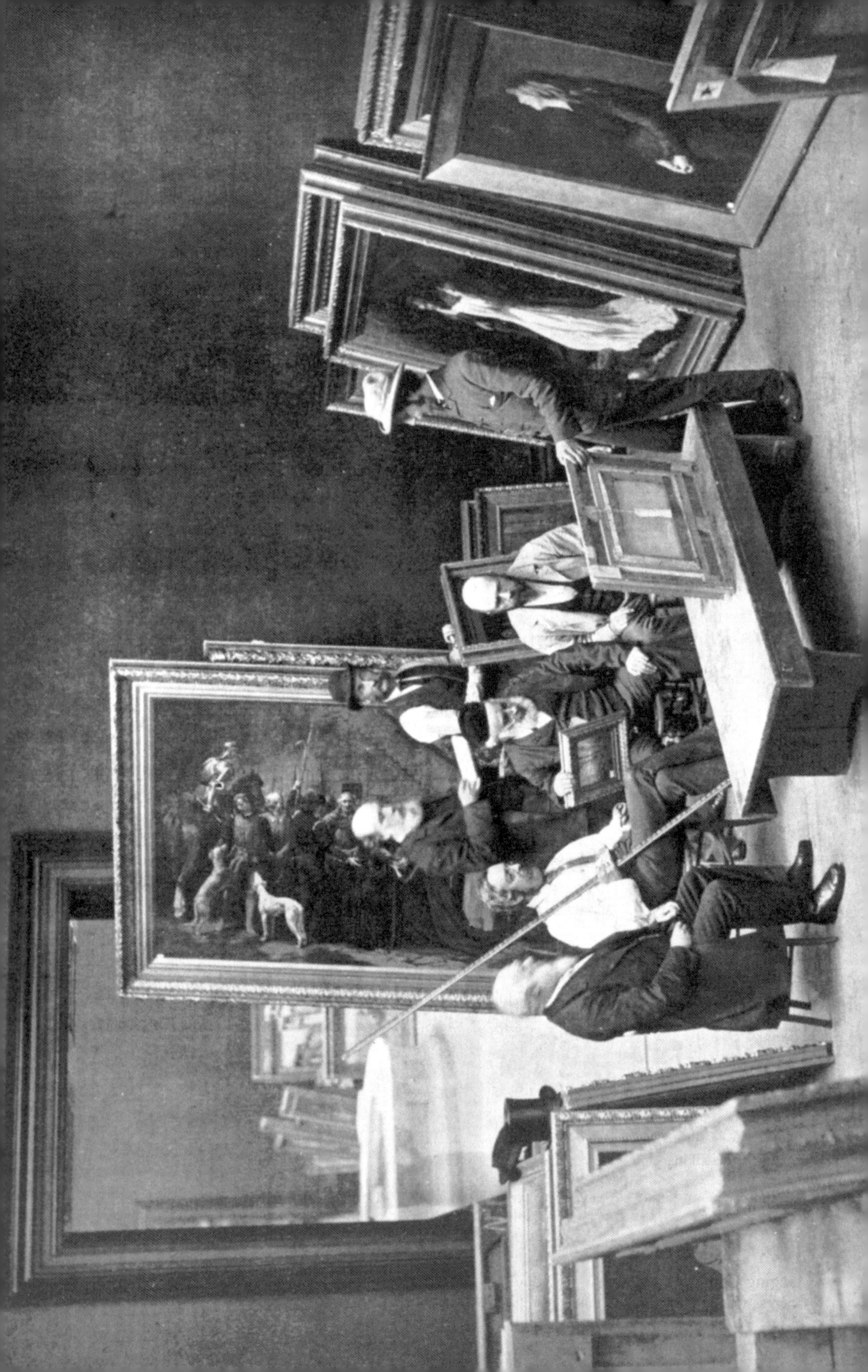

The 'spirit of self-improvement', as Ramsay Muir called it in his *History of Liverpool*,[1] revived after some thirty years with the Household Suffrage Act of 1867 and Forster's Education Act of 1870. With the Academy in suspense and the Royal Institution too stagnant to attract any public interest, the Corporation itself set up a Fine Arts Committee, sponsored a large Autumn Exhibition annually from 1871 to 1939, and at once began buying works for a permanent collection. Edward Samuelson, Philip Rathbone and J. A. Picton, the principal moving spirits, took matters up much where the earlier generation of reformers had left them, seeing the 'main object' of their exhibition as 'exciting a widespread interest in Art among the masses of the general population', with special reference to the tastes of 'the working man'.[2] To start with it must have seemed that they were brilliantly succeeding. Sales from the first exhibition amounted to £6,395, in 1874 to £9,526, in 1884 to more than £12,000. During the 1872 exhibition, which lasted for three and a half months, 22,894 tickets were sold at 3d, 6d or 1s, plus 332 season tickets; at least 10,000 schoolchildren were reckoned to have been let in free. 242 of the 960 works shown were sold for a total of £6,214, more than a third of it paid by individual members of the Town Council. A year later there was a public meeting at the Town Hall to discuss the provision of a permanent exhibition building, and nearly £7,000 was promised by those present in the room.

That November Andrew Barclay Walker the brewer was elected mayor in succession to Samuelson, and announced that he would give a gallery himself (he also paid for the gallery's extension in 1882). This was the origin of the Walker Art Gallery, which from 1877 onwards housed the Autumn Exhibition and the pictures which the Committee bought from it each year or acquired otherwise. By 1895 there were over 600 of these, including a large proportion of the works from the Royal Institution gallery, which the Corporation took over in July 1892; 103 of the total having been bought out of exhibition profits. As for their quality ' . . . The fact has not been lost sight of,' the Committee is quoted as saying,[3] 'that the public, for whose education and instruction the institution in a great measure exists, delight in subjects of a popular character, and, with this end in view, pictures have

[1] Written when he was Professor of History there and published for the University Press of Liverpool by Williams and Norgate, London. Second Edition 1907.

[2] Corporation of Liverpool: *Report of the Fine Arts Committee upon the second Autumn Exhibition of Pictures 1872*. The Committee felt that a good way to achieve this was to give official prominence to 'a large and striking gallery picture, telling some tale of human action and passion, with simple and effective power'.

[3] In the article by H. M. Cundall, 'Liverpool Walker Art Gallery' in the *Art Journal* for August 1895, p. 250.

o The Hanging Committee at an early Autumn Exhibition. Philip Rathbone
n shirt-sleeves, with Picton on his right and Charles Dyall behind him

from time to time been added which, by appealing to common feelings and sentiments of our daily life, have afforded a fine moral lesson and given great pleasure to the numerous visitors to the Gallery who are uninitiated in

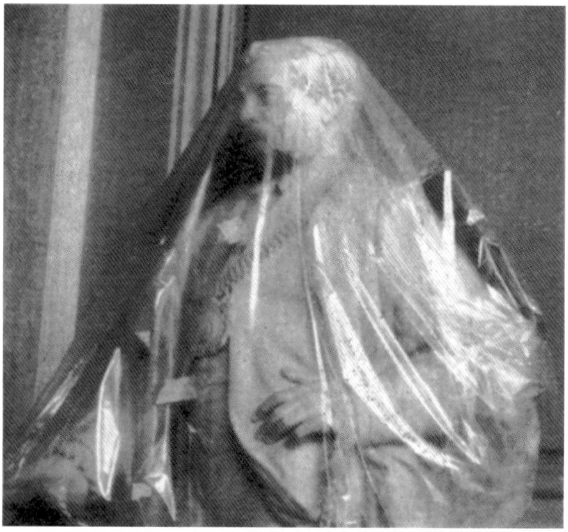

31 Brewer, mayor and patron of the arts: Sir Andrew Barclay Walker's statue in the entrance hall of the gallery he gave

higher forms of Art.' The object was popularization, a continuation of popular education by other means. 'There is, perhaps,' wrote the local antiquarian and dealer Joseph Mayer in 1876, 'no city in the world where the social duty of patronizing Art is now more firmly established than in Liverpool.'[1]

Alas, it now seems to us that few galleries have accumulated a larger number of valueless pictures. A wiser policy by the first two Curators, Charles Dyall (1877–1904), and E. R. Dibdin (1904–18) might have avoided this, for the exhibitions and the interest of the more enlightened patrons attracted the leading English artists and not a few from abroad. But Dyall was not in favour of highbrow or difficult works:

> Art has now taken deep roots in the intelligence of the people. . . . The free air of public opinion will help keep it clear of parasites, and all those enervating influences that prevent its growth and development. It must not be made an intellectual monopoly, nor be so lofty in its aim as to become abstruse and unintelligible.[2]

[1] Joseph Mayer: *Early Exhibitions of Art in Liverpool.* Privately printed. Liverpool 1876, p. 89. The book is dedicted to A. B. Walker. Nine years earlier Mayer had given his own collection to the Liverpool Museum, which had been built in 1856 on a site below that of the gallery.

[2] From his paper to the Art Congress of 1888 (*Transactions*, p. 295). See p. 53 below.

Under these conditions it was hardly surprising that the finest contribution to the city should have occurred outside the gallery, in the fourteen stained glass windows designed by Burne-Jones and executed by Morris for All Hallows' Church, Allerton, which was consecrated in 1876.[1] Yet there were perfectly reputable artists who sent to the autumn exhibitions: Legros, Tissot, Lhermitte, Scholderer and the excellent German realist R. Hirth du Frenes, for instance, in 1878; Sargent and Watts in 1896. There is still in the Walker Gallery a *Study of a Head* which Legros painted there in 1878 'before a large number of art students . . . as a practical lesson in art. Time occupied in painting, one hour and forty minutes'.[2] Herkomer seems to have lectured the same year. In 1881 Hall Caine read a paper on Rossetti's *Dante's Dream*, which the Committee bought from that year's exhibition; this was at an At Home, where the Band of the Liverpool Police Force also played and a Mr Aptommas performed on the harp.

Ruskin was the subject of three enthusiastic articles in the *Liverpool Weekly Albion* in 1872 (on 9, 16 and 23 November), and the next year wrote to an anonymous Liverpool friend suggesting that the Colonna Raphael should be bought for the gallery, the price asked being £40,000.[3] His letter was printed in the *Liverpool Daily Post* of 3 January 1874 and followed four days later by a hostile leading article. But the climate was changing, and only seven years later his secretary W. G. Collingwood, son of the Liverpool water-colourist William Collingwood and father of the philosopher, addressed a meeting of the Art Club with a view to forming a Ruskin Society; Philip Rathbone took the chair. There were also the lampoons – a common nineteenth century form of Liverpool self-expression – and the controversies: Samuelson and Rathbone falling out over the propriety of Alma Tadema's *The Sculptor's Model* in the 1878 exhibition,[4] the Reverend D. B. Hooke damning the gallery as founded on Drink. In a sense it may even have been quite a stimulating time, though only at a low artistic level and within narrow limits. For in the whole history of the Autumn Exhibition the city bought only one reasonably interesting contemporary foreign work: Segantini's strange

[1] G. E. Grayson of Liverpool was the architect. The church was built by John Bibby of Hart Hill in memory of his wife. One window, showing David mourning Saul and Jonathan, is not by Burne-Jones, as he apparently disagreed with Bibby's proposal that it should include portraits of two of the donor's children.

[2] *Walker Art Gallery, Descriptive Catalogue of the Permanent Collection of Pictures.* Compiled by Charles Dyall, Curator. 1890. (No. 179.)

[3] *The Works of John Ruskin*, Vol. XXXIV, pp. 512–13. The picture was on loan to S. Kensington. Pierpont Morgan bought it in 1901 and it is now in the Metropolitan Museum.

[4] Rathbone read a paper at the Social Science Congress that year entitled, 'The Mission of the Undraped Figure in Art'. It is included in the volume of 'Papers on Art' above. A topical ballad in *The Liverpool Lantern* for 23 November of the same year was called 'Nudity and Prudity, or the Battle of the Alma (Tadema). Art Cant – ata'.

allegory *The Punishment of Luxury* in 1893. It is impossible not to accuse the organizers of crass insularity; like most of Britain at that time they simply ignored the great French painters, whose works were not even shown.

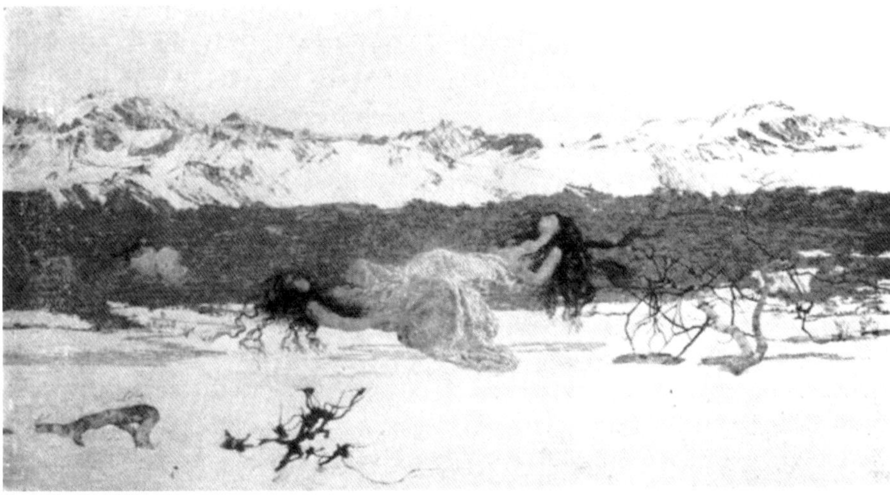

32 Giovanni Segantini: *The Punishment of Luxury*. The only modern foreign work of any merit bought by the gallery in its first thirty years

One minor Liverpool mystery is the absence from the gallery of any work by Whistler. For Whistler not only sent to the exhibition but was the principal artist supported – it can hardly be called patronised – by the man he flippantly spoke of as 'the Liverpool Medici': F. R. Leyland (1831–92), who had entered the shipping firm of J. Bibby, Sons and Co from the Mechanics' Institution, risen to be its book-keeper at eighteen and a partner at twenty-eight, and taken it over in 1872 to run it with great brilliance as the Leyland Line.[1] Leyland, a solitary man and a passionate amateur pianist, started collecting Rossetti's work in 1865, having come to know that artist through Miller; his son-in-law Val Prinsep said that 'it was the one real friendship of his life'.[2] He also owned three of Windus's principal paintings and a number of pictures by other relatively enterprising British artists, such as Burne-Jones and Albert Moore. In 1867 he bought Speke Hall, and there Whistler came to stay on a number of occasions, working lengthily on individual portraits (mostly not completed) of his hosts and their three children, and

[1] After his death Pierpont Morgan and Sir John Ellerman shared the ships, and the line ceased to operate around 1930. The present Bibby Steamship Co was a new foundation by the Bibby family in 1891.

[2] Val Prinsep, ARA: 'Rossetti and His Friends', in *The Art Journal*, London, May 1892, p. 134.

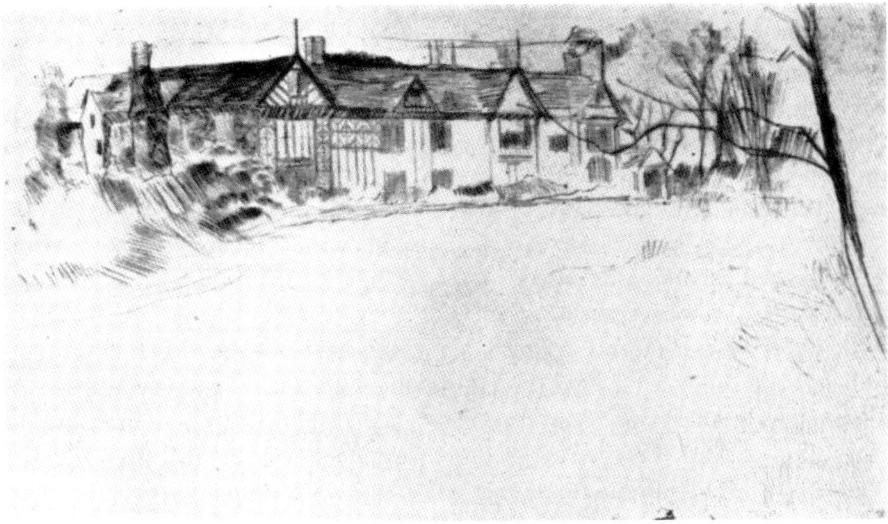

33 Whistler and Liverpool. *Speke Hall no. 2.* This etching of 1875 shows the home of his patron F. R. Leyland (now the property of the National Trust and close to the city airport)

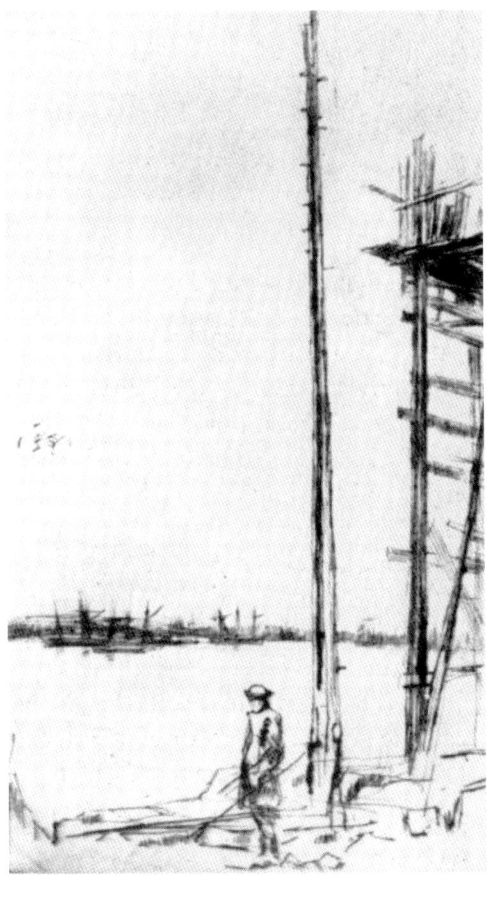

34 Whistler: *Shipbuilder's Yard.* Another Liverpool etching of 1875

producing some half-dozen etchings of various Liverpool subjects dated between 1867 and 1875. With Mrs Leyland Whistler's relations were reputedly close, certainly jocular; his biographers the Pennells make one improbable reference to an engagement to her sister.[1] Leyland however broke with Whistler after his high-handed behaviour over the decoration of the family's London house – the famous episode of the Peacock Room – and in 1879 figured as the chief creditor at the Whistler bankruptcy, thus earning himself three vicious caricatures.[2]

In 1891, a year before Leyland's death, the artist reappeared in Liverpool to help hang the Autumn Exhibition, staying with Rathbone early in August, apparently in the same room as Ruskin had occupied around the time of their libel action. The centrepiece of his gallery was to be Luke Fildes's *The Doctor*, and from the first he set out to poke fun at such typical Autumn Exhibition works, writing to Mrs Whistler:

> Well a great part of the Academy room is hung – and I fancy that the mischief of the intention is clothed in a certain delicacy – indeed so subtly is it that perhaps after all it will be scarcely perceived – however there it is – As much ridicule and exposure has been brought to bear upon the false sentiment and execrable colour drawing and execution, as one's own nerves could tolerate.[3]

Nor did this story lose anything in the subsequent telling:

> You know, the Academy baby by the dozen had been sent in, and I got them all in my gallery – and in the centre, at one end, I placed the birth of the baby – splendid – and opposite, the baby with the mustard-pot, and opposite that the baby with the puppy – and in the centre, on one side, the baby ill, doctor holding its pulse, mother weeping. On the other, by the door, the baby dead – the baby's funeral – baby from the cradle to the grave – baby in heaven – babies of all kinds and shapes all along the line, not crowded you know, hung with proper respect for the baby. And on varnishing day, in came the artists – each making for his own baby – amazing! his baby on the line – nothing could be better! And they all shook my hand, and thanked me – and went to look – at the other men's babies – and then they saw babies in front of them, babies behind them, babies to the right of them, babies to the

[1] Improbable because Mr Andrew McLaren Young tells me there is no mention of her sister, or of any engagement, in Whistler's correspondence with the Leylands, though the story has crept into some of the secondary literature.

[2] See Peter Ferriday: 'The Peacock Room' in *The Architectural Review*, June 1959, Vol. 125, p. 407. Two of these caricatures are lost. *The Gold Scab* is the third.

[3] From an undated letter in the Glasgow University Collection. This and other references to Whistler's 1891 visit were very kindly transcribed for me by Miss Helen Drabble.

left of them. And then – you know – their faces fell – they didn't seem to like it – and – well – ha! ha! they never asked me to hang the pictures again at Liverpool! What![1]

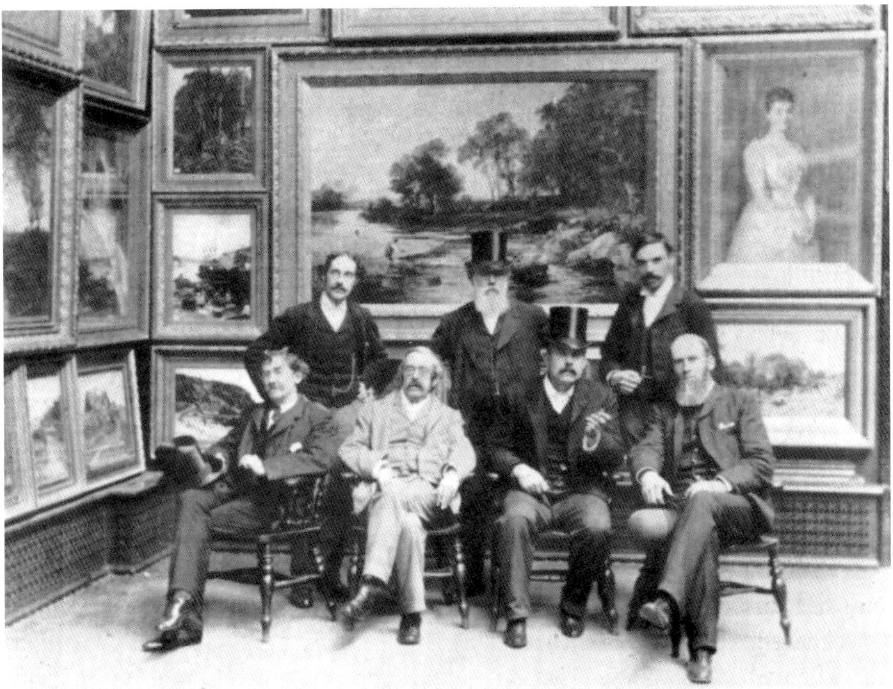

35 Hanging committee for the Autumn Exhibition of 1891. Seated, left to right: Whistler, Philip Rathbone, Arthur Melville, RWS, W. S. Boadle (Liverpool Academy). Behind them, the gallery officials: Alfred H. Frazer, Charles Dyall and John H. Hard

So he told it to the Pennells and D. S. MacColl at breakfast in Paris, as he strolled round the table filling their glasses. His own contribution to the show had been *The Fur Jacket*, but the gallery, not surprisingly perhaps, did not buy, though he had hoped that they might. The portrait of Leyland, which seems to have been all that that gentleman got in return for his advances and commissions, went to the Prinseps. The rest of the Leyland collection, fifty-eight old masters and twenty-nine modern British (including twelve Rossettis but no Whistlers) was sold at Christies on 28 May, 1892, going to swell a total estate of £700,000.

As Leyland for some reason played no part in the gallery's – or indeed the city's – affairs it was Philip Rathbone rather who embodied the spirit of this

[1] E. R. and J. Pennell: *The Life of James McNeill Whistler;* Heinemann, 1908, pp. 192–3.

period in Liverpool, much as Roscoe and Traill had embodied that of the early part of the century. He was however a woollier and less forceful man than they. The slightly absent-minded brother of William Rathbone the Fifth, he came of that remarkable dynasty of Quaker and Unitarian merchants who had initiated such enterprises as the Society for the Abolition of the Slave Trade (in the 1780s), the building of St George's Hall and the setting up of the Domestic Mission in Mill Street. He was chairman of the gallery from 1886 till he died, and was from the first a strong supporter of Ruskin, Morris and the Pre-Raphaelites; it was he who induced subscribers to present the three most important Pre-Raphaelite paintings now in the collection, beside himself giving Legros's *The Pilgrimage* in 1873 and bequeathing six fifteenth-century Italian works on his death in 1895. His portrait was painted for the gallery by Holman Hunt, and he also owned Albert Moore's *The Song of Solomon* and *The Marble Seat*.[1] A young and sceptical newcomer could describe him in 1893 as:

> a queer man, retired now from the Insurance business . . . a man always trying to be epigrammatic and sometimes succeeding (tho' seldom); a lot of common sense loaded with the unpleasant cant of continual posing for effect. He trundles the Art Machine about Liverpool and generally works public galleries and the like; lives in a bit of a house negotiating his way about among all manner of nice things packed together like stars in the Milky Way.[2]

His niece however wrote more charitably that he 'believed in strengthening corporate life and in quickening civic patriotism by appealing to men through their senses and making the visible city a place to be proud of.'[3] He expressed this aim in a number of lectures and papers, both in Liverpool and elsewhere, and tried to put it tangibly into effect by completing the sculptural decoration of St George's Hall.

[1] Whistler, on his visit in 1891, wrote to his wife that this picture was 'very sweet and really most beautiful!'. The letter, dated 3 August, is in the Glasgow University Collection.

[2] W. M. Conway to his future wife's stepfather Manton Marble, quoted in Joan Evans: *The Conways. A History of Three Generations*. Museum Press, London, 1966, p. 85.

[3] Eleanor F. Rathbone: *William Rathbone, A Memoir;* Macmillan, London, 1905, pp. 460–1. The author, who was Liverpool's first woman Councillor and England's first woman Minister, credits her uncle with a liking for 'the most modern schools of impressionism'. But it is clear from his own lectures on 'The English School of Impressionists as illustrated in the Liverpool Autumn Exhibition' (1883) and 'Impressionism in Art' (1890 – both in a mixed collection of his *Papers on Art* in the Liverpool Public Libraries) that this did not mean impressionism as we now understand it so much as the work of men like Stanhope Forbes and Albert Moore. Up to the 1950s the gallery's one French impressionist work was Henri Le Sidaner's *St Paul's from the River*, which was bought from the Autumn Exhibition in 1911 and had a thoroughly British subject.

The history of Stirling Lee's reliefs on the Lime Street side of the hall shows all too depressingly the difference between Liverpool's first and second rounds of 'self-improvement'. The huge building has always cried out to be completed by sculpture – it still does so today – and in 1885 Lee, a product of the Royal Academy Schools and the Paris Beaux-Arts, produced rough designs for five out of the first six panels. The theme, inspired by the

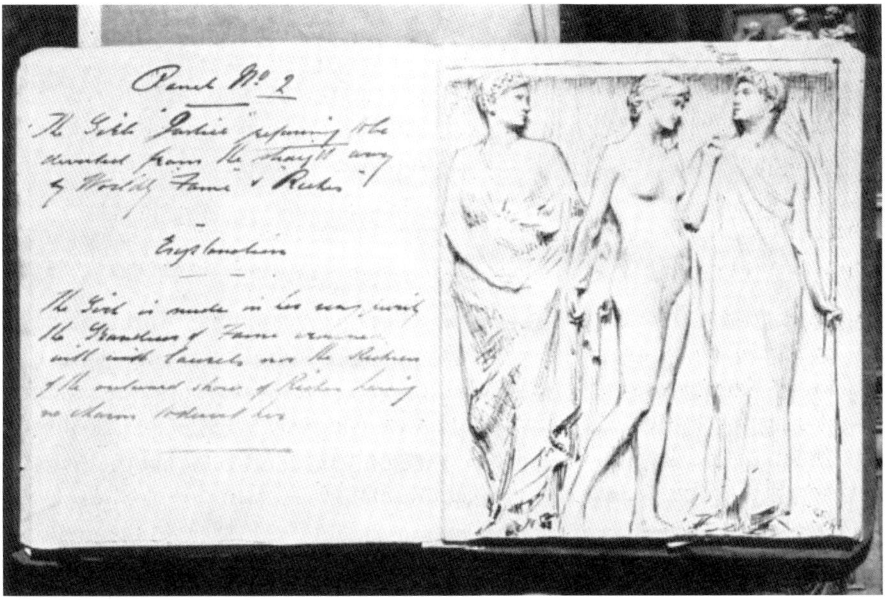

36 The crisis over the St George's Hall reliefs in the 1880s. Pen drawing for the second and, to the corporation, most controversial of Stirling Lee's six sculptures

law courts who are the building's principal users, was Justice: her 'Childhood, Girlhood, Womanhood, Administration, Result and Final End'. The designs were gently sub-classical, a sculptural counterpart to Albert Moore's style of painting, and as soon as the first panel was completed the Liverpool Architectural Society found that it was 'out of harmony with, and inferior to, the high standard of the architecture'. A move to end the contract was rejected by the corporation by twenty-seven votes to fifteen, but in the summer of 1886 Rathbone was sent up to London to report on the model for the second panel. Here Lee was rash enough to show Justice naked: 'Justice, in her purity' (so runs the inscription), 'refuses to be diverted from the straight path by Wealth and Fame'. Rathbone liked the figure; Armstrong, the director of fine art at South Kensington who went along to Lee's studio with him, 'thought the breasts required stiffening in order to look more monu-

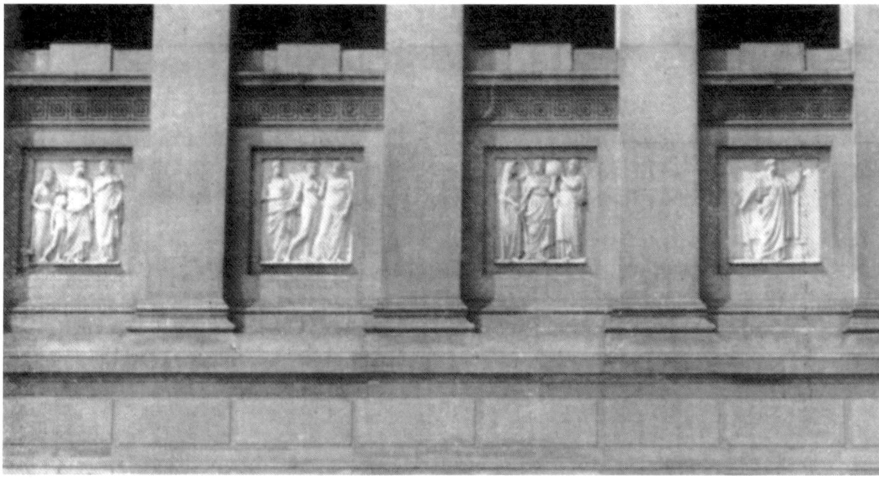

37 The first four of Lee's sculptured panels. With the third a greater rigidity and formality set in

mental and virginal.'[1] This however was too much for the city Finance and Estates Committee, who within a fortnight and without waiting to see the panel broke off the contract by twenty-five votes to three. Rathbone was left in the minority, and it was not till 1890 that he was allowed personally to pay for the four remaining panels, and then only on condition that the council could take them down after five years if it wished.[2]

In 1882, as part of the same great movement for wider education, the University College was set up. From the first it was intended to found a Chair of Fine Art there, known as the Roscoe Professorship and endowed by William Roscoe's admirers, with Rathbone as chief promoter. The Principal, Gerald Rendall, wanted to appoint William Martin Conway (1856–1937), the mountaineer, art historian, collector and subsequent member of Parliament. At first the university council havered, so that for three years he came as an occasional lecturer only. Twenty-eight at the time of his eventual appointment (and by then already tiring of the job), Conway was a man of considerable foresight, who saw 'a new architectural epoch'[3] arising from the use of steel for building, understood the importance of the *musée imaginaire* some forty years before André Malraux[4] and tried to get the university to set up a

[1] From Rathbone's report to the council, dated 23 July 1886, in a book of cuttings relating to St George's Hall in the Liverpool Public Libraries.

[2] Lee later became Honorary Secretary of Whistler's International Society. He is not known to have executed any other major work, and the remaining panels, looked at with today's eyes, are noticeably less freely designed and more insipid than the first two. If right eventually triumphed it was at the cost of being tamed.

[3] Sir W. Martin Conway: *The Domain of Art;* John Murray, London, p. 148.

[4] Ibid, p. 132.

Museum of Photographs. He had no pupils, but was 'used as a kind of free-lance'[1] to give lectures and represent the university on formal occasions; 'the

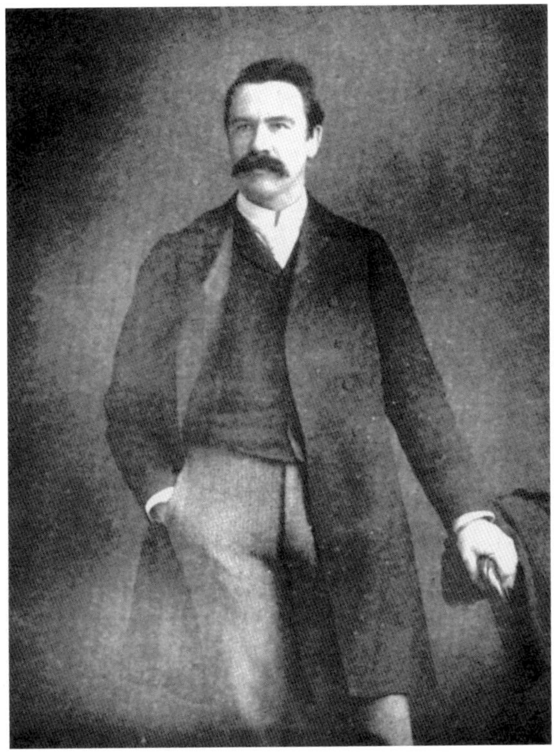

38 William Martin Conway, first Roscoe Professor of Fine Art in Liverpool University and one of the instigators of the Art Congress

function of the professor', so Rendall said, 'was to be to enlighten the public rather than to train artists.[2] . . .' His main Liverpool achievement was to act as secretary (and chief instigator with Rathbone) of a giant Art Congress on the lines of the British Association: the National Association for the Advancement of Art and its Application to Industry. This met annually between 1888 and 1890, the second and third meetings being held in Edinburgh and Birmingham; a further Congress was supposed to be held in 1891 at Nottingham,

[1] Lord Conway of Allington: *Episodes in a Varied Life;* Country Life, London, 1932, p. 84.

[2] Joan Evans: *The Conways;* Museum Press, London, 1966, p. 70. The lecture audiences it seems were often very small. Dr Evans says that on one occasion only eight people were present. However, when Conway first put in in 1886 for the Slade Professorship at Cambridge his Principal and colleagues gave him the most resounding testimonials, Oliver Lodge in particular writing of his 'earnestness and thoroughness worthy of a student of science . . . wholly devoid of that morbid or effeminate sensibility which sometimes accompanies keen artistic perception'. That time it was the architect J. Henry Middleton who got the job. The retiring professor, Sidney Colvin, wrote testimonials for both men.

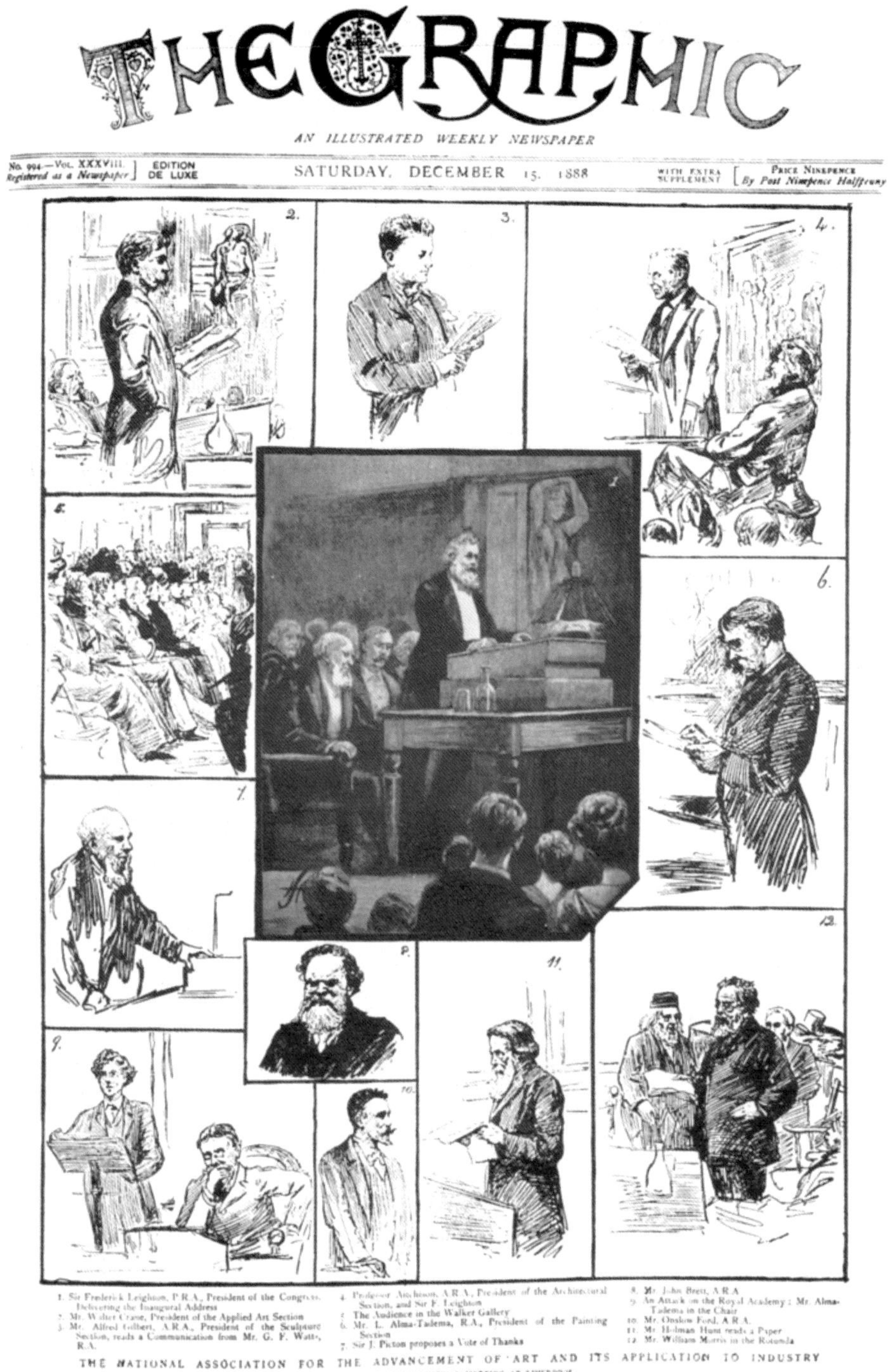
THE GRAPHIC

AN ILLUSTRATED WEEKLY NEWSPAPER

No. 994.—Vol. XXXVIII. Registered as a Newspaper | EDITION DE LUXE | SATURDAY, DECEMBER 15, 1888 | WITH EXTRA SUPPLEMENT | PRICE NINEPENCE By Post Ninepence Halfpenny

1. Sir Frederick Leighton, P.R.A., President of the Congress, Delivering the Inaugural Address
2. Mr. Walter Crane, President of the Applied Art Section
3. Mr. Alfred Gilbert, A.R.A., President of the Sculpture Section, reads a Communication from Mr. G. F. Watts, R.A.
4. Professor Aitchison, A.R.A., President of the Architectural Section, and Sir F. Leighton
5. The Audience in the Walker Gallery
6. Mr. L. Alma-Tadema, R.A., President of the Painting Section
7. Sir J. Picton proposes a Vote of Thanks
8. Mr. John Brett, A.R.A.
9. An Attack on the Royal Academy: Mr. Alma-Tadema in the Chair
10. Mr. Onslow Ford, A.R.A.
11. Mr. Holman Hunt reads a Paper
12. Mr. William Morris in the Rotunda

THE NATIONAL ASSOCIATION FOR THE ADVANCEMENT OF ART AND ITS APPLICATION TO INDUSTRY

SKETCHES AT THE INAUGURAL MEETING AT LIVERPOOL

39 The great Liverpool Art Congress of 1888. A page of sketches showing Lord Leighton (centre). Alma Tadema, Holman Hunt, William Morris and other participants

but apparently never took place. In Conway's eyes, so he explained nearly half a century later, the real purpose of the operation was to obtain the heaviest possible censure of the Corporation's conduct over the St George's Hall panels, which leading sculptors like Alfred Gilbert and Onslow Ford deplored. Once this had been achieved at the second meeting he organized the Birmingham Congress, then resigned 'having determined to undertake the exploration of the great, and till then unpenetrated, mountain region of northern Kashmir. No one else could be found to take on my job as Honorary Secretary of the Art Congress, so the movement came to an end.'[1] He subsequently became Slade Professor at Cambridge, where he had once got a Third in History, and almost at the same time was given a concession for all natural resources in the Acre Territory of Bolivia; in 1895 he was knighted. In 1918 he was elected Conservative Member for the Combined English Universities. His collection of photographs now forms the Conway Library at the Courtauld Institute; his house Allington Castle near Maidstone is attached to Aylesford Priory.

Utterly forgotten now, the Liverpool Art Congress of 1888 must have seemed a historic occasion. Leighton presided, supported by no less than thirteen vice-presidents, and there were sections for Painting (under Alma Tadema), Sculpture (Alfred Gilbert), Architecture (G. Aitchison), Applied Art (Walter Crane), Art History and Museums (Sidney Colvin, who was too ill to come), and National and Municipal Encouragement of Art (under the Edinburgh Professor of Art, Baldwin Brown). The main committee consisted of these six plus eighteen others, including Gosse, Herkomer, Poynter and Philip Rathbone, who was also secretary of the last-named section. About 1,000 people are said to have attended. Holman Hunt, Basil Champneys, Morris and Cobden-Sanderson were among those who read papers, Morris's on 'Art and its Producers' being relatively involved and dull. T. C. Horsfall of Manchester read one on 'How to make Workpeople care for art', Conway on 'Reproductions of Ancient Works of Art for Municipal Museums', Sir Philip Magnus on 'Some Notes on the Training of Industrial Artists', Rathbone on 'Lessons from France as to Imperial and Municipal Encouragement of National Art' – the result of a visit by him to the Paris art schools. Dibdin, Dyall and many others also spoke; Dean Farrar preached the introductory sermon.[2] At Edinburgh a year later Rathbone, now president of his section, chose as his subject 'The Development of Monumental

[1] Ibid, p. 87.

[2] Virtually all the papers are printed in *Transactions of the National Association for the Advancement of Art and its Application to Industry. Liverpool Meeting 1888*. London, 22 Albemarle Street, 1888. There are also volumes for the other two congresses.

Forms of Art, A Political Necessity of Civilisation'. However, Morris, who took over the Applied Art section from Crane, termed the second congress 'on the whole a dull affair' and accused it of 'ignoring . . . the working class except as instruments to be played on.'[1] The only papers of which he approved were those by Sir William Richmond and G. F. Watts.

In September 1888, i.e. before the Liverpool meeting, Conway was succeeded as Professor by R. A. M. Stevenson (1847–1900), Robert Louis Stevenson's cousin, who had worked as a painter at Barbizon and studied with Carolus-Duran in Paris in the 1870s. This very much less extrovert character, a gifted man of limited energies, was pushed into art criticism by R. L. S. and W. E. Henley, and is best known for his book *Velasquez* (1895) which was republished as recently as 1962; Whistler, who knew him, had a copy. More familiar than any other nineteenth-century Liverpool figure with the work of contemporary France, Stevenson attended the Liverpool and

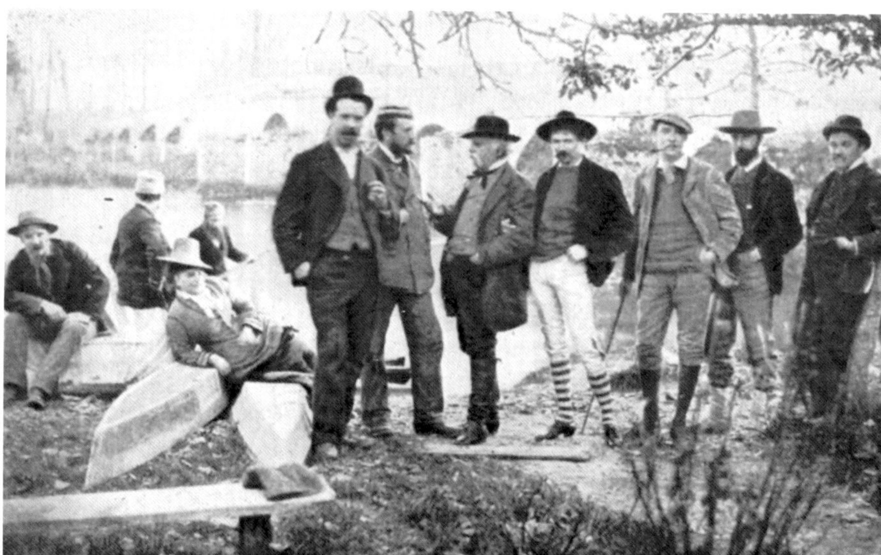

40 The second (and last) Professor of Fine Art. R. A. M. Stevenson with a group at Grez-sur-Loing in 1877, when he was still primarily a painter. Standing, left to right: Anthony Henley, Bentz, Palizzi, Stevenson, Frank O'Meara, Ernest Parton, Willie Simpson

Edinburgh Art Congresses, but was scarcely in tune with the local ideas. 'Art is not life', he wrote, ' . . . sentiment is not imagination', while his American friend W. H. Low reports him commenting on one of Millais's

[1] Quoted in J. Bruce Glasier: *William Morris and the Early Days of the Socialist Movement;* Longmans, London, 1921, pp. 86, 89.

pictures in the 1895 Royal Academy: 'Truly British art, a touching anecdote, poetry for the middle class'. There is (or was) a picture by Arthur Lemon for which he posed called *Hard Pressed*, showing an ancient Briton fleeing his enemies, and this became known to his friends as 'The Escape from Liverpool'. 'I thought I might hit it off,' was his account to Low, . . . 'But what I found was that, in addition to my definite work in the College, I was expected to wear a high hat and a carnation in my buttonhole, and talk mild gossip about Botticelli, Burne-Jones and Frith – actually Frith – at garden-parties and afternoon teas. And then there were a lot of pedagogues – duffers who talked about "schools", and attributions to this and that master – and queried about dates, and the *cinque-cento*, and that rot – and their wives, who wished to uplift the working classes by means of art, dear good ladies, of course, but – well, I held out as long as I could and then I simply cut it, for no human being could have stood it any longer.'[1] Stevenson's departure in 1892 seems to have put paid to the Professorship of Fine Art; the job remained vacant, and two years later, by some juggle that has never been explained,[2] it was turned into a Chair of Architecture and the present university School of Architecture took its place, with F. M. Simpson as the first professor.

The new arrangement was that the University College should contribute the Roscoe endowment and the City's Technical Education Committee £1,000 a year, which paid for a Section of Applied Art within the school. This section was a short-lived local offshoot of the wider movement associated with Morris and Walter Crane, and was under the direction of R. Anning Bell, RA, a painter and illustrator in the Pre-Raphaelite wake, with Charles J. Allen as instructor in modelling and Richard Llewelyn Rathbone as metalwork teacher. At the Walker Gallery's spring exhibitions of 1894–8 works by these and other members of the movement were shown, including Art Nouveau book-bindings by D. S. MacColl, so-called Della Robbia ware by Philip Rathbone's son Harold (second cousin of the metal worker) and work by the sculptors Conrad Dressler and Stirling Lee. Lee, Allen and Dressler were together responsible for the second group of six reliefs on St George's Hall (symbolizing National Prosperity and now suitably draped); R. Ll. B. Rathbone for the metal doors to the Unitarian Church in Ullet

[1] Will H. Low: *A Chronicle of Friendships, 1873–1900;* Hodder and Stoughton, London, 1908, p. 467. Low says Lemon's picture is in the Tate Gallery, but it cannot be traced there. For the fullest account of Stevenson see Denys Sutton's biographical study in the *Velasquez* reprint, Bell, London 1962.

[2] According to Lionel B. Budden (ed.): *The Book of the Liverpool School of Architecture;* Liverpool and London 1932, the idea originated with the Liverpool Architectural Society. On the other hand Roderick Bisson in *The Sandon Studios Society and the Arts;* Liverpool 1965, p. 4, says it was Stevenson's own suggestion.

Road. A third Rathbone, Harold's architect brother Edmund, meanwhile ran The City Beautiful Wayside Café, 'a home from home for aesthetes'[1] near

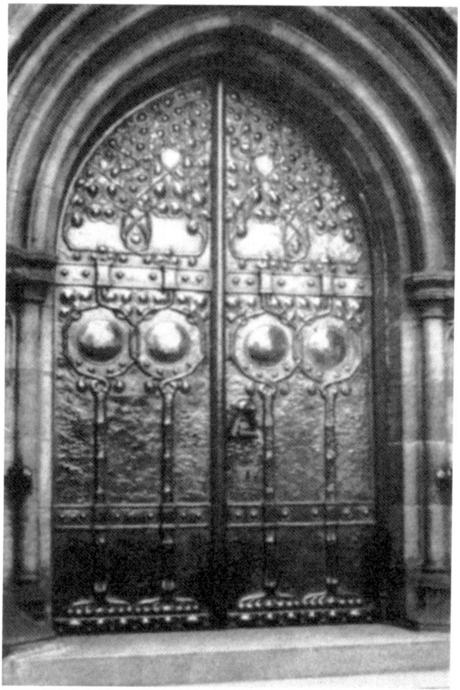

41 Liverpool Art Nouveau. Richard Llewelyn Rathbone's metal doors to the Unitarian church in Ullet Road

where The Cavern now is. The Applied Art Section's real monument, however, (as Dr Hughes has shown in *Seaport*) was the Philharmonic Hotel, built during the Walker brewery's late nineteenth-century spate of pub construction, between 1898 and 1900. The Philharmonic's metal gates by H. Blomfield Barr are one of the sights of Liverpool.

The section had some bright recruits, notably J. Herbert MacNair, who was Charles Rennie Mackintosh's brother-in-law, and in 1901 Augustus John. The 1902 Education Act however forced the Corporation to take over the School of Design, which since 1883 had been in a new building in Mount Street next the old Mechanics' Institution; and it seemed logical to detach the Applied Art Section from the university and fuse both to make a new city School of Art. Executed in 1905, this decision pleased neither the Applied Art teachers nor their students, and that year a number of them broke off to form an independent art school at 9 Sandon Terrace under MacNair and the newly-arrived painter Gerard Chowne. They had the

[1] Roderick Bisson: *The Sandon Studios Society and the Arts;* Parry Books, Liverpool, 1965, p. 66. Mr Bisson's book contains much relevant information about the old Applied Arts Section, together with the society which was shortly to emerge from it and the artists associated with both.

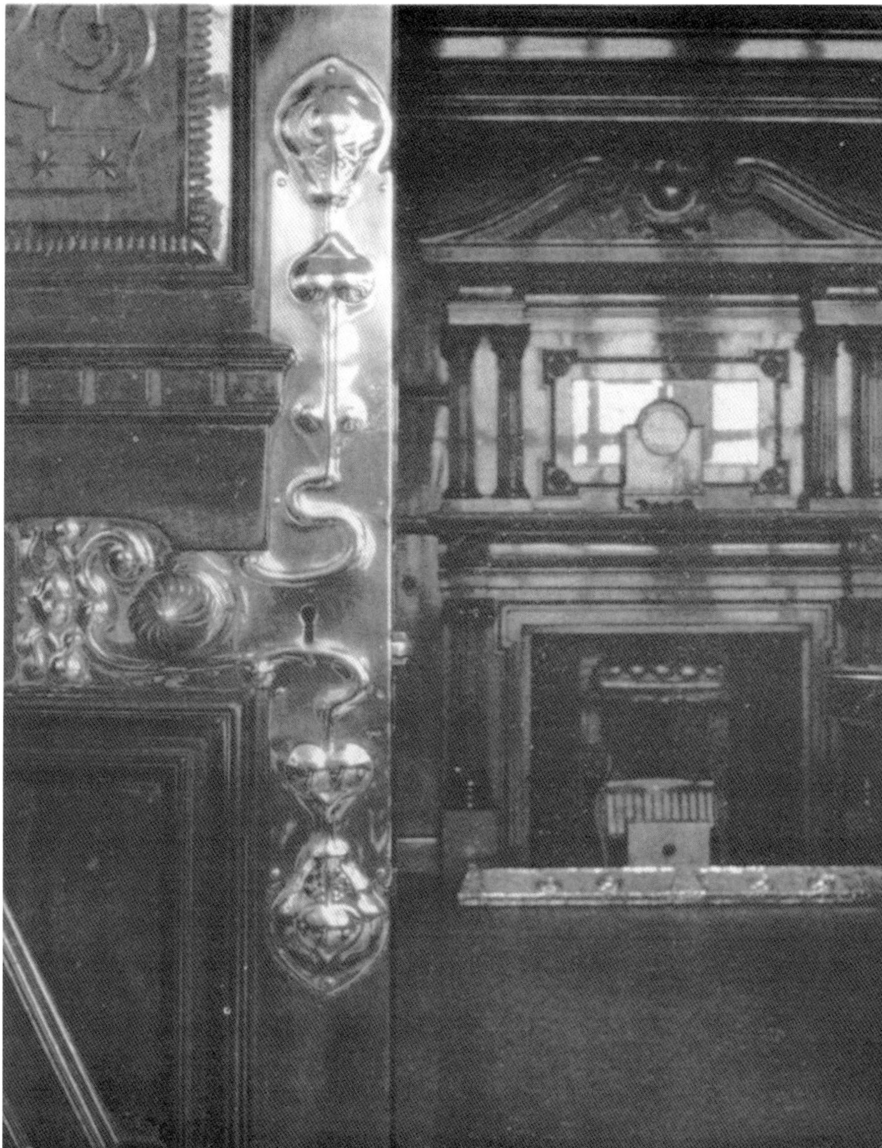

42 Liverpool Art Nouveau. Brass door furniture in the Philharmonic Hotel

support of the livelier teachers at the University (which got independent status as such in 1903 and was full of a new self-confidence), and John painted some of his best early portraits of such men as J. M. Mackay, E. K. Muspratt, Sir John Brunner and Kuno Meyer. 'Liverpool,' he recalled half

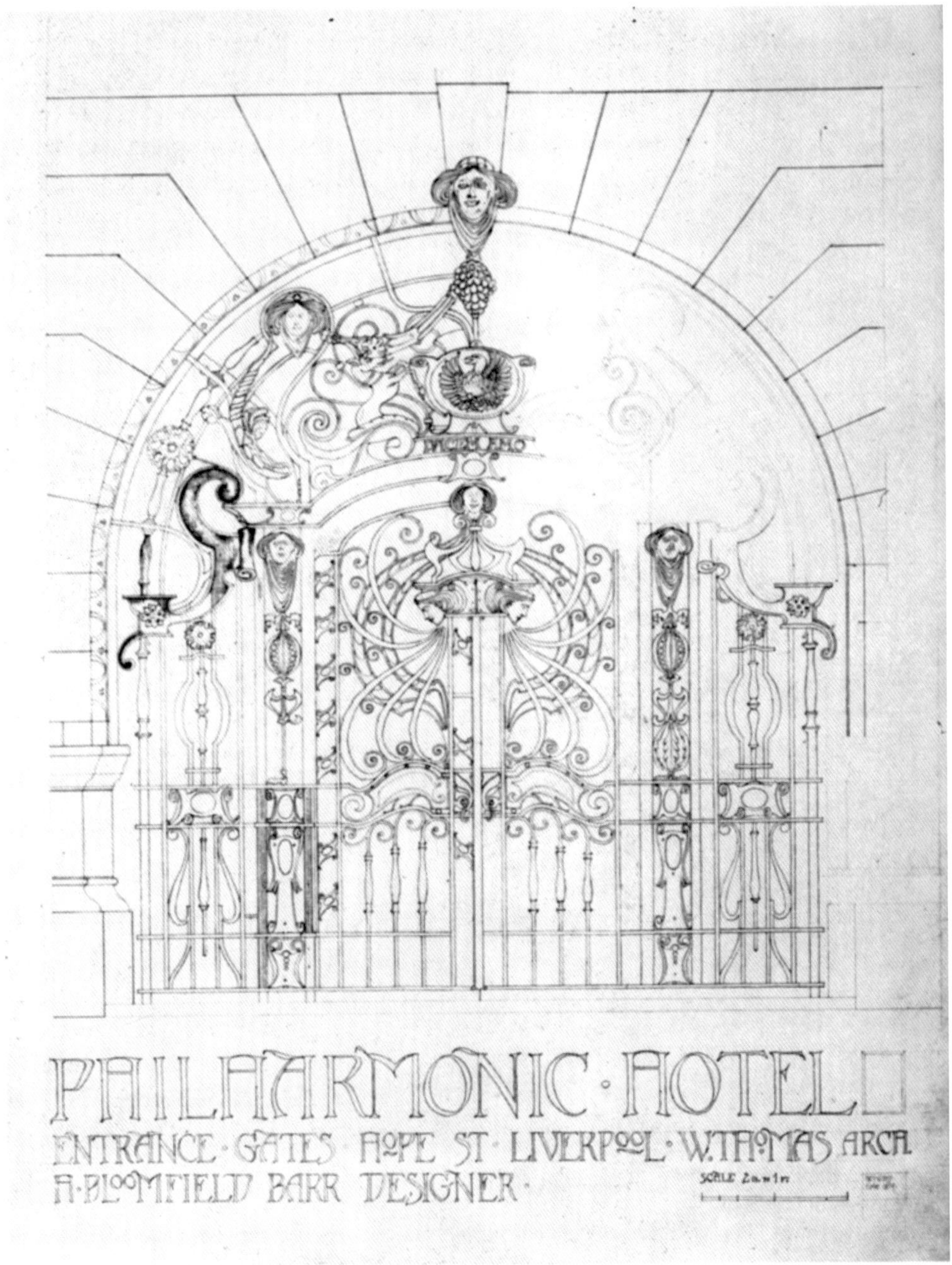

43 Liverpool Art Nouveau. H. Bloomfield Barr's metal gates to the Philharmonic Hotel, drawn by a student at the School of Architecture

a century later, 'commonly considered a dull, ugly and commercial city, for me abounded in interest and surprise.'[1] He had in fact given up teaching two or three years before the split, but he remained working close by in Chatham Street. Outside the Sandon group he was less appreciated. In 1902[2] the Liverpool Academy rejected his application for membership, and when that year a group of subscribers gave his portrait by Rothenstein to the Walker Gallery it was catalogued simply as *Portrait of a Young Man*.

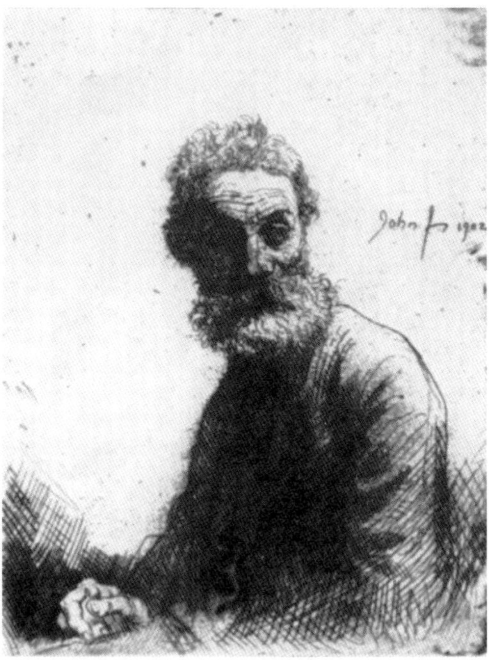

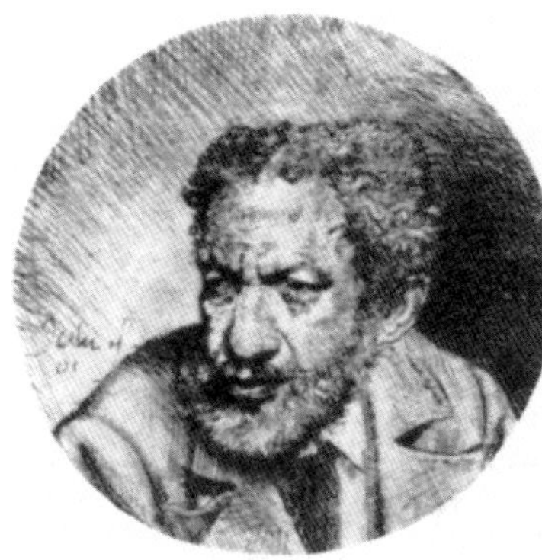

44 & 45 Augustus John's Liverpool period. Above: *The Mulatto*. An etching of 1910, first state. According to Campbell Dodgson,' The man was a man from Barbados, etched at Liverpool.' Left: *Old Man of Liverpool*. An etching of 1902

The brief Art Nouveau movement seems to have fizzled out as soon as the Applied Art section parted company with the architects. But the result was for the first time in Liverpool to create an organized group of artists outside and in opposition to the recognized art establishment. When Sandon Terrace was pulled down in 1907 to make a playground behind the Mechanics' Institution the new school moved down the hill to the Bluecoat School buildings (where the University School of Architecture, now under C. H. Reilly, joined it two years later.) There it transformed itself into the Sandon Studios Society, a mixed group of practising artists and amateurs with John,

[1] Augustus John: *Chiaroscuro;* Cape, London, 1952, p. 59. After leaving the city he painted further portraits of Reilly, Oliver Elton and Sir Charles Sherrington.

[2] *Not* 1905, as suggested by the Academy's 150th Anniversary Catalogue. Roderick Bisson established the correct date from the Academy minutes.

Steer, Lavery and Mackintosh as honorary members and Chowne and MacNair as teachers. The Liverpool Academy was at that time a dead body, though it had begun holding exhibitions again in 1897; the Autumn Exhi-

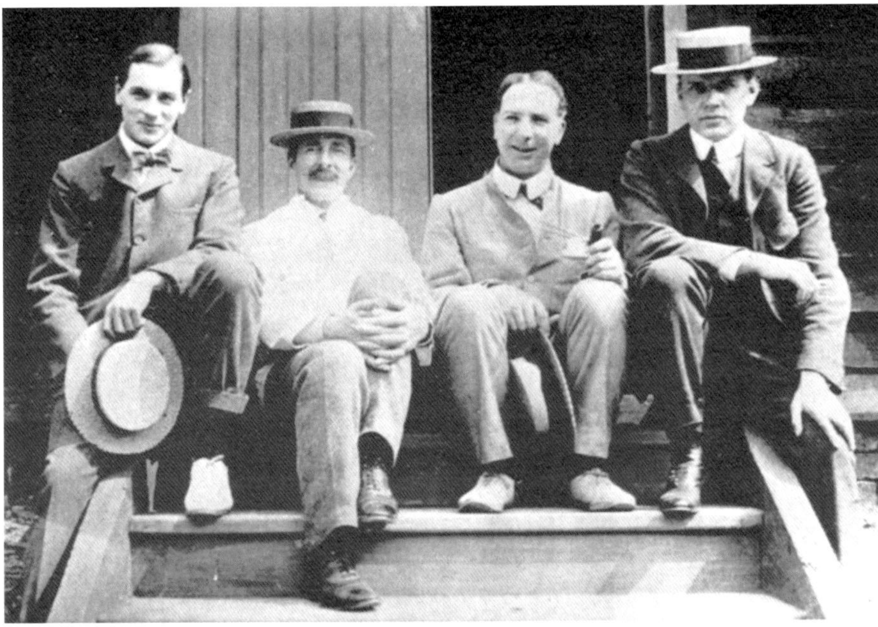

46 Teachers of the Applied Art Department with the Professor of Architecture. Left to right: Gerald Chowne, Charles J. Allen, J. Herbert MacNair and Charles Reilly

bition was largely controlled by the London artists, the Royal Academy having at one point threatened a boycott when the Liverpool influence seemed to be getting too great. The coal merchant (and total abstainer) John Lea, who had succeeded Rathbone as chairman, was 'slow to push out into new deeps' according to his biographer; 'he had certain intellectual and spiritual limitations'.[1] Dibdin took over at the Walker Gallery in 1904, and began the unhappy but not uncommon policy of taking members of his committee up to London each year for a tour of the studios. According to Sir W. B. Forwood[2] they would visit 200 in ten days, and always had the same cab-driver. He also wrote regular unsigned articles on art for the *Liverpool Post*, where he can be found calling Oscar Wilde an 'unhappy victim of

[1] *John Lea. Citizen and Art Lover*. A sketch by Frank Elias. Philip, Son and Nephew, Liverpool n.d. (1928), p. 25. Lea stood as a Liberal for East Toxteth in 1909 and was beaten by Sir Edward Marshall Hall; he became Lord Mayor in 1914. Frank Elias wrote several books for the Religious Tract Society and was a contributor to *The Boy's Own Paper*. His biography is generally eulogious.

[2] Cited by Elias (p. 34).

diseased propensities',[1] and writing of 'the jejune El Greco' and of Goya as being 'singularly ill-regulated as regards his life or his art'.[2]

So the irreconcilable gap was no longer between the art-lovers and the Corporation, as it had been at the time of the St George's Hall panels, but between the official bodies and the unofficial one. On the one hand there was the NEAC show organized by Chowne at the Royal Institution building in 1905 and attended by Steer and Tonks. There was the Sandon Society's spring exhibition of 1908, which included a Monet (*Etretat*) and twenty-one works by Augustus John. Above all there were the two Post-Impressionist shows, one in March 1911 and the other in February 1913, drawn from the famous exhibitions organized by Roger Fry at the Grafton Gallery in London and accompanied in each case by a section of Sandon artists. Against these enterprising ventures the Walker Gallery could set a belated show of the Barbizon school, including Corot, and of etchings from Georges Petit's Paris gallery in March 1908, while a batch of NEAC painters was admitted to the Autumn Exhibition of that year. In 1911 the Le Sidaner was bought. This lagging shift of taste however was hardly enough to excite the informed art lover, and there was no longer the old concern with the uninformed. Attendance at the gallery had been falling since the beginning of the century – 'doubtless due,' said Dibdin in his 1912 report to the city council, 'to the inducements offered in other directions, notably the attractions of numerous picture palaces and the tendency of many to spend their leisure time motoring'.[3] And Dibdin himself still reacted to modern art with a now all too familiar philistinism, comparing Vlaminck's *Pontoise* in the second Post-Impressionist show with 'Master Tommy's results with his first paint-box' and ridiculing van Gogh for the thickness of his paint.[4]

Opposition to the Sandon Society and its works reached a climax in 1909, when a lawyer friend of Augustus John's called H. Chaloner Dowdall was the retiring Lord Mayor and asked John to paint his presentation portrait, on the grounds that 'you will have the biggest gate the Autumn Exhibition has ever had, and I shall have a picture worth 500 guineas within five years' time'.[5] The painting, with Dowdall as a heavily dramatized civic Don Quixote and a rubicund footman called Smith as his Sancho Panza, took little account

[1] 'Art and Degeneracy', 29 December 1912.

[2] In a book review on 14 January 1914. These articles, together with two remarkable patriotic poems of autumn 1914 and other interesting items, are in a cuttings book 'Articles by E. R. Dibdin 1907–14' in the Liverpool Public Libraries.

[3] Quoted in Frank Lambert: 'The Walker Art Gallery. Growth of a Policy (2)' in *Liverpool Bulletin*. February 1952, Vol. I, no. 3, p. 3.

[4] Article of 15 February 1913, in the same cuttings book.

[5] Letter from Dowdall to Vere E. Cotton, 6 November 1945, in a book of cuttings and letters relating to the portrait, no. Hq. 759/2 JOH in the Liverpool Public Libraries.

of municipal dignity and affronted many of the citizens. Coming on it among the more congenial Autumn Exhibition pictures by Alma Tadema, Leighton, Luke Fildes and Solomon J. Solomon, the *Liverpool Post* critic called it:

> either an extremely bad practical joke or else the grossest exhibition of bad and inartistic taste we have ever seen on the walls of the gallery.[1]

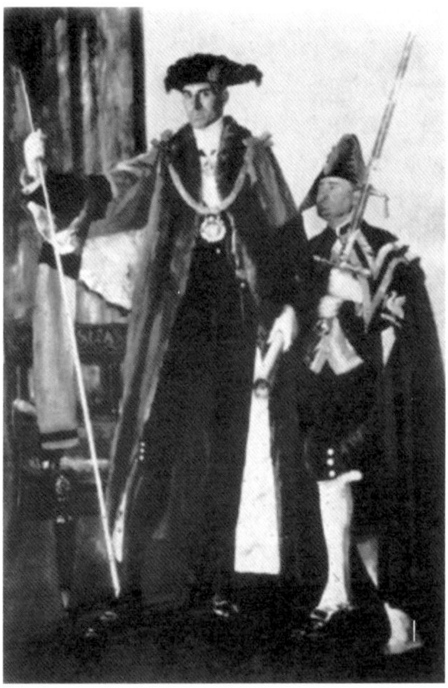

47 Another object of controversy: John's portrait of Lord Mayor Dowdall, 1909, now in the National Gallery of Victoria at Melbourne

Four days later the same writer was contrasting the 'hubbub among the long-haired gentry', which this verdict not unnaturally provoked, with the more laudable attitude of 'healthy-minded students of art'. Similarly 'Bent Briar' in the satirical *Porcupine* referred to 'long-haired neurotic commentators', arguing that

> If to coax Dicky Sam and his wife through our turnstiles we have to rely upon 'freak' pictures, the sooner we go out of the business, the better.[2]

John himself seems to have been taken aback by the venom of such attacks, which he found 'stupid, disgusting and unnecessary'.[3] Dowdall as ex-mayor defended him in a lecture at the gallery, but within ten years had sold the picture to a private buyer in Sussex who offered him £1,400 for it, or four-

[1] 18 September 1909.
[2] *Porcupine*, Liverpool, 25 September 1909.
[3] Interview in the *Dispatch* of 4 October 1909

teen times John's original fee.[1] It never found a home in Liverpool at all, and in 1938 went off to the National Gallery of Victoria – the year the Walker Gallery bought the *Two Jamaican Girls*, its first example of John's work.

The tensions of 1909 stimulated the Sandon group to produce a pamphlet called *The Sport of Civic Life, or Art and the Municipality*,[2] which set out to attack the official art policies all along the line. In this Henry Carr the Liverpool painter wrote on the Autumn Exhibition; the stage designer G. W. Harris, an ex-pupil of John's, on the Liverpool Academy, whose centenary was then impending ('When you hear the drums banging for the Liverpool Academy don't get up, it's not worth it. . . .'); Charles W. Sharpe on the commissioning of a London artist to paint four lunettes in the Town Hall vestibule; Frank Rutter on the cleaning of the Roscoe pictures and the building up of the permanent collection. There is also an amusing lampoon on John Lea, who is made to say:

> Now, this is a canvas we cannot well sky,
> It teaches a moral and catches the eye,
> If I say the word the City will buy [then a refrain].
>
> ART'S a fine thing and it's all very well,
> But COMMERCE is greater – it's harder to spell,
> So we'll hang up the works that are likely to sell.
>
> Lea, – lie – low!

[1] Dowdall was under some criticism for selling a picture in which Liverpool, despite its behaviour in 1909, still felt a proprietary right – especially as he at the same time bought a house and three acres of ground on Boars Hill near Oxford, to which he retired. He explained the circumstances in the letter to Cotton already quoted:

> . . . . a little later I was being good naturedly chaffed at the round table of The Conservative Club where the party leaders lunched. So I retaliated 'Well you may not like it, but you are businessmen, and I will bet I could get £1,000 for it.' Alderman Oulton was on my left and said 'Sell it', and it went right round the table everyone saying 'Sell it'. Sir Charles Petrie, Alderman Savage, Sir William Forwood (less confidently), and I think Sir Thomas Royden and others. Anyhow when I came here and had nowhere to hang it I wrote to Sir Charles Petrie who was then leader of the Council, reminded him of the joke and asking him if it would be generally agreeable if I took the joke seriously. . . .

Probably (as Colonel Cotton points out), Sir Charles and the other lunchers had been the chief donors of the portrait, which in those days was commissioned not by the Corporation but by a group of the sitter's friends. Then a month after Dowdall had had the offer of £1,400 from Mr Warren of Lewes House he got a letter from the Tate Gallery offering him £200 or £300 for the picture. This letter too is in the book of cuttings and bears a pencilled note:

> I asked my wife if she thought my son, who was then 10, would rather have his father in the Tate and a nominal price or the full market price and she said 'Don't be a fool'. H.C.D.

In the 1950s the Walker Gallery borrowed the picture from Melbourne, and Dowdall, now an old man, spoke about the circumstances of its painting.

[2] Edited and published by Charles W. Sharpe, Liverpool 1909. A successor appeared in 1912 under the title *A Bushell of Chaff*. Roderick Bisson says John Lea asked the School of Art and the local booksellers to boycott it.

The main item in the pamphlet however was an essay by William Rothenstein called 'Art and the Municipality', which no doubt related to the lectures given by him in Liverpool in early 1908 (on 'The Artist and the City') and at a Walker Gallery soirée presided over by Dowdall in October 1909; it may also reflect his discussions at Ditchling with Eric Gill. He was all in favour of making use of the local artist. 'I hold it to be more important,' he said, 'that such culture as is native in any city should be tended, developed, and ultimately employed than that a hundred masterpieces adorn the walls of the public gallery.' What should have been done was:

> to encourage a man of energy and discernment to settle in the growing city, capable of co-operating together in planning spaces and buildings, whether private or public, and of inspiring a circle of eager local craftsmen of every kind, who would thus have laid foundations for a living school of art.

He suggested that the Corporation should induce 'one or two men of tried character and attainment' to settle in Liverpool 'to advise and organize the collective efforts' of gallery, museum and theatre, which would remain under their existing management. 'Thus might be founded as it were a University of the Arts', with its students 'decorating schools, mission houses, chapels, halls, of any kind and however humble.'

> The necessary elements are there already – money *is* spent and work of various sorts is required, and local students, and enthusiasm, and latent talent. What is needed is to bring these elements into relation, and under modern conditions this can only be brought about by the devotion and energy of an enthusiast, working – and paid to work – for that end.

This would be much better than the prevailing situation, where the artist seemed 'little more than a parasite, waiting on the caprices of the rich rather than expressing the essential culture of his own time.'[1]

Simpson's successor C. H. Reilly invited Rothenstein to be his lecturer in art at the School of Architecture. The invitation (which was refused) and many of the ideas which Rothenstein outlined are part of a larger scheme described in Reilly's memoirs,[2] by which a powerful group would have moved into Liverpool cultural life under the wing of the university. The idea was to create a chair of Aesthetics for MacColl, who would also have become director of the Walker Gallery; John, Epstein and Elgar would then have been asked to become respectively professors of painting, sculpture and music. The Corporation were not keen, arguing that painting was their responsibility rather than the university's; but something of the plan seems to

[1] Ibid, pp. 5–9.
[2] *Scaffolding in the Sky;* Routledge, London, 1938, pp. 124–5.

have filtered into the 1914 project for a Lancashire Society of Arts centred on the Bluecoat School. This eighteenth century group of buildings now housing the Sandon Society was rented in 1909 by W. H. Lever (the subsequent Lord Leverhulme) for the benefit of the University School of Architecture and at Reilly's request. When it proved necessary to secure the freehold if the school was to be saved from redevelopment, Lever was persuaded to put up the money on behalf of the friends and tenants of the buildings. The idea was that the proposed society of arts should in due course take them over from Lever and run them as an arts centre. Part of its function as outlined was to give fellowships to eminent creative artists which might induce them to work in Liverpool for limited periods. Every year two fellows each in painting, decorative painting and design, sculpture, architecture and civic design, music, and literature and drama were to be appointed and lent rooms in the school on condition that they spent at least two months in Liverpool and discussed their work with other members of the society. In the event Lever changed his mind, and turned the scheme down flat when the Great War ended. But it remains the emasculated ancestor of the present Bluecoat Society of Arts.[1]

With that we have the main framework of the Liverpool art organizations as we know them today: the gallery, with the Roscoe collection of old masters; the Regional College of Art centred on its buildings of 1883 and 1905; the Liverpool Academy; the Sandon Studios Society; the Bluecoat Chambers and its studios; and the disappearance of any kind of art or art historical department at the university. Each of these phenomena was founded on a set of ideas which has not necessarily ever been fulfilled, yet arose from the local situation and the growth of the city and is still somehow hanging in the air like a very old radioactive cloud, even though few people are conscious of it now. It is almost as if there were a pattern in these things: a fresh social or philosophical approach to the problem leading each time to a small burst of activity as first the Royal Institution, then the Mechanics' Institution, then the Liverpool Academy, then the official Autumn Exhibition and finally the Sandon Society found new energies and an interested public. Each time it took some years for the word to get around and for the artists, local or metropolitan, to absorb the stimulus and produce their main works. By then the original approach had been forgotten or discarded, for the one man with the persistence and perhaps blindness to go on hammering away at the same

[1] The history of this society is given in W. S. MacCunn: *Bluecoat Chambers;* Liverpool University Press, 1956.

points from start to finish had been Roscoe, who came too early in the story for his achievement to take a very tangible form. His monument is in his collection; it is not in the structure of art in Liverpool.

Over and above this there was also a much larger shift of attitude which was not confined to Liverpool or even to this country. The social, educational, almost philanthropic view of the arts which evolved in the nineteenth century only appealed to the brighter spirits so long as it was not bureaucratized. As soon as it became official corporation policy there was a reaction against it in the name of artistic exclusiveness and good taste: that new emphasis on personality and technique which appeared in R. A. M. Stevenson's book. The Sandon Society, for instance, accepted the idea of the artist as gypsy, as gentleman or as scholar. It was more than doubtful about his role in civic life.

It is worth thinking how far this might have been avoided by a more intelligent corporation; certainly Philip Rathbone's death in 1895 seems to mark a turning point. For the real question in the arts in a city like Liverpool is how far the shift of patronage and policy-making into municipal hands can be used to stimulate rather than merely alienate the artist. Can the old concern with art's social function survive without turning him in on himself? All we can do here is try to show how history raises such questions; a far more detailed study would be necessary if they were to be answered. But the ideas and the events of those years are still there to be thought about, and so are the major monuments and many of the works which the local artists produced. A wider consciousness of these things would certainly help in the development of any new pattern for art in English provincial cities.

3 : ESTABLISHED INSTITUTIONS

Such is the background to the present art 'establishment' in the city, and the extension of central authority and central grants in the educational and cultural field has only confirmed it. Only the Liverpool Academy, of the institutions which we have mentioned, can today be considered as a purely local enterprise. The Walker Gallery is one of the four provincial galleries (the others being Glasgow and the university collections at Oxford and Cambridge) which the Standing Commission on Museums and Galleries regards as having been 'built up to national standard';[1] in 1960 it became the first provincial gallery to be substantially helped by the government to buy a picture it needed. The College of Art, the University and also the Public Libraries (with their Art Library and collection of prints) are geared into the national educational and library system, while the Bluecoat and Sandon Societies are seen as part of an embryo network of arts centres such as the present government, the Arts Council and the Gulbenkian Foundation all in their various ways wish to encourage. Bodies like these have changed in many respects since the nineteenth century, but broadly speaking they have not lost in importance. More than most English cities, Liverpool provides a strong and active structure for the visual arts.

The great transformation in the Walker Art Gallery dates from 2 April 1931, when Vere E. Cotton, Philip Rathbone's grandson-in-law, wrote a letter to the *Liverpool Post* denouncing its collection as 'utterly unworthy' of the place. He organized a petition of eighty leading citizens to complain that the gallery was failing to fulfil its purpose, which he proposed should be the formation of a balanced collection of British painting. This was true in that both attendances and sales at the Autumn Exhibitions had been falling off ever since 1904,[2] but whether the purpose had ever been quite what it now became is doubtful. Up to the time of Cotton's assault the gallery more or less rotated round the Autumn Exhibition, and the large collection of pictures which had been formed was mainly purchased thence; only the Roscoe

[1] Standing Commission on Museums and Galleries: *Survey of Provincial Museums and Galleries;* HMSO 1963, paragraph 22.

[2] Frank Lambert: 'The Arts – Painting' in *Liverpool Echo*, Centenary Edition, 1955, pp. 77–8. See also his two articles 'The Walker Art Gallery – Growth of a Policy' in *Liverpool Bulletin*, Vol. I. nos. 2 and 3, October 1951 and February 1952.

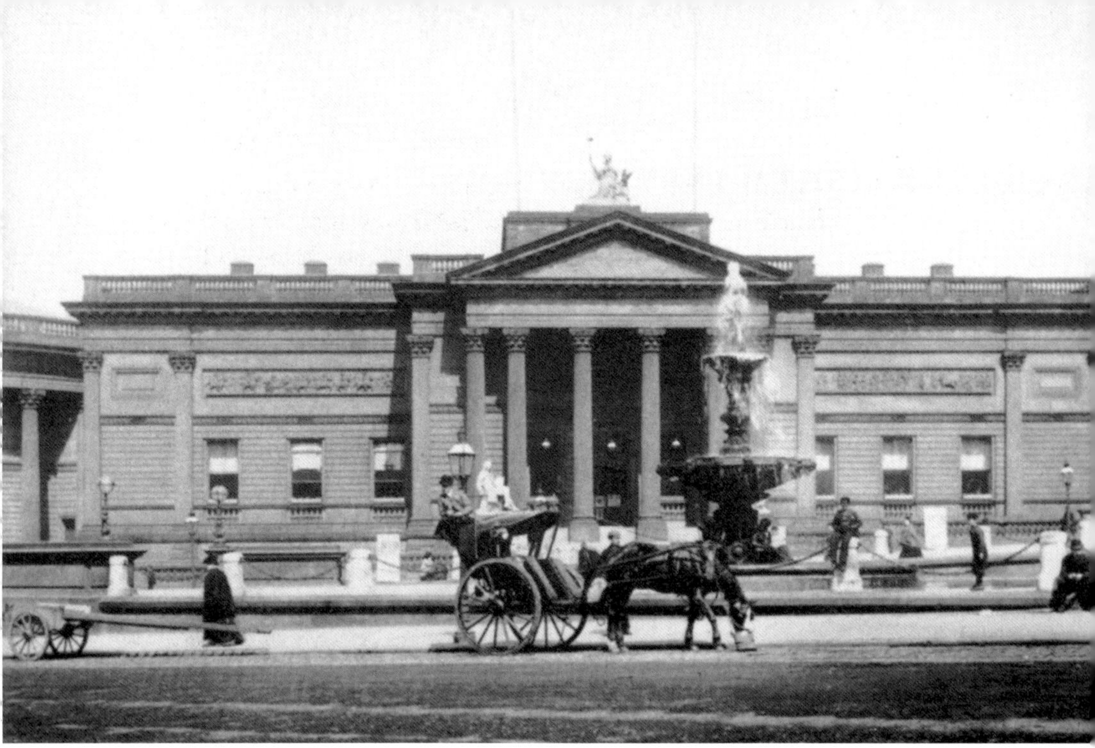

48 The Walker Art Gallery. An early photograph

pictures lent by the Royal Institution and the occasional legacy (like Rathbone's) provided a striking exception, actively disliked by the more philistine members of the public.[1] The only income for purchases up to 1929, apart from a bequest of £2,000 by Lord Derby in 1892, was the annual profit on the Autumn Exhibition, which dwindled over the years almost to the point of disappearance; it was in that year that the corporation first made a purchase grant: £750. Frank Lambert, however, who took over as director in 1932, with Hugh Scrutton as his successor in 1952 and Cotton himself as chairman of the city's Libraries, Museums and Arts committee almost uninterruptedly from 1939 to 1955, between them turned it into a place that artist and scholars all over the world have to take seriously. In 1931 it was near the bottom of the larger English provincial galleries. Today it is one of the small group at the top.

It normally shows a good representative collection of English painting from the seventeenth century to the present day, an outstanding group of Flemish and Italian primitives, a sprinkling of works by other great European painters, from Rubens through Rembrandt and Courbet to Seurat and

[1] See the unsigned article in *The Liverpool Review* 'A Chamber of Horrors' of 5 March 1887, when Roscoe's pictures were still hanging in the Royal Institution. 'The climax of horror is reached . . . when you come to the end wall, where the examples of the Byzantine school are hung which formed the main portion of the Roscoe bequest. Anything more terrible than this Byzantine chamber of horrors it would be impossible to imagine except it might be a nightmare.'

Matisse, and a few modern foreign paintings, not however of the first rank. It also attracts important loans; Christ Church, Oxford, for instance deposited its pictures in the gallery while its own new gallery building was being built, and twenty-four of Lt-Col A. Heywood-Lonsdale's pictures, including a Rembrandt and a Chardin, have been on loan since 1959. There is no Autumn Exhibition. Instead there is the annual show of the much revived Liverpool Academy, which has been held in the gallery since its postwar reopening in 1951, and, every two years since 1957, the John Moores Liverpool Exhibition, which has for young British painters become a biennale nearly as stimulating as those of Venice, São Paulo and Paris, and in every way more accessible. All this is a great achievement; it means that in thirty years the city has began to catch up with the main international current of taste and interest in pictures (instead of, as before, lagging thirty years behind it).[1] and that it is now known for its gallery to many people elsewhere who take no interest in shipping, football or pop music. It means too that within the new network of

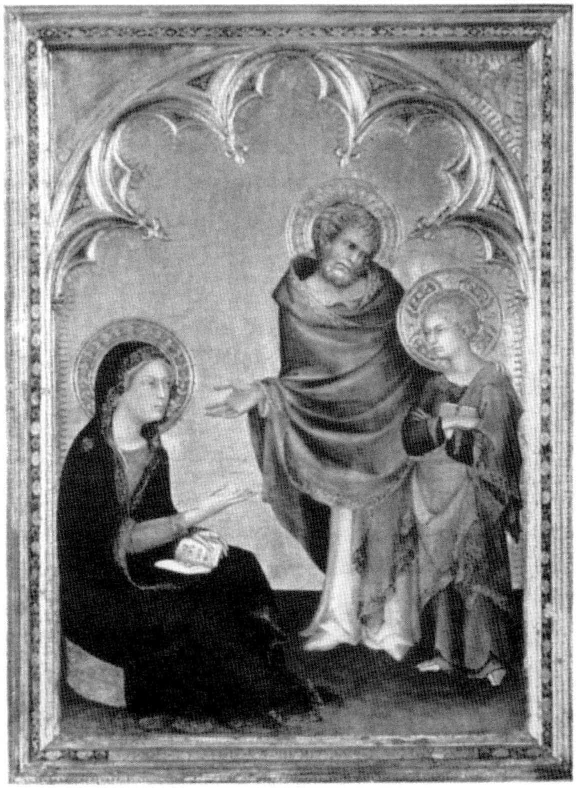

49 Simone Martini: *Christ discovered in the temple.* One of the outstanding masterpieces of William Roscoe's collection now in the Walker Gallery

[1] Dibdin's Barbizon show was in 1908. The Barbizon painters were internationally famous (and selling for high prices) thirty years earlier. They were painting their best works some thirty years before that.

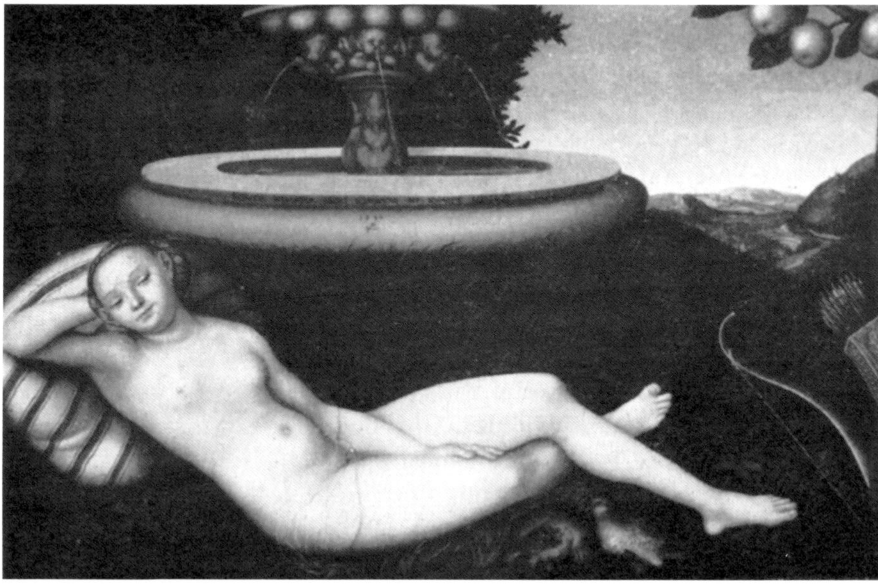

50 Lucas Cranach: *The Nymph of the Fountain.* Another of the Walker Gallery's Roscoe pictures

centralized art patronage and management – both official and private – Liverpool carries considerable weight. The remarkable thing is that all this is not more widely appreciated in Liverpool itself.

At least until very recently, the driving force in the gallery's development has come neither from the 150,000-odd visitors who are counted through its doors in an average year[1] nor from their elected representatives who govern it, but from a group of Liverpool's business leaders, with Cotton at their head. Until 1956 the purchase grant from the rates never exceeded £1,000 a year, and it was only six years later that it began to compare favourably with that available to other big provincial galleries; it now stands at £10,000 for 1964–5, which reflects the much greater interest recently taken by the council. The main burden however of those purchases which have so transformed the gallery's status has been borne by certain local firms, who have either individually paid for works the gallery has asked for or, more recently, subscribed to special funds in its support. Eleven major acquisitions in the past fifteen years, including the Rembrandt and the Rubens, have come about in this way, while some twenty of the most modern English paintings have been

[1] Attendance figures are not at all a reliable clue to the impact made by such an institution on the public, though they can be a reasonable guide to the success of a particular exhibition. For what they are worth, here are the attendances at the gallery for the period 1958–65:

1958/9	127,000	1962/3	125,427
1959/60	188,959	1963/4	125,427
1960/1	177,985	1964/5	127,596
1961/2	155,987	1965/6	213,191

given by the sponsors of the John Moores exhibitions. The kernel of the collection is still the Roscoe and other pictures from the Royal Institution, which were finally made over to the city in 1948; most of the 5,000 or so odd works in the cellars or out on loan come from the old pre-1931 purchasing policy; the seventeenth, eighteenth and early twentieth century English works added since come largely from a legacy of £20,000 from Lord Wavertree, a member of the Walker family who was deputy chairman of the Arts Sub-Committee and died in 1932. The development of the foreign collection and the extension of the English school into our own time have been due to the public spirit of industry, shipping, stores, insurance and banks.[1]

[1] This patronage can be analysed as follows:

(a) Seven works given individually by firms.
Gainsborough: *Sir Robert Clayton* (1950). The Liverpool Post and Echo.
Crome: *Landscape* (1950–1). Owen Owen and Co Ltd.
Stubbs: *Molly Longlegs* and *Three Brood Mares at Grass* (1951–2). Lewis's Ltd.
Flemish Tapestry: *Fortitude* (1952–3). Martins Bank Ltd.
Rembrandt: *Self-Portrait* (1953–4). Alfred Holt and Co (P. H. Holt Trust).
Van Dyck: *Portrait of the Infanta Isabella-Clara-Eugenia* (1954–5). The Royal Insurance Company Ltd.

(b) Given by Mr John Moores from the exhibition bearing his name:
1957–8: Paintings by Jack Smith, Ceri Richards, Victor Pasmore, John Bratby and Sheila Fell.
1959–60: Paintings by Robin Philipson, William Scott and Terry Frost.
1961–2: Paintings by Sandra Blow, William Crozier, R. B. Kitaj, Joseph Tilson and David Tindle.
1963–4: Paintings by Roger Hilton, Stephen McKenna and Christopher Paice.
1965–6: Paintings by Michael Kidner and Michael Tyzack.

(c) Firms subscribing to the purchase of Rubens: *The Virgin and Child with St Elizabeth and the Child Baptist*. (1959–60):
Alfred Holt and Co (P. H. Holt Trust)
Pilkington Brothers Ltd (of St Helens)
Peter Walker (Warrington) Ltd
J. Bibby and Sons Ltd
Tillotsons (Liverpool) Ltd
Continental Cinema, Wallasey
Sing White and Co
Tilney, Parr and Rae
Blackledge and Broughton

(d) Contributors of £1,000 and more to the Special Picture Purchase Fund Appeal (mainly seven-year covenants from 1960):
Peter Walker (Warrington) Ltd
Martins Bank Ltd
Royal Insurance Co Ltd
Alfred Holt and Co (P. H. Holt Trust)
John Holt (Overseas) Ltd
Lewis's Ltd
Owen Owen Ltd
Topham's Ltd
The Vernons Organization
Granada TV Network Ltd (of Manchester)
ICI
Liverpool Daily Post and Echo
Tate and Lyle Ltd
British-American Tobacco Co Ltd

There have also been outstanding contributions by Mr C. F. J. Beausire and the Misses Beausire, members of a Liverpool business family, who between them have given P. de Loutherbourg's *Landscape with Figures* (1953–4) and £7,000 to the Appeal.

The above list is intended only to illustrate the argument of the text, not to give an exhaustive account of benefactions to the gallery.

Common enough in America, such support of a city gallery is more rare in England, and because central grants (from the Treasury, from the Arts Council, from the National Art-Collections Fund or from the foundations) are often made conditional on a comparable local effort it is apt to snowball, bringing in two or three times the amount locally subscribed. Moreover it impels the city to take something of the same interest and keep up its own contribution if it is not to let the business oligarchy become predominant in the gallery's affairs. So far this has worked well in Liverpool, and the purchase of the Rubens *Virgin and Child* in 1960 is a good example. Here the

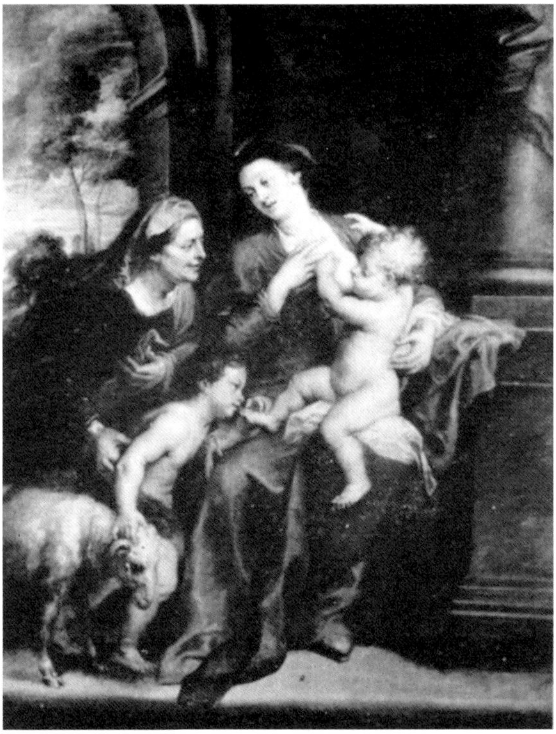

51 Rubens: *Virgin and Child, with St Elizabeth and child Baptist.* Bought by the Walker Gallery in 1960. Its most expensive acquisition yet, marking an important change in official policy towards the provincial galleries

subscriptions from private and business contributors and locally-administered trusts totalled about £10,000; the city matched this with £10,000 from the rates; £5,000 more came from the foundations and the National Art-Collections Fund; thus there was a total of £25,000 raised by the gallery which the government matched with another £25,000 to reach the purchase price of £50,000. Perhaps only 10 per cent of this sum came strictly from business, but without it the rest would not have been forthcoming. And the Rubens operation was doubly important as a demonstration both because it marked a change in government policy towards the provincial galleries (for which Cotton had been pressing since 1952; it was later formally set out in the 1963 Report of the Standing Commission on Museums) and because it provided a pattern for the gallery's subsequent Special Picture Purchase Fund Appeal. This fund, which passed £62,000 by May 1962 and has been used to buy the gallery's Courbet, Seurat, Monet and Cézanne, took advantage of the system of seven-year covenants under which any sum given is increased by tax concessions.[1] It was raised by a Labour Sub-Committee chairman, Ben Shaw.

I tried in conversation with one or two of the leading contributors to the gallery to discover just what it is that makes Liverpool business people willing to act in this disinterested way. Several of them are themselves collectors – Mr G. R. Kennerley of Vernons Pools, Mr Morton Oliphant of Tate and Lyle, Colonel Cotton (a former director of Martins Bank), Mrs Bibby, Mr S. Samuels, Mr John Moores of Littlewoods;[2] Mr Moores and Mr Kennerley indeed are also painters – and the obvious wish to pass on the pleasure they have derived from pictures certainly plays its part. There is also quite simply local pride, strongest with firms whose headquarters are in the area, though a branch of some larger concern is liable to contribute if it is autonomous enough. One director suggested that a firm should contribute as a duty to its employees, particularly if the gallery kept them in touch with its activities; another feared that the old family firms might soon become too impersonal for well-wishers like himself to be able to sway the board of directors, though much depended on the personal feelings of the chairman, who would often be allowed his own way over such commercial non-essentials. Whether these are so much motives, however, as explanations is more problematic, and it may well be that precedent and example are what really matters. The Liverpool business community is a close-knit one, whose most influential members are liable to find themselves meeting in a number of different capacities on different committees. When one of them in the

[1] Courbet's *Marée basse à Trouville* and Seurat's *Maisons Blanches, Ville d'Avray* were bought from Mr A. Chester Beatty for £22,500. This sum was met as follows:

£12,000 from the Special Picture Purchase Fund

£5,000 from the National Art-Collections Fund

£2,500 from the fund administered by Victoria and Albert Museum on behalf of the government.

£2,000 remitted as a gift by Mr Chester Beatty

£1,000 from the annual purchase grant

Cézanne's *The Murder* cost £32,400, of which £5,000 came from the National Art-Collections Fund and the rest from the Appeal.

[2] Mr Kennerley for instance owns paintings by Jawlensky, Soutine, Matisse, de Stael. Mr Oliphant has two Courbet landscapes, two early Fantin-Latours, a Gauguin landscape of 1884, several Sickerts, etc. The Samuels collection includes among much else a number of works by Pasmore, Sutherland, Eric Gill and Matthew Smith.

shape of Cotton made a really determined assault on his colleagues' generosity in the 1950s he created that most important of Anglo-Saxon attitudes, a tradition.

The building-up of the collection by these means has proceeded mainly on the lines of 'filling gaps'. That is to say that the gallery has aimed at showing

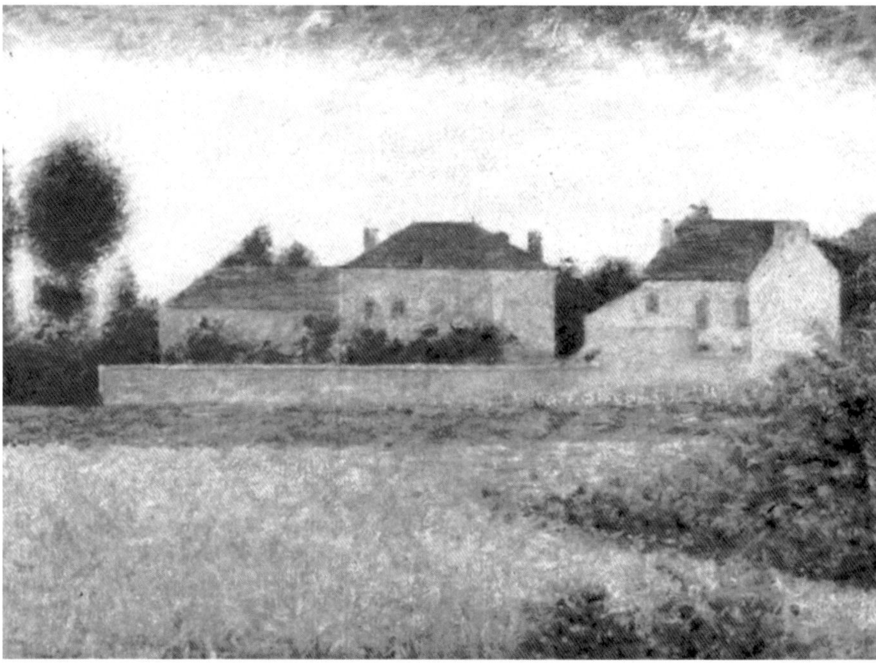

52 Seurat: *Maisons blanches, Ville d'Avray.* Bought by the gallery in 1961 as one of its first purchases from the new Special Picture Purchase Fund to which local businesses contribute

the work of certain schools and certain artists, and has bought its pictures not so much on individual merit as to fill in missing links in the intended chain. In 1951, when the gallery was reopened after its wartime occupation by the Ministry of Food, the director's intention was 'to provide an orderly survey of the whole course of British painting from Tudor times to the present day.'[1] The chief gaps he then saw were Hogarth, Constable and the Norwich school, and the 'younger and more advanced contemporaries', this latter being the result of Cotton's deliberate policy of not buying any picture until at least twenty years after it had been painted. The reopening coincided with the 1951 Festival of Britain, which the gallery celebrated with the first major

[1] City of Liverpool Libraries, Museums and Art Committee Annual Reports for the year ended 31 March 1952, p. 39.

exhibition since 1885 to be devoted to the work of George Stubbs. Three years later in his annual report the new director redefined the gaps as being

> in English painting of the sixteenth and seventeenth centuries, and in the continental schools from the seventeenth century onwards. The most urgent need of all is for a proper representation of modern art.[1]

From 1957 on this need for modern pictures has been met almost entirely from the John Moores exhibitions, so that there has been little occasion for those embarrassing conflicts which happen when a director who is accustomed to looking at modern works has to justify a purchase to a committee who are not. But this embraces modern English painting only. Where the continental schools are concerned most of the outstanding modern figures – Picasso, for instance, Braque, Klee, Bonnard, Léger – are still missing. They could have been bought cheaply enough in the 1930s, but where its own purchases were concerned the gallery virtually disregarded all foreign painting from its foundation until about ten years ago. This is its one real weakness.[2] 'Though the collection must be mainly British', wrote the retiring director in 1952;

> a group of French impressionist work would be most welcome, to demonstrate its influence on the New English Art Club and to illustrate the fundamental truth that art does not work in a social and historical vacuum. Their prices, however, are beyond the Gallery's resources. . . .[3]

This was over three-quarters of a century since the First Impressionist Exhibition and some forty years after the Liverpool impressionist shows, and although the Gallery's main purchasing effort has subsequently been turned in this direction it is a very late starter in the field.

It has held some important loan exhibitions. The chief in public appeal was the Van Gogh exhibition at the end of 1955, which was organized by the Arts Council and was essentially the exhibition shown that year in London; it had 44,209 visitors in six weeks. The most interesting as pieces of local enterprise were the Le Corbusier show of winter 1958/9,[4] which was partly

[1] Ditto for the year ended 31 March 1954, p. 43.

[2] A universal weakness in this country however. See Ronald Alley's devastating article 'The Representation of Twentieth-Century Foreign Art in British Public Collections' in *The Museums Journal*, London, Vol. 61, No. 1, June 1961. Mr Alley took fifty-six leading British galleries, excluding only the Tate, and found that they owned between them four Matisses, three small early Picassos, two Braques, two Légers and *no* paintings by Klee, Gris, Chagall, Miró, Kandinsky and other key figures.

[3] Frank Lambert: 'The Walker Art Gallery – Growth of a Policy' (2) in *Liverpool Bulletin*, February 1952, Vol. I, No. 3, p. 17.

[4] With 17,200 visitors in seven weeks this exhibition made a profit of £360. Local grants amounted to £475, those from the RIBA and the Arts Council to £900, admission fees to £840. It was subsequently shown at the Building Centre in London.

paid for by local architects and builders and was very largely initiated by the gallery and members of its committee, and the Ford Madox Brown exhibition for which Miss Mary Bennett was responsible in 1964. It has organized (as opposed to taking over ready-made) one-man shows for a very few contemporary artists: Uli Nimptsch (1957), John Napper (1959), George Mayer-Marton (memorial exhibition 1960), and Stuart Sutcliffe (memorial exhibition May 1964).[1] A great part of its effort has also in recent years gone to the proper listing and storage of the less presentable part of its collection, and to the overhaul of the loan scheme by which unwanted or specially purchased pictures can be borrowed at an annual charge of £1 per picture by public offices, schools and other bodies. It receives, shows and helps to judge the entries for the annual Topham Trophy competition for designs or models for a steeplechase trophy to be raced for at Aintree; in 1962 and 1963 this was won by two quite original small pieces of sculpture by John W. Mills of the College of Art at St Albans; in 1964 by N. Harding and in 1965 by Valerie Cooke. But the activity for which it has become most widely known is the holding of the biennial John Moores competitions, which in the last seven years have not only started drawing the London art critics to Liverpool but given the younger generation there that basis of familiarity with modern art which their elders lacked.

The objects of the Moores competition have remained virtually the same since 1957, and they are defined as

1 To give Merseyside the chance to see an exhibition of painting and sculpture embracing the best and most vital work being done today throughout the country;

2 to encourage living artists, particularly the young and progressive.

The exact conditions, the treatment of invited artists and the relative encouragement to be given to young and old, have varied each year, though the total prizes provided by Mr Moores have remained fairly constant at £4,000. Attendance rose from 10,000 at the first show (or about a third of that at the 1872 Autumn Exhibition) to 16,500 in 1961, when £3,915 worth of pictures were sold over and above the prize purchases. In 1959 there was an experiment, and a French section and a French judge (Professor André Chastel) were included; in 1963 there was no sculpture as Moores sponsored a separate competition in connection with the new Littlewoods building (discussed on p. 105 below). Broadly speaking the initial sorting of the 2,000 or so entries has been done by the gallery staff and the judging by a jury drawn mainly from the London art world (who also see the whole lot). The result has been verdicts which have sometimes anticipated, sometimes

[1] See pp. 164–7. This exhibition had 10,661 visitors.

confirmed those of London and are close enough to current international taste to be respected abroad. Such names as Jack Smith, for instance (1957), John Bratby (Junior, 1957), Souza, Joseph Tilson (both minor prizes the same year), Hubert Dalwood (sculpture, 1959), those of all the major prize-winners in 1961 – Henry Mundy, Sandra Blow, Leon Kossoff and R. B. Kitaj – as well as Peter Blake and David Hockney of that year's juniors and Antony Donaldson, Harold Cohen, Michael Kidner and Bridget Riley in 1963 were, if not wholly unknown in the London galleries, by no means recognized as they since became. Whether this alignment with the newest fashions is the best thing either for the artists or for the galleries who acquire their pictures is more debatable; some of these young artists' reputations have already started to slump again; others will no doubt follow. But such for the moment is the way in which the liveliest modern art progresses, and the exhibition of 150 or so selected entries in the Walker Gallery has each time

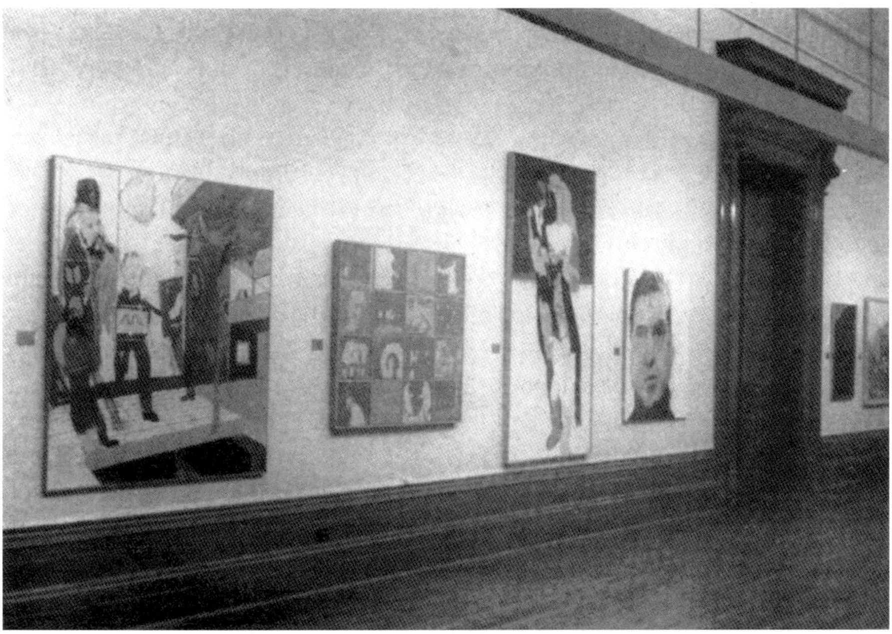

53 Modern pictures acquired from the Moores shows. Left to right: R. B. Kitaj, Alan Welsford, Allen Jones, Sam Walsh (a Liverpool painter). Beyond the door: Arthur Ballard (ditto) and Roger Hilton

been charged with a sense of discovery and surprise that makes it worth travelling a long way to see.

Liverpool's own artists are hardly prominent in the Moores exhibitions, though of course they are well placed to compete. Only four have been included in more than a single show; only nineteen have ever reached this stage at all, though Sam Walsh had a picture bought for the gallery at the 1963 show while John Edkins and (in the junior section) George Moore won minor prizes in 1965.[1] The gallery indeed is determined not to lower its carefully built-up standards just in order to give encouragement to local art, which the director feels is not part of its job, though it has a nucleus of works by leading Liverpool artists of the past which it will occasionally add to; thus it bought Windus's *Burd Helen* some seven years ago, and has also acquired a number of works and objects for their associations with William Roscoe. It has however developed a working arrangement with the Liverpool Academy, whose annual exhibitions have since 1951 been held in its rooms, and the president of the Liverpool Academy is ex-officio an advisory member of the Arts Sub-Committee by which the gallery is governed. It was in fact partly due to the director that the academy instituted an open section in 1955, which has since then been selected by two gallery and one academy representatives and one outsider. As a result of this move the academy now gets some 900 works sent in by non-members each year, and this has given it a new lease of life.

Unlike the gallery the academy has had to make do with its own resources, and if its progress in the 1950s and 60s has accordingly been a good deal more modest and parochial it matters no less to the artists. It is now one of the most flourishing provincial societies of professional artists, with some eighty members; in contrast with the tradition of the neighbouring academy at Manchester its exhibitions now include no London men; and altogether its position is better than at any time in the past 100 years. Admittedly things were better still immediately before that; for its sales before 1860 were said normally to total more than £1,000, with £2,500 in one record year,[2] whereas the average sales in the three years 1962–4 were only £185. But it is to some extent now caught between two forces larger than itself: the rising tide of amateurism and the steadily increasing attraction of the metropolitan (or even the international) art market for collectors and artists alike. This might be expected to deprive it of character; the insistence on professional standards,

[1] Edward Atkinson (1957), Arthur Ballard (1959, 1961), Martin Bell (1957), Sidney Bonner (1963), John Chadwick (1963), Austin Davies (1957), John Edkins (1965), Alfred Edwards (1965), Henry Graham (1957), John Hart (1957, 1959), Adrian Henri (1961, 1965), Nicholas Horsfield (1959, 1961), James Howie (1957), G. W. Jardine (1957), Noel McCready (1959), George Mayer-Marton (1959), George Moore (1965), Robin Riley (1959), W. L. Stevenson (1957), Stuart Sutcliffe (1959), Sam Walsh (1963), J. Coburn Witherop (1957).

[2] According to B. H. Grindley: *History and Work of the Liverpool Academy of Arts.* Lecture delivered at the Free Public Library, Museum and Gallery of Art, Liverpool, 9 February 1875. For earlier years Henry Lacey's *Pictorial Liverpool*, Liverpool 1844, gives the following figures: 1824 £10, 1825 £30, 1827 £489 and 1843 £840.

as quite rigorously maintained by the present committee, means that it depends largely on the professional teachers of art at the College of Art and elsewhere, most of whom have their eyes half-turned to London as the one centre where an artist can live by his work; the College itself moreover, under the new system recommended in 1960 by the National Advisory Council on Art Education, is drawing more of its students as well as its teachers from other parts of the country. Even in the 1840s and 50s however the academy had no very pronounced local flavour, to judge from those works of the time which have survived. With one or two isolated exceptions all the artists of

54 The conclusion of the 1965 Liverpool Academy, with Nicholas Horsfield, the retiring president

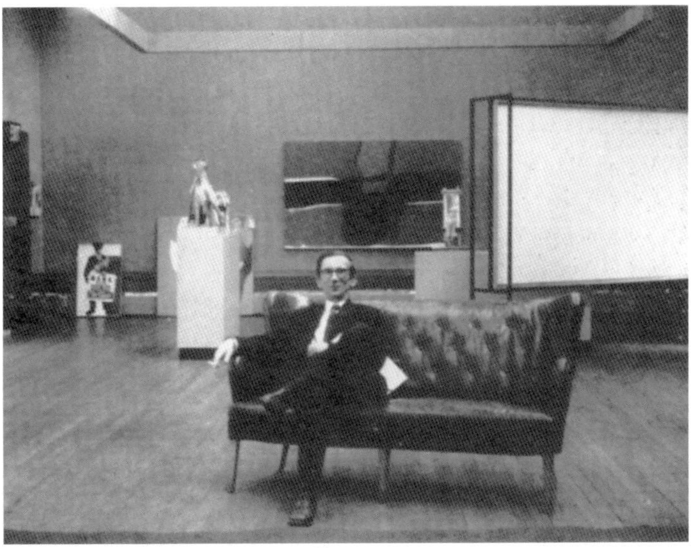

merit in the area now send to its exhibitions. As a result these are not only liable to contain the occasional work of what might be called national calibre – i.e., which would not disgrace a British Council show abroad – but are unique in modern England as the expression of a sizeable professional community of artists somehow surviving, without external grants, in a big provincial city. In 1965 it even began once more to find buyers for the pictures, selling £1,128 worth, or more than in any year since the Second World War. In 1966 the sales amounted to £774.

Not all the city's collection is in the gallery, for the engravings and etchings left by H. F. Hornby in 1906 were placed in the public library, and since then they have been added to, theoretically in consultation with the gallery; Goya's *Tauromaquia*, for instance was bought some four years ago with the aid of the Friends of the National Libraries and the National Art-Collections Fund, and altogether the City Librarian has about £1,000 a year to spend on purchases for the Hornby Library, which also contains rare books and manuscripts. £100 or £200 a year are additionally spent on the city's topographical collection of printed and watercolours by local artists, including

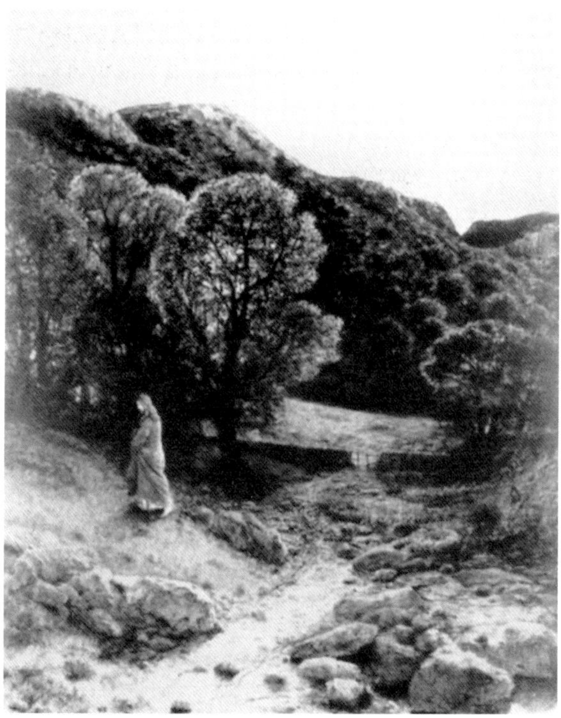

55 From the gallery at Sudley: William Dyce's *Gethsemane*

the commissioning of new works, and these two collections, totalling about 10,000 items in all, are drawn on for exhibitions both in the Central Public Libraries next door to the Walker Gallery and in branch libraries all over the city. There is also the Art Library, which comes under the City Librarian; owing to the peculiarities of the Dewey classification system it contains not only art books but books on sports and pastimes. It was opened in 1955 in a ground-floor room of the gallery so that it could be reached either from the gallery or from the library buildings next door. With the rebuilding of the Brown Library however, which now provides admirable new reading rooms at the other end of the buildings, it was removed and the way through blocked up.

There are a number of other public galleries on Merseyside, starting with

Sudley, an agreeable early nineteenth-century house in the suburbs of Liverpool which has been attached to the Walker Gallery since 1944 and contains Victorian furniture from the Melly family and a number of pictures formerly belonging to the shipping merchant George Holt (1825–96), notably a late Corot, Gainsborough's *Viscountess Folkestone*, three Turners and Dyce's strange *Gethsemane*. The most interesting of these galleries is the Lady Lever Art Gallery at Port Sunlight, built in Imperial-Classical style between 1914 and 1922 by the first Lord Leverhulme in memory of his wife and situated in the heart of this pioneer garden-city close to the very odd non-denominational Unilever church that is also the family mausoleum. At one end in the place of honour is Queen Victoria, flanked by portraits of Lord and Lady Leverhulme; at the other a large marble statue of Ferdinando de' Medici, no doubt symbolizing commercial munificence. In between it contains a good collection of furniture together with major works by the Pre-Raphaelites, Burne-Jones and Herkomer, plus other Victoriana, a Fantin-Latour, two good country scenes by Stubbs, Gainsborough's *Mrs Freer*, Raeburn's portrait of Telford, Turner's *The Falls of the Clyde*, several Richard Wilsons and some Spanish primitives. It is run by trustees and its Curator is the former deputy director of the Walker Gallery. Birkenhead itself has a well-designed gallery building of the mid-1920s, the gift of the Williamson family, which is chiefly remarkable for its paintings by Wilson Steer, who was born in that city though he never worked there. This and the single room at Bootle are looked after by the respective municipal librarians. All these bodies are quite independent of one another, though in accordance with the suggestion of the Standing Commission on Museums and Art Galleries they now form part of an area museum service for the North-West, which sees to the care and conservation of items from nine-tenths of the museums in the area. In the Walker Gallery's view the structure of committees which this calls for is too cumbrous, and the result not very inspiring. The director feels that a better solution would have been for the gallery to take some overall responsibility for Birkenhead, Bootle and others that are part of the Merseyside agglomeration.

The revival of the Liverpool Academy has taken place largely at the expense of the Sandon Studios Society, whose exhibitions are now very secondary to the annual academy shows. With the passage of time the society has seen many of its ideas accepted by the old establishment, until it too has become an establishment offshoot, and not one of the more important ones. Though its music and drama groups are active enough, people concerned with the visual arts now treat it primarily as a social club – its subscription is three times that of the academy, which keeps the younger artists at a distance – and

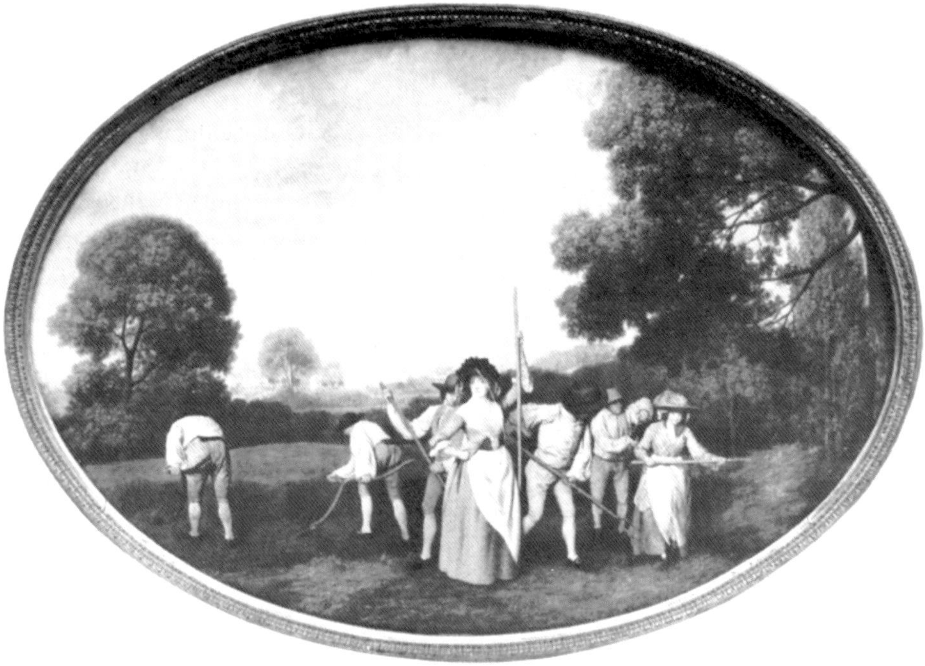

56 & 57 From the Lady Lever Art Gallery at Port Sunlight: George Stubbs's *Haymaking* and *Haycarting*

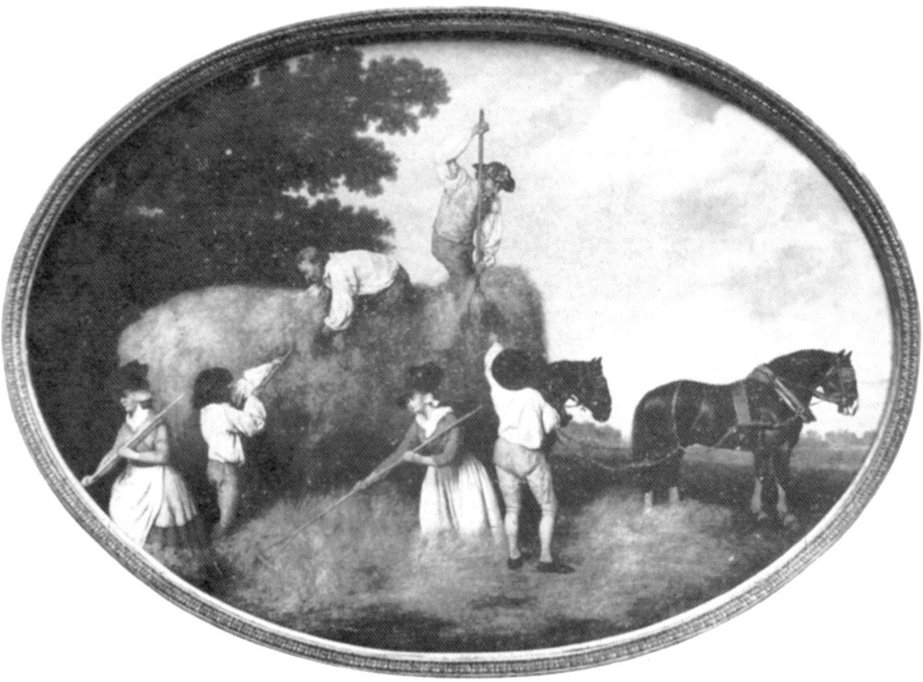

because its rooms are located in the Bluecoat Chambers it acts as restaurant, meeting and drinking place for the artists and organizations that centre on that early eighteenth century building. Its relations with the Bluecoat Society proper are not always very clear even to its members. In a sense however the Bluecoat was an offshoot of the Sandon, having been formed to manage the property after it was bought by public appeal in 1927, and consisting originally of twenty-four members actively connected with the Sandon Society or otherwise prominent in the appeal. These people constituted themselves into twelve committee members and six trustees, and have continued to function ever since by co-option, so that membership is not open to the outside world and no facilities are offered. Their purpose from the first has been to run the building 'as an Institution for the purposes and within the meaning of the Literary and Scientific Institutions Act, 1854, for the promotion of the fine arts, literature and science for adult instruction and the diffusion of useful knowledge generally.'[1] Tenants have been selected accordingly. A subsidiary intention was to organize lectures, concerts, plays and 'kinematic demonstrations' for the same educational objects. Mr W. S. MacCunn's history of the society however shows that major financial worries prevented it from thinking about any positive policy of this sort until after the Second World War. In 1961 it established the Bluecoat Forum as a co-ordinating committee to link the various other societies – artistic, architectural, musical, literary, photographic, cinematic, etc. – who now have rooms in the building (there are also a number of artists and architects who have studios there). The Sandon retains a special place as the largest and most sociable of these; it is the oldest tenant, and without the energies of its members (and specifically of the late Mrs Calder), the building would long since have been lost to commercial redevelopment.

The Arts Enquiry sponsored by the Dartington Trustees, in its report of 1946 on *The Visual Arts*,[2] spoke of the society as 'an arts centre to which there is no parallel in England', and with the increasing interest in the arts centre principle a certain amount of attention has been focused on the Bluecoat Chambers by those concerned with helping the arts. Under the new pattern of art patronage in England the Bluecoat Society can appeal for help to the Arts Council or the foundations and be sure that its claims will be given weight; the Arts Council in fact made it grants totalling over £5,000 in the period of postwar repair and reconstruction. It is only since about 1955 however that the society has been able to feel sure enough about the future of the building to think what the policy of an arts centre in Liverpool

[1] Deed of 28 January 1927.

[2] Oxford University Press, 1946, p. 56. See pp. 197–8 below.

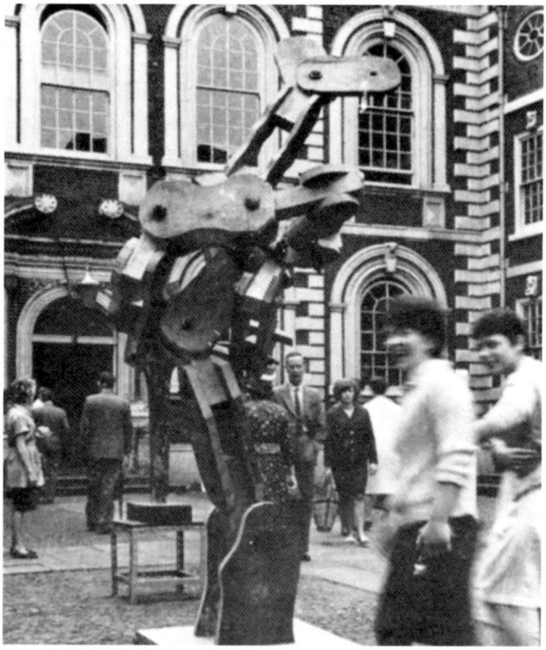

58 'Bluecoat 63'. The open-air sculpture exhibition in the front courtyard of the Bluecoat Chambers

might be and to wonder whether it is organized to provide it. This has always been the order of priorities, and it is reflected in the hierarchy of societies, for here the very concept of an arts centre, as defined in the 1914 proposal for a Lancashire Society of Arts and again in 1920, was devised as a means of guaranteeing the building's security against redevelopment, rather than vice versa. In 1955, however, the then secretary W. S. MacCunn suggested[1] that it might be time to put some of 1914's less ambitious principles into effect:

> Painters of distinction could be induced to visit and work in Liverpool; exhibitions and musical recitals could be sponsored; new works could be commissioned; a lectureship that, in time, might do for the arts what the Gifford lectures do for philosophy could be founded; the publication of books dealing with one or the other of the arts could be undertaken; and research could be helped.

Further ideas followed: scholarships for painters, a club for young artists, subsidized exhibitions for them, Merseyside exhibitions in a London gallery, the lobbying of Merseyside business people to buy more local works, Bluecoat fellowships and free studios for a year for promising artists, and, once again, public lectures on art. Some of this has been realized; the system of

[1] In his *Bluecoat Chambers;* Liverpool University Press, 1956, p. 68.

scholarships has been tried and (apparently failed), but two rooms in the building now make a slightly makeshift exhibition gallery, and the society is prepared to subsidize suitable shows there, with increasing success; indeed those of the early part of 1966 were of a consistently good standard, featuring work by John Edkins (one-man show), Margaret Dean, Frederick Bushe and Sean Rice. The main actions otherwise have concerned the two spring festivals organized by the Bluecoat Forum – Bluecoat 63, which brought large crowds to see (or hear) work by the building's tenants, and the equally popular Shakespeare celebrations in 1964. Another was to commission the present report.

I have cited these organizations as making up the Liverpool art establishment, and that is how they are spoken of by the younger artists and their friends. It is a loosely used word, and since a London journalist first coined it in the 1950s it has become charged with a certain envy and resentment which often vanishes once the user becomes a member of the establishment himself. None the less there is a sense in which institutions do become established, and that is when they are so generally accepted that they go on running without anybody having a very clear idea what their purpose is. In Liverpool as much as anywhere there is a reluctance to think clearly about these matters; thus the Town Clerk's report of June 1958 on the Cultural Life of the City speaks as if we were living in Roscoe's day:

> The happy relationship of commercial success and cultural encouragement is marked to a degree in this City, but that in itself is in no way unusual for it was common in the Italian towns of the Renaissance period, and indeed culture can only thrive where there is patronage to give it freedom of perception and development.

'Education' is still put forward as the aim of art, partly out of habit no doubt but partly because it is only for what the Bluecoat Society's 1953 Declaration of Trust calls

> the promotion and advancement of aesthetic education and the cultivation and improvement of public taste. . . .

that our present laws allow artistic enterprises exemption from tax. The only difference from the 1880s here is that, where once it was essentially self-education that was meant, the term now suggests an oligarchic condescension which some people, including some artists, much dislike.

'The public as a whole', wrote a correspondent to the *Liverpool Post* in 1956,

> does not ask for masterpieces: it just wants good paintings which can delight the eye, not pictures which conform to some obscure standard of technical perfection appreciated only by a group of art critics.[1]

This problem of creating a sense of participation, of common enjoyment and mutual respect, must strike all these organizations the more keenly their standards go up, and the gallery at least has already felt it, for both the director and those committee members with whom I talked have spoken emphatically of the need for a publicity drive to make Liverpool people more conscious of the treasures they own. It is a doubly difficult task, for not only does any nationally important institution often need to be impervious to uninformed local criticism but the means for informing the public is nowadays outside the local establishment's control. On the one hand the success of a gallery like the Walker is judged increasingly by the impression it makes in the wider field of art scholarship, international exhibitions and so forth – a field to which more and more attention is being paid by government, universities and the Press – rather than by any evidence of the satisfaction which it gives to the citizens. On the other the public no longer gets its taste for art from lectures and conducted tours such as the gallery itself can organize, or even from the local Press (though the daily *Liverpool Daily Post* has done a great deal to help[2]); but more from television and the illustrated Sunday magazines.[3] Even there any kind of 'educational' flavour is distasteful to most adults now that so many of us have undergone art education at school.

So long as an institution is confident of its purpose it can pursue it blindly and trust to the rapid evolution of our society's taste for pictures to support it sooner or later. Elsewhere however it is a matter of somehow capturing the local public's interest, or of giving it a sense of pride in the institution, or of getting it to identify itself with the latter's activities. These are in a way admissions of weakness; the very fact that a distinction is being drawn between institution and 'public' suggests that there is a cleft that can only be repaired by special measures. One such measure was the scheme put forward by a Labour Arts Sub-Committee member, Eric Heffer MP, for a special show, initially of working-class art. On the grounds that, as he put it,

[1] G. N. Ridley of Wallasey, on 9 October.

[2] In 1958 and early 1959, for instance, it ran a weekly series of quite large reproductions of the gallery's best pictures, together with short notes on them. In Roderick Bisson it has an unusually shrewd and well-informed critic; it has also published articles by the director and had helpful comments and leading articles on the gallery's problems. It was incidentally the first Liverpool firm to buy a picture for it.

[3] Radio and television programmes featuring the gallery have included the BBC television 'Animal, Vegetable, Mineral' on 6 October, 1955, a visit to the 1957 John Moores Exhibition by the BBC 'Critics', a programme on Granada TV on 9 May 1956, followed by 'One Hour in the Walker Gallery' on 21 November of the same year, and a thirty-minute tour of the gallery in BBC television's 'Looking North' programme on 6 March 1959.

art has largely become divorced from society. The mass of the people are little interested in it, and certain modern trends have not helped.

– he proposed an exhibition, possibly to become a regular event, of artists who because they work in industry or have lived or live in the environment of industry, reflect clearly the life around them, and in this sense marry art genuinely with society.[1]

The idea met with considerable criticism, both for its class bias and because in England now most realistic painting of working-class themes is likely to be amateur and to look it. It materialized however in somewhat different form in March 1965 as a small exhibition held under the title 'Industry and the Artist'. This included not only more or less realistic studies and actual industrial diagrams or working drawings but also sections of abstract, pop, optical and kinetic art which were held in one way or another to reflect the artist's view of the industrialized world. It was not a special public success, and it does not seem to have brought new visitors into the gallery.

[1] Letter to the *Liverpool Post*, 2 July 1963.

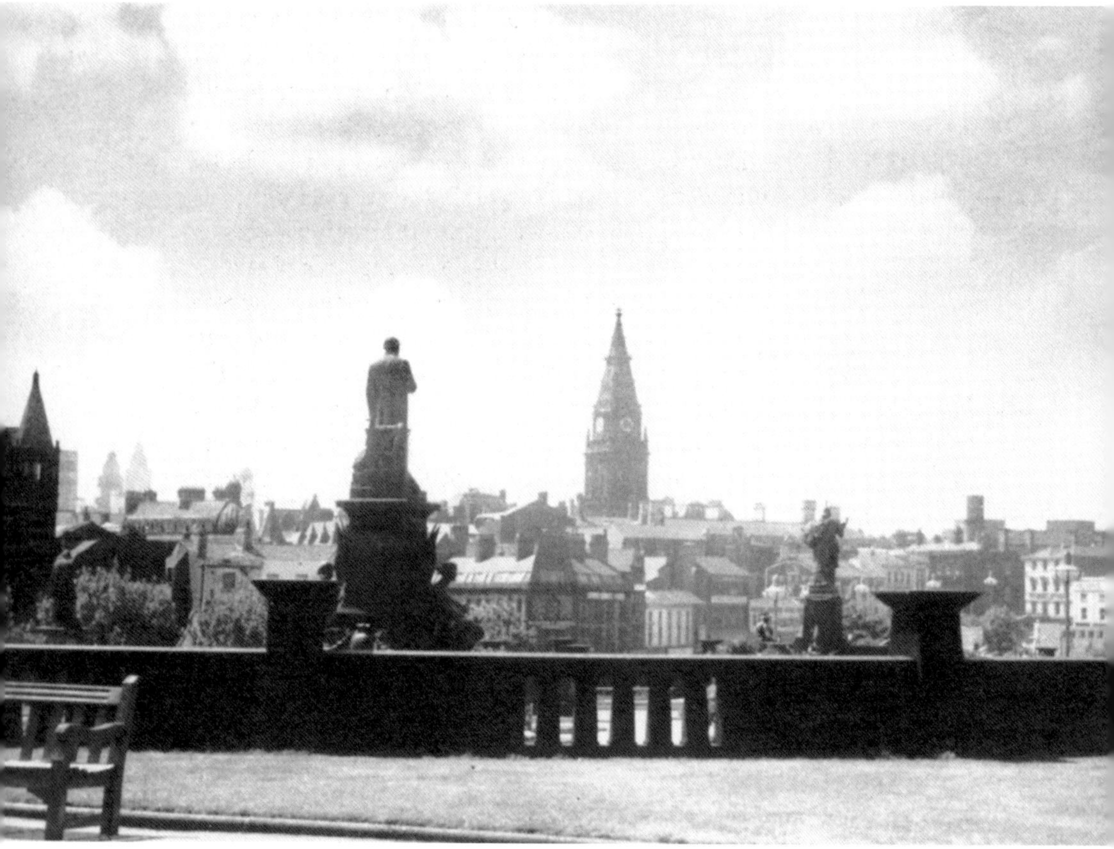

59 Art in public. Monuments to Liverpudlian and other worthies look out from below St George's Hall over the tunnel entrance towards the Municipal Offices (centre) and the twin towers of the Liver Building (left).

4 : ART IN PUBLIC

There is no 'establishment' to determine what we see around us in streets and buildings and in our places of work, for the visual arts no longer count as part of ordinary life. Ninety-nine per cent of what passes before our eyes has no conscious tradition or organization behind it, and in those few cases where it does rank as art, design or decoration, it cannot be attributed to any identifiable policy but at best to something vague, to a trend. This is the rule in our country, and Liverpool is no exception. That identification of art with the interests and ethos of the community which led to the building of St George's Hall largely vanished in the second half of the nineteenth century; the arts and crafts movement of the nineties was too weak there to produce more than isolated models and experiments; Rothenstein's rousing appeal for the embellishment of the city remained the rhetoric of an outsider. The legacy of public or deliberately socially-directed art that the present inhabitants were left with was a small one, so small that most of them would scarcely recognize its existence. Attempts to extend it have as a result been few; there is only one recent piece of public statuary that has made an impression on most people's consciousness, and that for rather special reasons. But at least the field can be surveyed as a whole, and because its pattern is not untypical of this country it is more worth studying than at first appears.

What *does* at first appear? A good deal can be seen from the steps of the Walker Art Gallery, for the main concentration of public sculpture in Liverpool stands around St George's Hall and the Mersey Tunnel entrance, with a second cluster a quarter of a mile away down Dale Street at Pier Head. Much of the siting of these worthy but largely boring monuments seems to have been decided piecemeal and almost by accident; thus in March 1927 Charles Bell Birch's Disraeli was shifted back into the St George's Hall portico, where it looks badly out of scale, to make room for the 1914–18 war memorial, while Sir Goscombe John's Edward VII at Pier Head was originally meant for the other side of the hall, but was banished on the insistence of Reilly and others.[1] The ruining of St John's Gardens, the open space that sweeps down from the hall to Herbert Rowse's Wembley-style tunnel entrance, by what Reilly called 'that forest of statues and unnecessary

[1] See C. H. Reilly: *Scaffolding in the Sky;* Routledge, 1938, p. 139. It looks no better where it is.

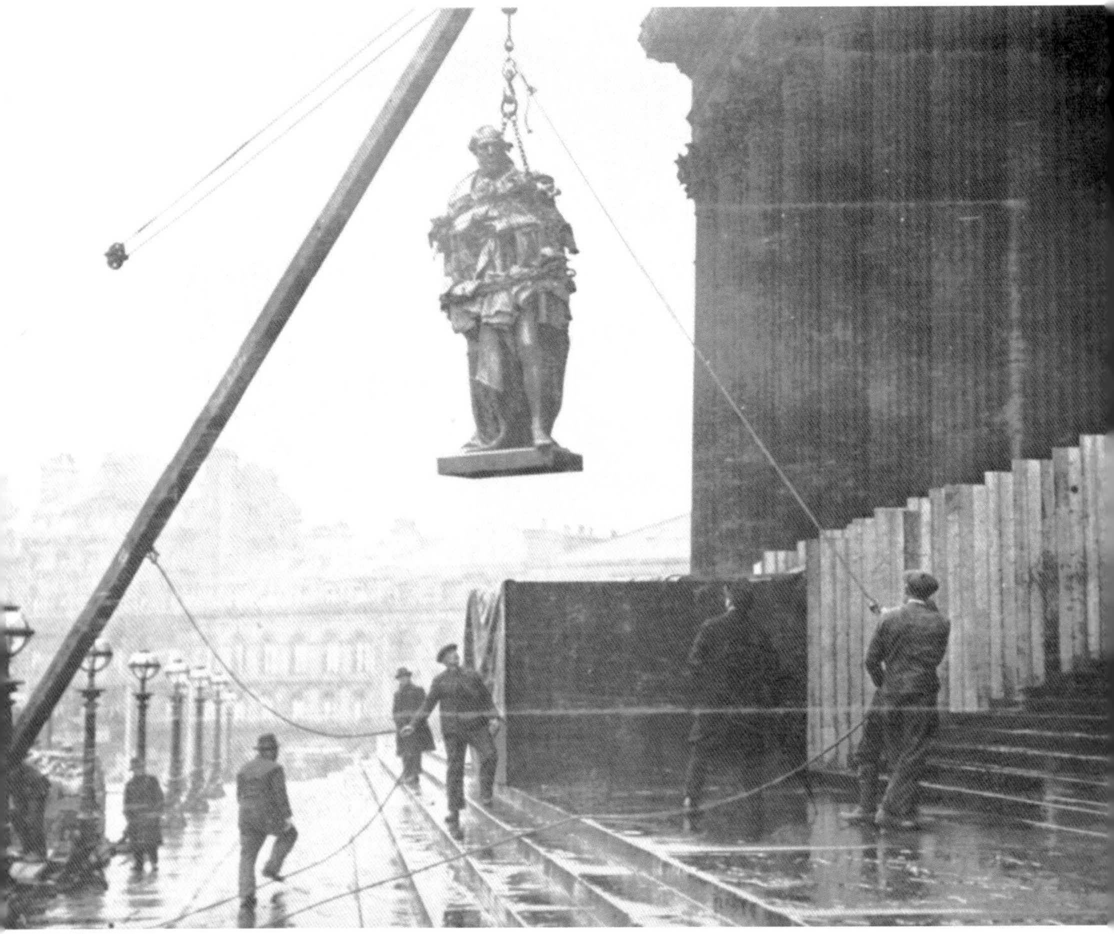

60 Art in mid-air. The Disraeli monument in front of St George's Hall being shifted backwards up the steps to make way for the War Memorial

stone piers'[1] was an unhappy series of concessions to our passion for commemorating not only national but local figures. The effect has been to bring monumental sculpture as such into disrepute. As we shall see later, it is now either ignored or actively resented. There has been no public critical discussion of it since Reilly's shrewd and amusing article with its description of Birch's Major-General William Earle (born in Liverpool in 1833 and killed in the Sudan in 1885) 'leading a charge from the safe retreat of the portico' and of Charles J. Allen's 'frieze of figures explanatory of insurance' on the

[1] C. H. Reilly: 'Some Liverpool Monuments' in *The Liverpool Review*, February 1927, Vol. 2, no. 1, p. 3.

Royal Insurance building. There cannot be more than a tiny handful of people in Liverpool who either know or care who such statues are by.[1]

And yet there are a number of monuments that do not disgrace the city or make it look in any way ridiculous. Gibson's statue of Huskisson in Prince's Avenue (illustrated on p. 29) is the outstanding instance,[2] though it was obviously not meant to stand where it now is; he was likewise respon-

61 More meaningless figures. Sir W. B. Forwcod, with the Picton Library in the distance and the western facade of St George's Hall

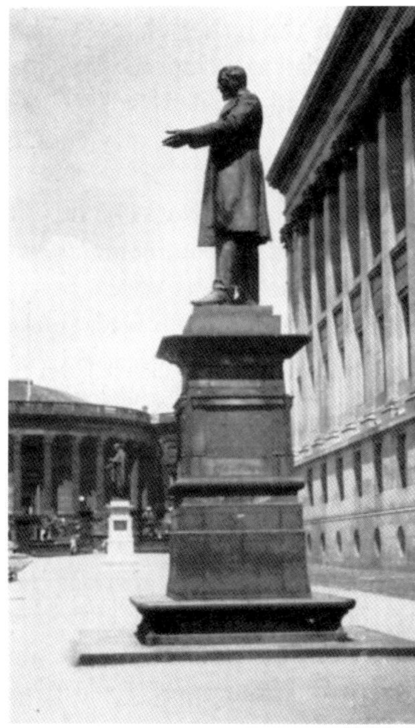

sible for a less visible figure inside the Huskisson Memorial below the Cathedral and a good statue of George Stephenson in St George's Hall. The unhappy fate of the sculpture for the hall's pediment we have already seen.

[1] They are here identified from an album *City of Liverpool. Photographs of Statues, Monuments and Memorials*, which was prepared in 1922 and is to be found in the Local History Library. The most sought after sculptors for such purposes seem to have been Sir Goscombe John (who also did King George V and Queen Mary above the tunnel entrance, and the Engine Room Heroes' Memorial at Pier Head), Sir George Frampton, RA (statues of Canon T. Major Lester and Sir W. B. Forwood in St John's Gardens and of Sir Alfred L. Jones at Pier Head), and Charles J. Allen RBS (bronze groups of Education, Industry, Commerce and Agriculture on the Victoria Memorial; two reliefs on St George's Hall; Florence Nightingale at the junction of Upper Parliament Street and Prince's Road; panels on the Rt Hon Samuel Smith memorial in Sefton Park).

[2] Gibson insisted on presenting his figures in classical draperies. His biographer in the *Dictionary of National Biography*, Cosmo Monkhouse, quotes him as saying that 'The human figure concealed under a frock coat and trousers is not a fit subject for sculpture. I would rather avoid contemplating such objects.'

But in the Nelson memorial behind the town hall and the equestrian George III in London Road (which is almost a straight copy of that of Marcus Aurelius on the Capitol in Rome) there are worthy works by a slightly earlier classical sculptor, Sir Richard Westmacott. This nineteenth century classicism was of course very much the style of Liverpool's early intellectual leaders. There are however also twentieth century works of merit in Herbert Tyson Smith's two war memorials, the one in the Post Office and the bronze frieze on the rather clumsily-shaped and-placed town memorial for which Disraeli had to be moved. The black basalt sculptures on the ventilating shaft at Pier Head are likewise excellent of their (1920-ish) kind, though they are rather lost at the back of a building which in itself is a large and deplorable architectural sham.

Nearly all such works of art – if that is the right word for some of them – are designed to commemorate rather than to beautify, and the generally funereal associations which have grown up around public art in Liverpool seem to have discouraged subsequent city councils from commissioning anything more. The great programme of municipal housing carried out in the 1930s under Sir Lancelot Keay was almost bare of extraneous decoration; about the only exception is Gerrard Gardens, a vast block of flats not far from the gallery (and innocent of course, of any vestige of garden), where there are two competent but tame sub-Meunier reliefs of idealized workers, much too small for the scale of the building. Since the war there has been just one such venture, a long abstract pattern in polystyrene by Antony Hollaway for some municipal flats at Primrose Drive, Huyton; otherwise works of art have been confined to new school buildings, mainly to those not built by Liverpool corporation. Even there they are less frequent than in London.

There was an obvious chance for the city to commemorate its return to life after the bombing, much as was done with Zadkine's statue on the waterfront at Rotterdam; however it was seized not by the municipality but by the firm of Lewis's, whose director the late George Breeze was an admirer and patron of Epstein's. The ensuing *Spirit of Liverpool Resurgent*, a male bronze figure on a prow jutting out of Lewis's exceedingly undistinguished new building, would have been badly placed for such a grandiose gesture even if the failure to rebuild the city's centre had not made it a rather premature boast. As it was not only was it one of Epstein's less successful works but the immediate focusing of the spectator's attention on the figure's genitals has remained distracting to the citizens, so that the three smaller but more impressive relief panels beneath it go largely unobserved. Yet all the same the commissioning of the Epstein was a bold effort, and a decade later the example still seems to nag at the corporation. Dr Ronald Bradbury, for instance,

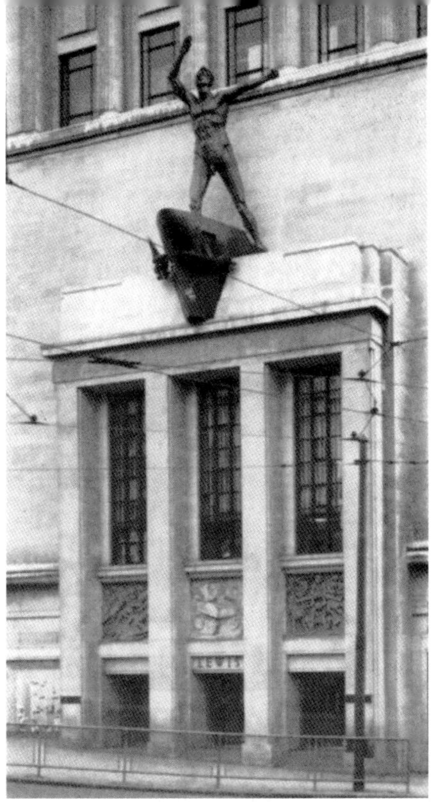

62 A post-war gesture by Liverpool, or rather by Lewis's stores. Epstein's figure *Spirit of Liverpool Resurgent* (photographed before the trams were abolished). It should be compared with Zadkine's *The Destroyed City* in illustration no. 139. Note particularly the three panels over the doors, which passers-by are apt to overlook

the present City Architect, told me that he had made tentative enquiries to find out if Henry Moore could undertake a work for the remodelled Pier Head area, only to be told that the artist was too heavily booked. More recently Eric Heffer has again proposed that there should be some major piece of sculpture on this site, symbolizing the new spirit of Liverpool as the Epstein is now felt not to do.

There has been no coherent policy for using artists in conjunction with the official building and planning schemes, and even in the new school buildings the occasional use of sculpture and (more rarely) murals has been on the initiative of the architect rather than on that of the Education Committee or its director. There are one or two quite striking pieces of work in the Liverpool area, but about the only schemes to have been carried out under the municipality have been Childwall County College, with its sculpture by Mitzi Solomon Cunliffe (then of Manchester), Anfield Technical College, which has a relief by the London artist William Mitchell, Herbert Thearle's Sandfield Park Special School, with decorations by Roderick Bisson, and Springfield Park Comprehensive School, with its rather forlorn small figure by Stanley English standing in a pool; these last two are local artists. The Lancashire County Education Committee and their architects seem to be more enterprising; certainly Ruffwood Drive Comprehensive School in the new suburb of Kirkby is well above Liverpool standards both architecturally and in it use of mosaics to symbolize the figures (Telford, Darwin, etc), after whom the 'houses' are named. Over at Birkenhead the Technical college building by Willinck and Dod has a cluttered and somewhat stereotyped mural by Eric Kennington – a kind of Birkenhead pot-pourri – but the newer and more important Liverpool College of Technology has nothing. The late city director of education told me that there have just not been the funds available for that sort of thing.

This is where the Roman Catholic schools differ. Built in many cases by the same architects as the new Catholic churches and subject to the same overriding concept (which the diocesan authorities themselves plainly hold) of art as a testimony to the glory of God, they have been a good deal less austere in their use of artists. These are mainly local, and not always of the first quality, but there seems to be a certain harmony of effort between artist and

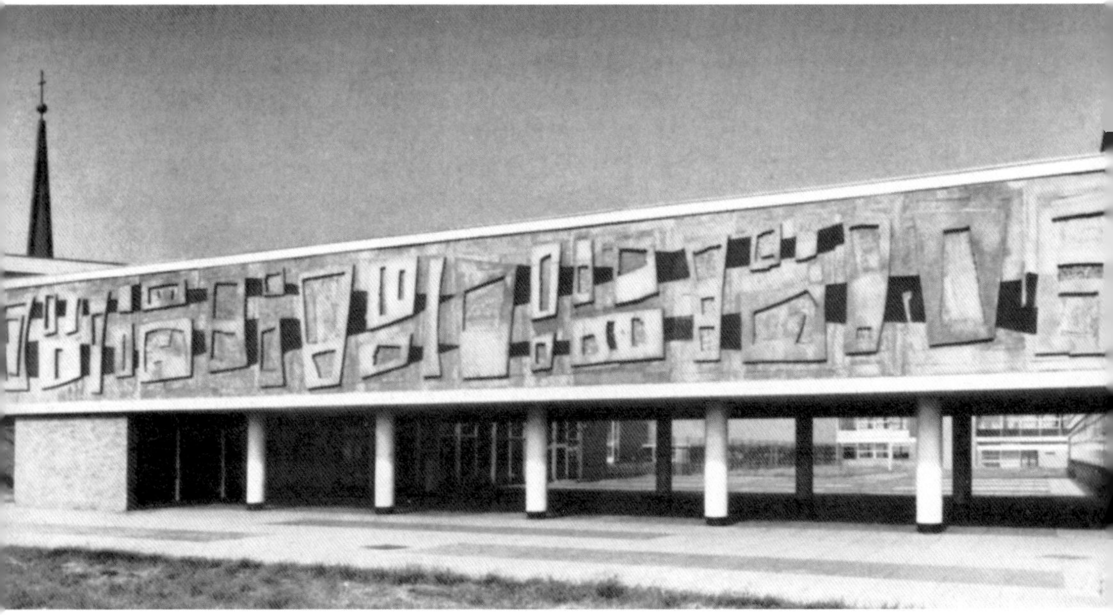

63 The Roman Catholic church as patron. Relief by the Liverpool sculptor Robin Riley on St Kevin's School, Kirkby

architect which surely helps the former's work, and in Robin Riley's long abstract relief on L. A. G. Prichard's St Kevin's School, Kirkby, the Catholic system has produced the most striking new public work of art in the area. The policy is the same for both schools and churches. Thus Weightman and Bullen, a Liverpool firm now specializing in this work who have built fifteen to twenty churches and over 100 church schools since 1949, told me that they try to convince the responsible priest in each case that work by an individual artist means more than, say, mass-produced Stations of the Cross from West Germany. Their principle might be defined as 'little and decent'; for instance, they will use clear glass rather than bad stained glass which they feel might never be removed. They pick the artists, discuss the exact number and nature of the works with the client, and decide their placing and probable cost before any building starts. They cannot afford Moore or Sutherland, but they have commissioned works by such local artists as Riley, George Thomas and Arthur Dooley (for sculpture), Robin Magee (for church furnishing) and the late George Mayer-Marton (for mosaics). The results are not spectacular; no art-lover's breath is going to be taken away, certainly, on entering one of these churches. They do however

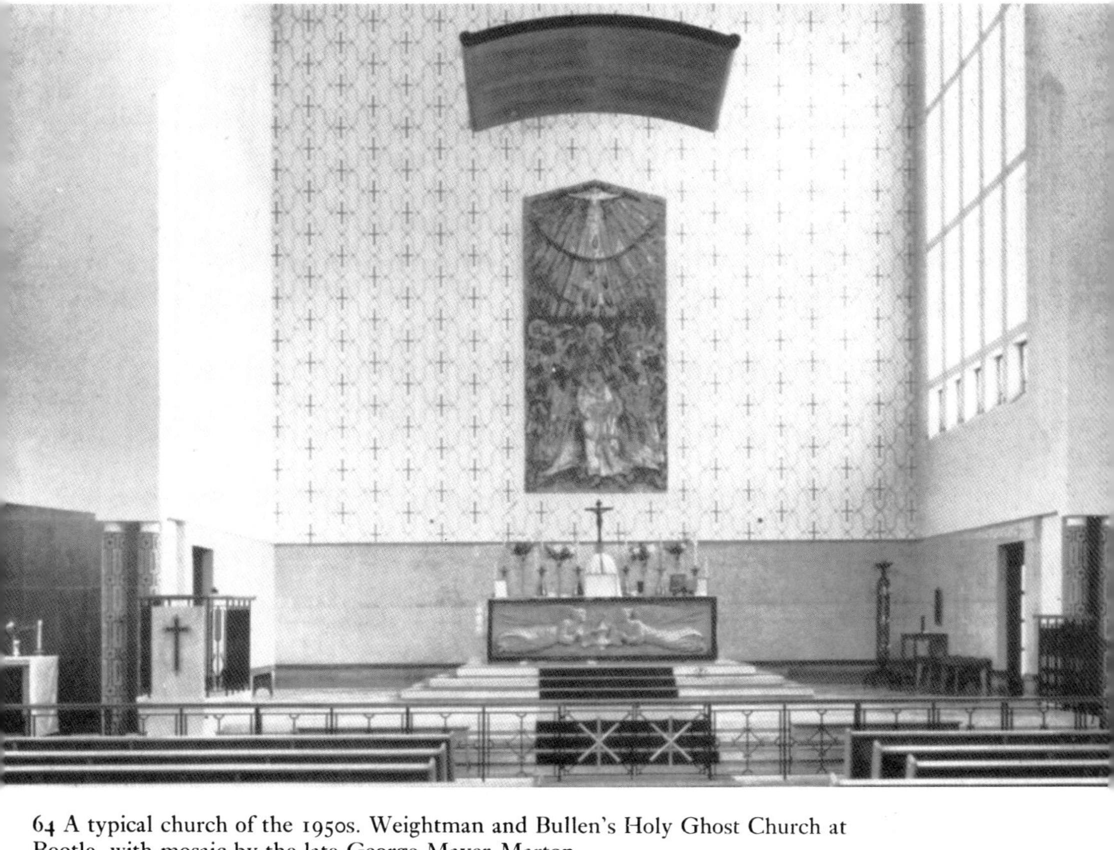

64 A typical church of the 1950s. Weightman and Bullen's Holy Ghost Church at Bootle, with mosaic by the late George Mayer-Marton

represent a considerable raising of the standard of Catholic church furnishing in the north of England and an unusual instance of local talent purposefully used.

In 1967 the new Roman Catholic cathedral will be consecrated. With its novel circular plan, like a vast upturned funnel, its windows by John Piper and Patrick Reyntiens and its sculptures by William Mitchell, Frederick Gibberd's great building quite possibly *will* take the breath away, and seems likely to provide for some years a religious-artistic sensation to rival Coventry. Scott's Anglican cathedral further along the same ridge is still slowly expanding and completing itself, but in a traditional style which made its impact many years ago and can add little fresh to the visual life of the city. Through its extra-mural department and the Reverend William Lockett, who is in charge of the art teaching there, the university has organized conferences on 'The Modern Architectural Setting of the Liturgy' (September 1962) and 'New Church Architecture' (September 1963), the first of which was attended by both Bishops of Liverpool and included a lecture by Gibberd on the new cathedral. At the same time there was an exhibition of modern church art at the Bluecoat Display Centre. In all these ways it can be said not only that the churches on Merseyside are conscious of the architectural use of the other arts as the lay authorities are not, but that they are specifically taking pains to learn about modern artists.

The university, which will incidentally have Gibberd's cathedral on its doorstep, is if anything even more ambitious in its commissioning of works of art for its buildings. Not only does it pursue a fairly consistent policy of spending roughly $\frac{1}{2}$ per cent of the cost of each new building in this way but it has bypassed the local artists in favour of men with something of a national reputation. Thus there is a group of three vertical hammer-shaped objects by Hubert Dalwood outside the Physics Building and a mosaic by Geoffrey

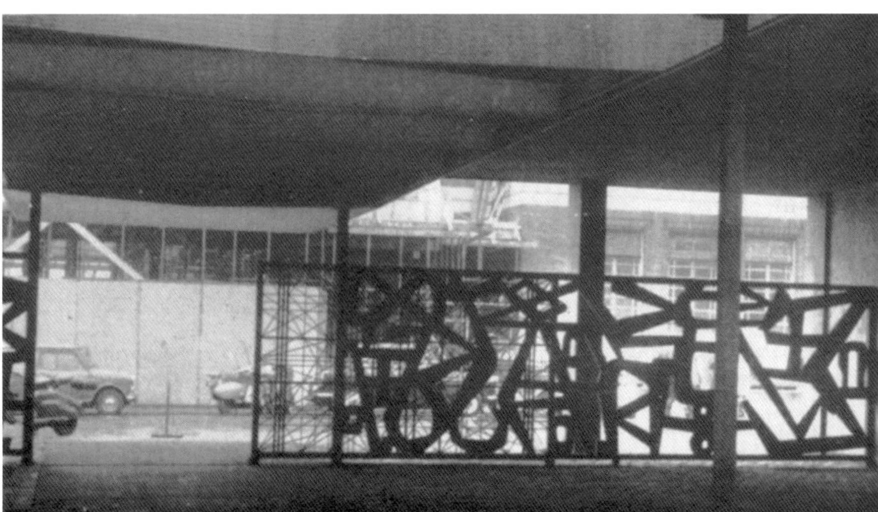

Clarke inside it; there is a mural by the late Peter Lanyon in the Civil Engineering Building, and a set of terracotta plaques by John McCarthy in the Mathematics Building showing 'the growth of mathematical ideas'. The same building has an iron screen and gate by this artist, and there are a rather dim horse and cow in brick relief on Maxwell Fry's Veterinary Building and a sculpture and a door handle by Mitzi Solomon Cunliffe in the Department of Civic Design. There are also a number of buildings still under construction or to come, each with a university committee in charge, though it has so far been the architects who have nominated the artists to be used. The object of this apparently progressive scheme of patronage, as the Professor of Civic Design explained it to me in his capacity as planning consultant to the university, is that students who will form the future leaders of the nation need to be brought into contact with works of art, and all the more so if these have been lacking in the environment from which they come. Unfortunately it largely breaks down on the quality of the works commissioned, which have turned out at best unmemorable. Why this should be so will be discussed later, but its bearing on the possible use of prominent but not top-rank modern artists for public tasks in Liverpool is obvious. It is an example to be learnt from rather than followed.

Occasionally a business in the town will buy interesting pictures for its own premises or commission work specially. Walker's the brewers first set the example, perhaps, with the nineteenth-century paintings which they bought for decorating their pubs; there are some fine Frith-like scenes hanging in the magnificent back room of The Vines in Lime Street. The chief case recently was Leonard Rosoman's forty-foot mural of the Liverpool waterfront for Barclays Bank in Water Street; an efficient but not very inspired compromise between the *genius loci* and the natural talent of the artist. But for his death this job would have gone to the local artist Mayer-Marton, who had done a quite successful smaller mural for the passenger department of Coast Lines. There is also a panel by another local painter, John Heritage, in the RAC office, and a mural of 1960 by a former Liverpool couple, F. H. and C. V. Lyle, in the self-service restaurant of Littlewoods Stores. British Railways likewise have good modern paintings hanging in the dining-room of the Exchange Station Hotel, though probably not as the result of any decision taken locally. But none of this is perhaps so promising for the future as one or two rather more inconspicuous instances: the metal panel representing a printed circuit which Arthur Ballard made for Johnson's TV shop in Lord Street at the suggestion of Quentin Hughes the architect; the paintings by Sam Walsh and Peter MacKarell in the bar of Dick Egerton's Royal Court Hotel, bought from them when they were com-

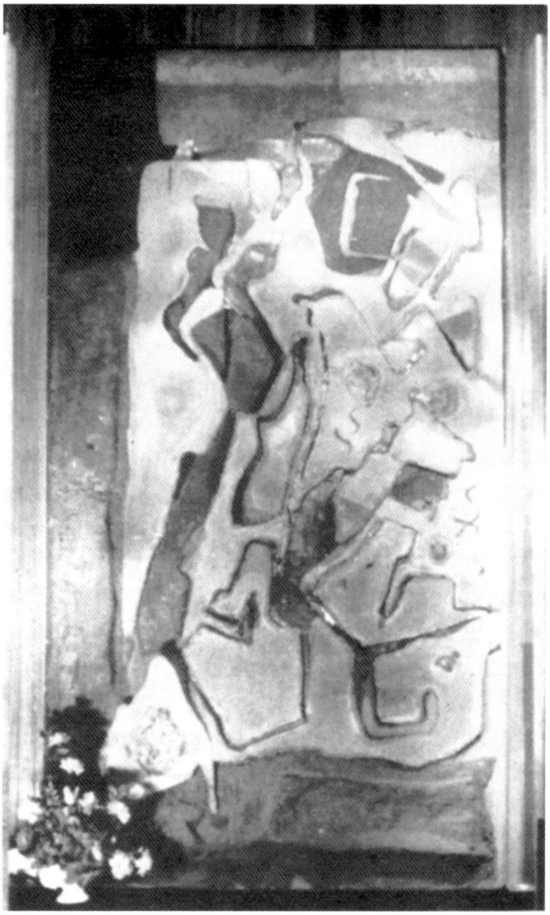

66 The best modern Liverpool mural: Arthur Ballard's metal relief in Johnson's T.V. shop, Lord Street

parative beginners; or the paintings by Walsh and Adrian Henri which Reg Mason has installed, to the apparent mystification of the customers, in some of his betting shops. Ballard's panel is the best mural work in Liverpool (in my knowledge and judgment), while the others seem to show a spontaneous taste for the livelier kinds of art, free from self-conscious feelings of patronage.

Wherever the visual arts are brought into the open like this it becomes hard to draw a line between art in the strict sense and civic and industrial design. The arts are no longer segregated in a gallery, to be looked at with specially-conditioned eyes; often they are stripped even of the largely reverential aura that accompanies their religious or educational use. They become woven into quite other activities, where they may be noticed or not according to their merits (and the observer's visual alertness) and must harmonize or compete with a thousand different sights, most of them man-made. This is a complex field for the art-lover to enter, and many of those supporters who helped to put the Walker Art Gallery so firmly on its feet have preferred not to explore it at all. It may be that their feeling for pictures is still in part an aristocratic one, and that they feel there is a risk here of art being profaned; moreover so far as their own business establishments and their own manufactures go they find that aesthetic judgments are subject not only to technical and commercial considerations but to the views of colleagues and the maintenance of smooth labour relations. This can make the redecoration of a factory a much more difficult business than the giving of a picture to the gallery, and the contrast between a firm's supposed taste (as judged

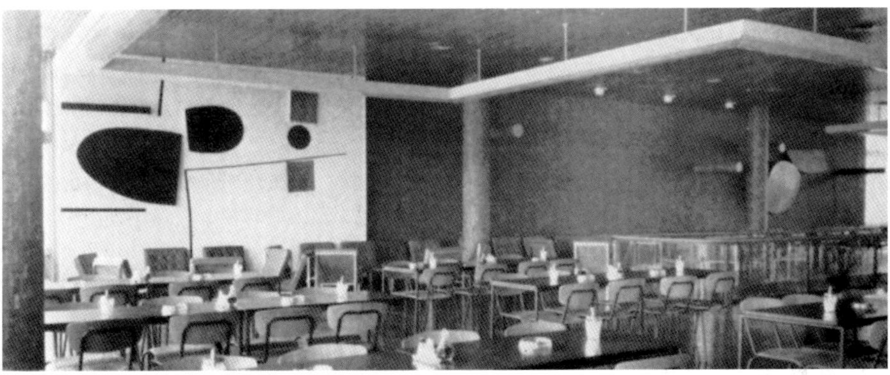

67 Outside Liverpool. Victor Pasmore's mural in the refectory of the new Pilkington buildings at St Helens

from its gifts and from the personal tastes of its chiefs) and the actual appearance of its premises and its products is often a little surprising. One eminent local cultural benefactor taxed with inconsistencies of this sort is reported to have replied: 'That's quite different. That's business.'

None the less there are some who have made considerable efforts to improve the look of their offices and factories, while others have acquired pictures of varying merits for their decoration. Admittedly as yet only two of them can be seen as a major visual asset to the area, and neither is strictly on Merseyside: Pilkington Brothers' new buildings at St Helens have a big mural by Victor Pasmore in the refectory, while in Ralph Tubbs's excellent Granada Television buildings over in Manchester – which are perhaps mentionable in this report because Granada covers Liverpool from there – a good collection of paintings has been formed on the recommendation of Sir Gerald Barry and a panel of advisors. These are outstanding in that both represent the development of a bold visual arts policy[1] within the daily affairs of a major organization; the similar attempt now being made by Littlewoods will be dealt with a little later.

With Lever Brothers' vast factory (5,000 workers) at Port Sunlight it was more a matter of the late chairman G. A. S. Nairn wishing to remedy the visual squalor of the place, which E. R. Scott the Civil Engineer then repainted according to new and most attractive colour schemes.[2] Part of the object was to reduce fatigue and sickness, but it cannot be proved that production has been affected, though the workers appreciate it. At Jacobs Biscuits at Aintree, a group of airy but architecturally undistinguished factory buildings with about 3,000 workers, the firm's architects in 1961 worked out a set of selected 'standards and finishes' for the offices which is followed and gives an impression of cleanliness and coherence. The directors here are convinced of the importance of environment. 'I am afraid,' writes Mr C. B. Barber,

> I cannot offer evidence on the importance of decor in factory working conditions. I am sure it is true that good design and pleasant appearance have their unconscious effect. I should add, we are fortunate in having at this factory a Sports Field and garden, and we pay great attention to the outside appearance and general surroundings.

This firm is glad to draw its labour force from a 1930s suburb rather than from the gloom and squalor nearer the centre or from a still unsettled area like Kirkby. At British-American Tobacco's factory (1,200 employees; the company chairman is also chairman of the Council of Industrial Design in London) redecoration is the responsibility of the engineer. The offices are fairly light and agreeable; in the canteens and dining-rooms, which are considerably less so, there are a few smallish reproductions by artists like Seago and Doyly John.

Pictures or murals in such places of work are a rarity.[3] Under its loans-out scheme the Walker Gallery lends works to English Electric and the Blue

[1] Though on no scientific basis. Thus the Group Welfare Advisor of Pilkingtons wrote to me that 'As one who is personally influenced by the appearance of the premises in which I work, I feel sure that many people are influenced in this way. However, we have done no research in this field, and therefore it is not possible to give any reliable information on this subject.' The directors wished to support modern art and asked the architect of the new buildings to recommend an artist. The firm also buys prints for its canteens.

[2] The operation is described by Mr Scott in an article in *Personnel Management* for October 1950.

[3] I circularized a number of firms with 1,000 or more employees, mainly those recommended by the Chamber of Commerce as likeliest to show interest. Here is a fairly characteristic reply:

> We do not have any policy for commissioning Works of Art for decoration, etc, in our communal rooms or canteens and with regard to colour schemes, these are usually taken care of by our own Architects Department who very often obtain complete colour schemes from Paint Manufacturers.

Funnel Line and for public display at Martins Bank and Holt's Arcade (i.e. to four commercial firms as against fifty schools and seventeen assorted municipal establishments to whom it lends); the Colour Print Gallery in London, which hires out sets of reproductions, has only one Liverpool industrial customer, R. Silcock and Sons (as against nine in Manchester, and six Liverpool schools). The late Sir Ben Johnson, however, whose dyeworks at Bootle started early this century on paternalistic lines and had one of the first industrial welfare departments in the country, owned a large collection of pictures which overflowed his own house and was hung all round the works; apart from a few watercolours of the works itself by Herbert J. Finn his trustees sold it through J. Davey the Liverpool dealer, 'without, so far as we know, comment or protest from the employees'[1]. Johnson was incidentally one of the founders of the Bluecoat Society.

Likewise J. Bibby and Sons, the cattle food business, had a collection which was auctioned by Outhwaite and Litherland on 15 November 1961. This was mainly 1930s British royal academic, though it included Maximilien Luce's *La Pleine* (sic) *de Bagneaux* and a painting by Maufra; in addition the same firm used to produce a publication for their rural customers called *Bibby's Annual* for which they commissioned original works, including many by a *Punch* artist and Royal Academy exhibitor (from 1880 on) called Gunning King, whose most famous work was *Come Along, Baby*. It would be true to say that art in the strict sense is less widely accepted in Liverpool industry than is the use of colour, whose managerial value is now more or less recognized. At Goodlass Wall, the Speke paint manufacturers, there is a Colour Advisory Service whose manager told me that colour photography, foreign travel, and the Civic Trust's 'facelift' schemes[2] have all helped sharpen

[1] Letter of 17 April 1963 to the author from J. L. Crockatt, the present managing director. Mr Crockatt's views on the whole problem are worth quoting further:

> The writer believes strongly that a high standard of painting and decoration is of psychological value in a factory. We think that regular re-decoration and freshening up is of greater importance than choice of colours. The question of colour choice has not had much attention in this factory, but was a matter with which the writer experimented to a considerable extent in a factory he managed before coming here just over two years ago. The practice there, which is now beginning to be felt here, was to select two or three colour schemes for a particular department using, generally speaking, the British Standards Institution colour card for factories. The employees in the department would then be consulted and allowed to choose which of the two or three available schemes they wanted.
>
> There is no way of proving that this technique has any commercial value, but as we have said above, we believe there is a psychological effect, particularly among female employees.
>
> A comparable effect is sometimes obtained and clearly seen in shops. We are all the time taking our oldest branches and modernizing them. We have often noticed that the staff, who may have been dowdy and not sufficiently careful of their appearance, suddenly take a new lease of life and become smart and well turned out when we give them a bright up-to-date shop.

[2] See p. 205. Goodlass Wall worked on the Holyhead 'facelift' and helped prepare the scheme for Ormskirk.

people's awareness of colour. It was interesting however to learn from him that an inquiry about murals from the Dunlop works there had led them to consider founding a mural prize for art schools. One of this service's young designers (themselves all art-school trained) produced a largeish abstract wall construction which his fellow-employees in the factory have come to accept, though many of them are said to have disliked it at first.

Much of what we have been discussing has been on a pretty low level, and it is no good pretending that the visual climate of modern Liverpool is exciting. The Walker Art Gallery may pursue a high standard, but too few Liverpudlians identify themselves with it; the nineteenth-century buildings may have a unique massive splendour, but despite the recent formation of a branch of the Victorian Society not enough people yet appreciate it for there to be any real certainty of its being respected or preserved. The visual results of the old industrial paternalism moreover, at places like Port Sunlight and Johnson's Dyeworks, may nowadays seem slightly absurd, but no newer and more intelligent attitude has come to replace it. Dominating everything is a twofold handicap which it would be wrong to pass over in silence: the shortage of inspiration among recent generations of Liverpool-based architects, and the willing acceptance by most sections of society of a very poor standard of design. Although first-rate architects cost no more than bad ones there is as yet scarcely a single modern building on Merseyside that is really worth looking at; in the centre office blocks like the new State House in Dale Street or competent-looking shops like Hendersons in Church Street or Walker and Hall in Lord Street are startling exceptions, while further out there are all too few new buildings to compare with Gerald Beech's sports pavilion at Wyncote, Nelson and Parker's Hamilton House at Blundellsands or the Ruffwood Drive school. To a great extent the revolution in English design since 1951 passed Liverpool by; there were fourteen Merseyside names on the Council of Industrial Design's 1963 register of designers and three in the 1965–6 membership list of the Design and Industries Association, for instance, as against forty and sixty-four respectively from Manchester; nor would anybody guess that Liverpool was a great printing centre from the design of the average local brochure or poster. This does not mean that progress even at a low level is unimportant, least of all from the point of view of the community concerned. But it does make for a distinction between those who are trying to apply the arts more constructively within these limitations and the smaller number who want to see a change of level as well as a more widespread use of art.

The issue has been raised above all by the new plans for the centre and subsequently for the whole of the city. The extent of the proposed rebuilding, the likely predominance of the modern architectural idiom with its absence of decoration, the new types of structure called for and the number of open spaces and pedestrian ways to be made visually interesting: all this is likely to pose some very large problems of commissioning and cooperation. It is not entirely easy to switch one's mind to the new scale; indeed the great risk, given the existing background, is that even those most familiar with the future picture of Liverpool may set their sights too low where the artist's contribution is concerned. The assumptions from which the planners are setting out, certainly, and the new 'overall conceptual framework' which they have outlined could hardly be bettered; the aim is not just to remedy the years of neglect and once again produce an efficient city but to shape what Walter Bor's Interim Planning Policy Statement repeatedly calls the 'total environment', that complex network of urban factors that at once expresses and influences the personality of the citizens. The approach is humane and far-sighted, taking account of the essential character of the place (whose coherence and exceptional 'city scale' both planners have emphasized) and of the need to retain a nucleus of those massive nineteenth-century buildings, industrial as well as civic, to which this is due.[1] Liverpool is to be a town, writes the present chairman of the Planning Committee, 'in which visitors will find visual pleasure, colour, excitement, activity and recreation,'[2] while Shankland cites the example of certain historic city centres, which he calls 'great collective works of art where the skill, care and love of the community has been most concentrated.'[3] Two concepts are accordingly emphasized in the City Centre Plan: 'The city as Art' and 'The city as Entertainment'. 'One of the basic objectives of the Plan,' says the same document, 'must therefore be to make Liverpool more beautiful.'[4]

If this is really to be so then the tasks for the visual artist – who can come from any part of the world, it should be remembered – will be very important indeed. As yet however they have not been elaborated except in the form of a

[1] This is made clear (and has been accepted by both parties in the City Council) in Section 2.19 of the *Liverpool City Centre Plan*, though to my mind the policy laid down there is too rigid and pays too little attention to areas like Nelson Street (the Chinese quarter) which are essential to the city's character though not architecturally distinguished. It is a bad sign however that the report on 'Preservation of Historic Buildings in Central Liverpool' which Dr Quentin Hughes prepared for the planners has now been shelved by the Council without discussion, possibly because of its emphasis on the merits of Albert Dock.

[2] W. H. Sefton's foreword to *Liverpool City Centre Plan;* City and County Borough of Liverpool, 1965, p. 1. Alderman Sefton is the leader of the present Labour majority in the council.

[3] *City and County Borough of Liverpool Planning Consultant's Report No. 10. Draft City Centre Map;* Graeme Shankland, 28 Bedford Square, London WC1., 1963, p. 19.

[4] *Liverpool City Centre Plan*, pp. 67–8.

few rather random suggestions thrown out by the planning documents. These have been more generally concerned with the importance of 'Townscape', of outdoor space and its handling, right down to such matters as improving the dismal Liverpool street furniture and planting more trees. Thus the two sections of the City Centre Plan dealing with 'Culture and Entertainment' (§2.5) and 'Advertisement and Display' (§2.21) call for the

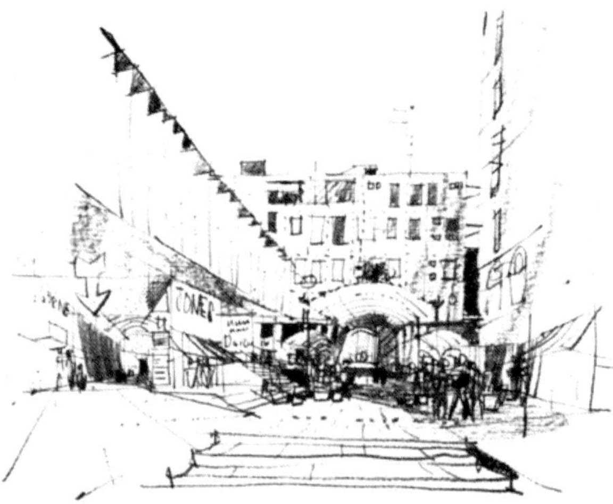

68 The possible shape of things to come. A drawing by Gordon Cullen for one of Graeme Shankland's planning reports

use of 'well designed illuminated signs and displays' to enliven the place at night; the former also for 'the generous use of sculpture and fountains', (thus tacitly by-passing other forms of art).[1] In Shankland's Draft City Centre Map the dispiriting title of 'Civic Husbandry' is given to a mixed bag of suggested measures including 'planting of trees, choice of pavings, design of light fittings and street signs, commissioning of works of art, building fountains'.[2] Fountains indeed are a favourite if rather damp hobby-horse for both planners, possibly because of the presence in Liverpool of a highly original artist in that genre. The *City Centre Plan*, once again, suggests that

> Water features strategically located throughout the pedestrian areas of the city could provide a unifying theme of a unique character for the new Liverpool.

'Water and fountains,' it suggests, 'will have a great role to play.'[3]

It is plain that these rather sketchily-thought-out propositions conceal a widespread will to see artists of all branches made use of. Bor for instance was responsible when at the LCC for commissioning the first sculpture for a

[1] *Liverpool City Centre Plan*, p. 68.
[2] *Draft City Centre Map*, p. 54.
[3] *Liverpool City Centre Plan*, pp. 87, 90. (From section 2.18, on 'Urban Form'.)

council housing estate – a figure by Trevor Tennant in Stepney (St Anne's) – and would evidently be prepared to take responsibility for such commissions in Liverpool. Dr Ronald Bradbury the City Architect is also in principle keen to cooperate with artists, though he lays more emphasis on the practical problems involved, arguing that so far he has had neither the staff nor the money to pay much attention to such things. At the University both the Professor of Architecture and the Professor of Civic Design are anxious to promote this alliance of the arts, while there is evident good will at the Walker Gallery, among the best Liverpool private architects (including notably the two firms working on the Strand-Paradise Street scheme) and in other influential quarters. How far this feeling is shared by the local politicians is slightly less clear. There is however a conscious feeling among leading councillors of both parties that it would help the city in many ways if it could earn a reputation for being visually more interesting and agreeable. This, in Eric Heffer's view, would not directly decide any firm to set up a factory in Liverpool perhaps, but it would be bound to have some influence on key members of its staff.[1] Talking to me, he quoted the example of Pittsburgh, where he had been told that the slum clearance and smoke abatement scuemes had brought executives to live in the centre of the city.

Under the new planning regime the most remarkable step taken so far has been by Littlewoods Mail Order Stores, John Moores's firm, which when building its tall new headquarters in the central area behind Exchange Station held a competition with prizes of £9,500 for a 'sculpture or three-dimensional design' to go in the high space under it. It was an important precedent both as representing an extension of the principle of the Moores Exhibitions into the field of public art – i.e. an attempt to open out the scheme of patronage in the city – and also as part of an all-round effort to raise design levels in a big firm, whose results can already be seen in smaller instances such as the company's printed matter and the signposting and layout of its Church Street

[1] The Public Affairs Officer at Ford's new Liverpool factory at Halewood (near Speke) wrote as follows (letter of 25 July 1963):

> On the subject of the effect of Liverpool environment on the recruiting of personnel, the Halewood factory is of course a fine example of what has been achieved to put the Merseyside image into its proper perspective. To launch the Halewood plant it was necessary to transfer 200 key personnel from Dagenham and other Ford locations to Merseyside. Many of these men and their families had false conceptions about life and conditions on Merseyside, and so we set ourselves the task of eradicating these impressions.
>
> Firstly we produced a film of life on Merseyside showing the beautiful countryside, fine shopping centres and housing developments, and this was shown to all the potential key men and their families at special social evenings at Dagenham. During these functions welfare officers answered questions on the important subjects of education and housing.
>
> The result of this social experiment was that we had 200 volunteers eager to start a new life in the North, and every one of them has settled down on Merseyside.

store. Already Littlewoods has an art society with about 800 members, and Moores lends pictures from his own collection for display in the two main office buildings; W. L. Stevenson, the former head of the College of Art, is in charge of the Department of Architecture and Planning. Perhaps the sculpture competition has not brought quite the results the firm hoped for, since none of the accepted big names in modern British sculpture chose to enter; the 2,000 employees in the new building are not going to be sitting over a masterpiece. None the less it stimulated a number of highly original designs – notably Peter Startup's brightly-coloured wooden 'maritime forms' and the 'hydromobile' by C. L. Crickmay of Liverpool, neither of which got

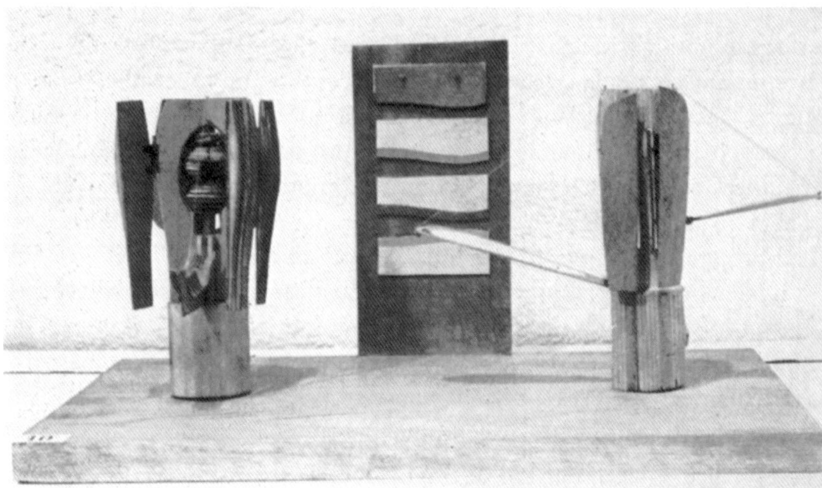

69 A subsidiary prizewinner in the Littlewoods Sculptural Design Competition (1964): Peter Startup's two changeable wooden structures

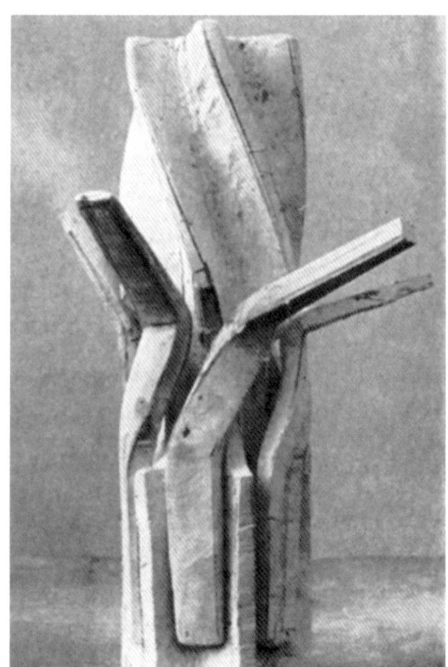

70 A John Moores prize for public art. Maquette by P. G. Heesom, first prizewinner in the Littlewoods Sculptural Design Competition for that firm's new building

prizes, as well as some good drawings by P. G. Heesom of Rhyl whose design was chosen to be carried out – and by making so many bright young sculptors think about the problem of public art in Liverpool and showing both their failures and their successes it may have done some very valuable spadework.[1] Its lessons need to be considered together with those of the university scheme.

As part of the 'Bluecoat 63' display at the Bluecoat Chambers a group of local artists and architects[2] set out to show how they too could contribute to the new city. The original idea evidently was to show collaborative schemes for particular Liverpool sites and buildings, in the hope of stimulating private and official interest in commissioning such work. In a modest way this succeeded; thus the WEBA group formed by Weston, Edkins, Ballard and Arnatt, four teachers at the College of Art, was subsequently asked to produce a work for a new building being put up by the Thames Investment Society behind the Liver Building, while at one time it looked as if ATV's new bowling alley in Wavertree Road might get a metal sculpture by Frederick Bushe for its façade, largely at the suggestion of Stephenson, Young and Partners, the architects.[3] Neither of these projects in fact materialized, and although the show itself was well attended it consisted either of completed works – including besides those already mentioned a good crucifix by Arthur Ballard for a chapel in North Wales designed by Quentin Hughes and Gerald

[1] The prizewinners in the first stage of the competition were divided into two sections. J. C. Dougill, Heesom, D. Troostwyk, J. M. Whiskerd, M. Kenny and R. M. Jones got £500 each and a commission to develop their designs further for final judging. H. V. Gregory, C. Sanderson, Miss F. A. M. Jardine, Roger Dean, Startup and F. L. Kenatt got £250 travelling scholarships. Kenny and Dean are Liverpool sculptors; Heesom is from Rhyl. At the second stage Heesom's model was selected for the main award of £5,000. The judges at both stages were Sir William Coldstream, Milner Gray and Peter Chamberlain.

[2] The committee, under the chairmanship of Dr Quentin Hughes of the School of Architecture, consisted of Arthur Ballard, Roderick Bisson, Nicholas Horsfield (painters); George MacPherson (sculptor); James O'Donahue and Roy Parker (architects); Graham Ashworth (of Shankland's town-planning team), John Patterson, Lucjan Pietka, and the Professor of Architecture, Robert Gardner-Medwin. The catalogue introduction spoke of the happier days when 'there was a welding of all visual arts under the leadership of architecture', and named the Constructivists as a modern school aiming at the same sort of synthesis. It listed twenty-eight local artists (six of them with studios in the Bluecoat Chambers) 'who have either had experience in producing murals, sculptural panels or other architectural features or have shown an interest in participating in this sort of work'.

[3] The client's first reaction to the idea is interesting for its realistic attitude to the problems involved. Mr L. S. Michael of Ambassador Bowling, ATV's subsidiary, told the architects that:

> It is of course an extremely dangerous thing to do, because there is a tendency for sculpture of this nature to 'date' very rapidly in appearance. One would obviously be looking for something as abstract as possible, without completely losing the bowling implication.
>
> A completely abstract piece of sculpture while having excellent decorative qualities would convey nothing to our prospective clients. . . . On the other hand a straightforward replica of bowling pins and balls might be extremely boring and inappropriate as part of the permanent decorations of the building.

Beech – or of purely hypothetical schemes by artists alone, sometimes without much architectural relevance. They were small-scale affairs when considered in relation to the immensity of the tasks which the new city plans might provide, and the only revelation of the show was the panels by G. W. Jardine, made by photographic enlargement from some of his collages; they were however hardly architectural.

The other body to concern itself with these problems is the Merseyside Civic Society, which has become active over the past four or five years in all matters affecting Liverpool's appearance and design standards and is now sometimes consulted by the corporation; it has about 500 members and is run by a mixture of architects and laymen. It has been concentrating of late on the appearance of the streets. Thus it has designed flowersellers' and newsvendors' stands as prototypes to raise the miserable level of the street furniture; it has pressed for a change in the Brunswick green colour of the buses; and it initiated a 'facelift' operation for Williamson Square, a process which normally brings economic as well as aesthetic benefits to the chosen area, but has in this case been held up largely as a result of the square's probable early redevelopment. Besides this it has started a move to encourage the main Liverpool stores to improve their fashion standards (as Browns of Chester are held to have done); and has taken part in various negotiations concerning the proposed municipal tidying-up of the neglected but highly romantic cemetery around and beneath the Anglican cathedral. Its boldest step was to commission the Denbighshire sculptor Richard Huws[1] to design a fountain, originally to be erected outside Liverpool, then switched to the city itself to commemorate the starting of work on the city centre. This cleverly-conceived hydraulic contraption, as striking in design as anything in the Littlewoods competition, long had no site allotted to it, but the corporation has now arranged with one of the developers for it to be put up above a new car park near Pier Head, and the Arts Council has given £750 towards the cost.

Such, in outline, is the present position of public art in Liverpool, and it is worth reflecting on it if anything further is to be done. For the unfortunate thing about the public use of works of art in this way is that although it is sometimes recommended as a self-evident desideratum the people who would have to put it into effect are left to act more or less in the dark. The subject is

[1] Huws, once a shipbuilding apprentice at Cammell Laird's Birkenhead yard and now lecturer in engineering at the School of Architecture, was responsible for the very successful water sculpture at the 1951 South Bank Exhibition.

71 Fountain by the local sculptor-engineer Richard Huws, commissioned by the Merseyside Civic Society and now being erected near Pier Head

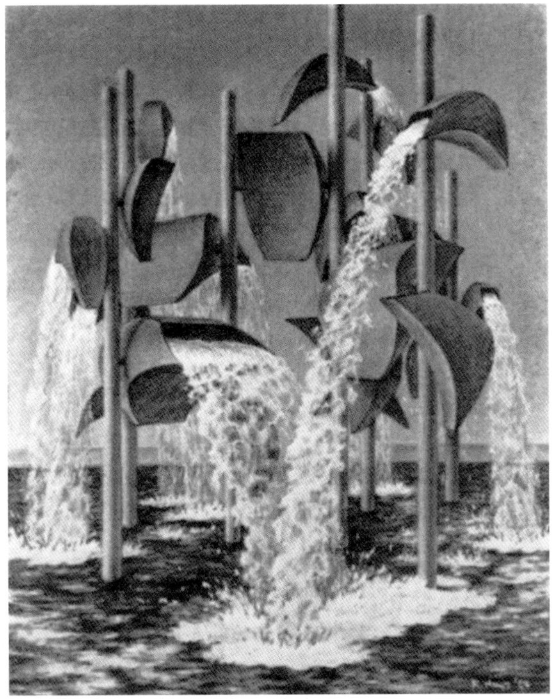

astonishingly neglected by critics and historians of art; there is (to my knowledge) *no* book in any country that even gives illustrations of the outstanding examples of such work in the world today, let alone an account of how they come to have been commissioned or their effect on the public for whom they were designed. The result is that potential patrons and officials in our cities, and artists and architects too, not only are often hamstrung by ignorance of the possible methods and mistakes, but are largely unaware of those achievements which justify public art today. In the circumstances if they have a sense of responsibility they may well refuse to act. If they have not then they are likely to act wrong.

This is why it has been worth looking at public art in Liverpool in this sometimes rather pedestrian manner. No doubt it has been a disheartening experience for readers accustomed to the grand sensations and technicolor scandals of books on modern art, but at least it allows art, architecture, design and other often disregarded elements of our visual environment to be brought into some sort of common perspective, and it raises problems which anybody who hopes to operate in this field has got to bear in mind. For who, to begin with, decides the commissioning of a public work of art? Segregate a picture or piece of sculpture in a gallery, and the role of the expert is at once admitted; the gallery's director, within certain limits, will have his way. Not so once art gets outside the ghetto walls; it is then normal for any councillor, company director or other patron to act on his own judgment, and the only question is whether it is he or his architect who will pick the artist, and site and specify the work. If there is no reason why the new type of patron should necessarily be the best person to decide this there is little more why the architect should, for although architects know well enough what is going to fit their own buildings they are not bound to have God-given qualifications to distinguish between good art and bad. Those Baroque artists who accepted 'the leadership of architecture' were sometimes pedestrian practitioners within their own particular fields, and the modern (post-Corbusier) architect's affection for artists whose geometric gifts outweigh their colour sense can easily be disastrous as soon as those gifts drop below the top (i.e. Arp-Nicholson-Gabo-Vasarely-late Pasmore) level.

All the signs in Liverpool are that the architect considers the nomination of an artist to be his province. And in a sense this is understandable, for the Liverpool artists evidently feel that public design issues are not their affair; they have, for instance, done nothing to support the new city plans and they play no part in the Civic Society. Moreover most artists (and not only in Liverpool) have to come a long way if they are to work with an architect at all. There is, in the City Architect's view, a new type of artist now evolving who is interested in structural details and what can be done with them; Mitchell or Hollaway, for instance, can see the possible sculptural implications of a plan at an early stage and agree them with the architect so that their work becomes part of the actual building process; but Liverpool has nobody trained in this way. The result, so Dr Bradbury feels, is that there is a gap between artist and architect which can only be remedied by quite small-scale experiments in collaboration. Similarly the late Stanisław Pater, the Polish-born architect who was mainly responsible for churches at Weightman and Bullen, found that artists tend to have a poor sense of scale unless they have done architectural work before, so that in most cases he would ask them to make a full-size maquette to be tried out on the proposed site. Not that it is necessarily the most efficient collaborators from the architects' point of view who will produce the best answer. Too much of the 'built-in' decoration on recent buildings – the Liverpool Building Centre is a characteristic example – is a humdrum regurgitation of modern art conventions which has no real identity of its own and could date disastrously as soon as the fashion supporting it has collapsed. Certainly the architect's assumed primacy in this field is subject to more qualifications than he normally admits.

Frequently, in the instances which we have been looking at, there has been an almost total divorce of the work of art from its site. This was ludicrous enough with the statues of Huskisson, Disraeli and Edward VII being shifted around like enlarged chessmen, but the case of the Huws fountain shows that sculpture can be commissioned without a site at all; (other possible homes suggested for it included Pier Head and Williamson Square, with a proposed public lavatory contending for the latter). This is the real weakness both of the works commissioned by the university and of the competitors in the Littlewoods scheme; they bear less relation to their background than to that of the artist. Dalwood's sculpture outside the Physics Building, for in-

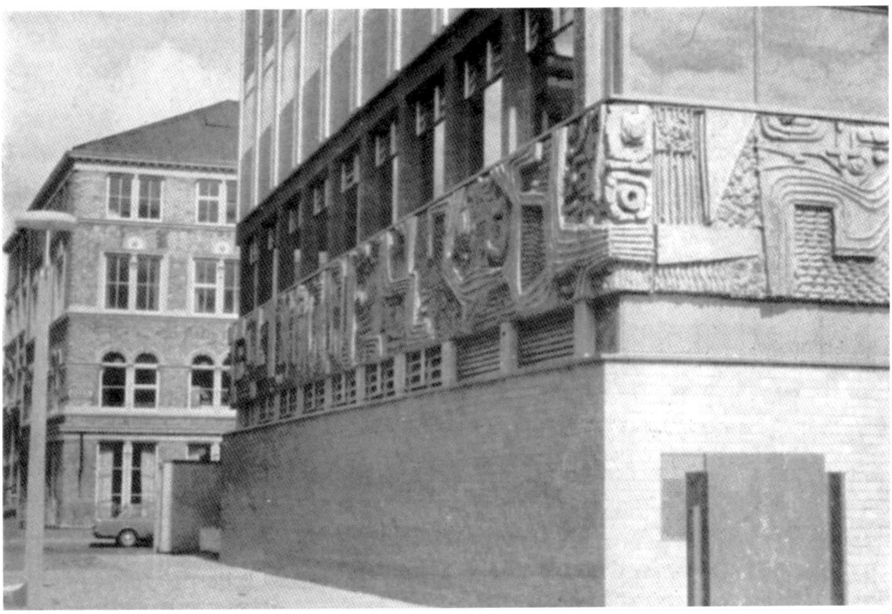

72 The danger of cliché: cast sculpture by William Mitchell on the new Building Centre in Hope Street, near the splendid Philharmonic Hotel. This is the kind of decoration that now tends to be appreciated by architects, since it is conceived and executed as part of the building.

stance, besides being blankly uninteresting in itself from too many angles, was out of scale with the building and out of character with the relics of nineteenth century Liverpool around it. Geoffrey Clarke's indoor mosaic, again, might well look good in a gallery, but it depends on a highflown written explanation alongside it to explain its symbolism, and unfortunately the light is too bad for the main symbol to be distinguishable. These artists are the choice of the architects, but they have not necessarily been brought in at an early enough stage; the fact that twenty-four different architects are being used makes for a certain disjointedness, while although they include some of the country's leading men (Lasdun, for instance, Spence, Fry), the buildings so far finished have hardly shown them at the top of their form. There has

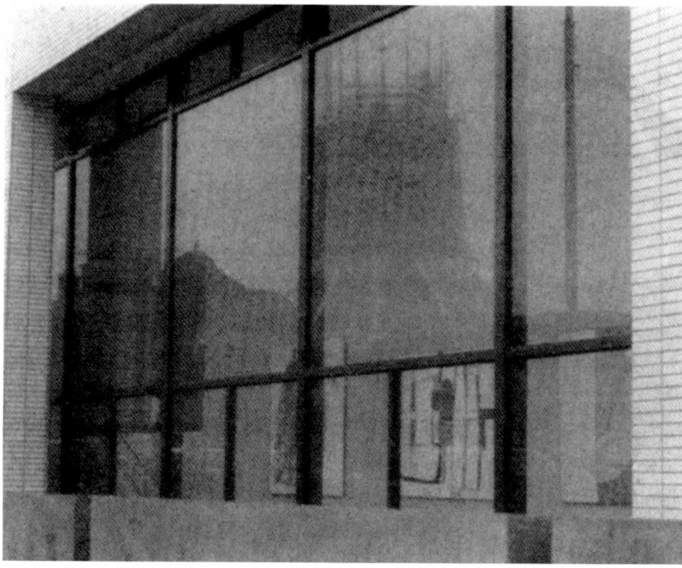

73 A new development in the University's art policy. Paintings hanging in the Electrical Engineering Building, seen from the street through a window reflecting the new cathedral

been a different policy in the case of Yorke, Mardell and Rosenberg's Electrical Engineering Building, where £3,000 was spent on original paintings and prints (of the architect's choosing) to be hung in corridors, common rooms and so forth; a number of the paintings – non-figurative works of no special distinction – are in a glass-walled basement corridor which can be inspected from the street. The prints are by leading contemporary English artists and mostly look very well. And most recently some £2,500-worth of paintings, half of them by Liverpool artists, have been bought for the new Social Studies and Modern Languages Building, this time under the chairmanship of Professor Ridley (himself a collector) and with the architect as a member of the selecting committee.[1]

It would be a mistake to blinker ourselves to the failures because of a commitment to the kind of modern artists concerned in them, or even a sense that failure on this level is better and more exciting than success in purely local terms. It would be a greater one to decide on this evidence that modern art is unfitted for public tasks or that the honest northern artist is preferable to the over-publicized Londoner. The lessons are surely more than the commission-

[1] The Science Lecture Theatres building subsequently built to the design of Professor Robert Gardner-Medwin in association with James and Bywaters includes work by two local artists: a tapestry by Geraldine Carmichael and concrete reliefs by Frederick Bushe.

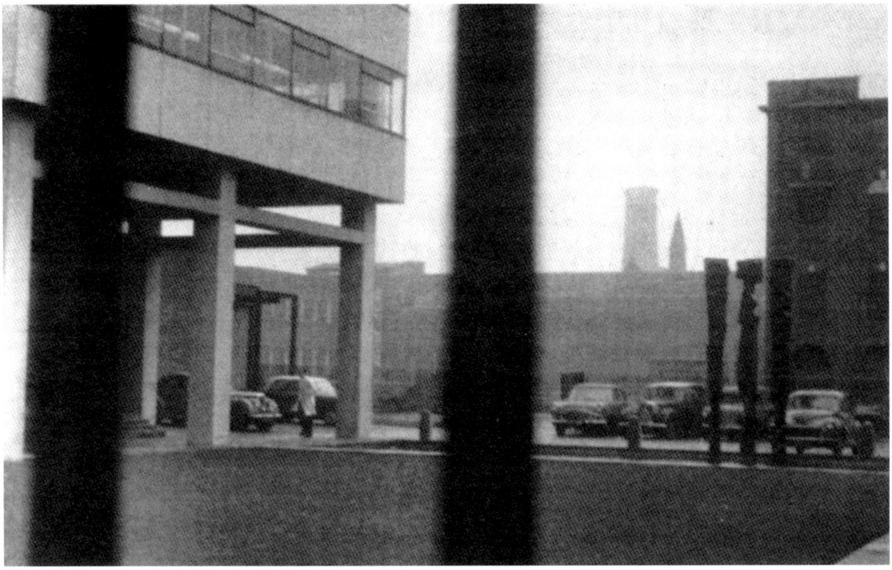

74 Out of place and out of scale. The three sculptural figures outside Sir Basil Spence's Physics Building. In the distance, the massive brick ventilating shaft to the railway tunnel

ing of public art is at present undertaken too amateurishly, without enough sense of site and purpose; that symbolizing pious sentiments like the resurgence of Liverpool is merely laughable unless they correspond to a strong public feeling; that the architect needs advice and the artist some awareness of scale and materials if their arts are to combine effectively; above all that once art gets out into the open the pseudo-philosophizing and the display of personal temperament which impress gallery-goers or magazine readers matter less than a real feeling for the background – the background not only of the building in question but also of the city's climate and architecture and the hopes and needs of the people who live there. This is something which to my mind emerged strongly from the exhibits in the Littlewoods competition; that attitude of 'take it or leave it' which the self-respecting artist now adopts towards patrons and dealers is likely to seem merely insulting to the public who find his work impinging all uninvited on their everyday lives. It must speak to them in some other terms if it is to become rooted there.

Moreover there is no system of change and exchange as within the segregated world of the gallery; there is no cellar for the dumping of unwanted works. Perhaps in due course public art will go off like fireworks or be stripped down like posters, but this is not how it operates at present. For better or worse it is there for good.

5 : QUESTIONS OF TASTE

In the years since the war this once philistine country has got caught up on a wave of interest in art, and particularly in the development of modern art over the past century. The booming prices in the saleroom, the establishment of art history as an academic subject in our universities, the vast increase in art books, the crowds packing the modern art exhibitions: all these are evidence of a great change in our attitude. Today art, even of the most seemingly outrageous avant-garde kind, is acceptable in smart English society; a topic for conversation, a good capital-gains investment, a subject for theses, a hobby for retired major-generals, an occupation for debutantes, it has become very nearly a reputable pursuit. The professional artist has altered; he is no longer expected to be a gentleman, like the painters of Bloomsbury or Camden Town or the fashionable artists between the wars; he is now accepted as a man of a race apart, a visual entertainer whose main function is to surprise. A whole generation of more or less classless painters and sculptors has come out of the art schools to meet the demand for short-lived sensations; they come often from ordinary provincial families and local art schools, then pass into the London machine, where the rewards are great so long as they are in fashion. The pace is hot in this world, which is very different from the one most civic and industrial patrons were brought up in. It is not easy to keep track of the movements of taste.

Yet each of the last two chapters has finally come down to this question, for both the public gallery and the unconfined art of streets and open spaces have got to mean something to the ordinary citizen if they are to justify themselves. How far then can the patrons and potential patrons of art in Liverpool count on this rapid rate of development being maintained on Merseyside too? Obviously there is a time-lag in such matters between Liverpool and London, and much that is accepted by a wide public in the capital is still disliked and viewed with mistrust in the provinces; it may indeed only be seen at all in Liverpool because of a certain itch to check up on the latest London craze. None the less it is clear that the general evolution is infectious. The figures for attendances at the Walker Art Gallery have improved, as we saw on p. 70; the increase in the sale of postcard reproductions shows that interest in the pictures is becoming less casual; the Bluecoat gallery is establishing itself; while use of the art library seems to have gone up very rapidly at first.[1] The books most in demand are monographs on particular artists and schools and the semi-popular (*haute vulgarisation*) illustrated books produced by such publishers as Skira, Thames and Hudson, Weidenfeld, and Oldbourne, typical results of the new international system of 'co-production' by which the expense of printing and block making is shared between a number of different countries. Admittedly these are only small straws to show which way the wind blows, but it would be wise to regard Liverpool taste too as changing, even if its development has so far been slower and more idiosyncratic than that of England as a whole.

There has been nothing in recent times to compare with the three great Liverpool art arguments of the past: the cases respectively of the Pre-Raphaelite prizewinners, the St George's Hall reliefs, and the Lord Mayor's portrait. Yet even with a gallery of the reputation of the Walker the elected representatives still intermittently dig in their toes and oppose the purchase of a work which they do not 'understand'. This has not happened often, first because under the Cotton-Lambert regime there was a practice of buying no very modern work;[2] more recently because the Moores gifts have created a strong modern department without much need for controversial spending of public money. Nor should it be taken too seriously when it does, for quite apart from the fact that a democratic opposition exists precisely to raise objections there is also a school of thought both in and out of the council which feels that controversy is an effective way of stimulating interest in the gallery. The first important case was in 1958, when the Arts Sub-Committee refused to allow the director to spend £247 on a painting by William Scott. 'I feel that this is an insult,' councillors were quoted as saying;[3] 'If we tell the City Council we have bought that we won't get any more money'; 'I cannot see any merit'; 'A monstrosity'; 'I would rather have Winston Churchill's *Still Life*'. Before the end of that year the picture had been bought by the

[1] The figures for postcards sold are: (year ending) 1958, 16,729; 1959, 17,518; 1960, 18,119; 1961, 24,151; 1962, 28,065; 1963, 22,138; 1964, 23,873; 1965, 22,924; 1966, 28,822.

The City Librarian's annual reports give the following details: 1958, an increase of almost 5,000 readers (on a previous total of about 15,000); 1959, no mention; 1960, lending issues up by 40 per cent, reference issues by 38 per cent; 1961, both up by about 15 per cent; 1962, lending up by 25 per cent and reference by 75 per cent. Since then there has been some falling-off, owing partly to rebuilding operations, partly to the provision of more art books in branch libraries.

[2] In Cotton's view there should be a distinction between what the gallery ought to show – which should be extremely catholic so that visitors can see as much as possible of what is going on in art – and what it should buy and keep.

[3] *Liverpool Evening Express*, 21 February 1958.

Musée de l'Art Moderne in Paris; it is now worth about three times the sum asked. Three years later the opposition objected to the purchase of the Henry Moore *Falling Warrior* in comparable terms: 'a phoney pot-boiler', for instance, 'Just a blob of metal', and 'Where is its face?'[1] In 1963 however the

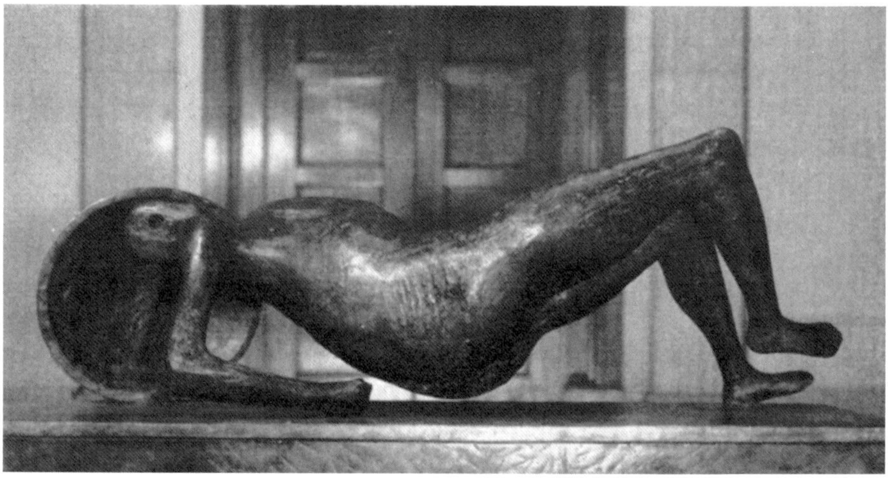

75 A purchase by the gallery that was opposed in committee: Henry Moore's *Falling Warrior*

city's first modern American painting – a smooth (and to my mind) superficial abstract work by Paul Jenkins called *Phenomena Votive* – was bought thanks largely to the enthusiasm of the Sub-Committee chairman, Robert Bessell, and it is possible that the tide may be changing.

Councillors do not necessarily sit on the Arts Sub-Committee because they wish to; 'the average councillor', so one of them told me, 'just couldn't care less about the gallery'. This attitude, slightly overstated perhaps, seems to many a fair enough representation of that of the public, and at one time it may have been so. Whether the same holds good today is more doubtful. Despite the director's complaints in his annual reports (of 1953–4, 1954–5, 1958–9, 1962–3) that the city is largely unaware of the treasures it owns a surprising number of the people whom I myself questioned, either directly or on paper, at least knew that the gallery was a proper subject for interest, even for pride. A feeling of this sort is perfectly compatible with a failure ever to visit the place, and what people get out of the collection and what it actually contains are two very different matters. The best-liked (or best remembered) pictures are a curious mixture; among the postcard reproductions Lowry's *The Fever Van* is a best-seller; while my own enquiries in 1963 put Daguerre's

[1] See the *Liverpool Daily Post* of 13 and 14 January 1961 for the sub-committee and of 2 February for the council meeting.

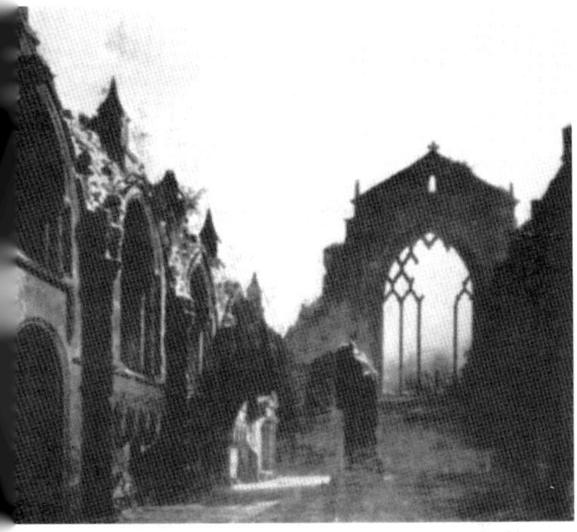

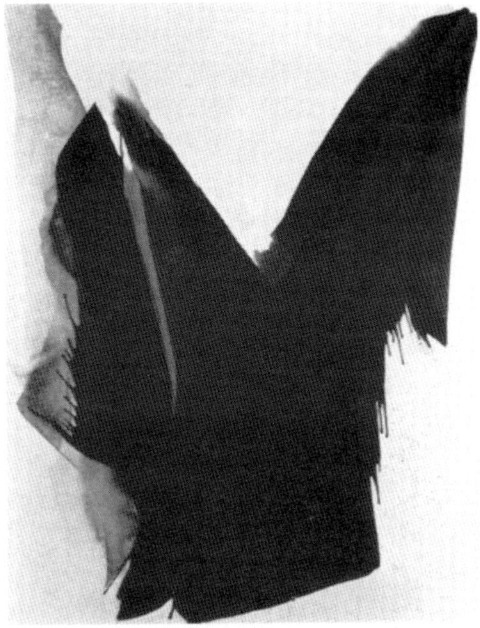

& 77 Two of the gallery's most popular ·tures. Above: A very popular work: Daguerre's ·ins of *Holyrood Castle by Moonlight*. This was ·inted 1823–4 and presented to the city in ·64. Right: Paul Jenkins: *Phenomena Votive*, ·rchased ninety-nine years later

romantic *Holyrood Castle* and the new Jenkins abstract (both at that time hanging conspicuously on the stairs up to the main collection) as the main favourites. The primitives found few supporters: one or two for the Simone Martini; none for the Ercole de' Roberti *Pietà*, which is surely one of the most beautiful pictures in England. One boy even suggested that all the old pictures ought to be put in a 'museum': an interesting indication that galleries are coming to be seen as places for new visual experiences, to which the study of earlier masterpieces is a positive obstacle.

A certain licence is allowed in a gallery, which is withdrawn as soon as art gets out into the streets. The difficulty facing public art in Liverpool is that when it is more or less traditional in style, nobody will notice it, while when it is not it is noticed all right, but is liable to be taken as a personal affront by the public. Most of the existing public statues simply are not looked at; the Liverpool citizens I questioned had only the vaguest idea of what was round St George's Hall, that great conglomeration of statuary in the heart of the city, and apart from the four Landseerish lions (which were no doubt imprinted on their memories as children) dismissed it as a display of militarism and royalty: something to which they automatically shut their eyes. This situation they are used to and accept. It was a different matter however when the Bold Street Association, representing the smartest and architecturally least disagreeable shopping street in Liverpool (which Shankland has sug-

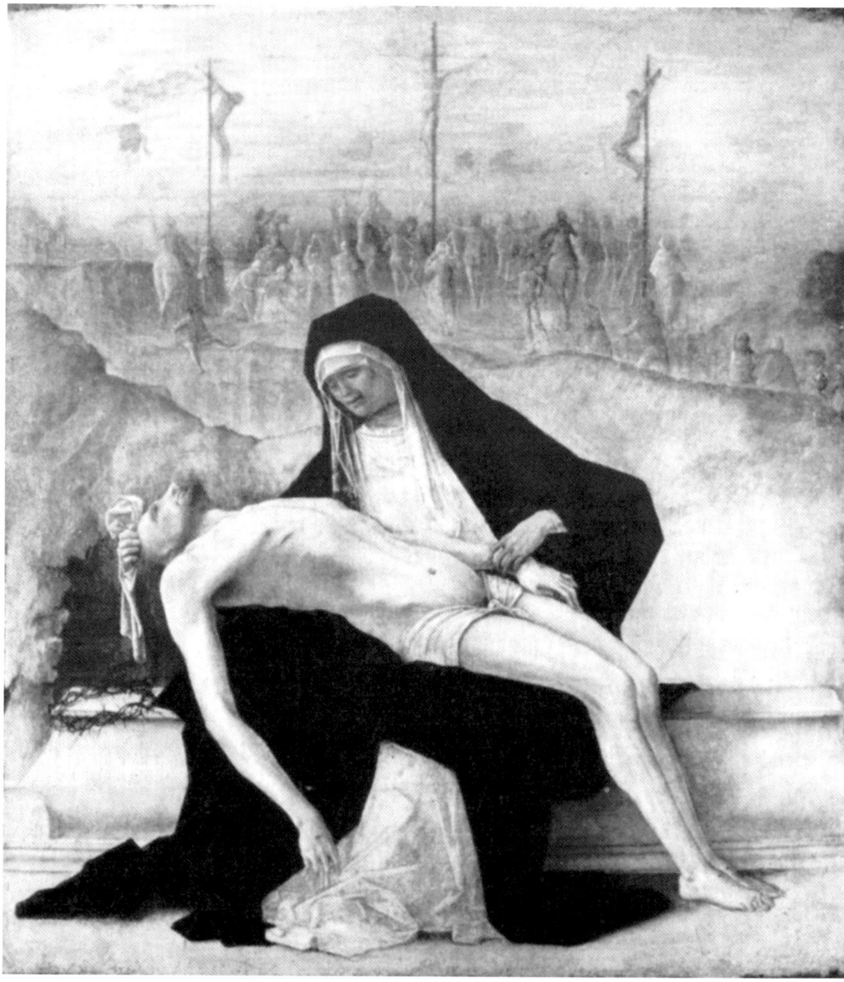

78 *Not* a public favourite: Ercole de' Roberti's *Pietà*, from the Roscoe collection in the Walker Gallery

gested glassing-over and turning into a pedestrian way), put a bombed corner site at the disposal of a local modern sculptor. This well-intentioned act proved a model flop. It started happily enough with a small unveiling ceremony at which the association's vice-president expressed his hopes 'that the public of Liverpool will recognize this work of art as an asset to the city and respect it. I personally think we should encourage young artists to create works like this and give them every opportunity to display them in Liverpool.'[1]

[1] *Liverpool Daily Post*, 19 September 1960.

Then, wrote the *Liverpool Daily Post*'s reporter:

> The draperies fell . . . and there was the sort of silence in which everyone is wondering to say . . . A child let out a howl. Then twenty-seven-year-old sculptor Robin Riley, of Catherine Street, Liverpool, tried to answer all those questions from the baffled and bewildered.

'I was primarily concerned in making a figure as a piece of sculpture,' Riley was quoted as saying. 'It was sculpturally unnecessary for it to have arms. I wanted to create the impression of the power in human beings, in humanity and in life itself.' Again. 'The figure is the reflection of my own personal awareness and it cannot be explained. It is just a figure. You either have a purely personal emotional reaction or you have not.'

There is an emergency meeting of the Bold Street Association; the statue itself is given police protection. Next Arthur Maiden Ltd, the poster hoarding firm who control the site, insist that it should be removed, on the pretext of 'reported public reaction against it, which might be directed against us when we are in no way responsible for it.' No, their managing director tells the *Liverpool Post*,[2] it wasn't that it was indecent,

> although people had said it was offensive and vulgar. Yes, it might be art, but they didn't think so. They were merely exercising their right to have it taken away.

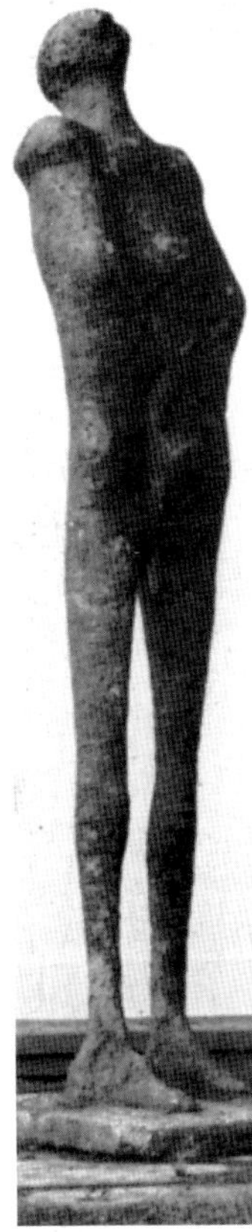

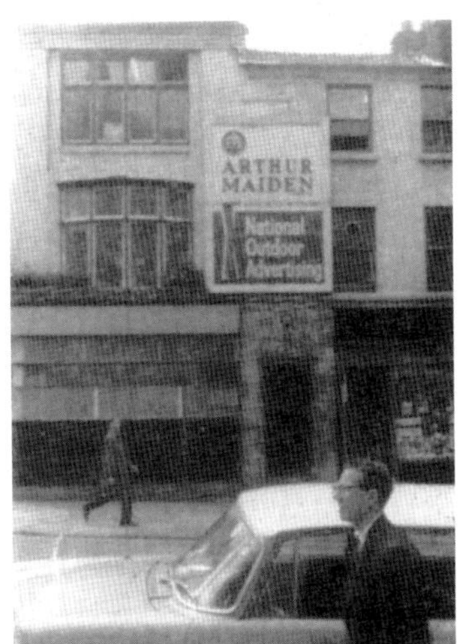

79 (*above*) Public art and public taste. Robin Riley's *Standing Figure* after its removal from the Bold Street site. 80 (*right*) Arbiters of this taste: Arthur Maiden Ltd's Liverpool headquarters

[1] *Liverpool Daily Post*, 19 September 1960.
[2] Ibid., 20 September 1960.

> A crowd gather; the statue is lowered to the ground. The vice-president rather wistfully says they had 'hoped that this site might become a showplace for many of our young artists'. Riley accuses his critics of being ashamed of humanity.
>
> A man with a beard said: 'Dreary old Liverpool strikes again.'
>
> An old man with a flat cap said: 'Get away, mate. We've got enough of that kind of thing with old Herbert on top of Lewis's.'

'Hardly anyone,' commented the *Post*'s reporter, 'could describe their objections to it. It's back to front, it's a prostitution, it looks as though it's got a nasty mind, it's revolting, they said. And, plaintively, what does it mean?' The statue was later given asylum in a Liverpool private garden, though Councillor Maguire of Crosby would have liked it put on the Blundellsands sea front. 'I think,' he explained, 'it typifies the struggle of our merchant seamen during the war.'

In the use and choice of works of art for homes the population of Liverpool lag not only behind London but behind their own past. So far as original works are concerned, there are now only two established picture dealers in central Liverpool – Boydell, and J. Davey and Son (who is also one of the principal frame-makers) – as against some twenty half a century ago. Davey told me too that in his father's time there used to be 240 gilders in the union in Liverpool and as many again who were not members; today there is one. Agnews had a Liverpool branch from 1873 to 1909 and there was also in those days a good market for local painters; thus in 1876 the *Porcupine*'s London correspondent was writing of the resentment felt by the London exhibitors at the Autumn Exhibition who suspected that 'the bulk of the twelve thousand and odd pounds resulting from the sales in William Brown Street found its way into the pockets of the local men.'[1]

Today this is all very much changed. Not only do the few noteworthy Liverpool collectors (such as Mrs Bibby and Messrs Oliphant, Kennerley and Samuels) do their buying in London – Boydell told me that he had never been asked for a work by any of the great French painters – but the Liverpool artist finds it difficult to sell. Though old Liverpool pictures, especially of a topographical nature, are in considerable demand, both Boydell and Davey feel there is practically no market for the present generation of artists. Of those whom I myself have talked with, certainly, only the sculptor Herbert Tyson Smith and, with considerable difficulty, Dooley, George Thomas and James Cliffe have been able to live without relying mainly on a teaching job. It was considered exceptional by his confrères when Nicholas Horsfield, by-

[1] *The Porcupine*, Liverpool, 5 February 1876, p. 708.

passing the dealers, sold some £750 worth of pictures in 1963 from a one-man show at the Bluecoat Chambers that represented the cream of two years' work, though in spring 1966 Sean Rice the sculptor also sold nearly all his works from a two-man exhibition in the same gallery. Generally speaking the uncertain income from local sales can only represent pocket-money to the artist, nothing more.

Both Davey and Boydell say that business has much improved in the past few years; the growing interest in pictures has affected people's furnishing habits, especially when setting up a new home, and the fashion for bare walls is disappearing. None the less there is no gallery in Liverpool such as artists and students would like to visit, or the leading painters to show in, or the chief patrons to support. Of the two survivors Davey finds that the market is for old pictures, including nineteenth century works, for which there is a demand in America. Boydell's is rather more interesting; it has dignified

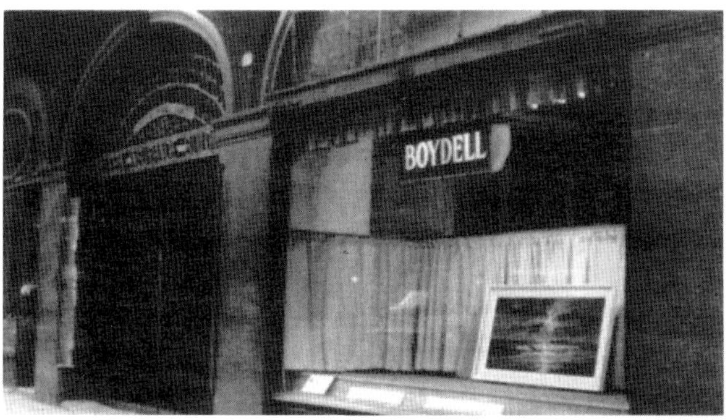

81 The Boydell Gallery, at the corner of Castle Street and Dale Street, the principal Liverpool picture dealers

premises and a good stock of early nineteenth century and the more conservative modern watercolours, and although many of the oils are stereotyped landscapes by unknown continental painters, imported in batches and selling for only £10–£30, Boydell himself commissions competent small paintings of Liverpool scenes by Gordon Ellis, an artist living in Scotland. He is beginning now to sell more abstract work, but only when, like that of the French artist Michel Mouly, it has already become familiar through reproductions, the pace-setters here being the Bristol print firm Frost and Reed. There is nothing in the activities of either of these establishments to replace the gallery run by Eric Rowan (lately of the College staff) for the New Shakespeare Theatre Club which the American actor-director Sam Wanamaker managed between November 1957 and January 1959. Here there were shows of Klee, Francis Bacon and Joseph Herman that are still talked about in Liverpool. Unfortunately the gallery was badly placed to catch the ordinary theatregoer, and had little success in selling pictures. It was doing a public gallery's work rather than that of a dealer.[1]

The main market in Liverpool is for coloured prints, and these are often by artists of whom the right-thinking art-lover rests in happy ignorance: painters of colourful landscapes like Doyly John, Deakins and George Hann, and above all the South African Tretchikoff, whose pictures show expressionless girls with huge smooth faces in a strange green and purple glow, exotically dressed against a flat wall-paper-like background. A few years ago when the Medici Society branch in Bold Street put one of these in the shop window it drew so many admirers that the police rang up to know what was wrong. Such works, which are stocked also by Boots's Art Department and by Owen

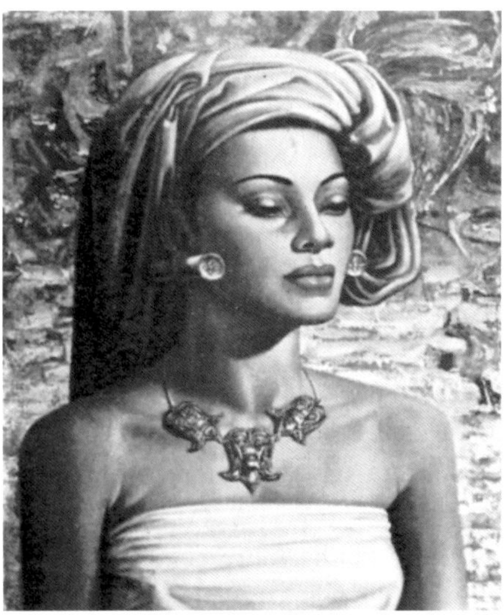

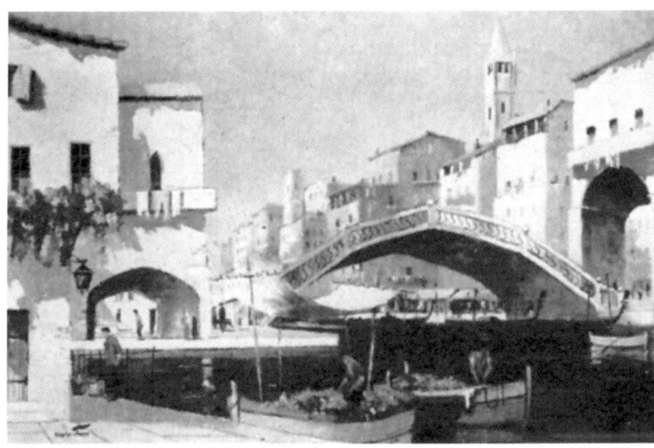

◄ 82 Best selling prints: (1) Tretchikoff's *The Balinese Girl*
83 ▲ (2) Doyly John's *A Bridge in Venice*. Both these artists are published by Messrs Frost and Reed

Owen,[2] sell for about £4 or £5; Boots furthermore have an interesting device called Craft Master, 'the original painting-by-numbers set' which is a do-it-yourself version of similar subjects in similar colours: Loch Lomond, for instance, Mountain Châlet, Spanish Dancers, Wild Stallions, St Tropez,

[1] I have not seen the gallery run by the painter Ray Fields at Bebington near Port Sunlight. This is combined with a working studio.

[2] The Central Buyer for Owen Owen told me in May 1963 that 'The fashion at the moment is for Spanish subjects, Harbour scenes, Mountain and Swiss-type scenes, and a colourful range of Italian Lakes. . . . Old Masters are not popular with the exception of Constable's *Haywain* and *Flatford Mill*.' He attributed this to the increase in foreign travel.

Mademoiselle and The Charm of Paris (showing the Sacré-Coeur).[1] Lewis's sell much cheaper so-called 'Canvatex' reproductions of Cézanne, Picasso, Matisse and Utrillo; I saw a reproduction of the de Stael footballers in the window of the Times Furnishing Co, and in Lewis's Show House, when I visited it, there was a really good selection of prints on the walls (including not only Braque and Dufy but the Uccello *Rout of San Romano*), for which the salesman in charge had had 'quite a few orders'. Once again it seems that the climate is changing. The Medici Society, which has had a Liverpool branch since before the 1914 war, held its first exhibition of truly modern prints, organized in conjunction with the Redfern Gallery in London and

[1] The following detailed report from Mr John M. Caven of Boots's picture department is dated 30 April 1963.

> In the last few years there have been two or three definite fashions in our customers' demands. First of all there was the period when only the large colourful bird pictures by Peter Scott, Vernon Ward and Hugh Monahan would be sold. We sold at that time about seven of these to any one other subject. Then we had D'Oyly John, and other painters of that kind, with their gay continental prints. These were very popular, and it is still very common to see them in people's homes. We still sell this kind of print, but nothing like the sales of a few years ago.
>
> Meanwhile the craze for two or three small pictures on a wall was in, mostly subjects of birds or flowers. The demand lasted quite a long time, and ended, as it had to, with the large pictures coming back.
>
> For a short while the V. Ward Flower prints sold very well, then Tretchikoff came onto the scene with his very colourful Chinese Girl, Lost Orchid, Weeping Rose, and many others. For the last two years his have been the best all round selling reproductions, and we are still doing quite well with them.
>
> Nevertheless the fashion is beginning to change once again, but this time there doesn't seem to be any definite subject or artist that our customers are following, but copies of the old masters, and French impressionists, seem to be selling better than ever. This however has been made easier for the public with the very exceptional value colour prints which 'Prints for Pleasure' of London have been introducing, also the Brush Stroke Mounted Prints at 19*s.* 11*d.*
>
> The 'Facsimile Reproductions' of Bristol, are very good, but are more expensive, and most people do not want to spend a lot of money on a picture when it may only be up a year or so at the most.
>
> The following have been our most popular prints in the last few months:

'Saw Ohn Nyun'	By Sir Gerald Kelly
'Moonlit Sea'	By R. De La Corbiene
'Balinese Girl'	By Tretchikoff
'Amanda and Harriet'	By Strevens
'Chinese Girl'	By Tretchikoff
'Red Skirt'	By R. Clemente
'Tumbling Waves'	By E. Mandon
'Freedom of the Plains'	By M. Bordi
'The Haywain'	By J. Constable.

> In closing I would like to say that, in the buying of pictures, we have found that the Liverpool public are about a year behind what is being sold in the South and London, and even longer in some cases. For instance pictures without glass were being sold in London in the larger shops two or three years ago, but are only now taking on in Liverpool.

Since then, Mr Caven tells me, there has been little change in the type of print that sells best. Customers have, however, been buying more in the £8–£12 range, and there is a new demand for original continental oils.

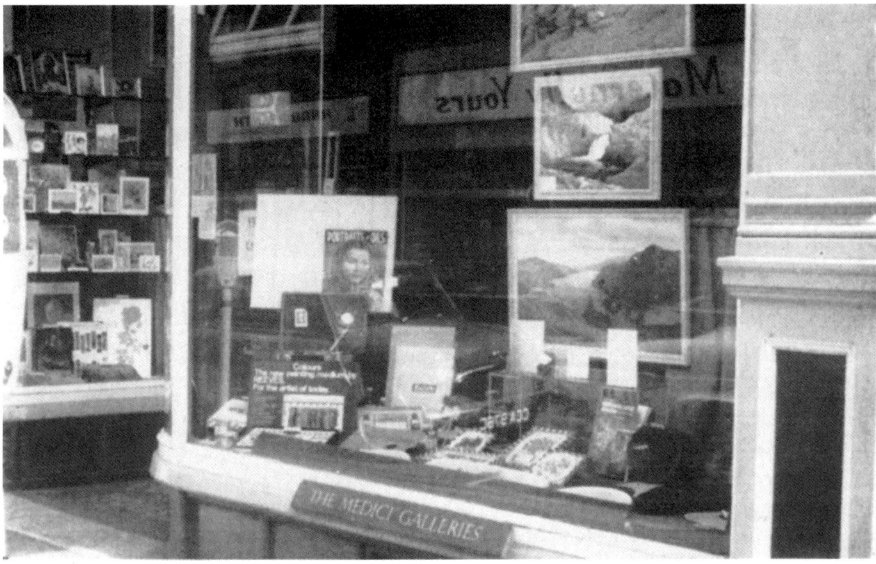

84 The Medici Galleries' Liverpool branch in Bold Street

including works by Kandinsky, Feininger, Chagall etc., in the summer of 1963, and its somewhat unexpected success led to its becoming an annual affair. Seven copies of the most 'difficult' picture, for instance, the Kandinsky *Accord Réciproque*, sold at ten guineas. The wishy-washy devotional pictures of Margaret Tarrant seem to be losing some of their old appeal; Vlaminck sells well, also Lowry and the Picasso child with the dove. Intellectuals, on the whole, tend to choose Brueghel, professional people Canaletto; Dali's Crucifixion does well with Catholics; Constable is the most popular of all. At the same time a rather indifferent abstract by a French painter called Jean Jacus, entitled *Ships of Thought*, has done well with schools. The title makes such a good essay subject.

None of these prints originates in Liverpool, of course, any more than do the best-selling modern oil paintings, so that even if the choices made are significant it cannot be said that the works themselves exactly reflect local taste. They do however to some extent determine it, to judge from the pictures exhibited in amateur art shows. *Bettwys-y-Coed*, *Rarin' to Go*, *Nr Matterdale*, *Late Roses*, *Sunset and Smoke*, *Call of the Sea*, *The Langdales*, *Spanish Fountains*, *Highland Cattle*: these opening titles in the Merseyside Artists' Association's 1964 Spring Exhibition give a good idea of the sort of themes prevailing among such part-time painters. There are other amateur societies besides this one, of course; the Liverpool Artists Club has become essentially a business men's club, but there are also the Liver Sketching Club and the Wirral Artists from across the Mersey, whose standard is rather higher. But both the Merseyside Artists and the Childwall Art Group, an energetic amateur outfit based on the Childwall Evening Institute, seem impregnated with the gaudy escapism of the print shops; there are colourful landscapes, scenes from the sunny south, exotic portraits like bad bible illustrations, and more recently a sprinkling of fearful abstract or 'symbolic' works. It is rare to find anything that tries to reflect the Liverpool scene or the experiences of everyday life; and though the Childwall group's 1963 show did have one quite original small painting its theme, a lowering bison, was as remote as any. There were also (besides idealized portraits of cats, and other horrors), a number of pictures by a student at the Walton prison art classes, mostly imaginary landscapes such as one might find in a furniture shop, but including one abstract. The Paul Jenkins in the Walker Gallery, the shows at the Medici and now this. . . . Half a century after its origins, some twenty years since the millionaires began to accept it, the battle for abstract art is being won in Liverpool too.

On this popular, amateur level there is a great deal of copying, sometimes of style and subject, sometimes of actual works. If there is any degree of self-expression here it lies simply in a choice of more or less conventional, predetermined themes (which change gradually with fashion), and in the actual craftsmanship of handling paint. This, certainly, is how it appears in the big mental hospitals round Liverpool – Deva, Winwick and Rainhill – where the therapeutic value of art is now accepted but the actual practice amounts to little more than a time-occupying hobby, to be ranked with old-time dancing, wool rug-making and occupational therapy in general. Sometimes childish, sometimes reaching a fair amateur standard, the pictures produced in these huge cut-off communities (of which Winwick and Rainhill in particular were unforgettably depressing) are not treated as guide to diagnosis; at Winwick copying prevails, often from travel brochures or from Walt Disneyish drawings, at Deva there is a proportion of original art of a kind, but much copying too.[1] The only truly personal works of art that I saw had been produced at

[1] A report by the art teacher in the Deva Group of Hospitals in 1963 said that a teacher was then visiting Deva Hospital twice a week for three hours, and Moston once. Patients with artistic talents and/or some previous training were given courses in drawing and painting, including abstract or imaginative painting in oils. The others, if amenable to being taught, were instructed in perspective and water-colour. The patients worked to music, particularly to that of composers unfamiliar to them, like Delius, Sibelius and Wagner. In good weather they were encouraged to work out of doors.

The most withdrawn patients were left to draw or paint on their own and tended, from a medical standpoint, to do the most interesting work. There was some clay modelling, that by an epileptic and certain subnormal patients being of special interest. Some of the patients showed great originality, one of them having a gift for 'caricature in abstract form'. Many were good at posters, and these were used on notice boards and elsewhere in the hospitals.

For special occasions the teacher might organize groups of patients to produce large paintings. One of these was used for the Christmas decorations in 1962.

Some patients were destructive, using sharp instruments to attack an image. The classes were of up to about twenty.

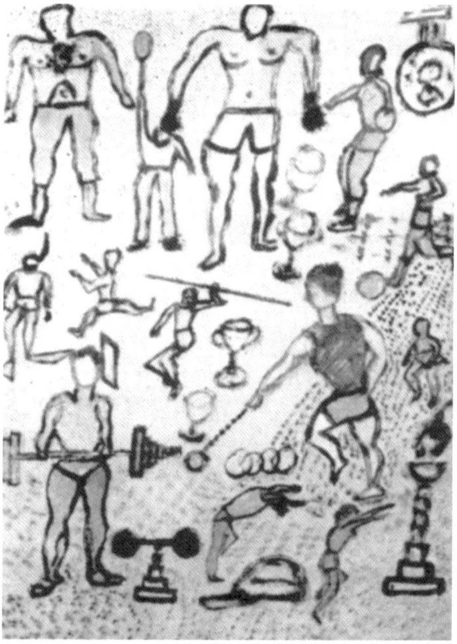

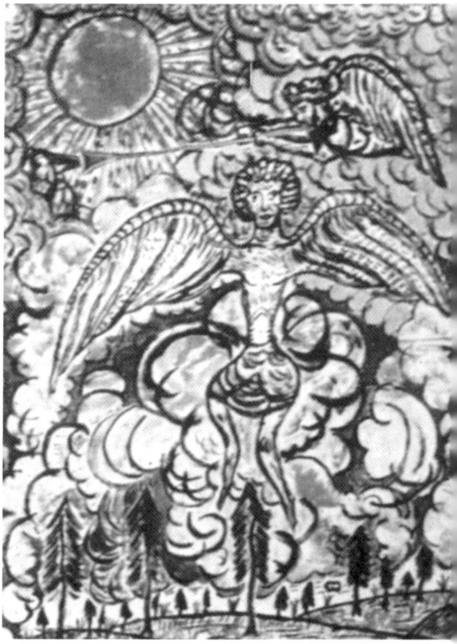

Rainhill (a building designed by the architect of St George's Hall, with 2,400 inmates and a main corridor a quarter of a mile long), where the education officer A. W. Fraser himself owns a picture of Arthur Ballard's and has decorated his recreation room and library with good prints. Here one patient had sculpted two quite original heads in stone, while another produced over a period of years drawings and paintings of extreme interest, pictures which not only progress through a steadily increasing competence and complexity towards abstraction and simplification but have a range of imaginative reference which nobody would have guessed to lie in the power of the uneducated and totally uncommunicative artist. Though this man gave up three or more years ago – he is still a patient, alas – his work deserves to be known for its own sake, quite apart from any bearing which it might have on his case. It is a remarkable instance of spontaneous gifts, and it makes one wonder what the Liverpool amateur artist might not be able to do if he used his own eyes and imagination rather more, and got away from the painting-by-numbers frame of mind.

So far in Liverpool there has not been much to suggest the emergence of any naturally self-expressive local talent in the visual arts which would match the astonishing outbursts of popular music over the last few years. As will appear later, however, there are local artists like Ballard and Arthur Dooley

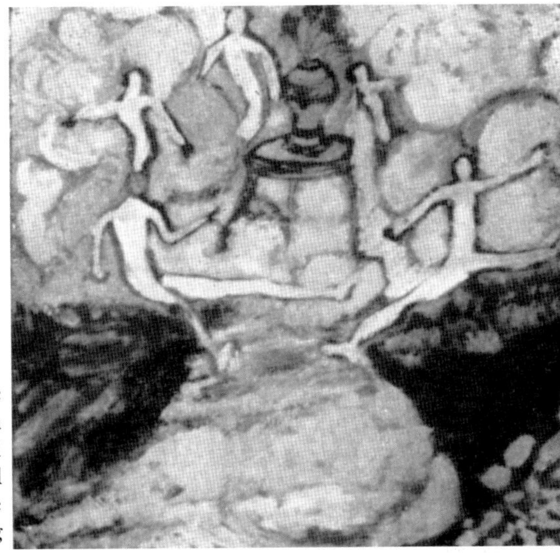

85-89 Art as expression: five pictures from a sequence by an untutored patient in Rainhill mental hospital. They are in chronological order, and after the last of them he stopped painting

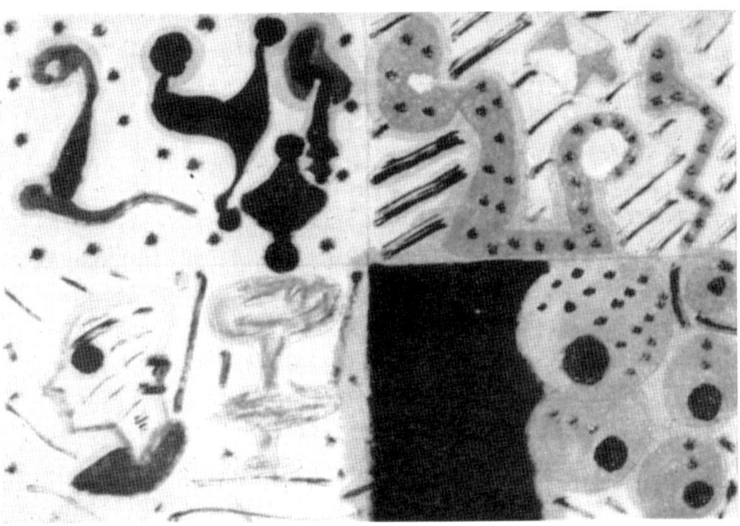

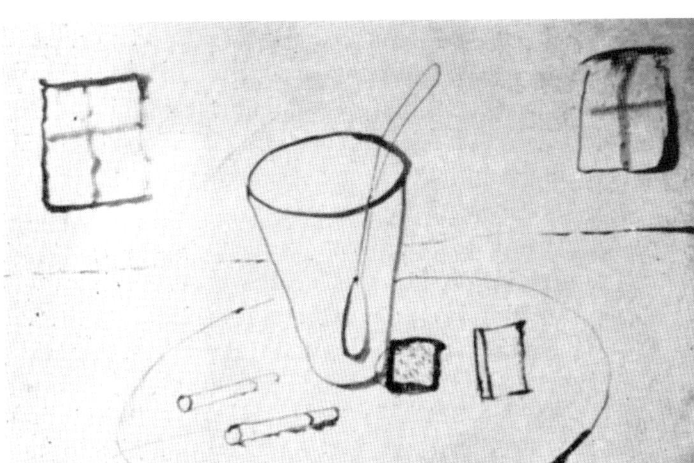

the sculptor who believe that the talent and the possibility of its expression are there, and that it is only a matter of time before it will break out. Whether this is so is a large question, bound up not only with the whole system of art education in the city but with the achievements and potentialities of the professional local artists themselves, two subjects which will be considered in later chapters. It is encouraging however that there should recently have been a couple of attempts to organize Liverpool arts festivals, of a quite non-establishment kind, that have set out to express the spirit of the place. The first of these, the South Liverpool Festival of Art, was originally held in 1960 and based on the Domestic Mission, a late nineteenth century Unitarian foundation in Liverpool 8; in 1964 it developed offshoots in Garston, Vauxhall and Speke and a selection from them all was shown at the Walker Gallery under the title 'Liverpool: People and Places'; in 1966 it spread to several other areas, which held their own District Festivals of Art, and the Walker Art Gallery's final selection ('Liverpool Today and Tomorrow') drew 15,410 visitors in a month.

The idea behind the South Liverpool Festival was the conviction of the Rev. J. Keir Murren of the Domestic Mission that art was at once a means of recording the life and character of the neighbourhood and a socially cohesive force. He had discussed at various club and committee meetings what forces of this kind could be found to set against those that up till then had been helping drag down that section of Liverpool and, he said, 'it was coming away from a John Moores art exhibition that art clicked with me.' He had when I saw him two Picasso postcards in his own small and rather dingy room, and there was a Picasso mother and child hanging in the chapel along with Della Robbia plaques made by Harold Rathbone in the 1890s; none the less he told me that he was 'not art mad at all', but just 'using art in this very real social sense'. The first two of the festivals, as eventually organized by Murren jointly with the neighbouring David Lewis Settlement, contained respectively about 450 and about 700 pictures, mainly by children, showing scenes, episodes and people of the neighbourhood; more recently the project has become part of a larger Community Council, which is concerning itself with a wide range of social problems, from housing and street improvement to the relations between residents and local industry. Though both exhibitions gave expression to a good deal of liveliness and amusing observation the artistic talent revealed was not at first very striking, but the cream of the later shows included works that were genuinely beautiful, as well as directing attention to the everyday environment and the hope of improving it. As an apparently successful example of a new kind of collective (or neighbourhood) art therapy they are a most interesting precedent, suggesting that a similar but wider sense of new artistic curiosity and vitality will be of very practical benefit to the city as a whole.

The two Merseyside Arts Festivals organized in August 1962 and May 1963 by John Gorman were held in the Hope Hall near the new Catholic Cathedral, with the support of Leslie Blond, cinema proprietor, property owner and patron-cum-landlord of the arts. They were the work of the younger professional or would-be professional artists and poets, though of such as the establishment has hitherto rather ignored. This group of people, which includes the poets Roger McGough and Brian Patten (editor of the

90 A poem by one of the participants in the Merseyside Arts Festivals and Hope Hall Events

MOTHER, THE WARDROBE IS FULL OF INFANTRYMEN

Mother, the wardrobe is full of infantrymen
i did, i asked them,
but they snarled saying it was a mans life

Mother there is a centurion tank in the parlour
i did, i asked the officer
but he laughed saying Queens regulations,
and it was out of tune anyway.

Mother polish your identity bracelet
there is a mushroom cloud in the backgarden
i did, i tried to bring in the cat
but it simply came to pieces in my hand.
i did, i tried to whitewash the windows
but there weren't any
i did, i tried to hide under the stairs
but i couldn't get in for the civil defence leaders
i did, i tried ringing Candid Camera
but they crossed their hearts.

i went for a policeman but they were looting the town
i went for a fire engine but they were all upside down
i went for a priest but they were all on their knees
Mother don't just lie there say something please
Mother don't just lie there say something please

Roger McGough

Liverpool poetry magazine *Underdog*) and the painters Walsh and Henri, contains, to my mind, a number of the brightest talents in Liverpool, though it was handicapped by lack of funds and organization and also by the dinginess of the Hope Hall, then a cinema and subsequently given over to the Everyman Theatre. The club in the basement of this hall – supposedly the scene of some remarkable Love Feasts in the last century[1] – was till recently the real meeting point for Liverpool popular music and the other arts. In the hall itself Blond has shown, besides local painters, an exhibition of paintings by Bomberg and mixed shows from the Waddington and St George's galleries in London; although neither the architecture nor the patrons have been ideal for such a scheme he evidently hoped it might fill the place of Wanamaker's New Shakespeare. For the 1963 festival Henri organized the exhibition in the hall; there was another in the Friends' Meeting House and an amateur show in Stanley House, where a number of coloured people live. There were poetry readings by McGough and Pete Brown (of London), also an international folk music concert, folk dancing at Pier Head, and a debate with Mrs Bessie Braddock. It seems characteristic of Liverpool, and perhaps of England, that there should have been no contact between Gorman and Keir Murren of the Domestic Mission, though both were based on Liverpool 8, and that although I was in Liverpool at the time of this festival, and seeing a number of people in the art world, I never heard about it. The establishment, it is not unfair to say, did not approve of the Hope Hall.

My own attempts to gauge Liverpool's natural tastes and needs and its degree of familiarity with art began with the questionnaires already referred to in connection with the Walker Gallery's pictures. As the detailed analysis of the results in Appendix A will make plain, they were worded so as to discover the recipient's awareness of art not only in the gallery but as a human activity, a possible environment at home and in public places, a means of embellishing the city; and then to establish by means of a series of twenty postcard reproductions how he reacted to different styles of painting and sculpture of our own day, ranging from conservative to 'advanced'. The original aim was to have these questions put verbally to samples in different quarters of Liverpool, but in the event the vast majority of interviewees filled in their own forms, and almost half of them came from a single school. The

[1] According to James Stonehouse's History of the Streets of Liverpool in James Boardman: *Liverpool Table Talk a Hundred Years Ago*. Liverpool 1882, p. 149. He says that Samuel Warren reported them in *Blackwood's Magazine*. The hall, then a dissenting chapel, subsequently became the church of St John the Evangelist.

final composition of the 368 replies – 84 from visitors to the Walker Art Gallery, 172 from children and 27 from staff at Gateacre Comprehensive School, 31 from employees at Littlewoods Spinney House offices and 54 from interviewees – was certainly anything but scientific. None the less I did find this a useful and suggestive way of communicating with a large variety of people – it is remarkable what an impression of personality a filled-in questionnaire can in fact give, and how much it says that is anyway not statistically analysable – and enough of the evidence which it provided seemed to tally with other impressions for its main pointers to be significant. In this odd mixture the conservatism of the children, taking similar directions to that of the non-Art Gallery adults but going rather further, offset the more 'aesthetic' tendencies of the art gallery visitors; both, for instance, agreed in preferring Peter Scott to all the other postcards, whereas the gallery visitors put him near the bottom. I would disregard the children however when it comes to questions not of taste but of knowledge; asked to identify a monument or name a Liverpool artist they clearly consulted one another as they did not where personal preferences were involved.

The first thing that struck me about the answers was the relatively high degree of what might be called accessibility and the small evidence of any total alienation from art. Roughly two-thirds of those questioned were in personal contact with some kind of artist (amateur or professional in the proportion of nearly three to one); about 40 per cent of all adults, or 25 per cent if you exclude the gallery visitors as unrepresentative on this point, indulged in some kind of visual art themselves; less than a fifth disliked the idea of one of their children going to art school. This was evidence more of open-mindedness than of any very active interest. Not more than one adult in six took part in any art group or art class, and although the vast majority had seen art programmes on the television – largely *Monitor*, but above all the programmes on Michelangelo – it was evidently in many cases as passive consumers, since only one in three of the total admitted to looking out for them. As for the proportion who confessed to having no pictures in their houses it was strikingly high for this visually-conscious age. Roughly a third of those who answered (and the same proportion of the non-gallery adults) said that they had none. The percentage among the children was higher, but that may be because some of them saw the question as referring only to their own personal possessions.

The local artists are largely unknown. Of my 368 informants thirty had heard of Arthur Dooley, no doubt because of his personality and his appearances on television rather than on account of his actual sculpture. Twenty-four named Stubbs and nineteen Arthur Ballard, the present Academy president, but all except eight of the former and six of the latter were form-mates at Gateacre School who were clearly helping one another. Adrian Henri got four mentions – this being before he too was the subject of a television programme – and, among others, Herdman two and Huggins one; but artists like Gibson and Windus from Liverpool's past and Horsfield, Jardine, Hart and Tyson Smith from the present all went unmentioned. Roughly two-thirds of the 368 and three-quarters of the non-gallery adults were unable to name anybody – an astonishingly high proportion for a city that used to pride itself on its achievements in the arts. Nor do the citizens notice at all clearly the statuary that is around them out of doors. Of the adult total roughly a quarter had no idea what was in front of St George's Hall; one half ignored the relief and figures above the main Mersey Tunnel entrance (which nearly 22,000 cars pass under daily); an eighth did not even know exactly what was above the entrance to Lewis's, while only one in ten was at all conscious of the reliefs below. Outside St George's Hall two in five knew the lions (though with some uncertainty as to their number); one in five knew the war memorial, one could identify Victoria and Albert, and another one had a vague notion of equestrian figures ('prancing horses with staid horsemen', as one informant descriptively called them). Very few mentioned the retiring Disraeli or the gallant General Earle.

Through these answers a picture builds up of a community which accepts the idea of art as something desirable, but largely shuts its eyes to its actual manifestations. This is so to some extent even with the Walker Art Gallery, though there seemed to be less indifference here than is often alleged. Very few indeed – only three adults out of 196 – condemned the gallery as a waste of money; the answers from the gallery visitors were naturally more enthusiastic, but of the remaining adults only about a quarter expressed indifference, as against 45 per cent who wanted the collection to be added to and a fifth who felt pride in it. Admittedly about a tenth of these adults (and, more surprisingly, a quarter of the Gateacre schoolchildren) had never yet set foot inside the gallery, but nearly 44 per cent had visited it within the previous two years, which is more than might have been expected. My invitation to 'name a picture you liked' however brought evidence of certain blindness, not so much because of the actual choices expressed – though the apparent absence of interest in the Roscoe collection and, to a great extent, in the Rembrandt and Rubens and other recently-acquired masters is disconcerting – as in the frequent failure to make any choice at all. Less than half those questioned were able to name a picture; some of them, thanks perhaps to the unclear wording of the question – it ought to have specified 'a picture you liked *there*' – named works which are not in the collection – and often I got the impression that the respondent was not expressing a preference so much as scratching his head for the name of any picture in the world he could remember. Much the same blankness occurred with the respondents who said that they did have pictures in their home; a substantial minority were unable to identify them in any way.

And yet these same informants seemed to show an overwhelming appetite for more art in their lives. Was this just the way the questions were worded? I don't think so, as I felt exactly this odd combination of tolerance, apparent blindness yet longing for beauty when trying the questionnaire on a group of mainly working class hospital patients (whom I have excluded from the results as the questions were subsequently slightly altered). There were two groups of questions widely separated: first 'what do you feel about the idea of seeing paintings, sculpture and so on at your place of work?', then the same *inside* public buildings, then the same outside such buildings and in open spaces. Here four-fifths of all adults said they liked it at their place of work, over 96 per cent inside public buildings and four-fifths out of doors (the children's trend throughout was similar, though the resistance was higher, especially among the lower forms). The second group asked if it was 'a good thing that the Council should spend money on works of art for (a) improving the look of the city? (b) the city collection in the Walker Gallery?', then went on to ask if the informant would be willing to see an extra halfpenny rate – a purely hypothetical figure, equivalent to over £50,000 a year – devoted to these purposes. It attempted to eliminate non-ratepayers from the answers and to make certain that any ratepayer knew what such expenditure would mean to his own annual rates. The result here was naturally to damp first enthusiasms, but less than I would have expected. Again, four-fifths of the adults said 'yes' to (a) and to (b); three-quarters in each case said 'yes' to the extra halfpenny rate. Eliminating the non-ratepayers made no change to the proportion willing to accept extra rate (a), and actually sent that for (b) (extra expenditure on purchases for the gallery) up once more to four-fifths. Only between 10 and 15 per cent of these fell off when they actually realized what they themselves would have to pay. About two-thirds of the eighty ratepayers approved the (conjectural) extra charges.

It is quite a striking succession of sweeping votes for a more active public art policy, though it is anybody's guess how far they represent Liverpool opinion as a whole. No doubt it would be rash to assume that four-fifths of the local electorate want these things. All the same I am convinced that the opinions being voiced were by no means those of a special stratum of art-lovers but would be widely repeated; and that the potential support for such a policy could be stronger than even the keenest advocates of the arts in

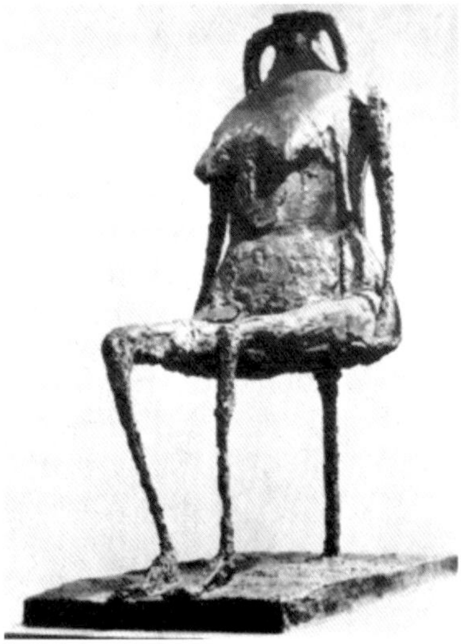

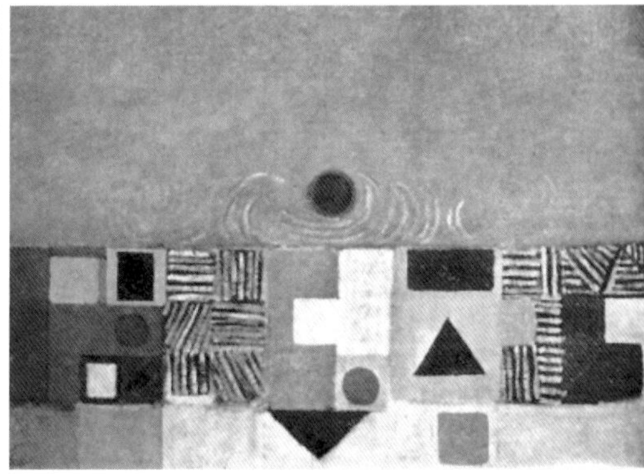

91 & 92 Germaine Richier's frightening figure, *Water* (black and white postcard), was predictably disliked, as was Victor Pasmore's *Square Motif* (coloured postcard). Both from the Tate Gallery

Liverpool at present think. But exactly what sort of art is it that they have in mind? The object of getting people's reactions to the twenty postcards presented at the end of the questionnaire was to see not merely what art was most congenial to them but where they drew the line between the modern art they could tolerate and that which they found jarred on them. These pictures fell into five main groups: the traditional, print-dealers' type represented by Peter Scott, Laura Knight, Doris Zinkeisen and Munnings; the modern figurative painting of Derain, Kokoschka (whose picture I expected to provide the highest common factor of Liverpool taste), Vlaminck and Augustus John; the more 'extreme' modernism of Picasso, Appel, Ben Nicholson and the abstract Pasmore; the impressionist sculpture of Renoir and Epstein; finally the modern sculpture of Henry Moore, Picasso again, Pevsner and Germaine Richier. There was also a Lowry (drawn, like the John, Vlaminck and Renoir, from the Walker Gallery's own collection) and, as an odd shot, one of the second batch of reliefs from outside St George's Hall. The point was not so much to conduct a democratic vote – which could be a deadly mistake in the arts – as to find out where we stood. If I was going in due course to make recommendations that flouted accepted tastes I wanted to know what I was doing.

This was where the opinions of the different sections – school children, gallery visitors and other adults – varied most widely; indeed, the element of unpredictability and variation between individual forms was far higher than for any of the earlier questions. It is impossible to tell, moreover, what weight

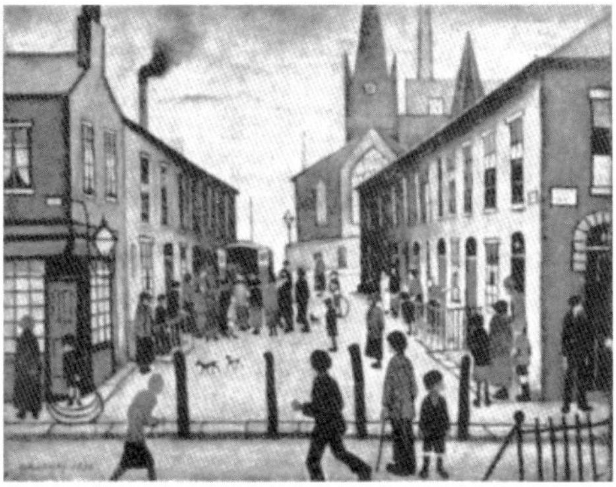

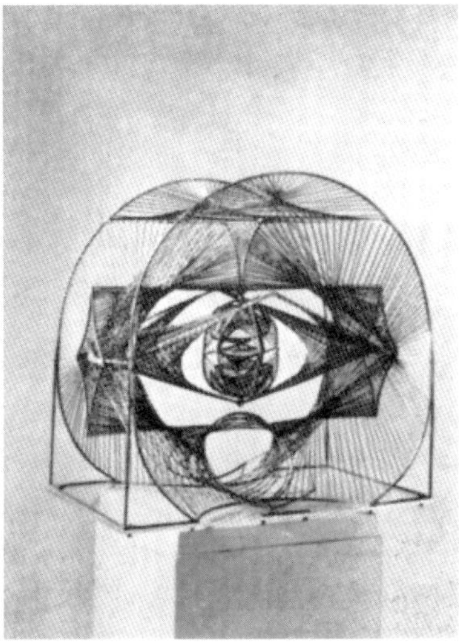

93 & 94 L. S. Lowry's *The Fever Van* was very popular and Antoine Pevsner's construction, was liked by a surprising number of people who had no use for other abstract work

of like or dislike attaches to any single opinion, or how much thought has gone into it, or how far certain condemnations, like the gallery visitors' verdict on Munnings and Laura Knight, are based on a sense of rivalry – a need to disapprove of certain names, or certain *kinds* of painting – rather than a pure aesthetic judgment. But that is after all how taste is made up, and certain conclusions did stand out. Thus I expected that the figures by Moore and (above all) Richier would be widely disliked since so many people seem to feel an empathetic pain when the human form is in any way maltreated by a sculptor (this, surely, was the real trouble with Riley's armless figure in Bold Street). Indeed they were, but it seemed most odd that on the one hand Pevsner's far more abstract sculpture should be viewed so very differently, while on the other Pasmore's beautiful and – I would have thought – wholly inoffensive abstract painting of 1950 was rejected, getting the largest score of 'dislikes' from the gallery visitors and having altogether 192 out of 338 voices definitely against it, a majority larger than that cast for any 'like' except the Peter Scott. Perhaps abstraction of a more or less 'machine' kind can be judged without the usual suspicion that the viewer is being hoaxed or insulted; it was remarkable that the Pevsner was liked by at least two people who otherwise only liked Munnings, Scott or Laura Knight; and it also has that element of intricate workmanship which matters to people who themselves work with their hands. That does not explain however why the Ben Nicholson and the Appel should be ranked by all sections well above the Pasmore, or why half the gallery-goers should dislike it.

The main likes are not surprising. Peter Scott came easily top, supported by 74 per cent of the children and 72 per cent of the non-gallery adults; the pictures which the gallery visitors and the rest could agree in liking were indeed the Kokoschka, but even more the Lowry, the Vlaminck (which showed a boat, a popular subject in a port), and the Augustus John. The significant point here was perhaps the general popularity of the Lowry, which came equal top (with the Picasso girl) in the gallery list, and fourth for the other adults and the children; this is partly no doubt because it is a thoroughly Lancashire picture, partly because it mixes the childish and the adult, partly because it is a popular picture in the gallery's own collection; familiarity is certainly an important factor in determining taste. It was also far the least disliked of all the cards, scoring thirty-seven dislikes only as against forty-six for the next-comer, the Vlaminck. The highest degree of indifference ('don't care') was shown – quite rightly, in my view – for Dressler's tame relief from St George's Hall, though the *fauve* Derain also scored highly (except with the children, a lot of whom disliked it), while the Ben Nicholson got roughly a third of 'don't care's from all sections. A minor oddity was the liking of many gallery visitors for Doris Zinkeisen's piece of impressionist pastiche, which comes out a particularly bilious green in the postcard. I can't help suspecting that this was a perverse tribute to Manet or to the general prestige of impressionism rather than to the picture itself.

After looking through all these it does seem that it is those who have had least education who are quickest to dislike works of art. Three of the Gateacre children, for instance, registered fifty-eight dislikes between them (out of sixty possible expressions of opinion); another, making up his own form as there were not enough to go round, put the 'dislike' column first in red ink (he had nine dislikes to six likes); while a young insurance employee who had left school at sixteen disliked all but three of the cards. The gallery visitors were certainly more tolerant; there was no card that more than half of them disliked, whereas for the children there were four (Richier, the Picasso sculpture, Pasmore and Henry Moore) and for the non-gallery adults five (the same plus Appel). The gallery-goers expressed slightly more likes per head than the rest and only four dislikes, as opposed to 6.17 dislikes per head for the other adults and 6.22 for the school children. The average ratio of dislikes to likes in each case suggests that for every eight cards they disliked the gallery visitors liked fourteen, but the other two groups only nine. Of course this is once again largely a matter of familiarity; when people actively dislike a work of art it is usually not because they judge it a bad one but because they find it strange. At the same time I suspect that there may be a broader element of resentment about it: that those who feel educationally handicapped in any way are hostile to what they cannot understand, where others would either try to puzzle it out or feel secure enough to suspend judgment. If this is true it could be an important consideration in planning the city's future art policy, though it should be noted that there is no such distinction where the general urge for more art is concerned, which seems to seize all alike.

I quoted the Bold Street fiasco at some length earlier because it so vividly illustrates the danger of meeting this urge in the wrong way. Despite the enormous increase in interest in art matters, despite the visual stimulus given by television and colour photography, there is still a great gulf between modern art and the public which is ignored only at the cost of pain to all concerned. Such art is not easily accepted; it contains, for many people, causes of offence which can only be cancelled out by the power of conviction of the work itself and of the manner in which it is presented to them – two things that were perhaps lacking in the Bold Street case. But that is only one of the hazards. It is all too easy to compromise on excessively tepid works, like the bulk of the existing Liverpool monumental statuary, which are just as likely to discredit public art by boring people until they no longer look at, or even notice them; indeed the difference between my informants' great desire for art inside public places and the somewhat reduced enthusiasm (often among the more knowledgeable of them) for open-air works is, I suspect, mainly due to the dismal example set so far. It is really a very difficult dilemma, for even the most intelligent (and often the most socially-minded) of modern artists tend to skate over these problems – which are not normally talked about except by hostile critics – while the public authorities responsible feel uncertain of their standards and ignorant of the precedents that might help them. Much could be done in Liverpool, perhaps, if the city had a policy for the visual arts which people could identify with the gallery. Many of the resentments and resistances we have been discussing might be overcome by local pride.

So far however the signs of any real identification of art with the city or with the people's lives there have not been encouraging. There is obviously no particular sense of association with the Liverpool artists, and although there is an active amateur art movement there it bears no distinctive local flavour; too much of it is a rehash of the very lowest level of accepted themes and styles, like many of the prints in Liverpool's under-pictured homes. Vaguely the citizens look to art as a benefit which they would like to have, but this may only mean that they are expecting too much of it. Despite the admirable intentions of the South Liverpool Festival the attempt there to knit the visual arts more closely into people's daily lives has still not done much to stimulate an indigenous visual tradition. It may well be that both things will have to go together: that a genuine basis of acceptance – and tolerance – for a more go-ahead official policy will only be created when Liverpool begins to feel that she can assert herself visually as she has already asserted herself in sound and in sport. This of course does not mean that a lot of Merseyside Lowrys have to be produced and put to work decorating the city, but that the sense of individual self-expression and of collective self-expression might turn out to be linked. It is not enough just to develop in the wake of London. If Liverpool really wants more public art she will have to strike out on her own.

6 : EDUCATING THE EYE

'The great need of the present day, from the point of view of the production of Fine Art, is the Education of the Amateur, the purchaser.'[1] Thus Conway, writing in 1901, some years after his Liverpool experience. But that is only one aspect of the problem. If we leave aside the subtle but surely very strong influence of a sense of educational deprivation there are still a number of different ways in which art education of one kind of another can affect the visual scene. There is not only the education of the amateur, who nowadays has to be seen as ratepayer, industrial administrator and local politician as well as mere private purchaser of Kandinskys and Tretchikoffs, and is catered for under the discouraging-sounding heading of Art Appreciation. There is also the more professional and academic field of Art History, which produces the experts to educate others: a subject which has enormously expanded since 1945. There is practical instruction in art, where the handling of visual ideas and the materials to express them with is taught to three main groups: children, future professionals (chiefly teachers and designers for industry) and the amateurs for whom art is anything from a time-filling hobby to a frustrated passion. Finally there is the teaching or preaching of design as an application of visual judgment and three-dimensional common sense to everything that we build, make or buy.

In an increasingly specialized world these different aspects of art teaching are rarely seen as parts of a single process. Our society has its accepted ideas about each kind – art appreciation, art history, child art, art schools, painting as a pastime and the preaching of good design – but everywhere they seem to be governed by different committees and pursued along individual channels; whether conservative or 'progressive' they are, as a rule, not brought into relation with one another. Yet you need only look at a city like Liverpool to see how they all bear on the situation which we have been discussing in the last two chapters. The enjoyment of the real treasures of the Walker Art Gallery (as opposed to *The Death of Nelson* or the latest subject of controversy), a keener interest in the work of local living artists, the understanding of the city's own architecture and the considered judgment of any works of public art: it all depends on some kind of 'art appreciation'. Simi-

[1] *The Domain of Art*. p. 24.

larly evolution of anything like a distinctive Liverpool style in art depends not only on the practical teaching given in schools and art schools but on the facilities offered to the talented individual to express himself, whether or not he is making art his job. And the whole visual level of life in the city depends on the half-instinctive adoption of decent design standards in what the people of the place buy in the shops, have around at home or in public places, and, above all, actually make. All four types of teaching are ultimately concerned with the same thing: with the sense of arrangement, balance and colour, with the eye and with visual curiosity. They act on one another; any progress made in the one must stimulate the rest.

At the time when Conway wrote this close interconnection was still taken for granted, so that the Walker Gallery, the University with its Roscoe professorship, the Workers' Educational Association – even the institution of drawing as a compulsory subject in schools – were parts of a general educational movement to which the Arts and Crafts exhibitions also belonged. Since then the whole concept of adult education has very much altered. It is no longer a matter of making up for the deficiencies of a man's formal education, which in those days ended at thirteen or even at ten, so much as helping to occupy his increased leisure. The old notion of works of art as a means of improving the ignorant mechanic's mind, based as it was on an association of goodness with beauty which few would make so confidently today, has given way to a less condescending but also a much less ambitious approach. In Liverpool at least the WEA has become virtually a part of the university's extra-mural department; both are concerned to teach their now much better-educated adult pupils what happens to interest them rather than what some higher policy considers they ought to learn. Art, in our leisure-haunted age, is certainly part of this. The politics, economics and current affairs that preoccupied classes in the 1930s have largely lost their audience; art and archaeology, sociology and psychology, even subjects like travel and jazz and 'preparation for retirement' have moved into the centre of the programme. This of course reflects the generally increased interest in art throughout the country. In England, Wales and Scotland there were thirty-nine extra-mural courses in the visual arts in 1945/6 and 518 in 1961/2; in the Liverpool extra-mural area the comparable figures were one (for 1946/7) and twenty-nine. Out of the thirty-nine WEA classes held in Liverpool itself in 1965/6 five dealt with the visual arts, and there were further classes in Birkenhead, Wallasey and other parts of the agglomeration.

The decline of the missionary spirit means that much of this apparently increased interest is now a more or less idle one. The classes are held in the university buildings or the Royal Institution or in middle-class suburbs; the Friday art-appreciation classes at the Institution are attended above all by housewives; only about one in twenty of the WEA students are manual workers; over four-fifths of the university extension students left school after fifteen. The Deputy Director of the gallery, who takes the chief Liverpool WEA class on the history of art, told me that there were not more than half-a-dozen males in that class. His attempt to stimulate greater keenness by describing something of the sheer detective work, both scientific and critical, involved in the history of art was discouraged by a Ministry inspector who thought that he should concentrate on 'appreciation'. And this purely passive appreciation seems to be the main objective of very nearly all the courses organized. Only now and again is there an attempt to relate the study of art to any constructive aim; thus the extra-mural department's staff tutor in art, whose conferences on modern church architecture have already been referred to, has also conducted courses on this subject in Preston and West Kirby, while in the 1963/4 session there was a class at Crosby on 'Merseyside Architecture: Old and New' taken by F. M. Jones of the School of Architecture: a subject vitally connected with the replanning of the city. Generally the system is geared to the production of consumers for whom art is a leisure-time luxury, a kind of holiday. The association of art with summer travel, already evident enough from the paintings in amateur art shows, is rammed home by the successful art tours which the extra-mural department has organized. These have taken bodies of mainly professional people and teachers to visit the Spanish or Italian museums for a fortnight at between £45 and £65 a head; in 1965 the department organized a Hellenic cruise, costing about three times as much.

For seven years between 1954 and 1960 the Walker Art Gallery and the extra-mural department together organized lectures of an altogether higher standard. They were held in the gallery's lecture theatre, whose 180 seats they usually filled; at those on twentieth century art indeed the audience was too big, so that they had to move to the university. For the first five years they consisted of a course in the history of art from the Renaissance to the present day, and they were lifted out of the normal sphere of adult education both by the setting and by the inclusion of such lecturers as Professor E. F. Jacob and Sir Kenneth Clark. There was also during this period one rather exceptional university extension course, where Victor Pasmore, Keith Vaughan, the late Stanley Spencer, Alan Davie, Joseph Herman, Robert Clatworthy and Arthur Ballard spoke on contemporary art; one or two members of the then audiences told me that they regretted the gallery's decision to break off the association. A modified form of this scheme was restored in 1964, with a series of lectures chiefly by outside authorities on the gallery's own pictures. In the interim the gallery had been turning its attention to the Liverpool schoolchildren, who since 1957 have had their own Schools Officer giving conducted lectures to some 5,000 or 6,000 of them every year. Ben Shaw the late sub-committee chairman would have liked there to be a special children's room, but the problem so far has rather been to attract the sixth-formers. A coffee and sandwich party was held for them in conjunction with the show of Miss Sonia Henje's collection of modern pictures (organized by the Arts Council and also seen at the Tate Gallery) in the autumn of 1962, and this was very successful. Otherwise the keenest visitors have been the primary schools.

As a means of exciting enthusiasm for art, lectures have lost much of their old importance, despite the new attractions of the coloured transparency – a dangerous instrument which can come to seem more attractive than the picture itself. Parties can bring people to a gallery and draw attention to an exhibition, but they make serious viewing of the works almost impossible and it is open to doubt whether they really further the interests of art by turning it into a social event. It is rather television and to a lesser extent the coloured magazines that give most people their impetus and their new ideas about the visual arts today, and this is true even of many artists (it was suggested to me that some embryo art historian ought to establish how much of current iconography is traceable to the *Sunday Times* colour supplement). Here the programmes organized for schools by Granada Television in Manchester set an admirably high standard,[1] but despite their Lancashire origin they are designed for broadcasting throughout the country, and neither they nor John Berger's Granada series *Drawn from Life* of autumn 1961, with its attempt to relate people's occupations and preoccupations to the work of great artists, had any special bearing on the problems of Merseyside. This inevitable squeezing out of purely local concerns, even from regional television, might be expected to have two effects on art education in Liverpool: to lead those responsible to make closer contact with the programme organizers on the one hand, and at the same time to make them use the traditional

[1] The series, each of ten weekly programmes designed for the 15–18 age group, have been:
- Autumn 1961. *Design.* (Reyner Banham, Misha Black, Sir Hugh Casson, Nikolaus Pevsner, Paul Reilly, etc.)
- Spring 1962. *Context.* Art in Life since Time Began. (Banham, M. I. Finley, Jacquetta Hawkes, George Lehmann, Bryan Robertson, Sir John Summerson, etc.)
- Autumn 1962. *Art in the Making.* (Robertson interviewing Ralph Brown, Denys Lasdun, Colin MacInnes, Bernard Meadows, Keith Vaughan, Vicky, etc.)
- Spring 1963. *Word and Image.* (Ten talks by the Rev Moelwyn Merchant.)

In 1963 three schools in Liverpool and three in other parts of the agglomeration were known to be watching.

media for matters of local importance rather than for the general encouragement of art. But this does not seem to have happened, and for better or worse the apparatus that exists is used to teach appreciation of almost anything except Liverpool's own assets, background and possibilities.

The principal art school, the Regional College of Art in Hope Street, is administered by the city and still lives next door to the Liverpool Institute School from which it separated in 1905. It has however become far more closely geared into the national art educational pattern, and its local character is reflected less in the direction of its teaching than in the fact that many of the local artists have jobs there. It is not merely, as its name implies, a school for the whole region, including Preston, Blackpool and North Wales; since the 1960 report of the National Advisory Council on Art Education under Sir William Coldstream it has become one of those art schools of quasi-university status that train for the new Diploma in Art and Design, with the result that standards in those departments whose work I have seen have risen rapidly even as the present book was being written.[1] Under this scheme, which came into operation in 1963 with the admission of the first Dip AD students, the composition of the student body was bound to change, for not only have the higher general educational qualifications demanded (five 'O' levels, including at least three in academic subjects) meant that art students from all over the country now compete for places, but the more general education provided makes this a possible university substitute for some who would not otherwise have become art specialists. The so called pre-Diploma course, or first year basic course for all students, can still be planned on the College's own lines, but is now virtually in the position of a lesser art school whose students must pass the new requirements if they are to continue; it is at present physically separated from the College proper. The Teacher Training Department, which trains for the Art Teachers' Diploma and is the main source of art staff for Liverpool's primary and secondary schools, is also outside the Coldstream recommendations; it is run in conjunction with the university Institute of Education. Otherwise where art is concerned – that is Fine Art (including sculpture since 1965), Graphic Design and Textiles and Fashion, but not Three-Dimensional Design, for which the College has not yet been recognized by the National Advisory Council – the College is the regional instrument of a national system.

There is thus nothing very distinctively Liverpool about the College, though both John Moores and Leslie Blond have helped it by giving scholar-

[1] That is to say in the Fine Art (including sculpture) and Graphic Design Schools. The school of Textiles and Fashion provided nearly all the prizewinning entries in a competition held by the Cotton Board in October 1965, when all but two of the art schools training for the new diploma in this subject competed.

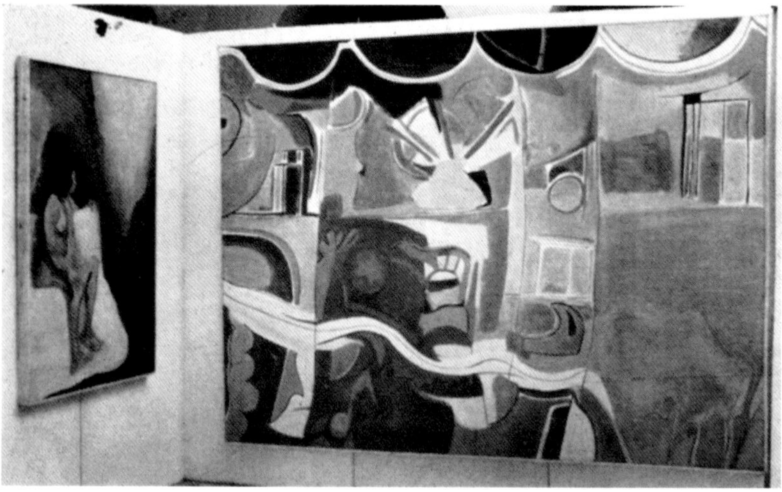

95 & 96 The Regional College of Art. A show of the

ships, nor has it any other specially remarkable characteristic on the art side; it is, from the national point of view, simply the best art school in a hitherto somewhat uninspired area, whose most famous postwar product, John Lennon of the Beatles, is not exactly an artist and was far from appreciated in his student days. Yet it has one unique asset in its printing school, which since 1960 has occupied a large and well-equipped new building adjoining the main part of the College. Liverpool is among the main centres of the printing industry in the country, and vocational training as a whole is a field which the National Advisory Council left 'for local initiative and organization by schools and colleges in consultation with industry and commerce.'[1] The Department of Printing accordingly continues to be guided by a special Printing and Allied Trades Advisory Committee and runs not only independently of the new Dip AD system but to a great extent independently of the rest of the college; except in the basement there is not even a communicating door between the two buildings. No doubt there are advantages in the freedom from interruption and distraction which this means for the 700 or so part-time printing students, who outnumber the full-timers next door by about two to one. All the same, one need only look at the lack of new graphic and typographic ideas in Liverpool printing – on poster hoardings, in locally-designed brochures, and in the Liverpool papers, despite all their purely technical pioneering – or at the graphic design work done in the College to feel that an opportunity is being missed. Far more than the Royal College of Art in London, whose designers have few chances to make personal contact with printers or study their machines, Liverpool has the equipment

[1] Ministry of Education: *Vocational Courses in Colleges and Schools of Art*. Second Report of the National Advisory Council on Art Education. HMSO 1962, paragraph 2.

Fine Art Department's work in spring 1965

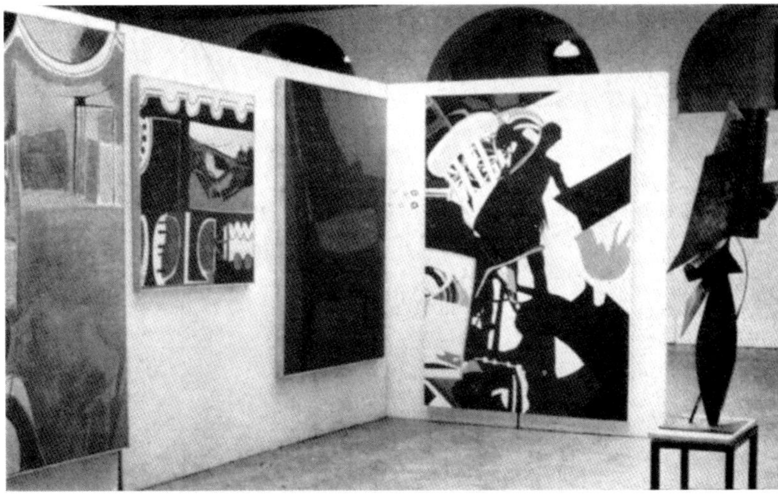

and the technical skill to become the country's main source of visual ideas in printing and book production. Yet both Ballard and MacKarell, of the livelier painters among the College staff, seemed to see it as entirely natural that they should never have done any work with the splendid apparatus next door, while conversely it was depressing to find one of the new colour offset machines in the printing department being used to produce pictures of the crudest calendar-illustration sort.

The part of the College which does seem to be generating new ideas is the Teacher Training department, which is interested less in the Bauhaus-like exercises in use of materials practised in the pre-Diploma course than in finding fresh ways of relating visual expression to interests and experience within a child's range. Some of the ideas tried out here or in schools co-operating with the department have been the plotting of movements (of the ball in football or of customers to and from a Wigan pub) as the basis for a picture; the use of plans, real or imaginary, for the same purpose; variations on everyday objects – just what, for instance, can be done with a chair –; the use of subjects like transport which command a wide interest and technical knowledge that can be expressed in drawing; the use of engineers' drawings as models; the making of some sort of construction by the pupil, which he then makes a picture of; development of micro-sections of plants, etc; imaginative variations of relative size, such as a flowerbed seen by a three-inch dwarf; or the putting of verbal and numerical structures (like a crossword puzzle or a list of engine numbers) into pictorial form. What the College is in effect doing here in a small way is to revive the Renaissance spirit of curiosity, of using visual creation as a means of understanding how our environment works, but to extend it both by calling on the visual discoveries of modern art

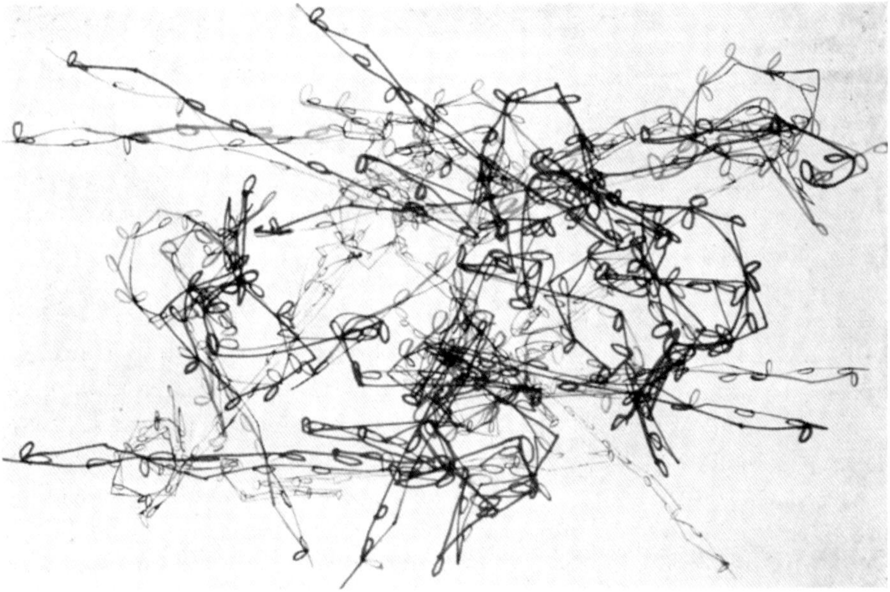

Children's work under the auspices of the teacher training department.
Above: *Gavotte*. Below: *Juke Box*

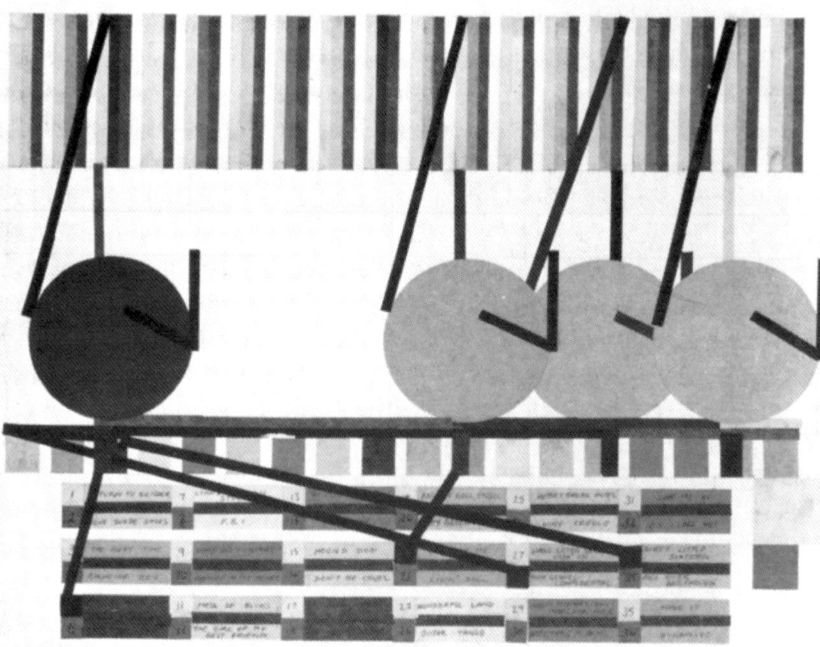

and by considering processes, movements and other relationships as well as immediately visible reality. It is an interesting direction in which to be experimenting, and it could easily prove a fruitful one in a wider sphere than that of art education. For there are the germs here of an approach to art which would be aligned with, and not merely to one side of, the modern technological world.

The Coldstream recommendations left the lesser art schools – which on Merseyside means those at Birkenhead, Wallasey and Bootle – to conduct vocational training according to the needs of local industry, to run preparatory courses for those hoping to go to a diploma course elsewhere, and to teach art under their own arrangements to part-time students. There was also a suggestion that they should try to become 'focal points for all those in their neighbourhood who are interested in the visual arts and that they should try to increase public interest in these arts by such means as lectures, exhibitions, etc.'[1], something that for the College would mean wasteful competition with the gallery and the Bluecoat Society but could well be of relevance for the lesser art schools. Birkenhead indeed would like to develop along these lines, if only it had more space. So far as the fine arts are concerned these have become overwhelmingly (and in the case of Bootle exclusively) schools for the part-timer, which in effect means the amateur; Birkenhead's prospectus for instance offers 'development of skill by those who enjoy art as a spare-time activity' and says that 'Beginners are specially welcome'. When I went to Bootle the school was living under rather makeshift conditions in a house formerly used as a salvage dump, pending removal to a proposed new College of Further Education; some of the painting and pottery students had been attending ever since 1945 and there had evidently been little turnover in the classes for some years. At Birkenhead the school is crammed into a solid brick building of the 1870s, with a forlorn looking area of terrace houses behind it; there are over 100 part-time painters of all ages, some retired and some just out of school. There are also part-time fine art students at the Regional College, but the Birkenhead Principal told me that there is an unsatisfied Liverpool demand for part-time painting and that there are many additional applicants whom he could take if he had the room, given the necessary permits from the Liverpool Corporation. These permits are a means of settling accounts between the different local authorities; in 1963 students over 21 were normally paying 37s 6d a year to come once a week, plus £1 for additional evenings; at Bootle they paid between 22s and 33s a year to come for three evenings a week.

[1] Ministry of Education: *First Report of the National Advisory Council on Art Education*; HMSO 1960, paragraph 60.

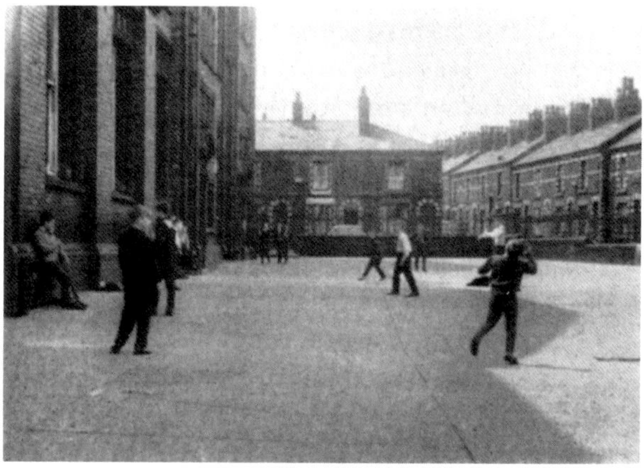

99 Boys at Breckfield Secondary Modern School, in old-fashioned buildings not far from Anfield football ground

100 An art class at Gateacre Comprehensive, one of the newer and larger Liverpool schools

There has also in Liverpool been an institution called the Art High School, with about 100 pupils. This was once a preparatory school for all departments of the College of Art, living under the same roof with it: one of a small number of such schools all over the country which were intended to fill the time between the school-leaving age of 14 and entry to art school proper. With the raising of the school-leaving age in 1947 its original *raison d'être* vanished; it moved to separate (supposedly temporary) premises in houses in Gambier Terrace that year and in 1960 broke off from the College altogether. Perhaps because of the name, perhaps because the headmaster was a trained artist, it tended to get boys and girls wanting to make art their main subject, and the head certainly wished art to be the backbone of the teaching. But the school no longer figured as prominently as it had among those gaining places at the College, and it became something of an unresolved oddity in Liverpool education: a niche for unorthodox pupils or for those who would like a straight academic education but were unable to get into a Grammar or a Secondary Modern School. It was closed in 1966 and the pupils were transferred to one of the comprehensive schools; the buildings reverted to the College of Art.

Besides these art schools I visited a number of secondary schools, some under Liverpool, some under Lancashire County Council, in order to get an idea of the native talent for art and the measures taken to bring it out. All of these were schools where I had been advised, from one direction or another, that the art department was of particular interest; thus although they varied very widely quâ schools (academically, socially and architecturally), they cannot

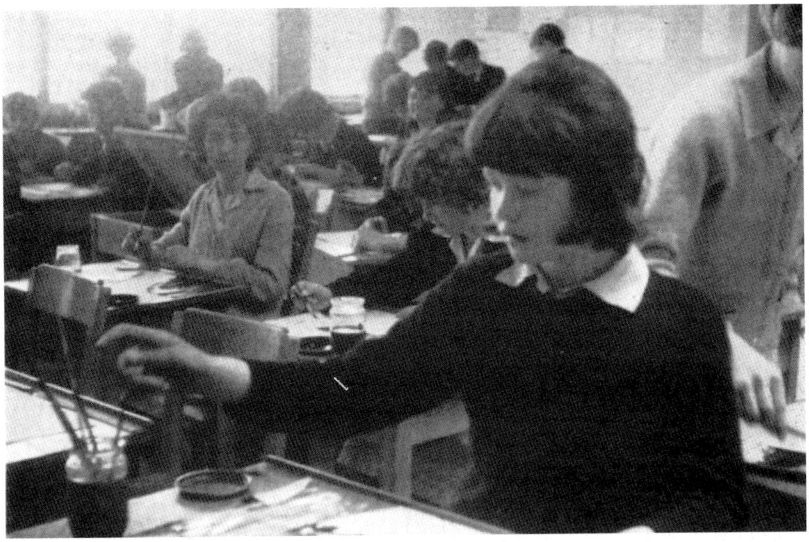

be taken as wholly representative of Merseyside art teaching. They were none the less extremely encouraging; indeed the real problem they raised was why the often quite original self-expressive energy found there was not found, in more developed form, in the art schools – a problem by no means unique to Liverpool. Where Liverpool differs is that this talent, contrary to the general conception of children's art – and in contrast with all the illustrations in Sir Herbert Read's well-known *Education through Art*, for instance – is not primarily pictorial but sculptural; it cannot have been sheer coincidence that all the most interesting work I saw was three-dimensional, whether in pottery, sculpture, wood and metal constructions or cut paper. The best drawings and paintings came from schools in poor areas – Breckfield Secondary Modern School in Everton and St Martin's SMS in Liverpool 8 – but they were also the most naive and conventional ones. In the former there were vivid pictures of daily life (including an episode at the dentist's and one at the police station) as well as bright geometrical designs and perspective exercises, (perspective being taught less as an aid to representation than because it interests the children for its own sake). At St Martin's, where there was at that time only one art teacher and the whole school did art because there was a shortage of staff for other subjects, the boys were sent out into the shabby streets and waste areas to pick up subjects (and objects too, which can be used as improvised stencils or stamps to print with or build into constructions and mosaics). The result was that their work reflected the Liverpool scene more closely and literally than any other I saw; it has figured largely in the South Liverpool Festival exhibitions at the nearby Domestic Mission.

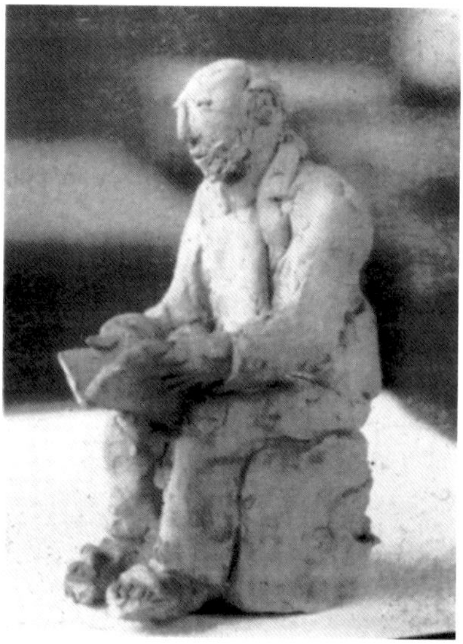

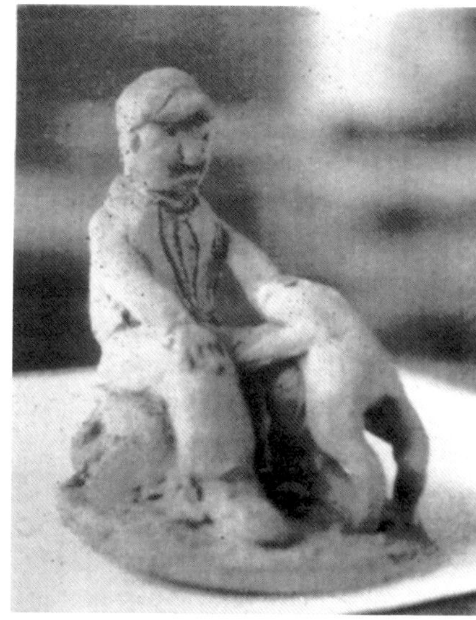

101 & **102** Pottery figures by boys at Breckfield SMS

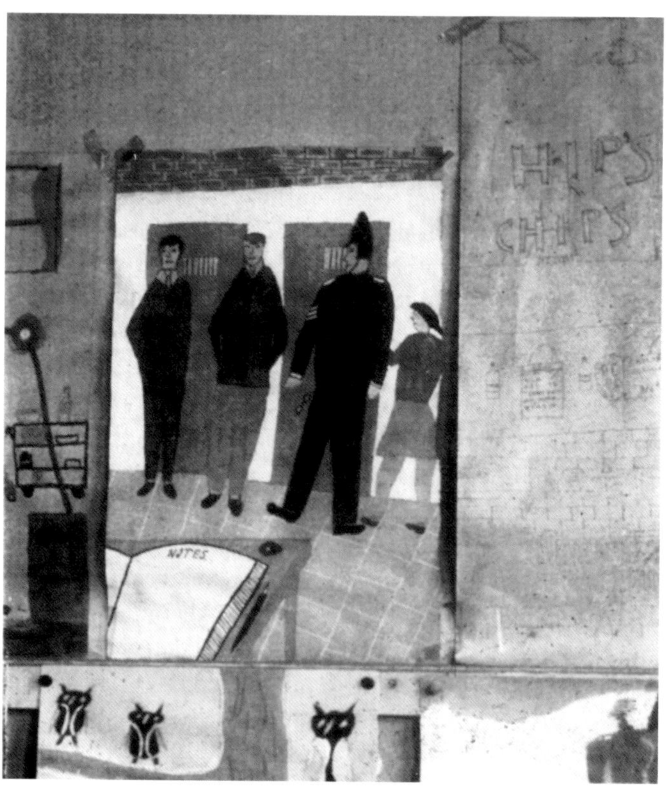

103 Drawings by boys at Breckfield SMS

BEFORE THE KICK-OFF

What a crowd,
Rattles buzzing like aggravated bees.
Policemen pulling kids out of the ground.
Flashes of light bursting out everywhere.
Children running onto the pitch for autographs.
The crowd swaying to and fro,
Like a piece of silk held into the wind.
The bright green pitch,
Clashing with the red and white of scarves and rosettes.
The men squabbling with each other about teams and players.
The Kop lets up a mighty roar,
Shouting the Liverpool chant,
As the teams come out.

Alan Jones. 2A

104 A poem from the *Breckfield Broadsheet*, Summer Term 1963

The methods of the Preliminary Course evolved by Itten and Moholy-Nagy at the Bauhaus in the 1920s are often reflected in these schools. Thus it is common to find experiments with materials of a more or less abstract kind, or prints made from embossed wall-papers, cigarette packets or whatever else comes to hand. At the Bluecoat School however – the boys' school that once occupied the present building of the Bluecoat Society but is now in a solid Edwardian scholastic edifice further out – there was a whole-hearted incursion into constructivism after the sixth form had been taken to see the Arts Council exhibition *Construction England* at the Walker Gallery in the spring of 1963. Within the (to my mind somewhat cramping) limitations of non-figurative art the work done here in scrap wood, bent metal, cane and string, and also in one or two instances in stone, was most impressive, and all the more noteworthy because the training is directed towards encouragement of a general visual awareness rather than particular proficiency in art. The other remarkable development was at Gateacre CS, one of the biggest (1,600 pupils) and newest schools, situated in one of the newer south-western suburbs and with a full-time art staff of six. Here one teacher in the metal-work department – nominally a craft teacher in the technical wing, and accordingly not included in the six – happened to be a Camberwell-trained

105-107
Constructions by
boys at Liverpool
Bluecoat School

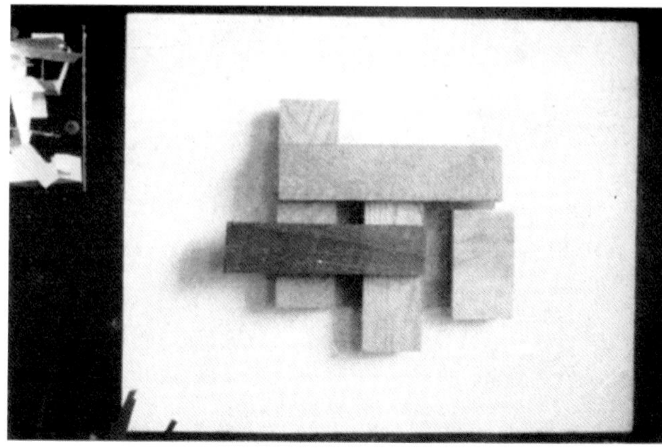

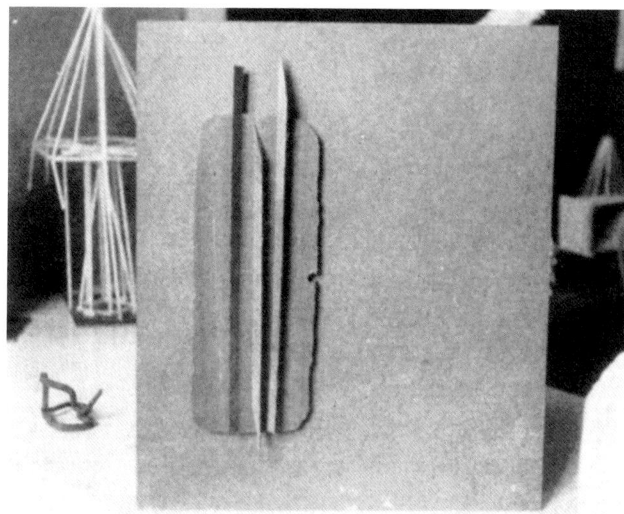

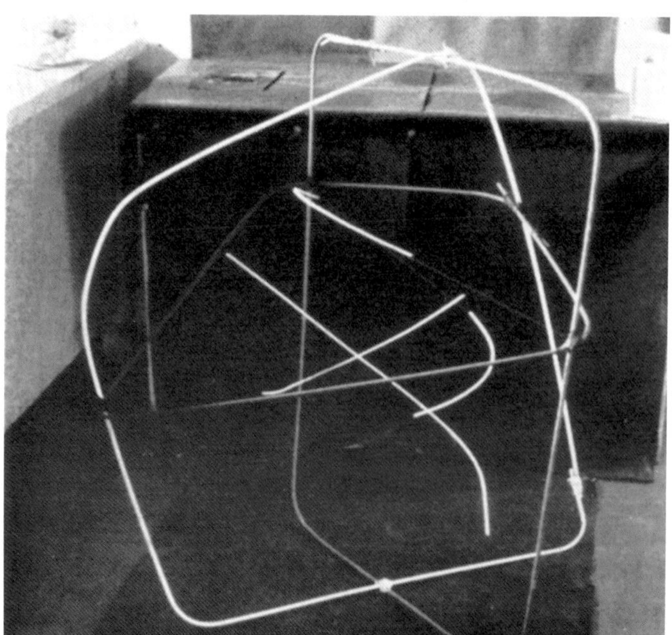

sculptor, who taught foundry and welding by getting the children to make metal constructions or figures out of scrap. These and related exercises have produced surprisingly expressive results; even examinations can be conducted on these lines, as is shown by the following paper which was given to one of the bottom forms:

Metal Constructions – Answer Question 1 and three others, four in all. Paper marked out of 40.

1 Name ten objects you can use in making a construction.
2 Draw, in line only, a construction it would be possible to make using a chair as a starting point.
3 Draw, in line only, a design using a H type TV aerial.
4 Draw, in line only, a construction you could make out of straws or wire. Base this on any objects you have seen on the way to school (the street lamps for example).
5 Draw in solid form (shade on one side only), a wooden model of this school as seen from the top.
6 Draw, in line only, as many different roof shapes and chimney stacks as you have seen.

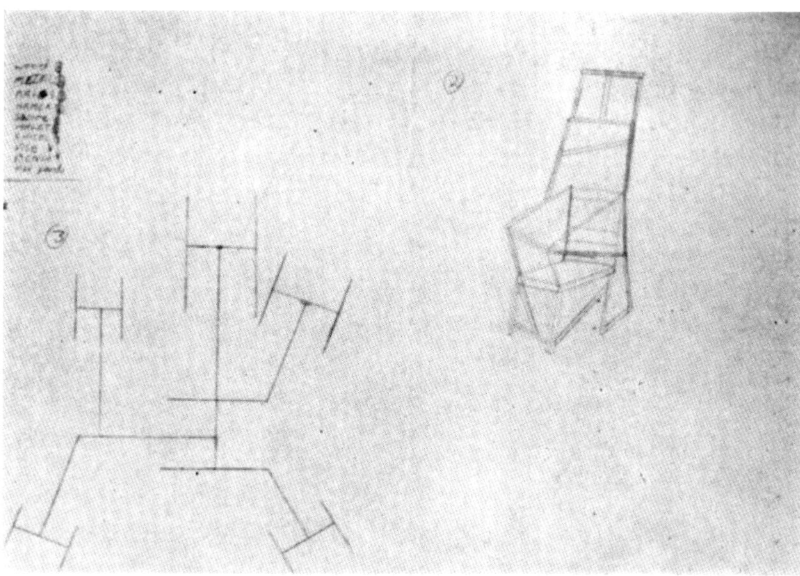

108 Gateacre CS. A page of answers to the questions above

Gateacre is one of several schools producing lively pottery figures and groups – Breckfield being another – and the former pottery teacher wrote a thesis for Manchester University on the apparent tendency for some of the

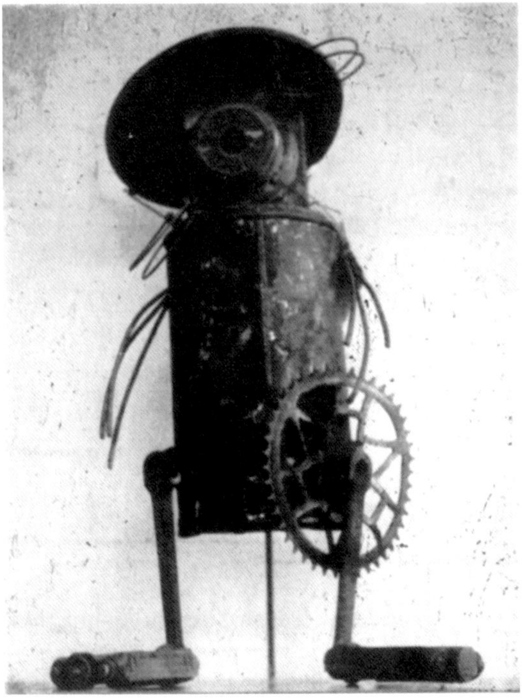

109 Scrap metal sculpture by three fourteen-year-old boys at Gateacre CS

110 & 111 Other sculptural work done in the metalwork class at Gateacre CS

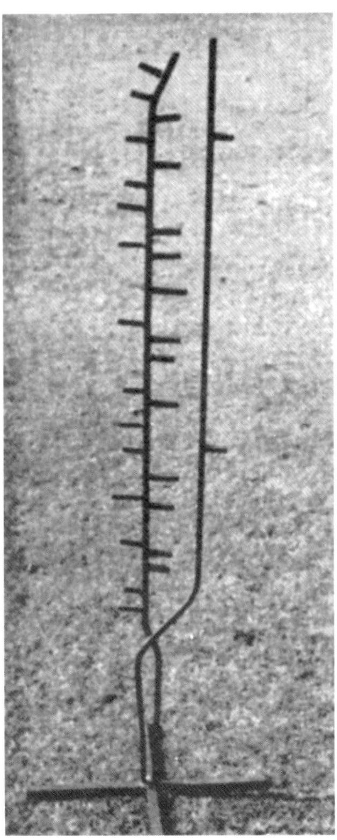

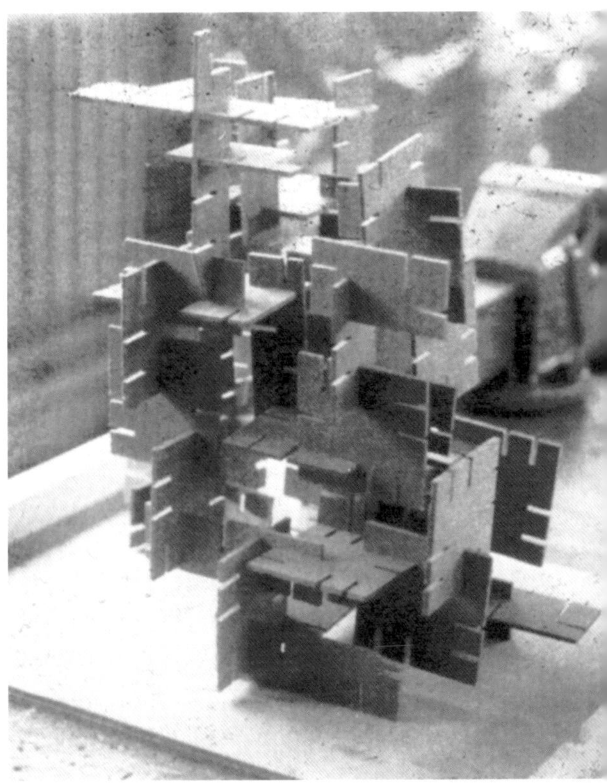

best work to come from the lower streams, a tendency also mentioned by other teachers, and one which conflicts with the new conditions for admission to the College.[1] At Stanley Park SMS, in an undistinguished building of 1938 by the cemetery in Anfield – it has subsequently been transformed into a girls' Comprehensive – I saw some entertaining mosaics made of lino and other more or less fortuitous (or *Merz*) materials; at Ruffwood CS (1,900 pupils), the Lancashire County Council school at Kirkby whose buildings were discussed earlier, there was fabric printing and a plan to do ordinary printing; at New Heys Girls' GS, another of the best and best-sited new school buildings in the area (designed by Herbert Thearle), the girls' paintings are framed and used to decorate staircases and corridors. I also saw a collective exhibition put on in the College entrance hall by Holly Lodge High

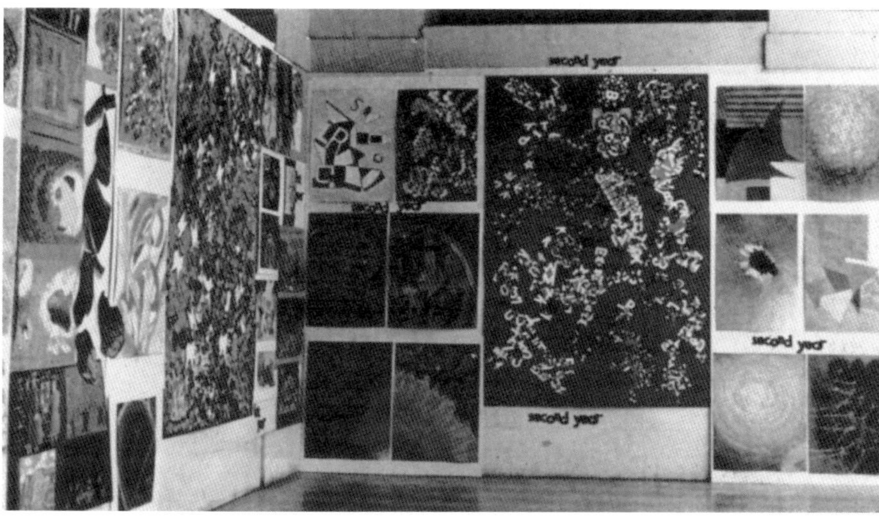

112 Part of an exhibition of work by girls at Holly Lodge Girls' Grammar School

School for Girls, which was interesting above all for the use of letters in some of the pictures, one of them a large collaboration by the bottom form. The best academic drawing I saw was one from Wade Deacon GS. Generally however the most striking work that I saw outside Gateacre and the Bluecoat was at Maghull GS (680 pupils), another of the Lancashire schools in the new

[1] Though it is sometimes forgotten that paragraph 5 of the first Coldstream Report specified that 'students of outstanding artistic promise' should be admitted to the diploma courses even without the required 'O' level qualifications.

northern suburbs, where every year the whole mixed school contributes to a big group exhibition on a single theme – a bullfight, a circus, the life of Lord Nelson – which demands a term's preparation and involves not only a wide variety of media but some costume study and historical and geographical research. The bullfight material included work by students who subsequently went to the College – a plaster head of a matador, a bull's head on bicycle handlebars – and a big tempera painting of a bullfight by three sixth-formers.

The struggle in the schools, it seems, is to get art recognized as something more than a suitable occupation for lower forms and a special subject among

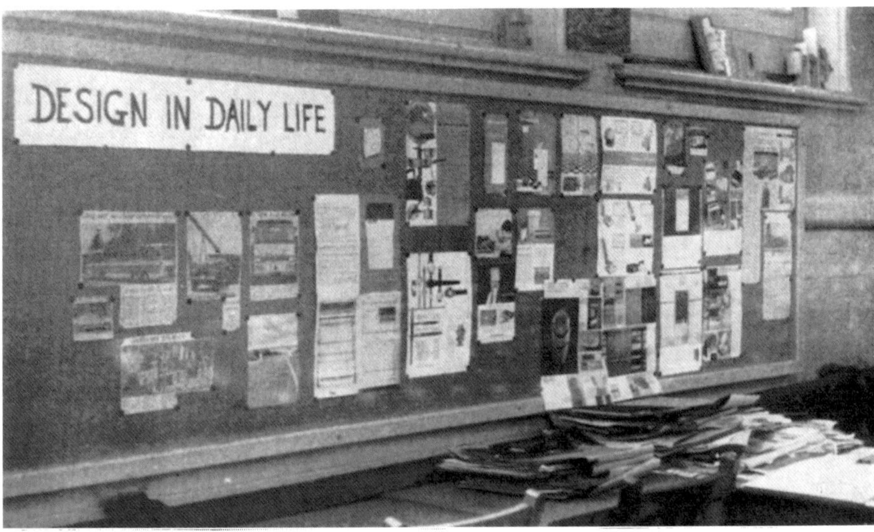

113 Breckfield SMS tries to teach awareness of design

'O' level candidates. It depends entirely on the headmaster (and on the degree of confidence existing between him and his art staff) whether sixth-formers are allowed to take art up again, as was happening in only about a quarter of the Liverpool selective schools at the time when I began my enquiries. The main question here is whether art is to be regarded as a matter of basic education, a field where any civilized man should feel at home, or to be treated as a speciality, even a sideline. So far the prevailing view in the Education Committee seems to have been the latter. This no doubt accounts for the iron curtain which has dropped down somewhere between the evident talent and interest visible in the schools and the rather uninspired amateurs and aimless lecture audiences mentioned earlier. Some schools try to avoid this by encouraging a few pupils to come back and work after they have left the school; thus Maghull has old pupils attending its senior art club and at

Ruffwood the headmaster hopes to act as a local community centre with evening activities for boys and girls who have left; similarly the Prescot Further Education Centre (run by Callendar Cables) in 1962 started an evening art class so that ex-secondary school boys could carry on work which they had been doing with a particular teacher. Both at Stanley Park and at St Martin's (360 pupils) however – two schools in poor areas – the art masters spoke of the difficulty of finding suitable jobs for their talented pupils and helping them to work further. Two from Stanley Park were then painting part-time at the Childwall College of Further Education; one was employed by Dollond and Aitchison the opticians, who were teaching him photography; one had a job in a library and was painting in his spare time. Two from St Martin's had gone to the Art High School; one clever potter was now making shoes; Robert Dooley (no relation to the sculptor) who got the first award at the South Liverpool Festival did a year at the Art High School, working in a butcher's shop at weekends, then became a manual labourer.

The teaching of the principles of good design, which is rare enough in the schools – I only saw evidence of it at Breckfield SMS and the Bluecoat School – seemed on the whole to be unheard of and unthought of at the technical colleges and Colleges of Further Education to which other pupils go on. 'No aspect of aesthetic design is dealt with', 'No element of art or design training', 'Have no call to introduce design training in any way'; these were typical phrases in reply to an enquiry to various Merseyside Further Education establishments, and even a new and apparently go-ahead place like the Kirkby College of Further Education had no use for the idea. Indeed the late Director of Education for Liverpool gave me the impression that my (quite hypothetical) suggestion of introducing teaching of industrial design into the College of Technology was something that he had never considered. This treatment of design as a subject apart, an intrusion of aesthetics into a domain where it has no business, as something no more essential to the grown-up than art itself, springs partly from misunderstanding. At least that is what I concluded both from Birkenhead Technical College and from the fine (and very stimulating) new College of Technology down the hill from the Walker Gallery. At Birkenhead, where (besides the Kennington mural) the students' union has bought good reproductions to hang on the walls, the Mechanical Engineering department seemed to be unaware of the connection between the beautifully-finished tools and measuring instruments made there and any wider concept of good design; 'design', to judge from an unflattering comparison made between two lathes, one with a mock-streamlined casing and one without, is thought of as a kind of coating of good taste put on after the job is complete.

In 1962 the Ministry of Education instituted a short annual course on Aesthetics and Engineering Design at Loughborough, where the main theme – stressed at the first course by the Chief Research Engineer for BMC and the Chief Designer for British Transport – was the need for co-operation between Art and Technical Colleges, the work of the Pre-Diploma course at Leicester being used to show how much closer the two vocabularies can be than is often imagined. Among others at the College of Technology I saw John Rees Jones, an engineering lecturer who had been on this course. He had since introduced a lecture on industrial design into the College's course on Engineering Design and Stress Analysis, but felt that there were two difficulties: that it was hard to get students to create instead of just working to pattern, and that there were no exploratory exercises in the use of materials as at the Bauhaus. In his view students would not feel the need to 'build in' good design from the start unless education on these lines began already at school. A fundamental trouble also is that engineers are attracted to management rather than to design, at least in the sense in which they understand it. Apart from this the only kind of visual teaching at the College was in the Department of Food Technology (an elegant term covering the training of bakers and pastrycooks), which is relegated to the basement of the college's old building. Here there was some drawing and painting and colour theory – much of it on a Walt Disney-cum-Mabel Lucy Attwell level, to judge from the resulting designs – with a view to the decoration of cakes.[1] And this was not untypical of the attitude of the other vocational colleges. Except in the Mabel Fletcher Technical College in Liverpool 15, where the student nurses who are its main raison d'être do art as part of their general education, the subject is only taught to those whose work demands an extra element of daintiness – not exactly an approach to appeal to the engineers.

Industrial design is however taught as part of the first year course in the Department of Architecture and Surveying at the Liverpool College of Building, a former section of the College of Technology which now takes part-time students in its own building just below the university and the College of Art. Here the students do experiments with materials and with mechanical principles – I saw for instance a harmonograph which one of them had devised for making rhythmical pen patterns – and they also learn letter-carving in stone. In 1958 they designed and built a sculptural-looking

[1] The best cake designs I saw were gingerbreads stamped from a plasticine mould, which had something of the quality of the modelling in the schools. They are said to be commercially unsuccessful.

crawling and climbing structure in concrete for an adventure playground run by the University Settlement below the Cathedral, using begged materials and borrowed equipment; unfortunately it is now in a sadly derelict state. More recently they were consulted by the Sales Manager of Bayco, one of Meccano's subsidiaries, who wanted to devise modern structures that could be made from Bayco toy building parts; designing these gave considerable entertainment to a group of students who had just taken the intermediate exam. This college, which is little known to those of the College of Art staff I mentioned it to, also produced one of the most original designs in the Liverpool Architectural Society's exhibition held as part of Bluecoat 63.

At the university there has been a move to institute a new chair of Fine Art. Nobody to whom I talked there seemed to have a very clear idea what a Professor of Fine Art would actually do, nor is it now known by what constitutional or unconstitutional process the original Roscoe Professorship of Fine Art became diverted to architecture: a question which it might be relevant to examine. The university however put the proposal before the University Grants Commission in its 1962–7 quinquennial estimates, which were cut; and since then it has been suggested that there should be a new Professor of Visual Arts as a kind of roving propagandist. There is already a small basis for fine art study there, in addition to the school of architecture and the department of Civic Design (which dates from 1909), in the provisions made by the late Sir Sydney Jones, a director of Alfred Holt's who was Treasurer and Pro-Chancellor of the university and also Lord Mayor. Thus there is a Sydney Jones Collection in the Tate Hall where university receptions are held – it proved to be locked when I was shown round it, and to consist of a very average lot of English watercolours – there are legacies for making additions to it, and three annual Sydney Jones Lectures on art or architecture. In 1961–2 these lectures were given by Sir Anthony Blunt, Alistair Smart of Nottingham University and Victor Pasmore, representing the three categories from which the planned chair might be filled: art scholar, university lecturer-cum-gallery curator (as Professor Smart then was), and practising artist.[1] This last is a type of appointment recommended by the Bridges Report of 1959,[2] but it meets with some scepticism in Liverpool as

[1] In 1962–3 they were given by Ian Nairn; in 1963–4 by Alan Bowness, Adrian Heath and Hugh Scrutton on different aspects of the John Moores competition. In 1964–5 they were devoted to the theatre. In 1966 John Hart spoke about art education.

[2] *Help for the Arts.* A Report to the Calouste Gulbenkian Foundation 1959. Paragraph 111. 'At very little additional cost universities could provide valuable encouragement to artists by employing them on short-term contracts. In return the artist could give occasional lectures and arrange exhibitions, and by being accessible so that students can see him at work in his studio he can show how in fact an artist paints . . .'

encouraging the artist to develop a flamboyant 'personality' rather than work. The Professor of Civic Design feels that as it is also unlikely that a first-rate art historian could be lured away from the London libraries and collections except perhaps in order to found an honours school of art history (which is no part of the plan) the best solution would be a professorship of industrial design. This is something that at present exists in no other English university, though industrial design is taught in the engineering departments of a number of universities[1] and there is a move on foot to found a chair at the new university of Warwick. At Liverpool however the current idea is only that there should be a new Department of Building Production, with an Industrial Design section included. The Director of the Council of Industrial Design, who is C. H. Reilly's son, thinks there should be an industrial design department in any university where engineering is an important subject.

Taken as a whole then, Liverpool's system of visual education seems to be lacking in purpose, consistency and continuity. There is too little evidence of co-ordination or common thinking even between neighbouring institutions whose age groups and subjects of study overlap; there is not even much contact. Everywhere there seem to be barriers, though nothing solid and outward such as could be demolished by order; more an unquestioned tradition of boundaries, sometimes drawn so constrictingly that a kind of no-man's land is left all round: the dead ground into which the visually alert child slips after the age of sixteen. Art, with which visual design is generally included, is still seen as unnecessary for adults unless they are to make a career of it; at best it is something for leisure, holidays and retirement, a way of making dull realities palatable, an aid to selling them – the decoration on the cake. Given such an attitude (and of course there are exceptions) it is not surprising that Liverpool's people's taste in art, whether as consumers or as amateurs, should so often be essentially escapist and exotic, or that art and manufacture, even that handsome Victorian couple Art and Commerce, should so often be strangers.

The local relevance of such education is as a rule not seen. Yet there is surely a connection between this failure to carry visual training into higher

[1] Glasgow, Newcastle, Manchester (Department of Building), Leeds and Leicester. The Royal College of Art has an industrial design department which has about thirty students and a staff of four; the course lasts four years. I was told there that the disadvantage of industrial design as a full-time subject is that there are not many jobs to be filled annually – perhaps fifty in the whole country – and to the university-trained engineer they seem like the bottom of those open to him. For Manchester's rather different approach see p. 206.

education, to 'build in' the visual element at all stages, and the actual level of design and decoration in shops and streets. People who had learnt to look about them more critically in everyday life would still find it a huge task to make Liverpool a beautiful city, but at least they would sweep away unnecessary horrors like the present bus shelters, and they would better appreciate what is good in the Liverpool scene. The same is true of any possibility of a visual self-expression to match the city's fierce vitality; the necessary sense of identity through art – even an awareness of the present Liverpool artists, their strengths and weaknesses, – can hardly be developed unless art seems actual and accessible, nor can promising beginnings like those of the Teacher Training department and the best secondary schools lead far if the talents they have found get no chance to develop after school. The interest in art among the population is undeniable. But unless the system develops clearer objectives the danger is that it will degenerate into a superficial concern with art fashions, with sensations and talking points and checking up on what was in the Sunday paper or on television. There is more to be got out of art than that.

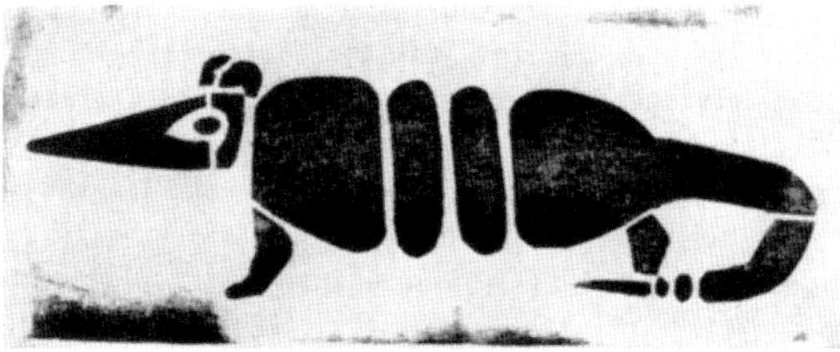

114 Linocut from Gateacre CS

7 : THE ARTISTS

Any plan for the future must depend largely on the presence or absence of notable local artistic talent on Merseyside. At the moment this is not an easy point to resolve, for not only are judgments of living art a highly subjective business but in this case we have to apply two separate sets of criteria at once. There is, as we have seen, a body of professional artists in and around Liverpool who must, as such, be judged by the same standards as the viewer would apply to professionals anywhere else in the world. They have also to be considered in terms of the jobs waiting to be done, many of which, given the state of modern communications, could as well be tackled by artists from London or from abroad. At the same time it is impossible to ignore the quite different problem of establishing a distinctive local spirit and tradition. We have already had small symptoms of this in work done in the schools and in the Teacher Training department of the College and at Rainhill hospital (though oddly enough not by the local amateur societies), and any signs of it among the professionals must be interesting almost irrespective of merit. Thus we have to look at these artists against a double background: first that of the city's plans, needs and tastes; secondly its character, both visual and social. Indeed art itself is a double business, as we are coming increasingly to recognize, where not only the finished work has to be judged but also the excitement and the social impact of its creation. Today nobody can view art as consumption or production alone.

This second aspect of the Liverpool scene has become widely familiar over the past three years. With its boxers, its comedians and its two great football teams (not to mention the Grand National) the place has always had its own clear identity in the public mind, but it has never been so well known as now. Television began it, perhaps, with the Z-cars serial and Alun Owen's plays and the very moving Liverpool television documentary by Denis Mitchell called *Morning in the Streets*; then the folk-song revival popularized Stan Kelly's performances of the old Liverpool songs.[1] But what took Liverpool's name around the globe was the so-called Mersey Sound and its most famous exponents, the Beatles. Commercialized as it quickly became, this

[1] His record of sea songs *Liverpool Packet* is Topic no. 27. The same firm publish a record by The Spinners called *Songs spun in Liverpool* (TOP 69).

was a spontaneous form of popular music that developed in clubs and cellars all over Liverpool at the end of the 1950s: small groups of very young, very un-slick and apparently un-professional musicians shouting and pounding out their tunes on electric guitars. The four Beatles were at first only one of the wildest and toughest of these; they came together in 1960, were top of the local popularity poll in 1961, started recording for EMI in 1962, then became a national institution the next year and a world-wide craze during 1964. Since then they have been pushed out of the top place in the national popularity charts by groups from other parts of the country, but they still stand in many people's minds for a special kind of Liverpool vitality, so that the artist who used once to say evasively to his southern friends 'Oh, I'm from Cheshire' now finds it is more creditable to admit he is a Liverpool man. 'The Beatles are the best thing that has happened to Liverpool,' the painter Adrian Henri told me. He was not thinking only of the noise they make.

For the particular creative ferment which threw up the Beatles and dozens of other rhythm and blues groups was more than a clever exploitation of old musical clichés and new techniques of amplification. Under the ballyhoo and the apparent banalities it was a fresh wave of young Liverpudlians, bright products of the post-war state school system, who had found their own way of expressing themselves without any noticeable advice or encouragement from anybody else. With their special brand of anarchy, aggressive yet human, they were just one jump ahead of their contemporaries in other British cities, and there is no real reason why their energies should not have found other channels. There is indeed enough of a link between the Liverpool pop movement and other forms of art to show that we are dealing with something bigger than sceptical critics think. Henri, for instance, whose pictures are discussed below, has worked with pop groups in presenting his 'events' (loosely organized stage performances akin to Happenings) at the Hope Hall or the home of the Mersey beat, the Cavern Club. Brian Patten and Roger McGough, the poets who have helped provide his texts, are associated with two of the country's most promising local poetry magazines: *Underdog* and *Phoenix*. Patten's poems are to be published by Allen and Unwin, McGough's novel by Michael Joseph; with Henri they are to feature in a Penguin Modern Poets volume and in Edward Lucie-Smith's anthology *Liverpool Scene*. McGough has formed a cabaret-type group called The Scaffold with John Gorman and Mike McGear, the latter being brother to Paul McCartney of the Beatles; they have made two records and under Brian Epstein's management are gradually winning an audience outside Liverpool. Lennon of the Beatles was a student at the College of Art; his Thurber-like drawings decorate his short books of Joycean prose and nonsense verse, *John Lennon In His Own Write* and *A Spaniard In The Works*.

It is only recently that these people's undoubtedly lively minds have been applied to raising the popular song lyric above the bottom level of banality. But Bill Harry, the founder-editor of *Merseybeat* (subsequently renamed *Music Echo*, a local equivalent of the *Melody Maker*), is another ex-student of the College; he has printed unusually interesting photographs of the groups by the Liverpool photographers Peter Kaye and Graham Spencer, while the Beatles' own photographer Robert Freeman, besides supervising the excellent colour effects of their rather poor second film, designed Lennon's books, of which the first was one of the most elegant and original pieces of British book production in 1964. All these may seem straws in a lot of wind: small matters compared with the stupefying boom of the music and its more commercial accompaniments, or even with the main tradition of visual art in Liverpool. But they do show the possibility of generating visual and poetic counterparts to this music in the autonomous cultural life of Merseyside, and there are other artists besides Henri who are aware of it. Arthur Dooley the sculptor, for instance, told me that he had talked to the young members in clubs and cellars where the groups perform (he reckons that there may be 300 such groups in Liverpool altogether, while the City Centre Plan estimates some eighty beat clubs in the centre alone) and tried to show them that there were analogies between his sculpture and their own means of self-expression in music and dancing. They have become interested in his sculpture as a result, he says; they have come down to his studio and have bought or commissioned pieces. He and other artists have been financed and befriended by Alan Williams, owner of the Jacaranda and Blue Angel clubs and original manager of the Beatles before Brian Epstein (himself a picture collector) took them over.

The most striking instance however is that of the painter Stuart Sutcliffe, who died of a brain tumour in Hamburg in 1962 at the age of twenty-one. Sutcliffe, a Scot by birth – his father came to Liverpool as a ship's engineer – went to Prescot Grammar School and the College of Art, where he was a friend and contemporary of John Lennon. He had a picture in the John Moores exhibition in 1959 while still a student, and the College gave him considerable freedom to work on his own, though it refused to accept him for teacher training after he had passed his diploma as a painter. He became a founder-member of the Beatles, playing bass guitar with them on their Hamburg trip in 1960, staying on to attend the State High School for Art there, but playing again on their second Hamburg visit the following summer. At first he was totally disillusioned with painting after having been turned down (for a mixture of good and bad reasons)[1] by the College, where his works seem to have reflected the influences mainly of Bratby and Bomberg. But at Hamburg two artist friends encouraged him to come and work under Eduardo Paolozzi, then the visiting professor there, and this un-

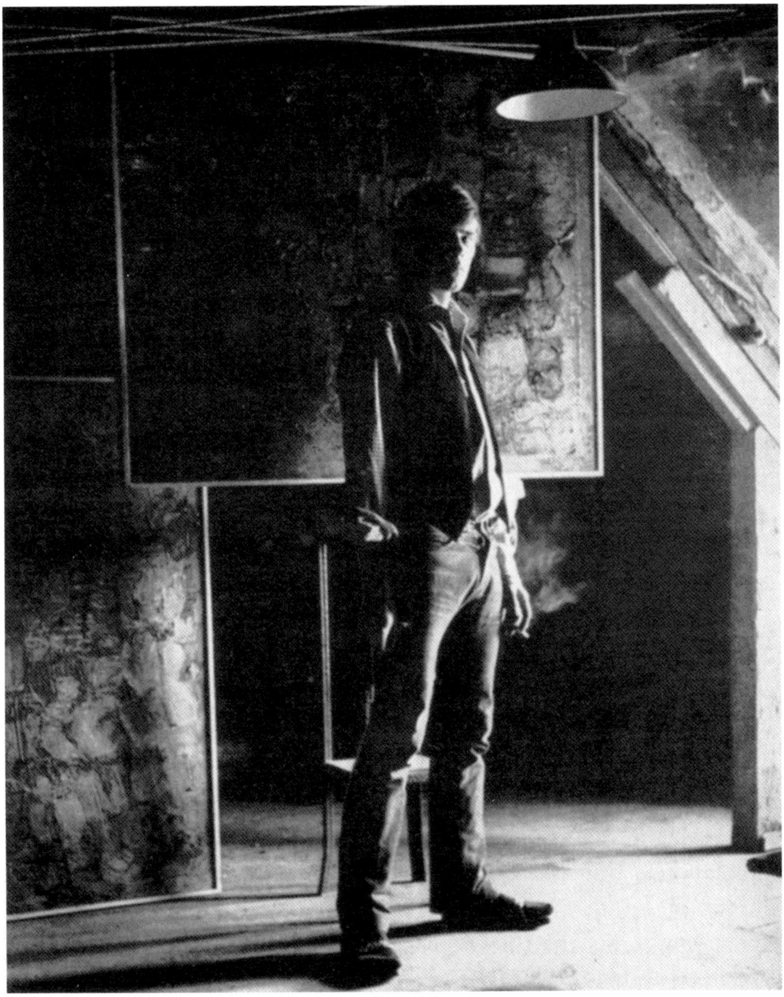

115 Stuart Sutcliffe, the fifth Beatle, in his Hamburg studio, with two of his black paintings

leashed a remarkable burst of creative activity in a much more personal and original style. Probably no recent Liverpool painter has worked with anything resembling this intensity, and the range, variety and colour of his last few months' works made a very strong impression when they were shown

[1] Among other things it was felt, understandably, that he was a painter and not a teacher.

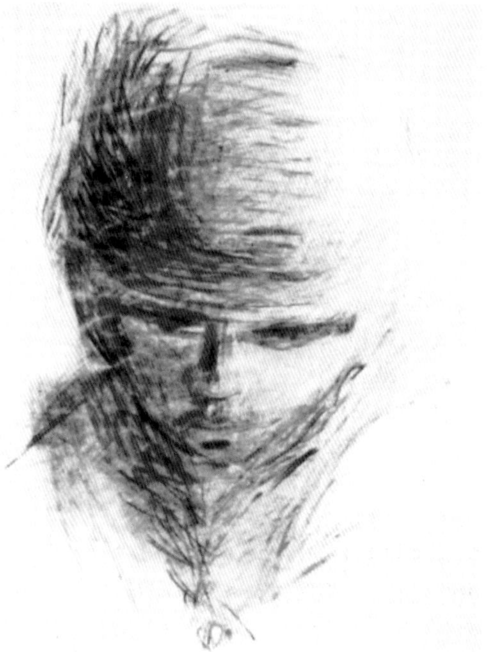

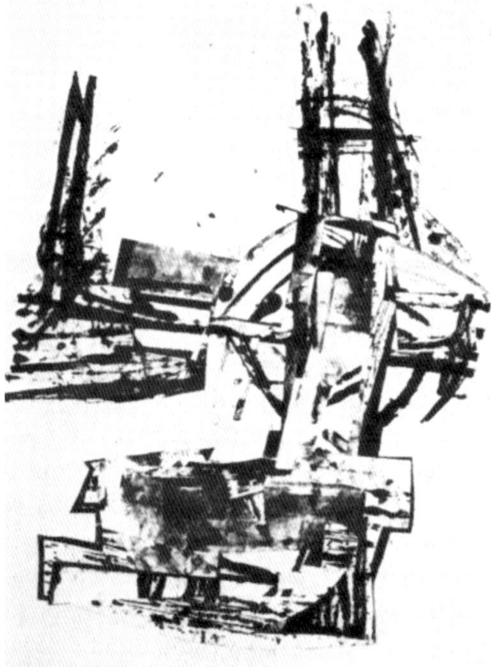

116–117 Hamburg drawings by Stuart Sutcliffe

at the Walker Gallery in May 1964. 'A very perceptive and sensitive person, and very restless', Paolozzi called him in an interview, and again:

> There is that sort of marvellously desperate thing about the whole Liverpool business now. I always felt there was a desperate thing about Stuart in his life. . . . I was afraid of it.

He was an outstanding loss to Liverpool and quite possibly to English painting. And over and above the merit of his pictures he has a special significance as somebody whose burning creativity switched from art into pop music and then back again. He showed the way.

Not that Sutcliffe himself, by all accounts, saw any particular connection between his music and his painting; he seems rather to have treated them as two distinct channels. But the very existence of this alternative is important in a community where the one medium has so far utterly overshadowed the other, and the simple fact that he was a Beatle immediately makes painting accessible to those of his own and younger generations who might otherwise be put off by the heavy curtain of cash, plush and gloss surrounding so much of modern art. Outwardly one would not think of him as a specifically local painter; though some of his Hamburg drawings seem to identify him as a pupil of Paolozzi's they give little clue to his nationality, let alone his Liverpool background. Yet undoubtedly in the Liverpool context he means something quite special. He was not only a small, tragic, self-consuming figure in the tradition of Jackson Pollock and the actor James Dean (with both of whom he seems to have felt some affinity) but a link in something larger: the shadowy chain relating a pretty low form of music to the most high-brow brands of modern art.

Considerations like this perhaps seem remote from conventional art criticism, but in Liverpool the city's particular self-awareness and the aggressive energy of its young people are both socially and culturally important. It becomes impossible to overlook them, so that although my first acquaintance with the art of the area was made without any great knowledge of such factors I have thought it best to outline them before moving on to discuss individual artists. For they did in fact largely alter my view of modern Merseyside art as I was getting to know it; familiarity for once bred interest and hope rather than the more usual contempt. To give some idea of my quite sceptical starting-point, here is my first introduction to Merseyside art en masse at the Liverpool Academy Exhibition of 1963:

> It has been hung so as to feature a large wall of the more with-it painters which faces you at the end of the big room. And you feel that everyone

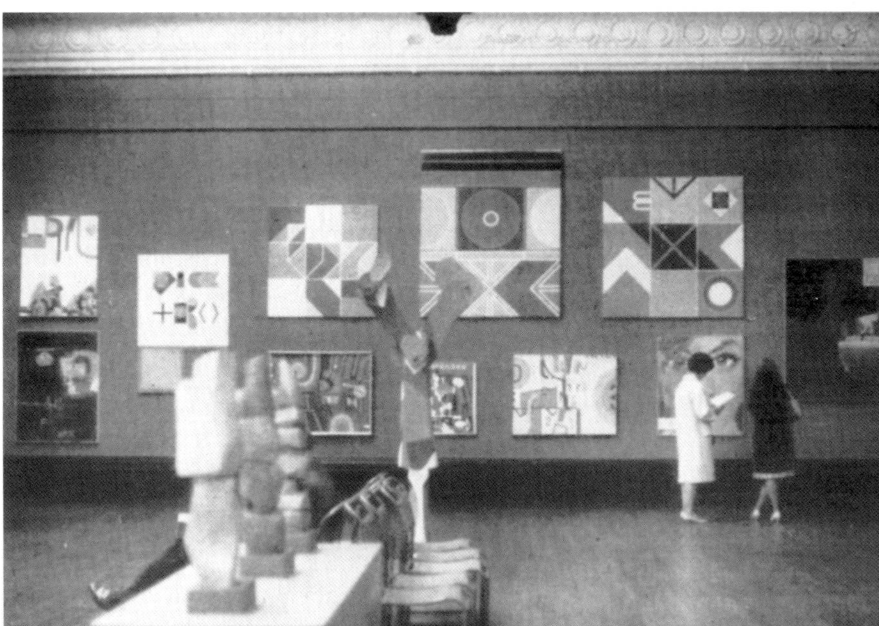

118 In the 1963 Liverpool Academy show. The four large pictures hanging at the top are by John Edkins. Extreme left and right are by Adrian Henri. The two women are in front of a painting by Sam Walsh. The remaining four are by Philip Meeson

> is rather striving to keep up, though in fact they are a long way down the line. The less the striving, in most cases, the better the picture: the two *Still Life with Guitars* by G. Gwyn Evans (Birkenhead) and Sylvia F. Forster (Heswall) are un-modern but good, and there are excellent straight pencil drawings of domestic subjects by Margaret Hughes. But clearly these are fish out of water nowadays. It's all tagging after other movements; thus on the large end wall the hard-edged abstracts of Edkins and the pop pictures of Adrian Henri are really would-be London pictures. Henri at least is below London standard for the kind of thing he's trying to do. And nowhere in the whole shooting-match is there any kind of flicker which one can say is specifically Liverpool.
>
> The best are indeed on this end wall: one of Edkins's (*Nomex*) and *Restricted Area* by Philip Meeson. But it's something done years ago in Germany and France. Nicholas Horsfield's (half way on one side wall) I know too well to judge in this context – it just looks out of place to me. A good pinkish Arthur Ballard opposite fighting with the red of the wall; A. says it's the only painting he's done for ages (is dated '62). Peter MacKarell's (derived from battleship construction sets) were all right in design but spoilt by black-green and orange colouring which I found strident. Martin Bell was unexciting but professional, and again moving with the times in square patches of colour. John Heritage, a big black-on-white like a blown-up drawing, which seemed rather good to me but called forth a snort from N.H. I understand better why after seeing one or two other things by him – notably a horror in the Sandon dining room.
>
> Also quite a pretty, Mundy-ish painting by David Breese and professional-looking etchings by John Roberts. Christopher Leyne's painting also professional in a cubist style. And then of course two of Jardine's surrealities, but not up to his best. Good piece of sculpture (skull) in steel by B. S. L. Rice.

In the months that followed my opinions of Henri and MacKarell changed a good deal; the Edkins picture was bought by the Walker Gallery and came to look rather impressive among paintings by much better-known modern British artists, some of them acquisitions from the John Moores shows. It would be wrong to disguise such changes by trying to give only final verdicts, and I propose to quote largely from my notes and set down my impressions as they came.

At that time I knew Nicholas Horsfield, the then academy president, and his pictures extremely well; I had some slight acquaintance with his successor Arthur Ballard and had seen his work at Roland, Browse and Delbanco's gallery in London; I had seen the odd picture by Martin Bell, G. W. Jardine and John Hart in mixed exhibitions outside Liverpool. All these were (and are) on the staff of the College. Ballard, I knew, had spent several months

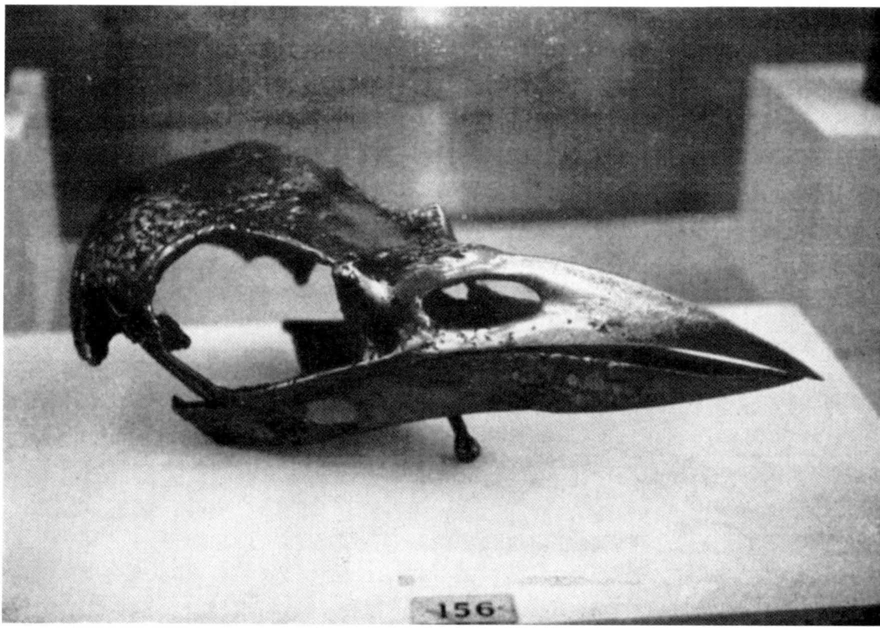

119 Sculpture by Sean Rice

painting in Paris in 1957 under an admirable Liverpool Corporation scheme which allows teachers an occasional spell of paid work or study abroad; the works of his I had seen were subdued, often earthy in colour, and non-representational in a rather negative way. He used to give the impression of forcing himself into abstraction not because it came naturally to him but out of some misplaced sense of obligation – to the spirit of the time, perhaps, or to the prevailing critical trend – and something of the same sense threatened his friend and colleague Horsfield: a sense which can be dangerous in an art community like Liverpool's, where there is not the same plethora of styles to choose from as in the great art capitals and it is easy to feel out of the swim.

Within his own conventions, which are those of a post-Sickertian impressionism combined with a Fauve colour sense, Horsfield is an outstanding artist whose best works – nearly all of them landscapes remote from Liverpool – could hang in a national collection. Extremely well-equipped technically, he is however not at all a facile painter, and in the Liverpool atmosphere of self-doubt he is apt on occasion to worry himself and his pictures to

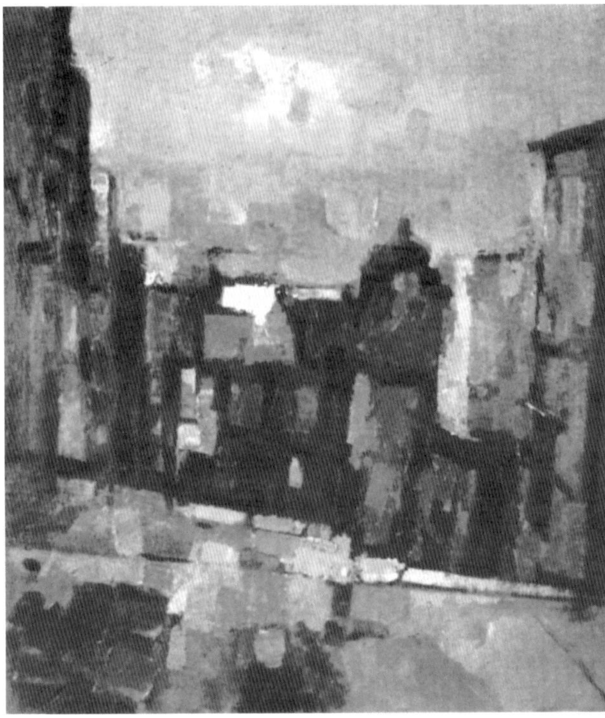

120 Nicholas Horsfield: *Mount Street* (Walker Art Gallery)

a virtual standstill. He feels that today the real revolution in art, and one which he dislikes and rejects, is the turning of the artist into an exhibitionist. The conflict, he writes

> seems to me to lie not, as formerly, in the rather tame squabble between so-called 'abstract' and figurative painting, but between acts of public declamation and private sensitivity.

In this climate, with its extraordinarily rapid consumption of artistic personalities,

> I begin to feel left on the shelf and sometimes doubt the values which have guided me without question for twenty-five years. Perhaps others of the middle generation, those whose ideas were formed, say, in the last years before the war (a bad time) may feel similarly.

He and Ballard spring from utterly different backgrounds, Horsfield being a southerner trained at Charterhouse and the Royal College of Art who fell in love with Liverpool when working as an Arts Council regional official in the North-West, while Ballard is a native Liverpudlian, son of an artisan, and an ex-student of the College. But Ballard too, I noted after my first visit to him in 1963, was

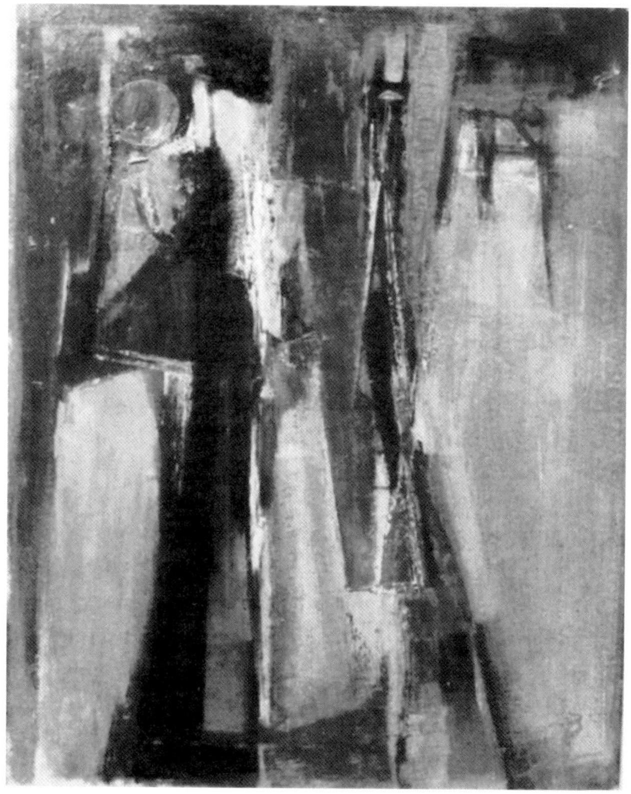

121 Arthur Ballard: *Non-figurative painting* (Walker Art Gallery)

uncertain of his values, or of the very existence of meaning of values, and hesitant about his own motives for doing almost anything he does. In the last two or three years he has painted very little, and what he has painted has been in no consistent style. The picture in the 1963 academy was the last of his characteristic abstract works I saw; since then he has experimented rather unenthusiastically with pop art and in the 1965 academy showed two very different but equally elegantly-painted boxing pictures, recalling the Liverpool heroes of his youth. He has been more interested in commissions of an almost sculptural kind, such as the 'printed circuit' panel and the chapel cross referred to earlier. But both he and Horsfield could be doing a good deal more, and although they have revolutionized the academy their influence on the painting at the College is now only indirect, the one being head of the pre-Diploma course there and the other jointly directing[1] the department of General Studies. It is a real criticism of Liverpool as a community that it does little to induce such highly gifted people to paint.

Horsfield had a one-man show at the Bluecoat Chambers in 1963, Ballard one at the New Shakespeare gallery in 1958. Horsfield sold nearly all his

[1] With Jack Bevan, translator of the poems of Salvatore Quasimodo.

pictures, Ballard two. Otherwise Ballard has shown locally only in the academy, selling roughly a picture a year except in 1956, when one of his works was hung upside down and the ensuing Press controversy brought him six purchasers. From the first Moores show his picture was sold to George Holt the shipowner, who presented it to the university via the P. H. Holt Trust; it was last heard of hanging in the metallurgical department. From the second show W. L. Stevenson bought the picture for John Moores, in whose office it now hangs. Nor can it be said that any of this has been

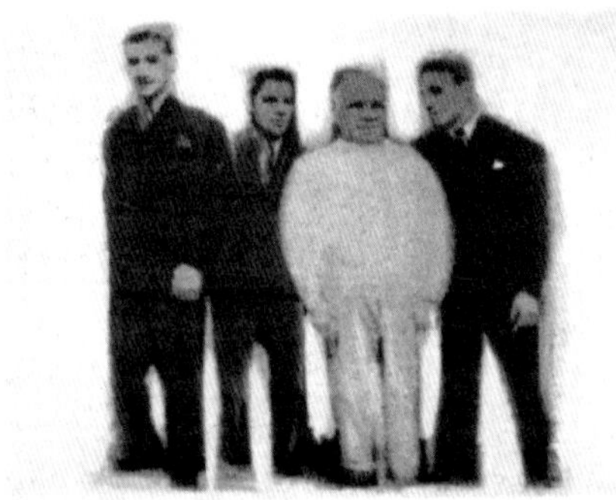

122 Arthur Ballard: *An original Liverpool Group.* (*Nel Tarleton, Stan Rowan, Ike Bradley, Stan Clayton*)

particularly rewarding. He made some £250 a year from sales through his London dealers while they were still taking his pictures, but they have not given him a show now since 1959. His two commissions in the TV shop and the school brought him about £40 each; neither he nor any other Liverpool artist I talked to has had commissions from the shipping lines,[1] though Holt bought one of his boxing pictures to put in a training establishment. The most he has made altogether from painting in any year has been some £400. He is certainly the best-known living Liverpool painter and, as he himself says, 'I could have worked as a charwoman and earned more money.' And yet (I noted)

> He very strongly supports Liverpool art, or rather its possibility. He has great faith in Liverpool individuality, which he thinks will assert itself in art sooner or later; we'll see something 'better than the Beatles'. He's proud of the efforts he's made to support individualists in the College, e.g., precisely, Lennon of the Beatles, whom the Graphic Design department were reluctant to accept. The boy was no good as an artist, he claims, and an intolerable rebellious nuisance. But he had character.
>
> Ballard thinks that the distinctive Liverpool art will come, and for that reason he's very much against the Moores show, which he regards

[1] I wrote to all the local shipping firms who might employ artists for the embellishment of their passenger vessels, and of the four that replied at all none used artists from Liverpool. Cunard, for instance, leave such matters to the 'design consultants' for the ship in question, who are unlikely to have the same local roots as the company itself.

as too broadly national. He argued that Moores ought not to 'bring this bloody great umbrella to cover us up' and that Biennale towns like São Paulo and Venice have failed to develop any art of their own. At the same time as all this I'm sure he himself minds very much about succeeding on the wider scale.

At the Hope Hall one night he and Arthur Dooley the sculptor came to blows over the question of working-class children and their chance of getting into the College, Dooley claiming that the system favoured what he called 'doctors' daughters'. To Dooley it seems that there is too much teaching either for commercial ends or to produce further teachers in a kind of self-perpetuating circle. Like Ballard he is a native of Liverpool of considerable physical toughness; his father is a docker and he himself served nine years with the Irish Guards and worked in Dunlop's Speke factory before establishing himself as a self-taught sculptor in 1961. Now well-known locally, he works in bronze, and his figures of men and animals, at once religious and revolutionary in conception, have considerable strength and feeling for their material and in their clumsier way belong to the same tradition as those of Henry Moore (despite his professed dislike for that artist and his contempt on finding that Moore's massive compositions are less solid than they look). Here are notes of three meetings with him:

1 James Cliffe took me round to see Dooley, but we didn't find him. A side street off Seel Street, with small old specialized shops and artisan-like outfits: goldbeaters across the street and a signwriter in the front room. Above the door a carved wooden sign saying A DOOLEY SCULPTOR. A black dirty entrance passage leading through to a padlocked door on the left: at the end a collection apparently of junk metal. A dark and poky courtyard glimpsed beyond.

We were just leaving again when Dooley's mate came in, a very pleasant sober and respectable-looking chap in specs, who is a wood-carver and shares the room. He opened the padlock easily enough without a key. Inside, a dark jumble of carvings, 18-inch high Moore-like figures in draperies, architects' drawings for a church at Leyland, rather a good watercolour drawing by Dooley's friend John Watts, a big expressionist-style painting by another friend now doing time in Walton for housebreaking. And, taking up quite a slice of the room, the enormous bed in which a fellow-sculptor had assured me D. would be reposing.

He had in fact gone off to the foundry, apparently re these figures which he is doing for the Leyland church. His friend described Dooley's visit to Faczinski the architect to ask him for £400. F. told him architects didn't do business quite like that. Dooley: 'All right then; give us five pounds.'

No hesitation about what he says, evidently. A TV interview for *Tonight* couldn't be broadcast owing to his language.[1] And on art schools and the jobs people get there: 'Three thousand a year and as much crumpet as you can eat.'

2 I managed to catch him rather briefly in the coffee bar. A big, dirty, sad-looking chap humped over a tiny coffee table, with two apparent acolytes in jeans, one each side of him. Conversation punctuated regularly (and no doubt automatically) with swearwords. Utter contempt for the College, for the Walker Gallery, for pretty well everything. Obviously thinks it's more important that anyone who wants to should be free to pursue art than that the art produced should be any good, or should find a home.

He approves strongly of the Rev. J. K. Murren, some respect for A. Ballard, much for this chap Watts. Thinks kids in school have all the natural art stifled in them; no idea of what the Teacher Training department does, or of the effect of such teaching methods. He and his friends were in favour of Berger's TV programmes, which the pale-faced, red-headed one (quondam Liverpool University, evidently) had certainly seen.

3 Again I found Dooley in the cafe over the Jacaranda Club, staring sadly out of his big face with one arm round a pale, silent girl in trousers and a light blue pullover. He offered me tea; the girl slipped off, evidently operating as a waitress. After talking for the best part of two hours I finished up feeling that he was genuine and likeable in his complaints against our society and in his sense that social and artistic activities must be linked; that he was wholly cynical about the art set-up and about exploiting the publicity which he sees as the key to it; that as an artist he *could* be personal, if a bit unskilled still, but is perhaps coming to take the easy way out of problems, even when it is work he genuinely cares about. I am sure he could do quite a bit for art in Liverpool, but whether he will do it through his work I'm not so certain.

He's obsessed with education. Nobody leaves school knowing how to *think*; they're just fed facts, and thinking comes (if it comes at all) at university. The practice of art, he feels, can change this, though he despises art teaching in Liverpool schools, which he evidently judges from his own experience, not knowing how it has improved since. The teddy-boy type, for instance, has been turned out with no thinking equipment, no relation to anything larger, simply with his self, and all

[1] Dooley himself denies this. 'That bad language is a fable'.

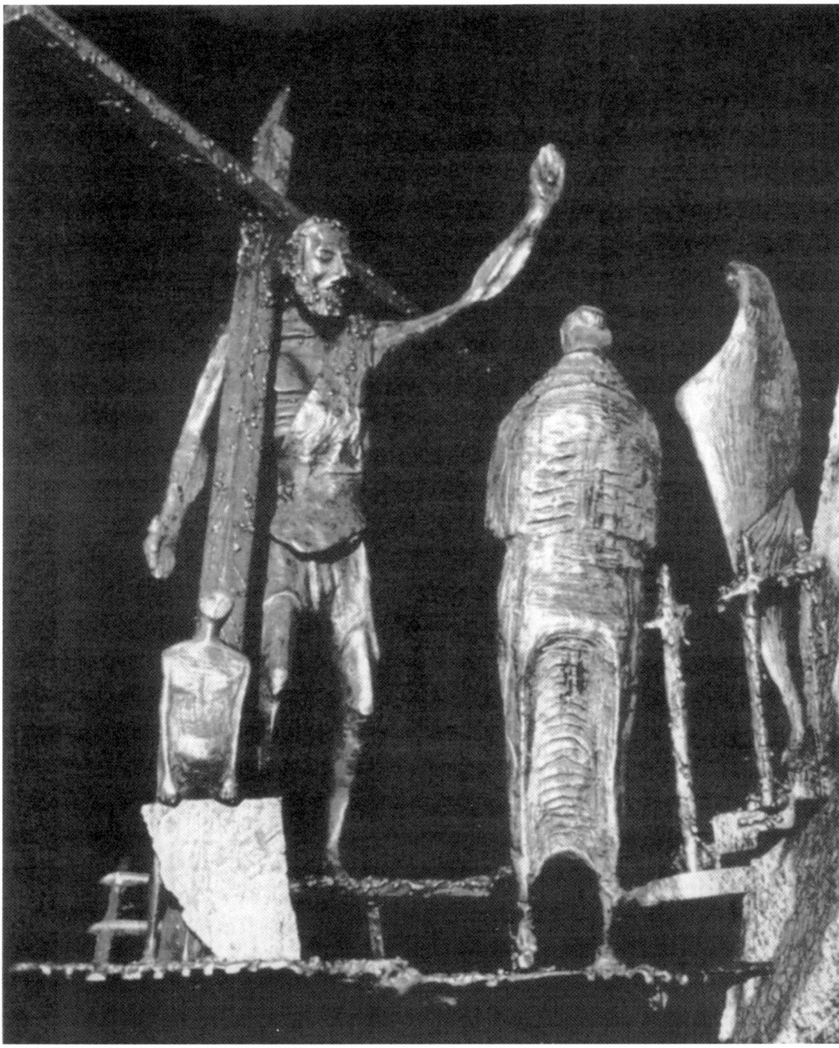

123 Arthur Dooley: one of the Stations of the Cross for St Mary's, Leyland

he can do is look after that self and dress it up. And this he sees as deliberate, quoting one schoolmistress down in Toxteth speaking of some child's educational handicaps: 'Well, it isn't going to matter. He's only a docker's son.' Thus (a) he wants wholesale revolution; (b) he feels there's a class barrier round the College; and (c) he sees art as something which can and should provoke thinking, and also self-fulfilment. This is because of his own experience: obviously his sculpture has been immensely liberating to him, and has enormously stimulated his ideas on all kinds of subjects.

He himself went to school in Upper Park Street, still a slum school today, where there was then no art teacher, only plasticine (or modelling

> clay?) and pans of paint set out on the desks. His conversion – it clearly was that, by his account – took place in the army in the Middle East. There he was appalled by the conditions in which people lived, and felt at first that orthodox Catholic charity and redemption was the answer. He sold Catholic papers on coming home, throwing himself into his religion and (I think he said) writing sometimes about it. Then, he said, he wondered if he couldn't express his ideas about these things better by making them. I saw what he says is the first piece of sculpture he made: a small, very abstract and rudimentary, knife-edged bronze figure: rather good, and from an autodidact remarkable. He is now a communist, he says, though he is a Catholic too, if not a very good one. In a sense he does think with his hands: he was not only no good at maths at school but even abhors the sight of a ruler. Like a French carpenter, if he has to measure something he'll just mark it off on an odd bit of wood.

Dooley has shown in Liverpool University, at the St Martin's Gallery, London (1962), at Blythes' Stores, Edinburgh (1963, during the Festival) and at the Bluecoat Chambers in 1964. On the recommendation of Lucjan Pietka of the School of Architecture he was commissioned to produce the Stations of the Cross for Weightman and Bullen's Church of St Mary at Leyland. Besides the young pop group supporters referred to earlier he has sold his work to London television commentators like Michelmore and Allsop, and to Professor and Mrs Frederick Ridley of the university, who own six of his pieces and were at one time coming to the studio almost weekly. He has also sold a figure to the Walker Art Gallery. Altogether he reckons that in his first two years of whole-time work as a sculptor he sold 150 items, which is probably more than any other Liverpool artist could say.[1]

The other man who has made a slight dint in local awareness is Adrian Henri, though in his case it is probably the 'events' and the poetry readings with which he is associated that have made his name known outside the art community, rather than his actual pictures; he was the subject of a short film in the BBC's *New Release* programme in June 1966. At the time when I first heard of him he was living in the early nineteenth-century residential area behind the Cathedral and the university but teaching part-time in the Manchester College of Art; he later joined the staff of the pre-diploma course at Liverpool. Born in 1932, he was educated at St Asaph Grammar

[1] Messrs. Tinlings, the printers and owners of the *Liverpool Post*, illustrated their well-produced engagement diary for 1966 with photographs of Dooley's work, annotated by the artist, and gave it the title *A.D. 65*.

School and trained at Kings College, Newcastle, notably under Richard Hamilton, and this together with his considerable literary interests has made

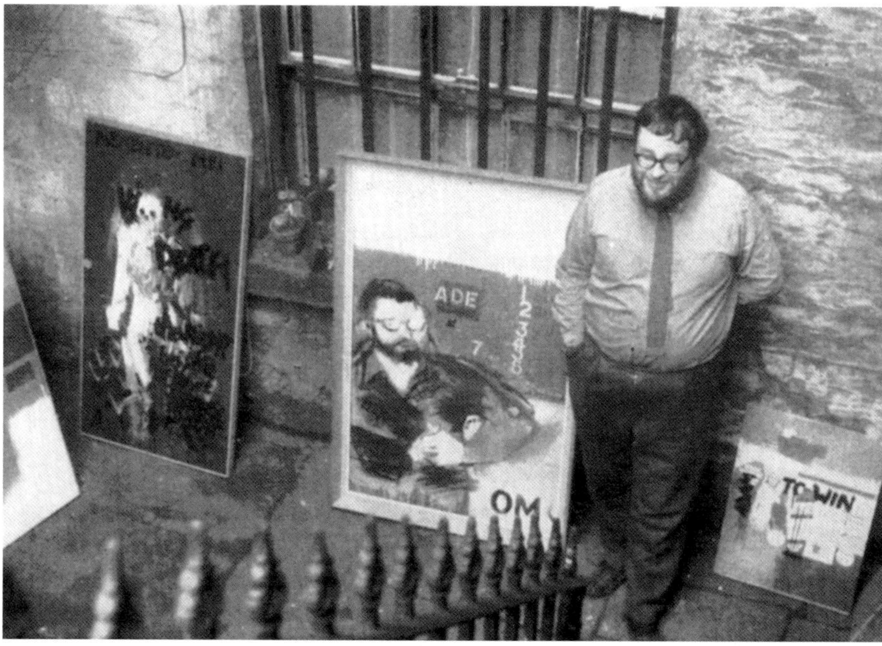

124 Adrian Henri with some of his work in the area of his Falkner Square house

him unusually at home (for an English painter, and even more so for a provincial one) in the Dada and 'pataphysical traditions of the continental avant-garde and among the modern American works that reflect them. His special contribution has been to sense the relevance of these and other apparently rarefied manifestations of the modern movement to the particular climate of Liverpool, for which he has great feeling and affection. 'The neo-Dada artist of today may use shock tactics', he has written,[1] ' . . . but the shock tactics are used to make a positive affirmation, events dedicated to cities "with love and squalor".' As a poet he has been able to put the key figures in his mythology, from T. S. Eliot[2] to the film *Ashes and Diamonds*, into a Liverpool context and make them seem at home there; it was he, for instance, who organized a Père Ubu procession to Falkner Square on Alfred Jarry's ninety-first birthday. As a painter he has shown inter alia at the

[1] In an article 'Events are Happening' in *The New University*, Oxford, number 12, 1963, p. 17.
[2] See his 'In Memoriam T. S. Eliot' in *The Times Literary Supplement*, 11 February, 1965.

THE NEW 'OUR TIMES'

(For Felix Fénéon)*

At 3 p.m. yesterday, a Mr Adolphus Edwards, a Jamaican immigrant, was pecked to death by a large bronze Eagle in Upper Parliament St. A U.S. State Dept. spokesman said later, 'We have no statement to make as of this time.'

2
Police-constable George Williams, who was partially blinded by a 15-lb jellybaby thrown at a passing pop singer, is to be retired on half-pension.

3
Bearded Liverpool couple put out of misery in night by drip oil heater, court told.

4
A certain Mrs Elspeth Clout, of Huyton, was killed by an unidentified falling object. It was thought to be a particularly hard stool evacuated from the toilet of a passing aeroplane.

5
2 chip-shop proprietors were today accused of selling human ears fried in batter. One of them said, 'We believe there is room for innovation in the trade.'

6
Fatality in Kardomah bomb outrage: Waitress buried Alive under two thousand Danish pastries.

7
At the inquest of Paul McCartney, aged 21, described as a popular singer and guitarist, P.C. Smith said, in evidence, that he saw one of the accused, Miss Jones, standing waving bloodstained hands shouting 'I got a bit of his liver.'

Adrian Henri, Jan. 1964

*(*a free 1960s Liverpool version of Fénéon's great 'Our Times'*)

125 A characteristic Liverpool poem by Henri. Fénéon was the late nineteenth-century art critic and anarchist

1961 and 1965 John Moores shows, at the Portal Gallery in London (two-man show with Sam Walsh), at the British Pop Art Show at Nottingham in 1963 and at the Northern Ireland Arts Council painting competition in Belfast in 1964, where his *Père Ubu in Liverpool* won the third prize of £200. But above all, perhaps, he is a showman, for he has worked six or seven summers in a fairground at Rhyl (for which he has painted decorative panels), and he has the rare gift in an age of exhibitionists of being able and anxious to present other people's work besides his own.

The address I had been given proved to be:

> A mysterious, virtually abandoned house in the corner of Falkner Square. No bell, no names on the door; push in and up anonymous stairs and there's nothing but shut doors on every landing. No sound or sign of life. I think I called out in the brown hall, but no movement. Then as an afterthought I tried the area steps and found a bell by the basement door and pushed it. That was Henri's, and on about my third visit his wife asked me in to wait for him in a room with books, sofa, cast-iron nineteenth century fireplace, some own painting and some (as it turned out) Walsh's, where I took up a Calendrier Pataphysique which some friend had sent them. No Henri that time, but Mrs told me there would be some form of Event, plus a bar extension, in the Hope Hall that night. Adrian was chasing around in connection with it.
>
> So in due course I went there. People were crammed smokily into the further room in the basement, waiting agog for something unknown to start. A broad, mildly Turkish-looking figure with beard and glasses came up from behind: this was Henri. Then a mixed programme: sketches, chap reading poems, two nice young girls singing folksily to guitars. Some of it rather good; most of it inaudible. No kind of décor, but the spare performers, or perhaps initiate onlookers, sitting round at the back. Not enough effort made to keep up the tempo, and interest rather slackened off. But altogether a good and lively atmosphere.
>
> Next day Henri at home with the gramophone playing Shostakovitch violin concerto while his wife tried to sleep. He teaches at Manchester but likes living in Liverpool; about to move somewhere else in the same quarter, which is plainly congenial, with its streets full of dirty ragged kids playing, black and white mixed, and its slumping Georgian houses. He himself comes from Birkenhead, but the family settled there from Mauritius; hence the name, which is pronounced Henry but no affectation. Has worked with Pete Brown, so knows of Michael Horovitz and his lot; is patronized by George Melly, who has three of his pictures and

POPILUDE for the artist Adrian Henri

America your stars have been eaten by reindeers.
I can almost smell the scent of the pines on the canvas.
I knocked on the pink cottage but no one answered.

Colourblind artists protesting against the nylon stocking.
Camp journalists protesting against the blood.
In the handbag secret gaschambers are being prepared for the
extermination of the few remaining poets.

On the obscure snowscape
lyrical mice nibble poems. You can almost hear the crippled musicians
playing sad tunes in damp green gardens, you can almost hear
the spastic lovers weeping straight bones beneath the trees.

A delicate moth struck by polio. I can see the sad skulls
of bleak artists studying me through many years of night.

The painting has a hole in its corset
through which drop atomic grandparents with strange and terrible ideals.
With sizzling faces. And the sun rocking itself to sleep in the living room.

In the white distance Ubu stands alert.
I'm an ant lost in the vast brylcream jar. I am the weird eggshell
whispering in the blue lakes, he tells the hidden reporters disguised as mirrors.

Adrian. There's a mutilated chinaman in your breadtin.
On some mornings I hear him screaming/wailing sad things/trying to find
the yellow prince who cried to Africa.

But now we are too late. My bedroom has been invaded by 8 pregnant birds.
And many other secret things rode jeeps across the landing.
Midnight. I wait in the dark corridor for england to come out of the w.c.

The birds were screaming in the wrong canvas.
The desert invaded by tulips/by the fantastic virgins
by the gunslingers from distant planets/O
merciful Dada limping across the asylum on a rocking horse.

Brian Patten

126 A poem by Brian Patten, who works with Henri and McGough

one of Walsh's.[1] Enjoys the matière and sheer luscious technique of painting, as well as having this strong literary-dramatic bent. Themes: Ubu in Liverpool; birds in the big brutal city; the ordinary pop imagery of Omo packets and so on. His 'events' have been televised, so he is not entirely shy of putting himself across, but I thought him genuine none the less, and the pictures were in many cases better than his exhibits in the academy show. But was rather repelled by a thing with a bloody pillow stuck in it and some ironic title. Henri himself quite pleased with.

Unfinished: a big painting on unusually coarse-textured canvas of the Entry of Christ into Liverpool. Modelled on Ensor, who figures in it

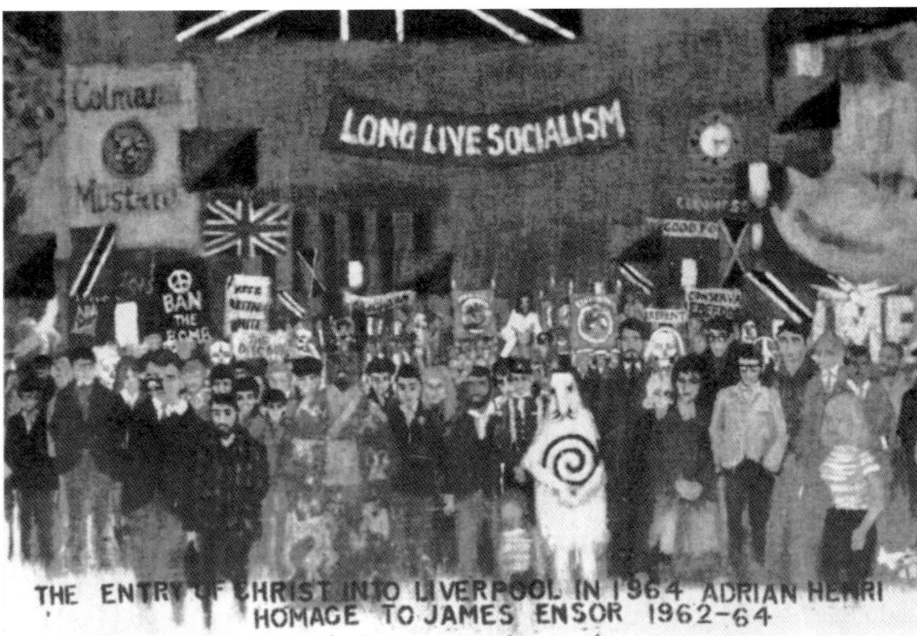

127 Adrian Henri: *The Entry of Christ into Liverpool*

along with Dooley, Melly, Pete Brown, Ubu, Charlie Mingus and other such. He and Walsh, who made his appearance nowabouts, had a 2-man show at the Portal Gallery in June 1962, and also one more recently in the Hope Hall on the cinema walls. Do local people buy their pictures?

[1] Melly, member of a well-known Liverpool family – George Melly, MP's furniture is in Sudley, and there is a plaque in the Cathedral to an uncle who fell serving with the Red Cross on the last day of the Italo-Abyssinian War – is the blues singer and co-author of the *Flook* cartoon in the *Daily Mail*. Brown is a London poet who does a good deal of public reading; his collaborator Horovitz is editor of *New Departures* and organizer of the 'Live New Departures' shows at the Institute of Contemporary Arts and elsewhere.

Not much, it seems, though they have sold one or two to an economics lecturer [Frederick Ridley, now a professor]. Walsh has had the occasional commission: he has a painting (no good, I fear) in The Crack and

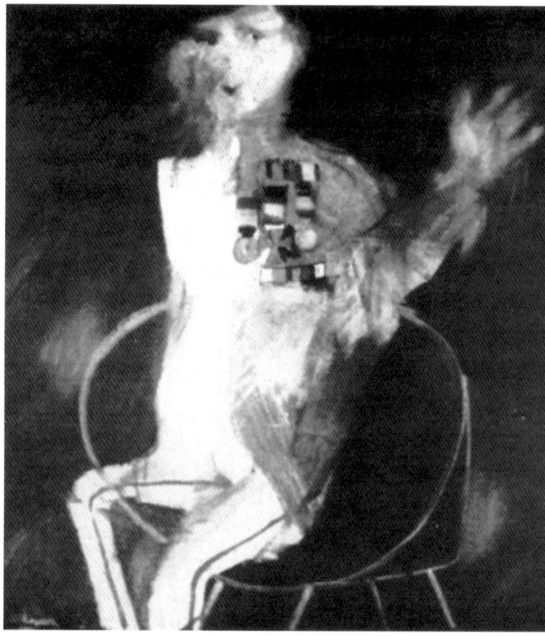

128 Painting by Sam Walsh, a Dublin artist working in Liverpool

one in the Royal Court pub, and he has done three for betting offices for Reg Mason, one of them in Ivy Leigh, West Derby, next Mason's house. Dick Egerton, son of Ma Egerton at the Royal Court, accosted him: 'You look like a painter. Will you paint a portrait?'

Walsh, some three years younger than Henri, is an Irishman, who studied painting at the Dublin College of Art, and came to England in 1955 to lead 'a double life as a portrait painter for money and an abstract painter for love'. From this uneasy compromise he moved, under the combined influence of Larry Rivers and Francis Bacon, to a kind of pop art based on huge blown-up faces (like his Bacon portrait in the 1963 Moores show, which the Walker Gallery bought), on advertising and the cinema and on the satirizing of sexual jinks in high society. 'For long,' wrote Henri in an article on him,[1] 'the man who painted was not the man who read Galaxy and likes monster movies'; but now he is. He also, as is evident from his latest pictures, finds the obsessive disgust of W. S. Burroughs's books congenial, though his own

[1] In the Liverpool undergraduate paper *Sphinx* for spring 1962, p. 24. The same issue contains a note on Henri by Walsh, a joint manifesto (Point 6: 'We would like children to find our pictures at the bottom of cereal packets') a d some illustrations.

reflection of it seems at once more modish and more sardonic than the writer's. No Liverpool painter has developed faster in the past three or four years, and his paintings are in increasing demand. Of the six works which he showed in

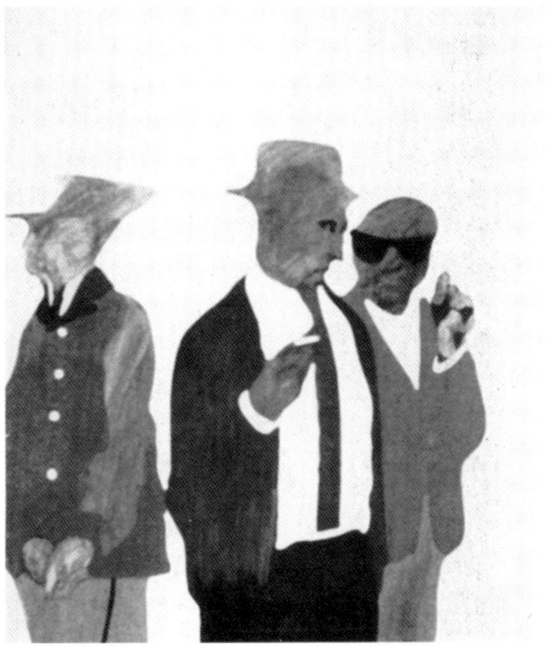

129 Sam Walsh: *Three Figures in a Warm Climate* (Walker Art Gallery)

the very successful 1965 academy five were sold, two of them to the Walker Gallery. The following year he sold four.

Recently Henri has twice put on his Events to the authentic pop music fans in the Cavern Club, apparently with great success. I saw the first show which he organized in autumn 1963 in the Hope Hall cinema (as against the basement room); despite total lack of publicity it drew an audience of about 350, which was better than many of the films:

> It also included some really good things, especially by Roger McGough, and was accompanied by an electric-guitar group called the Roadrunners: the first time I've heard poetry-and-jazz that really came off. There were two good poems by McG – the second called 'Summer with Monika', describing his stay-at-home, kitchen-sink holiday in the summer of the Profumo scandal – and also a very effective turn with all three poets, Gorman, him and Brian Patten, reading verses to a pet tune of the group's, which then let its own vocalist loose. A piece of pure knockabout: two mysterious men breaking up an elaborate structure like an oversized hatstand, which Henri had now and again been hanging some

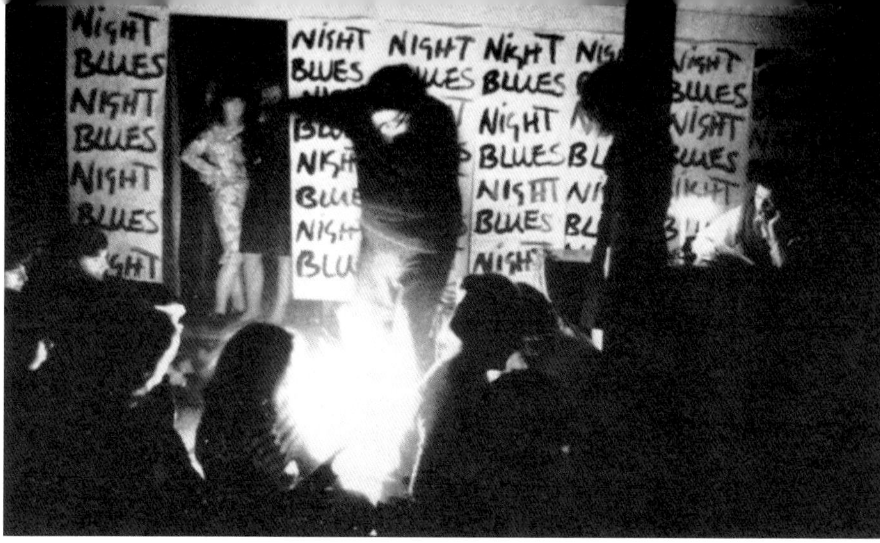

130 *Night Blues*, one of Henri's 'Events', with the artist (centre) and Brian Patten (at table on right)

object on. And a really very funny, originally-conceived and-written sketch by McG with a nuclear disarmer in a bomb-proof suit being questioned: this acted by Gorman and himself. A girl dancer from Oldham (I think) who capered around in the outer aisles – there being very little room on the stage. Occasional interruptions from the balcony. Henri as compère. Patten now and again disclosed by the curtain, typing away at a great epic poem which finally he never read. Large pictures by a painter called Don McKinlay who used to work with Walsh and Henri and went off to live near Bury, propped against the proscenium. A finale with all the company running round and round the cinema, waving flags; I later found out that this signified 'Roadrunners'.

There really was something there. Staging was poor, owing partly to amateurishness, partly to unsuitability of the stage; but there were no awkward lulls. And it was spontaneous, unpretentious, I thought, and above all indigenous. It seemed to meet the demands of a young and attractive audience, who later packed out the club downstairs. So presumably it was a success from the Hope Hall's point of view too.

A very different kind of artist is Peter MacKarell, who took part in Henri's exhibition 'New Images from the North' at the second Merseyside Arts Festival. The son of a Liverpool charge hand shipwright, he was a pupil at the College and is now on the staff of the Teacher Training department there; physically he is of much the same type as John Lennon. He too is writer as well as artist; he is a regular contributor of articles and drawings to *The Times Educational Supplement*, and he has written two unpublished novels that are sometimes untidy and undisciplined but contain excellent comic passages based on his own experience of teaching and his highly critical view of various aspects of modern art. I had admired a large battle picture of his which I saw

131 Poem by Roger McGough for another Henri 'Event'

DEATH OF A BIRD IN THE CITY

You should never have said that
Now
Your smiles are whiteelephants
and your face a photograph
to be comeacross
some slow brown Sunday

You should never have said that
Your tongue is a mother without pity
Now love is gone
and anonymous
like the death of a bird in the city

Roger McGough

in the College: a work that bypassed the whole modern movement, including the formalism of his own 1963 academy pictures, and went back to nineteenth century romanticism of a most vivid sort. He and a colleague, I found, are making a kind of sand-table model on which they propose to fight the American Civil War as a game of 'L'Attaque'.

He lives on the ground floor of one of a group of early nineteenth century houses at the cathedral end of Huskisson Street. A sympathetic place, with not much furniture (but that solid) and nothing but MacKarell's pictures on the walls. Curtains etc. good modern design. The odd wall in a strong colour. Plenty of books.

Immediately inside, a striking picture with little white circular labels, some rimmed in red, some in blue – both these lots numbered – and a third lot blank, dotted around on a glowing green ground through which a brown base shows streakily. This is Liverpool v. Everton, the product of MacKarell's interest in plotting moves; there is some connection with a sort of tiddley-wink soccer game which I don't quite understand. Also in the same passage, early pictures of grotesque heads, built up to some extent three-dimensionally, which he did as a student and now dislikes but his wife won't throw away. A bathroom with wall made into a scrapbook from colour photos, ads and God knows what else. In kitchen, one or two other such pictures, with an old bus on one. In front room, paintings developed from drawings of boats, etc., somewhat in the vein of his academy ones: one of them in fact, over the mantlepiece, having been rejected much to his annoyance.

In the bedroom MacKarell showed me a set of photos of tugs etc. in docks, and the model of the Prinz Eugen. A group of outline drawings from this and from the Hood: drawing silhouette of shadow with light at different angles so as to give umpteen different (slowly varying) outlines of the ship. Then pen and wash drawings done at Birkenhead docks, basis of some of the paintings in the front room: decent but not spectacular. Out in the passage the big battle picture. A smaller but

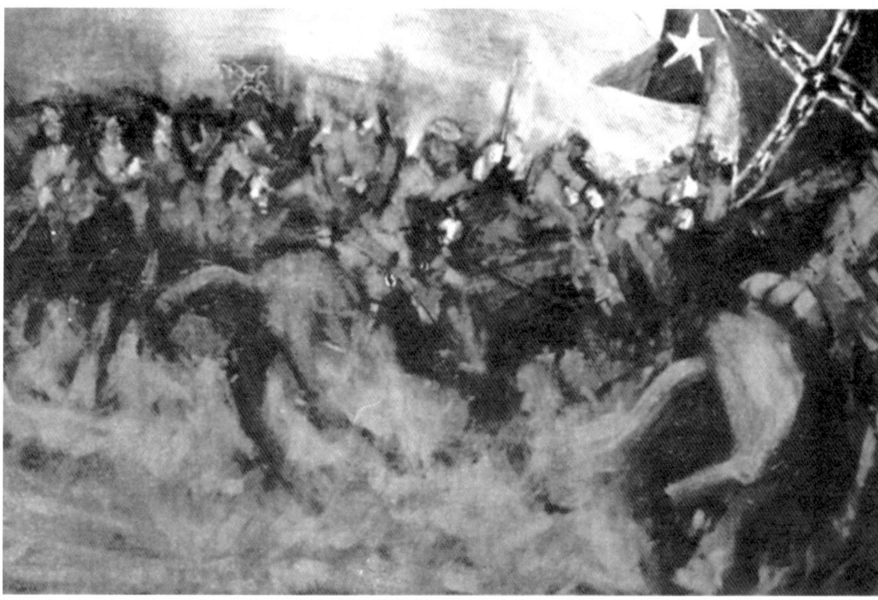

132 Peter MacKarell: *The Charge of the Texas Dragoons at Bandoleer Crossing* (detail) (Social Studies building, Liverpool University)

similar Civil War painting above his desk in the bedroom; in honour of it he put on a United States Seventh Cavalry cap given by a student. Also hanging there: a watercolour of Singapore docks done when he was in the army, and one of a shored-up yacht at Pwllheli. Besides ships – he is rare, incidentally, in finding a genuine Liverpool subject - he has another source in maps and charts. Throw-out admiralty charts on one wall; some earlier drawings in folder, not very good, based on map ideas.

I asked him re showing and selling. Mostly to friends or friends' friends, who will come up after the Academy and offer him £20 less than he's asking for a picture there. He once had a portrait of his wife in the academy, and as a result several people asked him to paint portraits. But he had done it because he wanted to, he says, and had little wish to paint other people. The New Vision Centre in London took some of his pictures, but he doesn't know what they did with them; he has also shown twice in the theatre at Lincoln, where one of the people responsible is a friend of his. Besides that he gives his pictures away: to Alun Owen the playwright (and script-writer of the first Beatles film), to Budd Schulberg (author of *On the Waterfront*), to Ben Johnson the eminent cowboy and others such. One is destined for the present commander of the Confederate forces in this country, who lives somewhere like Henley-on-Thames. He says he enjoys doing this: these people have given him pleasure (or more), and how else can he show it? Plainly he is someone who loses interest in his work once he's done it. He doesn't seem to be discontented with his outlets, and hasn't tried to do very much about improving them.

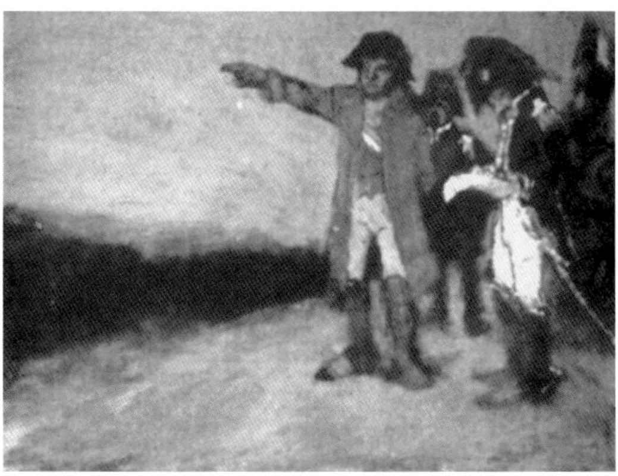

133 Peter MacKarell: '*You know we French stormed Ratisbon a mile or two away*'

Since then MacKarell has done further battle pictures and a striking *Dante and Beatrice in Liverpool*, part parody, part social realism; and moved house. He himself feels that his work as an illustrator is in some ways more important and more rewarding to him than his painting. 'Highly descriptive graphic drawing is integral to my work as an artist,' he writes; but although his drawings are perhaps more disciplined than his paintings, they also seem stiffer and less spontaneous. The great merit of his work as a painter, to my mind, is that it arises from an absolutely genuine *interest* each time. If the result is near-pop – something he hotly denies – it's not because pop is the fashion but because this subject (football, e.g.) is what he happens to be immersed in. If it is different (as with the American Civil War) then the approach can be quite different too. In this he is himself putting into practice the methods he and John Hart have devised in the Teacher Training Department for canalizing the ordinary Liverpool child's curiosity and observation into various kinds of art. His considerable aggressiveness and effervescence have been set purposefully to work.

The complete contrast is Jardine, who is a romantic rooted in the English nineteenth century and in the international surrealism of the 1930s, and works steadily away in his studio on the top floor of the Bluecoat Chambers, paying little apparent attention to other people's fashions. Born in Liverpool in 1920, he went to Wallasey Art School at a time when it consisted of six students and one master, he says; then in 1939 got a scholarship to the Royal College of Art, where he won the Travelling Scholarship for graphic design and studied mural painting under E. W. Tristram. 'The murals painted on wall-sized sheets of board,' he has written of his work there,[1]

> I found could be successfully sawn up into little bits and the bigger lumps discarded. This way I could get down to a nice little head or composition as small as four inches square. Even now if I am not satisfied with the composition of one of my pictures I saw it up into smaller ones.

Now he is a lecturer at the College of Art, and at the moment is probably of all these local painters the one who sells best in London. There he has had three successful one-man shows at the Portal Gallery, whose director Lionel Levy was formerly a student of dress design at the College. He has also had shows in Brussels (Galerie Vendôme, 1961) and Chicago (Callard Gallery, 1962). I myself (to return to immediate impressions) first saw his pictures –

> two of them, if I remember right – around 1950, when Nicholas Horsfield got up his Arts Council exhibition of Lancs painters. That, he now says, is about when he started to become known, and his work hasn't really changed much since. He is a strange-looking chap: a broad face with bright eyes, sticking-out ears and little motion in it: a slightly ungainly and awkward figure, though it would be difficult to say why. He gives an extremely self-contained impression, an air of living within himself, knowing his limitations and calmly going on pursuing his own aims. Of all the painters here he seems the least restless, though he says he lives here primarily because he has a job at the College; unlike John Hart, with his intense affection for the place, he says he'd sooner work anywhere than where he was born and bred.
>
> At the College he teaches in the graphic design school, which has its

[1] George Wallace Jardine: 'Another World', in *The Painter and Sculptor*, London, spring 1962, Vol. 4, number 4, pp. 18–23.

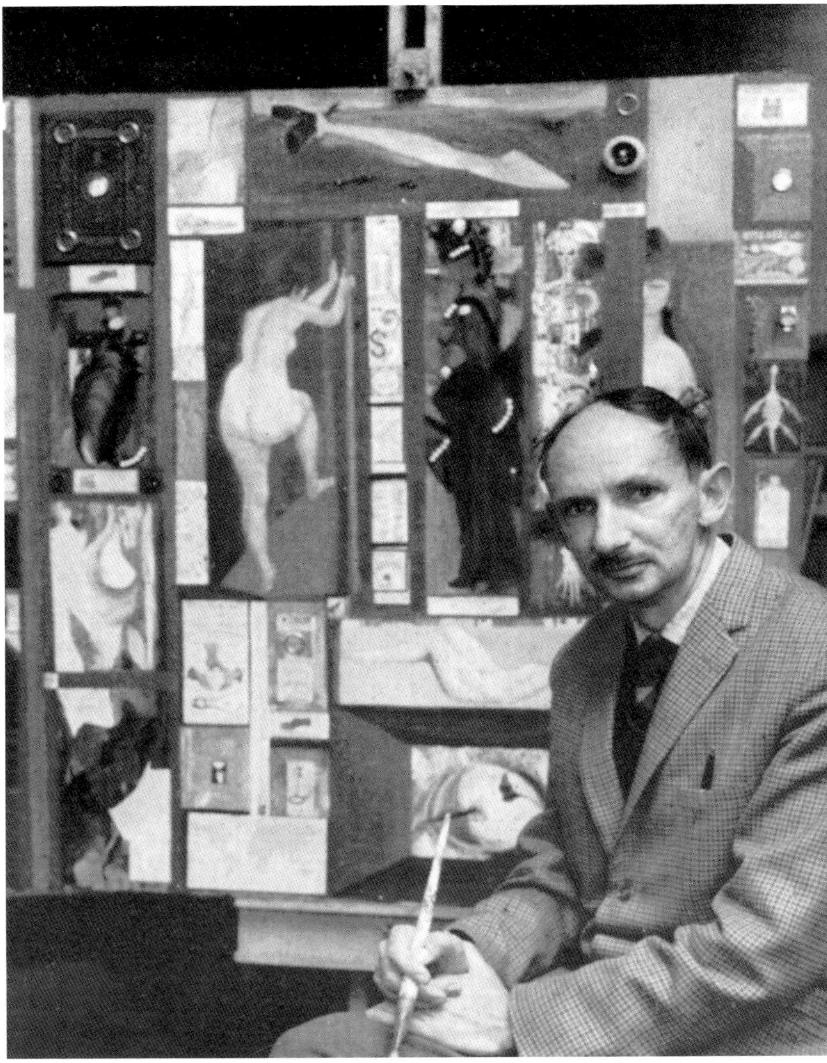

134 George Wallace Jardine, in his studio in the Bluecoat Chambers

own presses for woodcuts and lithographs. Some time ago he introduced a class of apprentice lithographers from the Printing School to the notion of collage, and says they were hopeless at it; instead of juxtaposing the incongruous or unexpected they tried to stick things in their right place, putting a bus against the background of a street, and so on. This concept of collage he derives consciously from Max Ernst, and the other artist he mentions as affecting him is Klee. [More lately he has become interested in Klimt and Schiele.]

The painting of his I liked best (on this first visit) was a shell collage over the fireplace, and obviously he likes it too. Otherwise his recent pictures are a bit more preraphaelitey than they used to be: partly because he is including very literally painted nudes, girls painted sometimes from the imagination, sometimes from one of the College models,

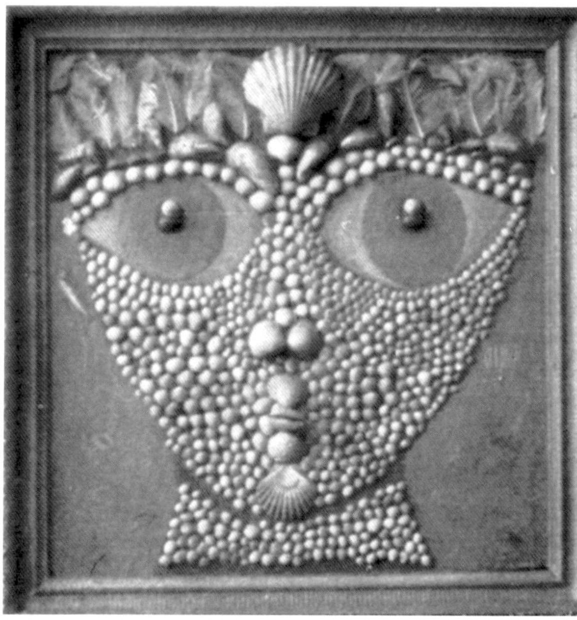

135 Shell collage by G. W. Jardine

and partly also because he finds himself putting in more and more arabesques of foliage etc. in a way that seems to link up with the art nouveau revival.

This kind of picture, with its overtones of Moreau, Watts, Böcklin, isn't my cup of tea, but they are personal and pretty genuine, and they are often very well painted. Colour is not impressive, the flesh especially having the air of pastry; they are now sweet where they used to be quirky in a rather primitive way, a kind of Lancs surrealist H. Rousseau. Nor is there much to their composition. There is a real poetry about them, however.

What I liked much better were the small portrait heads, of girl students apparently, which I don't think he shows. These are quite straightforward, carefully literal paintings of matt texture, which have been painted with love and have a quite personal flavour even though the element of fantasy has been deliberately kept out of them. They are certainly the best portraits I've seen in Liverpool, apart perhaps from Nicholas Horsfield's of Eric Goldrein the barrister.

The blown-up collages shown in Bluecoat 63 were an afterthought almost, a development from his albums which he is showing in his next Portal Gallery exhibition. At these shows – the first was in 1960 – he sells quite well, evidently. An American dealer bought all the leftovers from the first two: 20 out of the 60 pictures he had sent. Local buyers: Melville Curlender – six. Peter Rockliff – some. O'Donahue, Kingham, English.[1] But he doesn't sell from the academy for some reason. And the Walker have never bought. In fact he doesn't particularly need to sell here. He has not had commissions because he didn't want them; he was asked to do murals but turned it down.

The collage albums were remarkable: worthy successors to Ernst's *La Femme 100 têtes*. And Jardine has been steadily producing both paintings and collages since that date, notably a fair-sized mosaic on the subject of *Midsummer Night's Dream*. Perhaps he is more of a Liverpudlian than one might think; certainly his stubborn, almost pig-headed imaginativeness has something in common with the tenacity of his fellow-Lancastrian L. S. Lowry, and although he rarely exhibits in the north of England the fact that he is admired and respected by such a very different younger artist as Henri indicates that he is an ineradicable part of the Liverpool scene.

These are just the handful of artists whose work I chose, arbitrarily perhaps or accidentally, to study. There are many others. John Hart, for instance, a slight spectacled figure of buzzing energy, not only runs an outstanding department at the College but produces a steady output of non-figurative paintings; the last batch I saw were brownish abstractions on hardboard with much deep scratching. Like Charles Burton, the head of the department of painting, he no longer sends to the academy, but his work is in a number of Liverpool collections, including the students' common room at the School of Architecture. I have already mentioned John Edkins, then at the College, a hard-edge abstractionist from London who before coming up to Liverpool had not exhibited since his student days; the picture which the Walker Gallery bought in 1963 was the first he sold in Liverpool, though he was offered (and turned down) a commission to do a church mural for Weightman and Bullen,

[1] Melville Curlender is a successful Liverpool builder, who gave the Walker Gallery its new coffee bar. Rockliff, a prominent amateur musician and chairman of the Bluecoat Forum, works in the family printing firm. James O'Donahue and Norman Kingham are architects, with offices in the Bluecoat Chambers; their two firms are collaborating on the new Strand-Paradise scheme. Stanley English is the sculptor and a member of the Liverpool Academy.

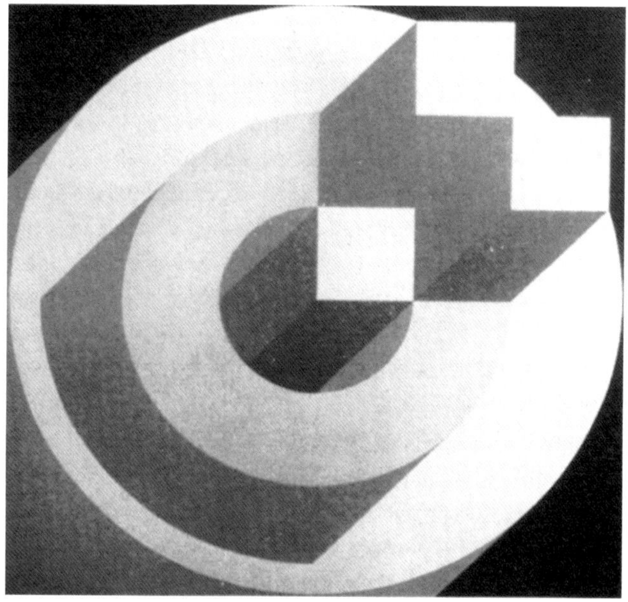

136 An artist revealed by Liverpool: the late John Edkins's *Fortification*

137 John Edkins: *Seven Answers*. Bought by the Walker Art Gallery from the 1965 Liverpool Academy

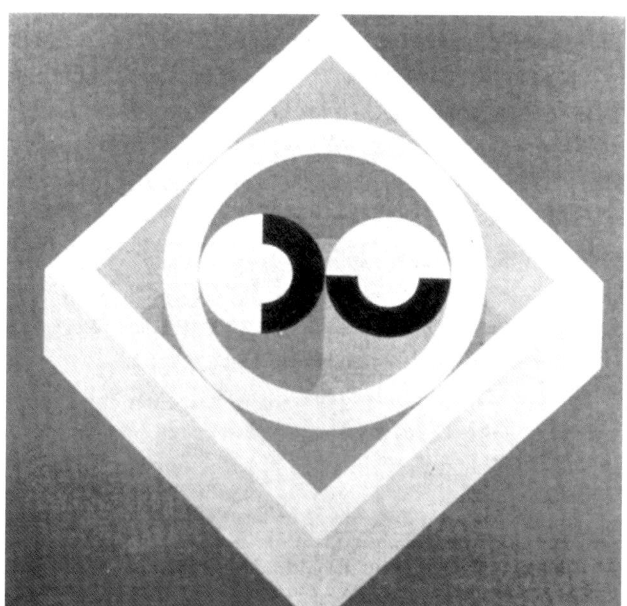

apparently because he felt unable to make any aesthetic compromises. Long plagued by illness, he died on 20 August 1966, only a few months after his first one-man show at the Bluecoat Chambers. He was an artist of unmistakably high quality who found Liverpool stimulating and felt that the academy had given his pictures their first external contracts; his colleagues quite rightly had a high respect for him and are sure that sooner or later he would have achieved major success.

Among the others there is Robin Riley the sculptor, who lives in Liverpool 8 though he teaches at Preston; he was responsible for the excellent relief at St Kevin's School, Kirkby and for the recumbent Christ in one of Weightman and Bullen's churches at Blackley near Manchester (St Clare's, Victoria Avenue), as well as for the unhappy Bold Street figure. There is Don McKinlay, now making very sensitive and original wooden sculptures

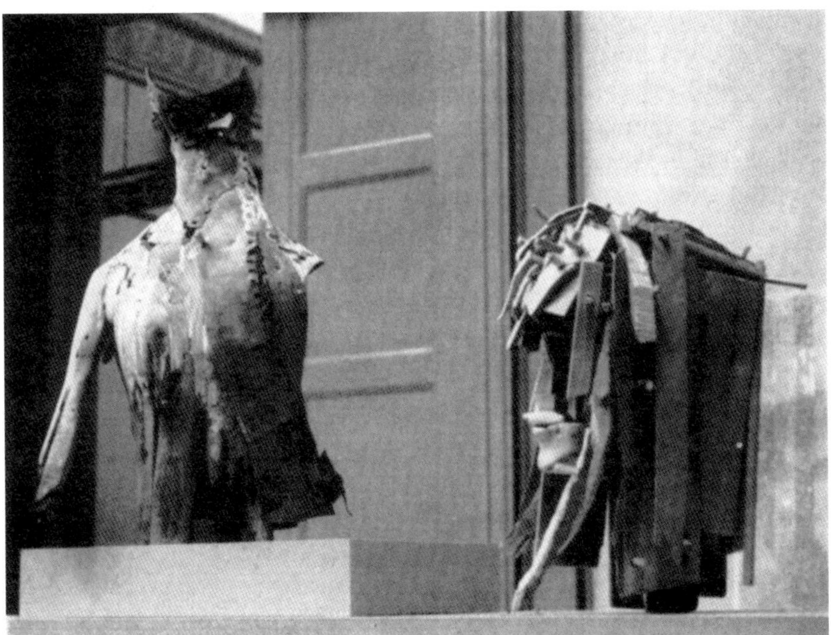

138 Two wood sculptures by Don McKinlay

in a strange patchwork style. There is Sean Rice, already mentioned, and Fred Bushe, two good sculptors in metal. There is Herbert Tyson Smith, still working at all kinds of stone carving jobs at the age of 82 in the back yard of the Bluecoat Chambers, and other long-standing pillars of the Sandon Society in Edgar Grosvenor, a clever caricaturist slightly in the Beerbohm tradition, J. Coburn Witherop the Walker Gallery's restorer and Roderick Bisson, a pioneer of the modern movement generally in Liverpool, who was exhibiting abstract work as long ago as 1936 and recently had the pleasure of seeing one of his prewar paintings in a respected London dealer's, priced at £400 and attributed to Albert Gleizes.

They and a number of other more or less wholetime artists (there are about eighty members and associates of the Liverpool Academy alone, all but six of them local and few of them amateurs) play a considerable part on the local art scene: probably as much as some of those singled out for discussion above. There are also those now working outside Liverpool, like Gordon Fazakerley, a former student of the College, who became interested in the Situationist movement and went to live in Copenhagen. Likewise Fanchon Fröhlich the engraver does much of her work at Hayter's studio in Paris. But it seemed better to concentrate on a few varied figures, in the hope that not only their work itself but their very different temperaments and circumstances, their beliefs and doubts, their attitudes to art and their contacts (or otherwise) with their fellow-artists and with the Liverpool public, would throw some light on our very complicated subject. For it is not just a matter of who are the 'good' artists in the area. Public art and private art each demand different qualities in an artist; moreover a man may have a local importance which the outsider might never guess from seeing his actual work, either as a source of pride and encouragement to other artists or as a reminder (discouraging to some, certainly) that the highest standards can and must be pursued even in a provincial community, or again (as happened with Augustus John at the beginning of this century) by the sheer infectiousness of his energy and brilliance. People's interest in art; the uses they find for it; the relations between ephemeral and permanent, act and product, personality and its sublimation: the whole business is changing, in a state of flux. And on top of that we have the particular Liverpool situation and climate, and the possibility of its spontaneous expression in art.

I don't think myself that any artist in the area, though Edkins might have been the exception, could be trusted to make a success of a major public work of art; there are a few (by no means as many as Bluecoat 63's 'Artist works with Architect' show hoped to suggest) who could produce smaller public works that would not actually disgrace the city; there are perhaps half a dozen whose work on a more private scale might attract a knowledgeable collector or gallery director from any part of the Western world, including Liverpool itself. There are one or two artists who matter to the city also because of the standards they represent, or because they have shown the Liverpool flag (as it were) in galleries elsewhere or on the television screen, or because they form a small focus of creativity for their fellows. It is not a tremendous score if one thinks about it in relation to the city's reconstruction plans, to the public appetite for art there, or to other art centres in Europe and the USA. All the same it is a good deal more than most English provincial cities can boast, and if there is also the beginning of a distinctively Liverpool approach to artistic creation it could be important.

In my view there are signs of this, though so far it emerges more in the character of the artists concerned and in their closeness to the city's other media of expression (not excluding soccer and verbal argument) than in anything that could be called a recognizable style. But there is just a possibility that some spark might be struck in the visual arts which would lead the gifted schoolchild to turn to them again after leaving school, and attack them with the same passion as he has been attacking his drums or his electric guitar. The impetus of course need not come from Liverpool itself; familiarity with modern art and a certain active curiosity about it are growing throughout the country; the old snobberies have to contend with a new feeling that 'anyone can do it'; in short, for better or worse, art is opening up. But there are these local links with pop music and poetry and popular mythology, and any sense that things were really beginning to move in the Liverpool art world might provoke surprising reactions. Excitement stimulates excitement, especially in such a temperamental community, and there are many factors which might contribute: more signs of local interest, for instance, or a greater consciousness of Liverpool art on the part of other centres, or any purposeful involvement of artists in the city's reconstruction. Once a distinctive movement started it might be almost as hard to hold back as the Mersey Sound.

At the same time depression does breed depression, and Liverpool artists are vulnerable to discouragement, very much like the Liverpudlians as a whole. They are not yet a confident community, for all the advances of the past few years, nor are they a very cohesive one. It is a question of striking the right balance, for of course an artist who has no doubts of himself at all is likely to be rhetorical and boring; moreover, if group activities (with their -isms, manifestos and the rest) are good for publicity, solitude perhaps makes for more serious and more truly original work. But the rather poor support which the artists seem to have got from local collectors cannot help matters much. The very existence of a body of professional artists in Liverpool is a bit of a sham, for there are only two or three in the whole city who do not rely on teaching or some other primary employment, treating the sale of their works as a more or less irregular windfall. It is an unhappy fact that the average Liverpool patron no longer buys Liverpool work. In 1965, as we have seen, the academy sold thirty out of 137 exhibits for a total of £1,128: as against an average total of £185 for the three preceding years. In present-day terms this is a remarkable achievement, but it seems pathetic when set against the nineteenth-century figures quoted on page 78, just as the sales from (and attendances at) the Moores shows have been pathetic by comparison with the early days of the Autumn Exhibition. Pathetic, that is, even when matching pound for pound; but in those days a pound meant rather more – to both patron and artist – then it does now.

Under such conditions the position of a painter without a teaching job to fall back on is bound to be extremely exposed. I only met one man in this category; nor did I hear of any other, though the sculptors can sometimes struggle through. He is James Cliffe, a portrait painter and decorative artist who has a studio in the Bluecoat building and did rather a good unsolicited portrait of Dooley for the 1963 academy show. His independence is not exactly an advantage to him. Thus he is not only frustrated and upset by the concessions to clients' taste which he sometimes has to make – a form of guilt which has held him back from applying for academy membership – but dreadfully vulnerable to any illness or disability. He told me that he feels outside the circle of Liverpool artists; very conscious that he cannot paint as he wishes, and anxious to break free from this bondage. But alas, if it isn't one kind of bondage it's another, and those who are free to paint as they want are tied to teaching jobs and to the place itself. This is the artist's dilemma, not only in Liverpool but in any other community which treats him primarily as entertainer or self-exhibitor, and has nothing it specially wants him to do.

8 : THE WIDER SCENE

In England as a whole the great change in the situation of the arts dates from the 1939–45 war. Four things seem then to have coincided to bring about an entirely new policy of state patronage, encouragement and diffusion. There

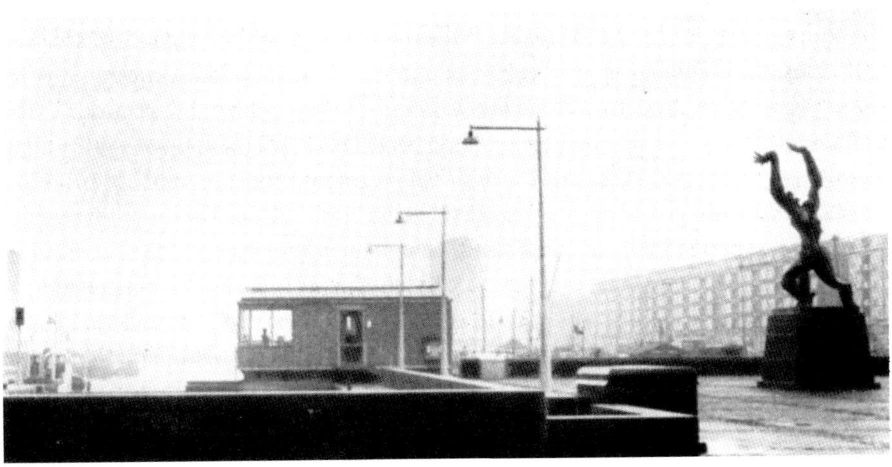

139 A successful public symbol. Zadkine's *The Destroyed City* on the Rotterdam waterfront

was a new public interest in the arts (and also in serious reading), brought about by the stress and boredoms of war. There was the general upheaval and destruction which forced people to innovate and extemporise without much regard for accepted tradition; thus there were concerts in music-halls, plays in factory canteens, art shows in pubs. There was a widespread concern with planning a new Britain, from the Beveridge Report down to those city plans so many of which seem to have remained on paper. And there were at the Treasury a group of officials and advisers genuinely anxious to promote the arts, the best-known being that brilliant member of the Bloomsbury circle, J. M. Keynes.

From this combination sprang first such wartime devices as the War Artists Advisory Committee and the Council for the Encouragement of Music and the Arts (CEMA): the first two bodies in this country designed to give systematic state patronage to the arts. At the same time an Arts Enquiry was set up by the Dartington Hall Trustees which, with a good deal of ministerial support, produced four reports almost equivalent to official Blue Books on the Visual Arts, Music, Drama and the Factual Film; the Visual Arts volume,[1] by a committee of fourteen under Dr Julian Huxley's chairmanship, being published in 1946. The position as set out in this extremely competent study was different in many essential ways from what it is now. The new rich had not yet begun buying modern pictures; prices were generally low. There was no municipal gallery approaching metropolitan standard; the Phaidon Press were the only publishers of art books worth mentioning; there were few instances of notable artists being commissioned to embellish churches or public places, and such as they were they dated from the war. But the Enquiry's ruling concept of 'State assistance to the visual arts' (p. 34) still dominates official and 'establishment' thinking on the subject, and its eight pages of suggestions (first formulated in November 1944) outline the system and many of the still unrealized objectives that have governed policy in this field for the past twenty years. Thus it proposed the setting up of an Arts Council and a Council of Industrial Design, which was put into effect before the report came out, and simultaneously a 'corresponding increase in the responsibility of local authorities', which was not. It favoured the grouping together of galleries, concert halls, civic theatres etc. to make cultural centres in large towns, and the establishment of Arts Centres in smaller ones.

Rising on the ashes of CEMA, the Arts Council was formed with a double task: in the terms of its Royal Charter,

> to increase the accessibility of the fine arts to the public throughout Our Realm, to improve the standard of execution of the fine arts . . .

At the same time its main financial effort was quietly directed to a third objective, the building up of a national opera: something that was passionately desired by a number of influential enthusiasts but was not specified in the charter at all. These three aims are not necessarily incompatible, but it can hardly be said that the Council has pursued them all equally – thus in the year 1963–4 out of a total budget of £2,751,676, £1,215,000 went to subsidize Covent Garden and the Sadler's Wells Trust and £117,007 on other operatic and ballet ventures, as against £55,199 for the visual arts for the whole of England (excluding the North East) – and since the closing down of its regional offices accessibility has taken very much third place. It is not that the Council is reluctant to support local initiatives for restoring the balance, as the case of the North East will show when we come to it, but it has largely abandoned the effort to think such initiatives out for itself. As far

[1] *The Arts Enquiry. The Visual Arts.* A Report sponsored by the Dartington Hall Trustees, Oxford University Press 1946.

as the visual arts in Liverpool go, for example, it plays no real role apart from the rare despatch of an important exhibition to the Walker Gallery and the still rarer purchase of a local artist's work. Intermittently the Director of that gallery sits as a member of the council's Art Panel (twenty-four strong), but its composition is mainly metropolitan, and most of the Council's work for the visual arts consists of organizing exhibitions without specific regional interests in mind, though it is prepared to make small grants to artists' societies and to non-profit-making commercial galleries. Its local influence is an indirect and intangible one, springing from the general stimulus which it has given the arts in this country, from the exhibitions which it circulates,[1] and the effect of its big London exhibitions in promoting the greater visual curiosity to which we have already referred.

In 1958 the Calouste Gulbenkian Foundation, an international philanthropic body set up under the will of the oil millionaire, formed a committee under the chairmanship of the former permanent head of the Treasury, Lord Bridges, to review the needs of the arts in Britain. The committee quickly decided that it was in the provinces rather than in London that the arts particularly needed help,[2] and Liverpool was one of the six cities where they went to gather evidence. Like the founders of the Arts Council, they wished both to pursue high (but undefined) standards and to further accessibility; at the same time they called for 'more scope for experiment' in the arts and a greater effort to promote their appreciation among the young.[3] They criticized the existing system of state patronage on three main grounds: that it operated through existing bodies instead of helping new needs; that it was weighted against experimental art (a contention which could hardly be put forward today); and that it did 'far too little' for the provinces.[4] To remedy this they made a number of proposals, of which the most original was the grouping together of local authorities (on the analogy of the Area Museum Council for the South West) to work with an arts officer paid, initially, by the Foundation: a scheme subsequently put into effect in Newcastle and the North East. They supported the provision of more Arts Centres, the institution of picture loan schemes by universities and colleges and the appointment by the former of artists on short-term contracts. They were concerned at the dropping of art

[1] In the year 1962–3 five of the temporary exhibitions in the Walker Art Gallery were organized through the Arts Council.

[2] *Help for the Arts.* A Report to the Calouste Gulbenkian Foundation 1959. United Kingdom and British Commonwealth Branch, the Calouste Gulbenkian Foundation, London 1959, paragraph 4.

[3] Ibid. paragraph 16.

[4] Ibid. paragraph 43.

by many schoolchildren after the age of fourteen, and hoped that both private and public patrons could be induced to include works of art in plans for new buildings. What exactly could be done about these matters they did not say, but they pointed out that a trust or foundation had great advantages over bodies like the Arts Council: it could back individuals, and it could afford to make mistakes.

Such examples of comprehensive thinking have been infectious. In 1958 the chief provincial art galleries banded together at Sheffield to press for greater state recognition, both in the matter of sharing new accessions to the national heritage (such as works given to the state in lieu of death duties) and in that of direct government grants. This move, in which Cotton of Liverpool was prominent, resulted first in the special grant for the Walker Gallery's Rubens, the first ever made to a provincial gallery, then in the stepping up of the purchase funds made available through the Victoria and Albert Museum from £2,000 to £25,000 a year (for 1960–1), and finally to a full *Survey of Provincial Museums and Galleries*[1] by the Standing Commission on Museums and Galleries originally set up in the 1930s. The Commission, whose members included the chairman of the Arts Council's Art Panel and one of the Bridges Committee – indeed the views expressed by these bodies are often close to the extent of overlapping – recommended the organization of further Area Councils on the lines of that in the South West, an increase in School Museum Services (i.e. organized visits to galleries, and loans to schools from them), greater co-operation between cities and their universities, and, among much else, the further increase of the purchase funds from £25,000 to at least £200,000 a year. They now stand at half that sum.

Private industry and organized labour have been caught up in the process. In 1963 the Institute of Directors, after Sir Kenneth Clark had addressed their annual conference, set up their own Arts Advisory Council under the general direction of the Arts Council's retiring secretary, Sir W. E. Williams. This will advise businesses about buying works of art, developing amateur activities and choosing worthwhile artistic enterprises to support; and it is clear from its composition[2] that its judgments will not differ greatly from the Arts Council's own. Patronage of this sort has of course been exercised independently by individual industrialists with a personal or professional interest in the arts, notably John Moores and Sidney Bernstein, whose Granada Television has not only built up the excellent collection of pictures and sculpture already referred to but formed a Northern Arts and Sciences Foundation to support the arts in the provinces. Granada has its own adviser

[1] Her Majesty's Stationery Office, 1963.
[2] Given in *Investing in the Arts*, Institute of Directors, London 1964.

in these matters – Sir Gerald Barry, the director of the 1951 Festival of Britain, which set new standards for the public use of modern works of art – and it specifically hopes to revive the individualism of the regions and make our provincial cities comparable with those of Italy and Germany. Its first measures have been in Manchester, where it has endowed a chair of Drama at the university and set up a school of acting. It has made grants to Sheffield and Lincoln repertory theatres and founded fellowships at York University and Manchester College of Art. In 1962 it bought Epstein's *Genesis* and *Jacob Wrestling with the Angel* for public exhibition.

The Trade Union movement has so far confined itself to gestures. At its 1955 congress it pressed the government to increase the Arts Council grant, in 1959 it called for a comprehensive review of state and municipal patronage; which the Prime Minister declined. Then in 1960, on the motion of Ralph Bond of the Association of Cinematograph, Television and Allied Technicians, it passed a resolution (number 42 on the paper) headed 'Promotion and Encouragement of the Arts':

> Congress recognizes the importance of the arts in the life of the community especially now when many unions are securing a shorter working week and greater leisure time for their members.
>
> It notes that the trade union movement has participated only to a small extent in the direct promotion and encouragement of plays, films, music, literature and other forms of expression including those of value to its beliefs and principles.
>
> Congress considers that much more could be done and accordingly requests the General Council to conduct a special examination and to make proposals to a further Congress to ensure a greater participation by the trade union movement in all cultural activities.[1]

As a result of this vote the TUC general council's statement to the next year's congress included a carefully-reasoned twelve pages accepting that 'public support for the arts is at present totally inadequate' but rejecting all idea of direct promotion by the movement as unnecessary and liable to encourage propaganda art and 'sectarian "workers"' cultural activities'.[2] In the council's view it would not help attract working class audiences any better if works of art were to deal more with working class experiences and aspirations, nor was there any reason to distinguish between workers' tastes and other people's. Local trade union bodies ought certainly to become more closely associated with the available cultural enterprises – by organizing visits by trade union parties, for instance, and keeping members informed about

[1] *Report of Proceedings at the 92nd Annual Trades Union Congress;* TUC, London 1960, p. 506.
[2] *Report of Proceedings at the 93rd Annual Trades Union Congress;* TUC, London 1961, p. 197.

cultural events – and trades councils should 'initiate or support'[1] anything that might promote a wider trade union interest. But the criteria must simply be those of 'integrity and of a respect for the highest standards'. In short, said the council,

> They do not wish the trade union movement to seek to exploit the arts for narrowly trade union purposes; nor do they wish, or intend, to commit the trade union movement to uncritical support of any particular cultural interest. But they are convinced of the need for closer relationships at every level between the trade union movement and those concerned directly with the arts . . .[2]

None the less on the strength of the 1960 resolution the playwright Arnold Wesker launched his Centre 42 with a number of eminent trade unionists on its council and the double aim of taking good art, both highbrow and low to trade union branches throughout the country, and at the same time stimulating local creativity. This interesting scheme was more radical than anything else since 1945 – it was the only one to look like developing new art forms, for instance – and in 1962 six 'trade union festivals' in provincial towns were staged whose visual component consisted of a nine foot high triptych by John Bratby and exhibitions of work by schoolchildren and local artists. Receipts however only covered a tenth of the expenses; the TUC's Trades Councils' Joint Consultative Committee got alarmed at so many unauthorized costs; the audiences were not, it seems, fired; and the local art was bad. Liverpool Trades Council was among those which Wesker visited, but it showed no enthusiasm for such a festival; Henri and Gorman called on the centre in London, but felt that it would not combine with their own ideas. The connection with the unions seems thereafter to have become more tenuous, the element of social pioneering less. Apart from the General Council's complaint about costs, nothing more has been said about art and culture at the TUC's annual congresses. On its side, Centre 42 is now concentrating almost entirely on raising funds from other sources to build a threatre-cum-arts-centre in the splendid Victorian ex-engine shed which has been given it in Camden Town, from which teams can be sent to any provincial communities that ask for them. Provincial centres are to follow; the ultimate ideal is that all artistic work should be presented to the public free.

In 1964 when the Labour party was returned to power – with the Liverpool constituencies leading the swing and Huyton returning the new Prime Minister – Miss Jenny Lee became an Under-Secretary responsible for the Arts: initially in the Ministry of Works but later transferring (as from 1

[1] *Report of Proceedings at the 93rd Annual Trades Union Congress*, TUC, London, 1961, p. 202.
[2] Ibid., p. 203.

March 1965) to that of Education. It was the first time a British Government had made such an appointment, though it had in fact been proposed two years earlier in a Conservative Political Centre pamphlet called *Government and the Arts*.[1] There is not really much difference between the parties in this field; thus the Conservative pamphlet dealt in the now accepted way with problems of patronage, the need for an increased contribution to local authorities, and the filling of gaps in public collections; and when in February 1965 Miss Lee produced her own White Paper *A Policy for the Arts. First Steps* (Cmd. 2601) it represented above all an attempt to accelerate the whole existing process. According to her paper the Arts Council in 1965–6 was to get nearly £500,000 more than it expected (for 1966–7 the grant went up another £1,800,000); the purchase funds allotted to local galleries and museums through the V and A were to go up to £104,000; arts centres and regional associations were to be specially encouraged; in the words of paragraph 43, 'A network of this kind should be developed to cover the whole country.' The work done for the arts in the schools was praised, though concern was felt that after school 'the impetus seems to weaken' (paragraph 60); it was hoped that local authorities and other public bodies would take to including works of art in their new buildings and displaying good pictures in their old ones; the government undertook to set an example. At the same time there is by implication in this same paper a certain criticism of existing assumptions; thus responsibility for the Arts Council has now been removed from the Treasury to the Ministry of Education, and when the paper was debated in the House of Commons on 27 April 1965 Miss Lee spoke of the danger of the Council's becoming a clique, and promised to bring in more regional representatives. Nor is she a member of Centre 42's council for nothing. For her paper may pay the usual tributes to high artistic standards, but it also states that:

> It is partly a question of bridging the gap between what have come to be called the 'higher' forms of entertainment and the traditional sources – the brass band, the amateur concert party, the entertainer, the music hall and pop group – and to challenge the fact that a gap exists.

– a sentiment, and a sentence, that has clearly not come from a civil service pen.

Such have been the main developments in the country as a whole, and they project a continually moving picture behind the Liverpool scene. For we now live in a land whose policy-makers recognize an obligation to see that the

[1] *Government and the Arts;* Conservative Political Centre, 1962.

arts flourish. This is partly the charitable approach of the helping hand, partly a genuine concern with high artistic standards, which private patronage alone would not be able to maintain. What actually constitutes high standards in the visual arts is decided neither by academic (or other) principles nor by public feeling but by taste: the taste prevailing among dealers and critics and virtually the whole of the official art world outside a few bodies labelled Royal. The maintenance of these consequently rather volatile standards matters more to the policy-makers than the satisfaction of local demands for art; but they recognize this as an obligation too and are increasingly uneasy about their relative neglect of it. Like all administrators they have a tendency towards formal simplification, seeing virtue in arts centres and regional or area associations rather than a confusion of different cities and individual artistic enterprises. They are apt to applaud reflections of their own taste – witness the *Survey of Provincial Museums and Galleries*'s criticism of purchases from the Royal Academy and enthusiasm over the penetration to the smaller galleries of more acceptable modern artists (paragraphs 25–7) – not perhaps realizing how easily this can lead to a tasteful uniformity. But they have fired a growing number of industrialists with their view that the arts must be supported, and now that it has become accepted orthodoxy the local authorities are increasingly following suit.

Thus if Liverpool wishes to pursue a more active visual arts policy it can call for support from several quarters, with good hope of getting it. And there are a number of lesser bodies and schemes, some of them dating from long before the developments of the past twenty years, which are also there to help. It is worth briefly noting these, as it is surprising how often they are ignored or the subject of misunderstanding. On the exhibition side, to start with, there are the travelling exhibits available to schools, training colleges, etc., from the Victoria and Albert Museum Circulation Department and the Council of Industrial Design. On the public art side there is the Society of Mural Painters, which is a professional body including such well-known artists as Ivon Hitchens and Leonard Rosoman and able to guarantee a workmanlike job at a set scale of fees; there is also a register now being maintained for the RIBA by the International Association of Plastic Arts, which lists more than 100 artists capable of working in collaboration with architects and gives photographs of their work. On the design side the Council of Industrial Design already in 1960 mounted a show in the Bluecoat Chambers which was seen by 37,000 people in fifteen days and linked with specially-selected displays in certain shops. On the civic design side there is an RIBA scheme for studying 'urban renewal' – i.e. methods for the more or less economic rescue of declining streets and districts which might otherwise be pulled down – and there is also the Civic Trust, which was started in 1957. Besides offering an annual prize to stimulate schemes of local self-improvement this industrially-supported body has successfully propagated the idea of street 'face-lifts' where shopkeepers and property owners carry out a co-ordinated plan of redecoration and redesign under a single architect. Such efforts have been found to pay in terms of increased trading, though the first examples have tended to reduce interesting visual idiosyncrasies to pastel shades, Festival of Britain plastic lettering, and a common level of accepted good taste.

Many of the measures that a provincial city might adopt, some of them blessed by the senior policy-makers, have already been put into effect in one place or another. The biggest and in some ways the most interesting of such schemes is the North East Association for the Arts, which was founded in Newcastle at the end of 1961 with Arthur Blenkinsop, now the Labour Member for South Shields, as its first secretary. This is a joint enterprise of some fifty local authorities stretching from Berwick-on-Tweed to the North Riding, who have set up what is in effect an Arts Council for the region, based on Newcastle. It is supported by the proceeds of ⅛d rate (more or less) all round; by private industry to the extent of about £6,000 in 1964–5 (three-quarters of it from ICI, Procter & Gamble and Tyne Tees Television); and, rather more symbolically, by trades unions and working men's clubs, who together contributed just over £100 for the same period. It also administers the Arts Council's subsidies for most of the enterprises in its area (£22,000 in 1964–5), while the Gulbenkian Foundation pays the salary of its full-time arts officer as the Bridges Committee suggested. So far the federation has not been able to do much for the visual arts apart from subsidizing certain galleries and exhibitions, notably in Billingham, where a shop has been turned into an outpost of one of England's finest and most oddly-situated provincial museums, the Bowes Museum at Barnard Castle. It aims however to treble its effort in this direction, giving direct help to artists, supplying transport and catalogues for travelling exhibitions from the public galleries, and possibly sponsoring a big competition on the lines of the Moores shows. Both its last two annual reports have asked for showings of the major exhibitions normally confined to Edinburgh and London. The association would also like to see more patronage of the arts by industry, commerce, hotel owners and the unions, and has mooted the idea of 'a service of advice and contacts'. As yet however, it has only been able to illustrate the odd item of public sculpture[1] in the *North East Arts Review*, a magazine

[1] The sculptures illustrated are by Colin Davidson (stylised Vikings on the central parade at Jarrow), Kenneth Ford (abstract work outside Scotswood Road housing development, Newcastle),

which it published as a means of generating interest and giving an outlet to local writers. The magazine itself, a good idea in principle, seems to have fallen slightly flat and has now been replaced by adapting the existing poetry magazine *Stand*, edited by Jon Silkin and previously published from Leeds.

Likewise in the provinces there are a number of redbrick or new universities which have some sort of art department. Newcastle and Reading are special cases, for there the split that occurred in Liverpool never took place, and the university has remained responsible for the local college of art; that at Newcastle now being one of the best in the country, with its own gallery, the Hatton Gallery. But Bristol and Hull have lecturers in art history attached to their history department; Birmingham has the Barber Institute 'for the cultural benefit of all students', with some fine paintings in its collection; Aberystwyth has an arts and crafts section in its education department. Three such universities in England have actual departments of art history: Leeds, Manchester and Nottingham. So, in Scotland, do Edinburgh and Glasgow. The latter also has the Hunterian Museum, which includes a marvellous Rembrandt *Entombment* and an outstanding group of Whistlers, while Manchester, helped by a £10,000 grant from the Gulbenkian foundation, has taken responsibility for the Whitworth Gallery, previously an independent foundation devoted mainly to drawings and watercolours. In these cities, as in Birmingham, the university collection has been established in a place which already has a good gallery of its own.

In Manchester there are courses in Industrial Design Technology within the College of Science and Technology, now a part of the university. They are run by two lecturers in Industrial Design in the Department of Building, but are intended also for engineers and industrial designers proper, and in fact bear on much wider problems of management and modernization. Aesthetics has little place in this teaching. Ergonomics, or the study of working conditions, the handling of design information, statistics, computer programming, the design of systems: the subjects taught there have a much more scientific slant, with 'exercises in visual appreciation' only appearing at the end of the list.

Other universities have adopted the American system of short-term appointments for 'resident artists': an idea first introduced into this country some twenty years ago at Leeds, where the late E. C. Gregory founded fellowships for a sculptor, a painter and a poet, to be held in each case for three years. Nottingham followed suit, then York, where the Granada fellow-

Edwin Hawking (relief outside police headquarters, Middlesbrough), and Geoffrey Dudley (*Fertility* outside entrance to ICI main offices, Billingham). Mr Dudley is the late lecturer in sculpture at King's College, Newcastle; Mr Hawking teaches at Middlesbrough College of Art.

ship has been held in turn by a composer, a novelist and an artist; the latest to adopt this practice is Trinity College, Cambridge. Brighton is going considerably further by setting up its own arts centre, supported by the Gulbenkian Foundation to the tune of some £50,000 (spread over three years), with (it is hoped) studios, music rooms, gallery and theatre, as well as a number of resident practitioners. The object of such attachments, as has often been said, is at once to give the artist an agreeable atmosphere to work in and to let other members of the university see him in action and learn something of his point of view. Whether in the case of the visual arts the object is actually attained is another matter, which is much less often discussed.

Outside the universities there is a wide variety of other relevant schemes. Thus Manchester now has not only an industrial design exhibit as part of its Building Centre, but also its own Civic Trust for the North West which is run by a committee of local industrialists and guaranteed by thirty firms subscribing £500 a year apiece; its present director was formerly a member of Graeme Shankland's planning team. Coventry has the only new municipal art gallery to be completed since the 1930s, besides Basil Spence's cathedral and some rather melancholy sculpture in the shopping centre. Leeds runs a picture loan service from its art gallery; Birmingham has a privately-sponsored kiosk called the Ikon Gallery now showing modern art in one of the open spaces of the Bull Ring shopping centre, and is building an ambitious Midland Arts Centre for Young People with theatres, cinema, a 'visual arts pavilion' and other facilities for the under-26s grouped together in a park; while, to come back to the capital, there is a very successful scheme for providing works of living art for London hospitals. This was started by the Almoner of the National Hospital for Nervous Diseases, who some ten years ago began borrowing pictures from artists for hanging in waiting-rooms, wards and corridors that had remained bare ever since the hospital was built. The Nuffield Foundation then allotted £2,000 (later increased to £3,000) a year so that pictures could be bought, and lent to other hospitals too; a committee was formed which appoints two buyers every year; and today there are twenty-seven hospitals co-operating and eleven more on the waiting list, while forty of the borrowed pictures have been sold to impressed visitors, to the not unnatural satisfaction of the artists. There is also one rather different London venture that is worth mention because of its bearing on the problems of urban renewal. Areas of previously down-at-heel Georgian housing, notably on the Northampton Estate in Canonbury and at Kennington, have been improved and redecorated since 1948, with the result that rents approximately trebled over fifteen years and individual houses sold at a profit of about £5,000 apiece. This indicates that such areas can be made to attract the better-off; preserving them can be not only aesthetically right but also economically rewarding.

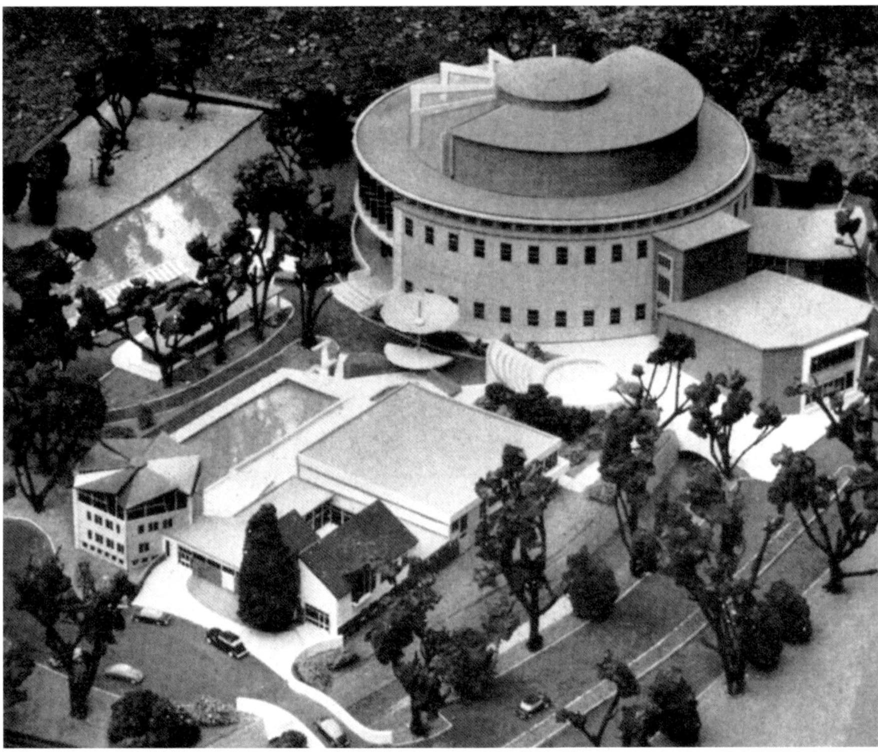

140 One of the best-known of recent English schemes: the Midlands Arts Centre for Young People, now under construction at Cannon Hill Park, Birmingham

Above all, London has progressed faster and faster than any provincial city in the public use of works of art. The sculptures, murals and mosaics that have gone up in the last twenty years or so, from the big Morley College murals by Keith Vaughan and Robert Medley to the Barbara Hepworth sculpture on John Lewis's Oxford Street store, are beyond counting, so that it is difficult now to go into any new office building without finding some example of modern art: not understood perhaps, and no doubt not liked, but accepted none the less, and indubitably there. The problem was well expressed by J. M. Richards in a survey of the new sculptures for the *Design and Industries Association Year Book* 1962–3, which incidentally illustrated

Geoffrey Clarke's big works on Thorn House and in the entrance to the Castrol building. He denied that the old aristocratic patrons

> always had a well-trained eye. It was often no more so than that of the modern businessman, the difference being that there used to be accepted standards to conform to. Now there are none, and the patron is thrown on his own resources. If he is sensible enough to know his own limitations he will seek advice – but whose advice?

The Greater London Council (ex-LCC) has been infinitely more enterprising than the Liverpool Corporation in commissioning works of art as part of new housing schemes and schools, and it has its own Advisory Committee on Art Acquisition (Patronage of the Arts). This body has existed since 1958 and is composed of equal numbers of Council members and members of the Arts Council's art panel, plus the Chief Architect and the art inspector from the Education Department who seems to have been the moving spirit. It plans schemes and nominates artists – normally to the Architect's, Housing or Education Committees, who may reject them – and has an allocation of £20,000 a year. Most of the works commissioned or bought have been for schools.[1] Mr Maurice Wheatley, the art inspector in question, told me that the resistance to purely abstract works is stronger among secondary than among primary schools, evidently because the former are at once more observant and more opinionated. In his view artists often work better for existing schools than in new buildings, where they deal only with the architects and make no contact with the people who are going to be in daily relations with the finished work. At the same time Mr Wheatley himself is responsible for buying prints and pictures for circulation round the schools; there is a library of art films, some of them made by teachers and financed by the Council; and about seventy schools are now taking circulating showcases from the Council of Industrial Design.

The great shift to public patronage, the new popularity of the arts among the young and the official acceptance of the modern idiom have all been paralleled elsewhere. What we are seeing in England is only part of a much wider movement which exists in all highly industrialized countries and spreads out from them as part of their influence on the rest of the world. Traditionally

[1] Artists commissioned in 1961 included Victor Pasmore (mural in Barnsbury Boys' Secondary School and mobile for Fairlawn School, Lewisham); Bernard Meadows, Ralph Brown, Karin Jonzen, George Ehrlich (all sculpture) and Robyn Denny (mosaic). Work was in progress by William Turnbull, Keith Vaughan, Robert Clatworthy, Uli Nimptsch and others. Details and locations are given in E. Lidbetter: 'An Experiment in Patronage', *Museums Journal*, London, June 1961, Vol. 61, no. 1, pp. 30–38.

we have been apt to lag behind the neighbours where the practice and enjoyment of the visual arts is concerned, but today this is hardly so, and the situation in a number of towns roughly comparable with Liverpool suggests,

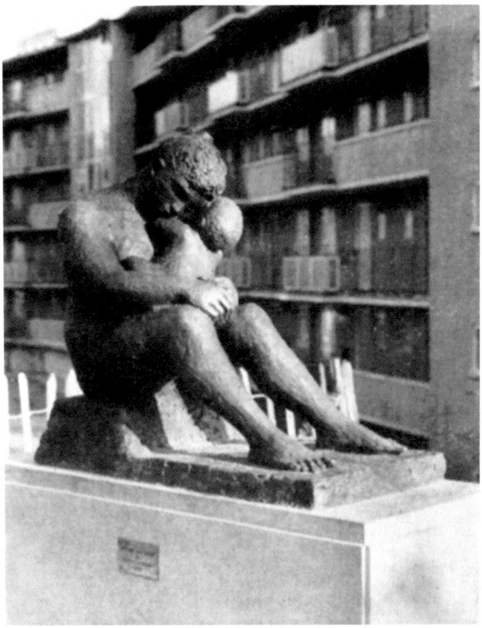

141 The London County Council art patronage scheme. A conservative work: Karin Jonzen's *Mother and Child* on the Sydenham Hill housing estate

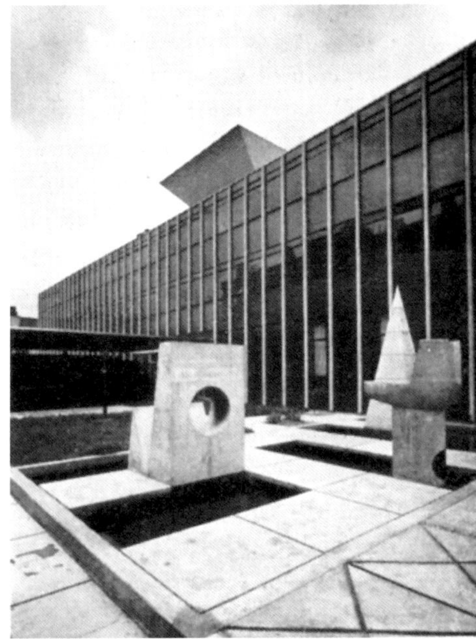

142 More advanced: the Rutherford school in Marylebone. Sculptural shapes by the architect, Leonard Manasseh

perhaps surprisingly, that the latter's effort and resources are now relatively good. Of course such comparisons cannot be exact; city finances, museum and art school administration, even the basis for reckoning art gallery attendance figures, all differ from one country to another, and much depends on the age of the town in question and its particular national status. None the less the details for such ports as Rotterdam, Marseilles, Boston and Genoa, all of which also have a population of about three-quarters of a million, as well as the smaller but still comparable Antwerp, do not wholly disgrace Liverpool. The galleries in Antwerp and Rotterdam are world-famous; they are older and better endowed than the Walker Gallery; yet they had fewer visitors over a comparable period. Only the privately-supported Boston Museum of Fine Arts, with six times the number of visitors and about twenty times the purchase money, implies a substantially different attitude to art. To quote the director of the Walker Art Gallery, who went there with his Chairman in the autumn of 1963: 'The fundamental impression is of a society using its art galleries far more intensively than we do.' Yet public art in Boston seems to be as neglected as in Liverpool, and there is no evidence of any strong local creative tradition.

In both Rotterdam and Antwerp however there has since the war been a development of public art, and particularly public sculpture, that makes even London's performance look trivial. In the former case this resulted naturally from the city's reconstruction after the bombing of 1940, and from the provision that sets aside 1 per cent of the cost of any public building for its decoration by works of art. At the beginning of 1963, for instance, there were eighty-two works listed there as commissioned or bought for new municipal buildings, mostly schools; the artists being all Dutch, though not necessarily local, and the average price in the £200–£600 range. A section of the art department (or *afd. Kunstzaken*) in the municipal offices is devoted to such projects, and where whole areas are concerned, as in a housing scheme, the percentage can be spent on the open spaces rather than the buildings themselves. This system however might not have caught the public imagination if it had not been for certain outstanding works, the two most important of which, Zadkine's *The Destroyed City* on the waterfront and Gabo's great abstract construction outside the Bijenkorf store, were due to private commissions. They and other sculptures by major international artists – Henry Moore's brick relief on the building centre and Marini's horseman on the Zuidplein – helped to stimulate a whole tradition of including sculpture or other forms of decoration in any new building whether official or not: the post office, insurance buildings, the new Unilever headquarters and so on. Undoubtedly Rotterdam is proud of the results. And as if that were not enough there is the municipally-financed Rotterdamse Kunststichting, which sets out to bring the public into contact with the arts by means of its own theatres and small galleries. There is the Kunstkring, an art club with about 1,000 members and a municipal subsidy of some 8,000 florins a year. On top of everything else the Ministry of Education will subsidize private purchases from certain approved exhibitions to the extent of 35 per cent of the price of the work.

At Antwerp, only sixty miles away and lying like Rotterdam (and Liverpool, for that matter), on a river estuary, there is a historic town with a great artistic tradition, a national gallery and comparatively little new building. Here in 1950 the first great open-air sculpture show was held in the Middelheim municipal park, some distance from the centre. This exhibition, which was the model for that at Battersea in London, has become a regular biennial event, and in 1958 it blossomed out experimentally into '*Het Beeld in de*

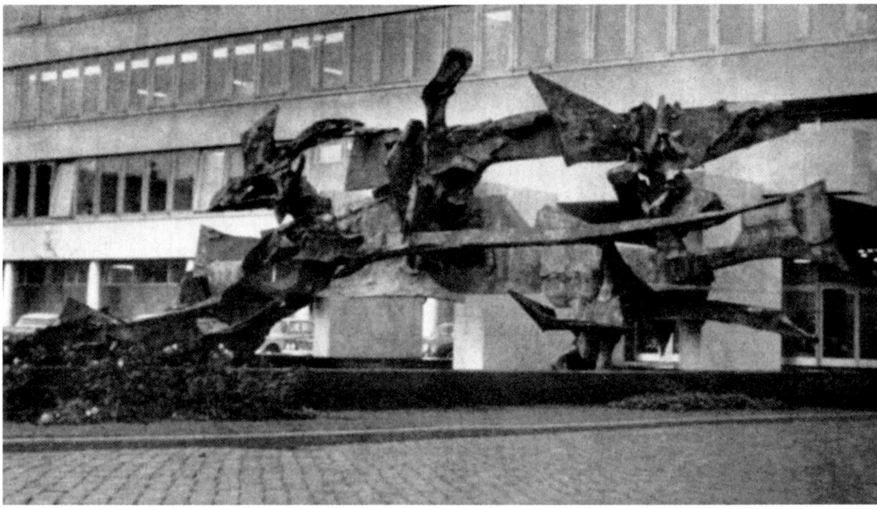

143 The example of Rotterdam, another bombed port. Wessel Couzijn's *Unity Embodied* outside the Unilever building

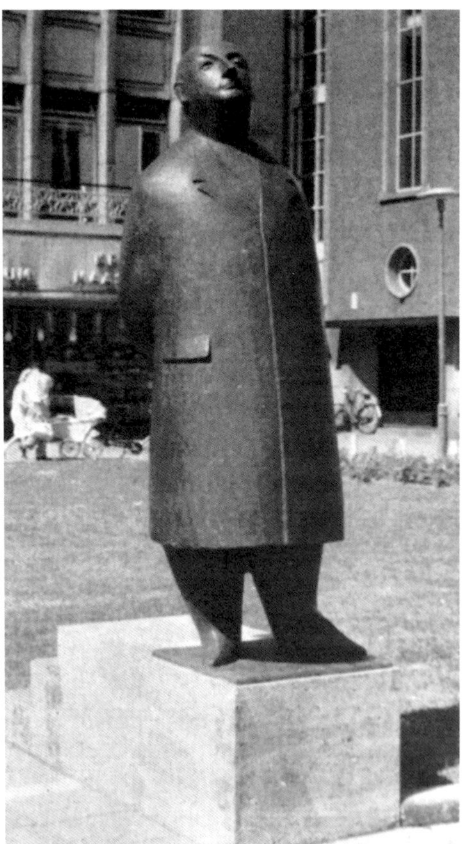

144 Oscar Wenckebach's *Jacques*. A popular public figure

Stad', an exhibition of similar works of modern sculpture scattered in streets, open places and other more or less suitable sites throughout the town. Simultaneously, starting in 1950, the municipality has built up the Middelheim park into an immense permanent open-air sculpture museum, with representative works by all the internationally best-known figures, including Moore, Hepworth, Reg Butler, Kenneth Armitage and others from this country. It is the only enterprise of its kind in the world, and the city spends some £10,000 a year adding to it. Leaving aside drawings and projects, it now contains over 200 works.

The closest to Liverpool of these continental ports is Hamburg, despite its much greater size, longer history and greater autonomy, and in recent years there has been a lively interchange of pop musicians between the two cities; it was indeed thanks to this that Stuart Sutcliffe was working there. The main art gallery, the Kunsthalle, is marvellously well off for nineteenth-century French paintings and modern works, mostly acquired when they were still quite cheap. There are good examples of the major impressionists, two particularly beautiful Corots, good Légers, Gris, Picasso, Munchs, Kokoschkas, Klee's *Der goldene Fisch*, a splendid Ensor still-life of 1896 and much else that no English provincial gallery could now hope to match. Similarly Bremen, with less than a third of the population, has two world-famous pictures in Monet's *Camille* and Manet's portrait of Zacharie Astruc; it also has a small museum devoted to Paula Modersohn-Becker, still little known in this country but a unique early twentieth-century painter and the outstanding artist of the local Worpswede school. But from our point of view the most remarkable thing in these two Hanseatic cities is Hamburg's collection of local scenes and subjects by distinguished modern artists. There are portraits and landscapes by Bonnard and Vuillard dating from 1913, a good Marquet and two slight but perfect Liebermanns of the Elbe. There is also a recent view of the city by Kokoschka and a portrait of Herr Brauer, its socialist president. (He is not a Lord Mayor, since Hamburg is not merely a city but a constituent province of the German Federal State.)

In Western Germany it is up to 2 per cent of public building costs, whether Federal or local, that has to be spent on decorative works of art, though there are many anomalies and variations as between provincial governments. In Hamburg, where there is a nine-man 'Art Commission' consisting of artists and officials, over 1,500 works have been commissioned in this way since the system began in 1951; the sum spent is now more than 1 million marks a year, and something like 130 local artists have recently benefited, with the lion's share going to about twenty-five. Likewise in France there have been regulations since 1951 laying down that 1 per cent

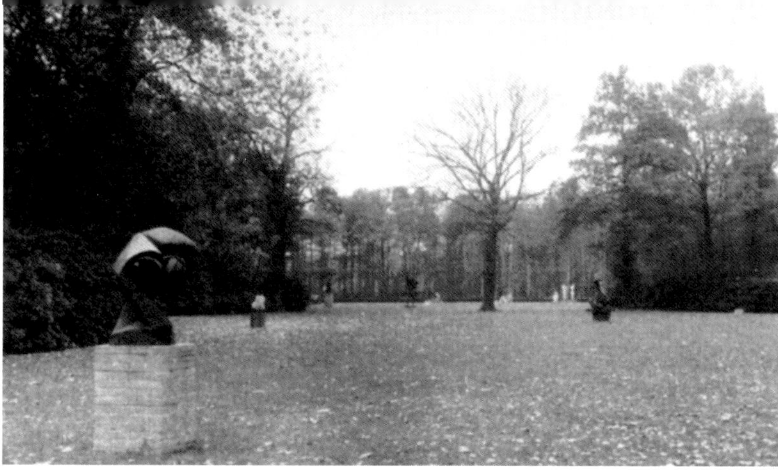

145 The example of Antwerp. The Middelheim sculpture park. (The work on the left is by Duchamp-Villon)

of the cost of any school or university building above a certain size must be applied to 'un ensemble de travaux de décoration', the artist responsible being nominated by the architect and approved by a special committee at the Ministry of Culture. It is said that there have been long delays in clinching such commissions[1] there, and that some two-fifths of the funds theoretically available have not in fact been used. None the less 6 million (new) francs were spent in 1962 – about £450,000 – and by the end of that year 467 schools had been dealt with and nine out of ten French sculptors were thought to be dependent on such jobs for their living.

Neither in France nor in Germany however, have the results been satisfactory, and on 19 January 1963 the French Minister of Culture made a statement in the Assembly proposing that the system should be changed. Instead of the frequently wretched works of art by living sculptors that had been more or less gummed on to so many new buildings he suggested concentrating on a few first-rate artists and using the rest of the money to provide schools with good reproductions of the (national) classics – works

[1] See the report in *L'Express*, Paris, 14 February 1963.

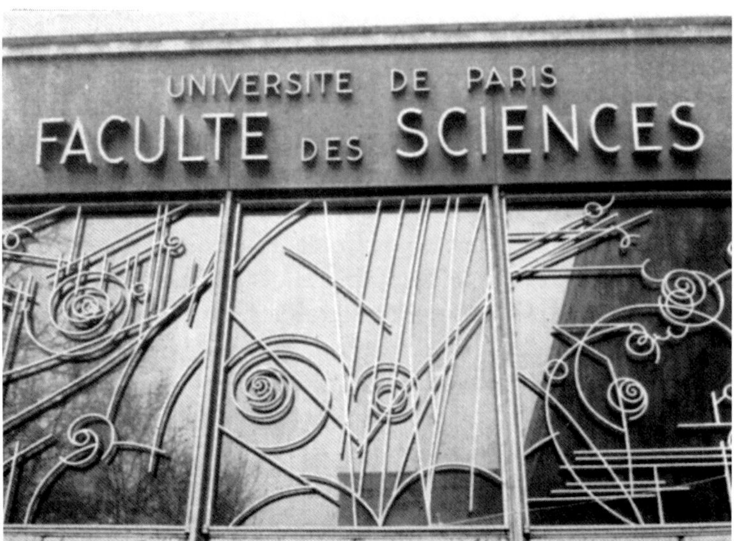

146 The French example. One result of the 1 per cent law; jazz decorations on the new science buildings for Paris University

specifically 'qui ont fait la gloire de la France'.[1] And true enough even an alleged 'ville d'art' like Barentin in the Seine-Maritime, which had the former Minister of Education André Marie as its member and accordingly contains public statues by Rodin and Bourdelle, a vast mosaic by Gromaire and much else, appears as a hotch-potch of largely irrelevant objects, dotted among ugly buildings. But intelligible as Malraux's suggestion was, it met fierce opposition from the artists, Zadkine (for one) arguing that 1 per cent was already too little, and did no more than cover the cost of a preliminary maquette.[2] And if the French had erred by putting their bad art on public show the opposite policy in Germany evidently worked no better. For part of the objection, according to a report by the Hamburg Rechnungshof (or committee on public expenditure) for 1962[3] was that

> so far the public has hardly had a chance to become aware of all these works, as they are mainly situated in places or buildings to which few people have access.

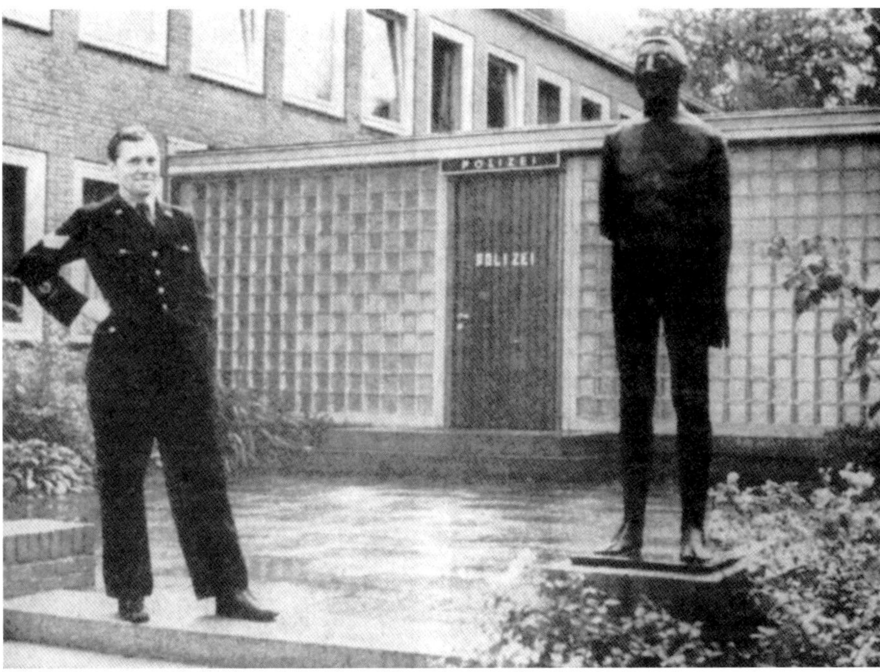

147 The example of Hamburg and the 2 per cent rule. The right art in the wrong place

[1] *Journal Officiel*. 19 January 1963. *Not* 'la gloire de l'humanité', note.

[2] This and twenty-five other individual or collective protests are quoted in *Arts* (Paris), 20–26 February 1963.

[3] Quoted by Gottfried Sello in *Die Zeit*, Hamburg, 24 November 1964.

Thus situated they might well be even less appreciated than they would be out in the open: a nude statue by the excellent sculptor Gustav Seitz, for instance, seemed hardly appropriate to a police station, where it was liable to be thought to portray a naked policeman. As a result of such anomalies the 2 per cent rule (or *Verwaltungsanordnung über Kunst am Bau*) was amended by the city senate early in 1966 to allow the pooling of the sums allotted, more concentration on the more important (or more suitable) buildings and – a complete innovation in Federal Germany, this – the employment of non-local and even foreign artists.[1] It will be for the Art Commission to decide whether a given building is to be embellished or the money put aside, though they are still not empowered to commission work for existing buildings or for open spaces.

Such instances are a warning that the mere multiplication of works of art is not enough; nor is greater generosity with public money. Even the employment of the most eminent artists, as insisted on by M. Malraux, is a much more precarious business than enthusiasts seem to imagine; the UNESCO building in Paris, for instance, includes big works by Moore and Picasso, Arp and Miró, but none of them seems to have been designed with much awareness of the site, the building or its probable atmosphere (a function of the people using it, their interests and activities) and once the prestige of such names has worn off a bit the works themselves are going to look misconceived.[2] This lesson is driven home by the experience of Rotterdam and Antwerp. On the face of it theirs sound like astonishingly enlightened projects, examples to be quoted wherever the question of public art is under discussion. That does not stop the realization from being in many ways depressing. The Middelheim sculpture park is a solemn place, and there is something aimlessly funereal about the discreet placing of the statues among lawns, shrubberies and trees; sculptures conceived *in vacuo* and designed for galleries or competition juries look sadly out of place in so elegiac a setting. In Rotterdam the Zadkine is, like much romantic sculpture, a rather dated work, but at least it is a successful public symbol in the way that the Epstein at Liverpool should be but is not. The Gabo, if the spectator can forget the pretentious explanations that get tangled around such structures, is a sheer delight. But there is also a frightful lot of mediocre work on mediocre buildings, and the creative excitement, the new ideas and interests that ought to spring up as a result of so huge a scheme, are not in evidence.

[1] See Herr Sello's article 'Keine Angst vor Henry Moore' in the same paper of 29 April 1966.

[2] Already pointed out in Professor Edgar Wind's *Art and Anarchy*; Faber, London, 1963, pp. 94–5. 'In this building devoted to the cultural work of the United Nations the arts loiter about the place without function, distracted and disunited.'

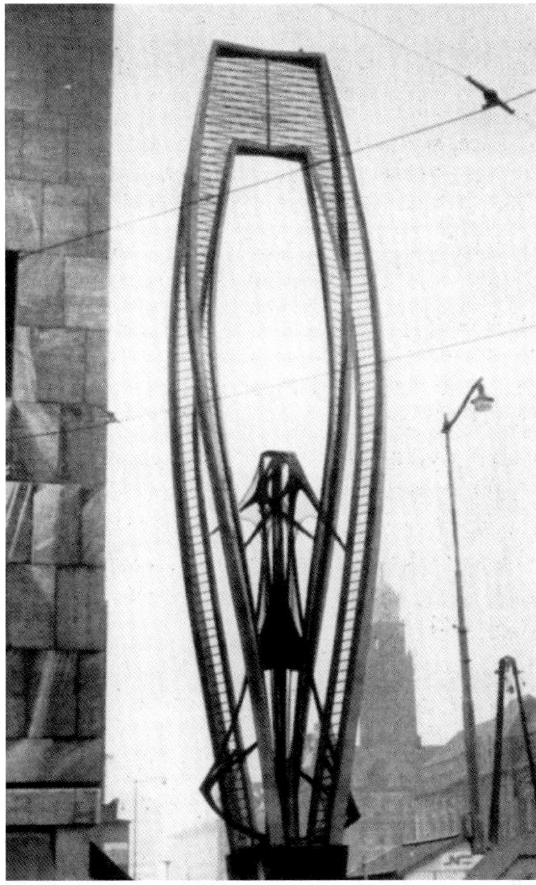

148 Rotterdam's masterpiece. Naum Gabo's great construction outside the Bijenkorf store. (The derrick beyond, like the sheds, was connected with the building of the underground railway)

If Rotterdam were a success the Dutch artists would once again be the liveliest in the world. The fact that they are not shows that something has gone wrong.

Perhaps there has been too much tendency since 1945 to think simply in terms of patronage: to treat the problem as one of finding new patrons in the state, the local authorities and the great industrial and social institutions, to take the place of the self-glorifying monarch and the rich private collector. Abroad, provisions like the percentage rule have been thought up less because there is a real public demand for embellishment, or a school of artists whom it would be criminal not to employ on it, than as a means of giving people jobs. Too little distinction is made between those whose style and talents are suited to such work and those who are not. This applies whether the public patron chooses, like the French Ministry of Culture, to go only for the most eminent artists, or prefers to distribute his funds more evenly and thinly. The great lesson of the Baroque has not been learned: that it is not necessarily the best individual works of art that fit best into an architectural scheme. It is still common, even among architects, to think of decoration as something to be glued on to the building once finished; neither the kind of integration practised at Peterlee (where Victor Pasmore was a con-

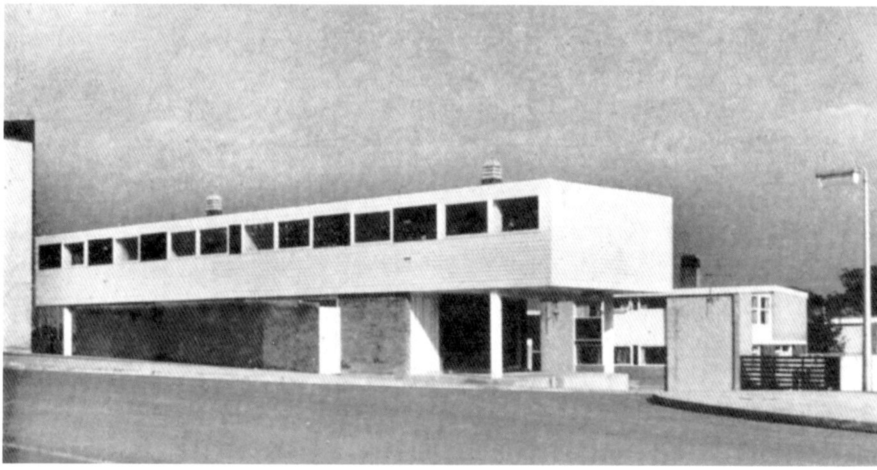

149 A building at Peterlee in County Durham, where Victor Pasmore helped with the visual planning

sultant from the first, helping to decide even the siting of the houses), nor the possibility of shorter-lived, more changeable and adaptable forms of decoration have yet been much explored. In this country concepts like 'arts centre' and 'regional federation'[1] have passed into our cultural shopping lists without any very precise definition of what they involve. It is not clear, for instance, whether an arts centre is a centre primarily for creating the arts or simply for consuming them. Creation, as opposed to interpretation, does not benefit from having the audience on the spot; the studio and the gallery are best kept separate. Nor indeed is there any reason why the consumer institutions should all be centralized, unless this simplifies their introduction to cities which (unlike Liverpool) lack them. Ideas like the arts centre now seem to be bounced by our cultural planners like a football for rival players to tussle for and hope to kick in a particular direction;[2] there is no

[1] On 20 June 1966 a meeting of interested groups under the chairmanship of the Lord Mayor of Liverpool decided to set up a Liverpool Arts Association which would act as such a federation, and a working party was formed to plan it. The visual acts were not at first represented. One object of a federation is to permit the state to distribute funds which it is not allowed to give to individual organizations or groups. What the others are remains slightly unclear. It is apparently less difficult to set up new cultural administrative bodies than to remove such restrictions on the existing ones.

[2] Thus in Liverpool the Bluecoat Society would like to be regarded as an arts centre, while an independent claim for an arts centre of a primarily theatrical nature has been put forward from a

knowing where they may end up. Above all, the immense problems of the public's remoteness from much modern art and the artists' frequent indifference to its views have been left to solve themselves. The new patrons seem to think that they have a duty to be passive – as if patrons in the great ages of art had ever been that – and that there is nothing incongruous in introducing gallery-, even Biennale-type art into a lay public's daily lives. Such failure to face obvious difficulties, though not bound to be disastrous, is fair neither to the public nor to the artists, and generates among both parties an unfortunate sense that the whole position is false and slightly ridiculous. Getting the money and establishing the administrative framework are only the start of it. The development of a stimulating climate depends on other things.

Merseyside Arts Centre Association organized by the Royal Institution and Merseyside Unity Theatre. The Town Clerk has suggested the formation of a number of smaller centres to serve outlying areas as well. The City Centre Plan proposes a new arts centre building behind the Bluecoat Chambers to meet various currently unsatisfied needs. In my view it might be better if the magic words 'arts centre' were left out of such discussions.

9 : POINTS OF DOCTRINE

The weakness of the policy of the last twenty years is that it rests on assumptions which are very seldom discussed. Admittedly this saves a great deal of argument, and to those who feel that the assumptions are on the whole the right ones it may seem safer to establish them on grounds of authority, snobbery, faith and (strongest of all) custom than to thrash them out before a possibly unsympathetic public. None the less it is wrong, because under the surface they become widely and uneasily doubted, above all at a certain distance from our taste-making metropolis. 'The visual arts are integral to a civilization'[1]; 'in any civilized community the arts and associated amenities . . . must occupy a central place';[2] 'support for the living arts';[3] 'the needs of the arts';[4] 'the maintenance, improvement and development of artistic taste';[5] 'the healthy progress of artistic practice and appreciation':[6] phrases like these from the basic scriptures of the previous chapter obviously beg enormous questions. We are taking too much for granted, and artists and public alike know that we are, and once we start doing so it is difficult to know where to stop. The tacit assumptions breed an equally tacit[7] suspicion that the whole edifice is founded on make-believe; it becomes a castle in the air with no visible connection to our individual problems and hopes.

The rethinking of the relationships between art and the rest of life seems to go in waves, usually in response to the stimulus of great political events. Thus the French Revolution, taking up certain ideas of Rousseau's and Diderot's, evolved the notion of giant popular festivals and made the Louvre into the first great public gallery. The early nineteenth-century reformers in England saw art philanthropically, as a popular educational force; it was also they who most strongly pressed for a proper system of training in design for utilitarian ends. 1848, with its second, abortive outbreak of revolutions

[1] *The Arts Enquiry. The Visual Arts*, p. 42.

[2] *A Policy for the Arts. First Steps*, paragraph 14.

[3] Ibid, paragraph 25.

[4] *Help for the Arts.* Paragraph 1.

[5] Constitution for the North-Eastern Association for the Arts. Clause 2(a).

[6] *The Arts Council of Great Britain. The 19th Annual Report.* 1963–4, p. 13.

[7] It may be starting to find its tongue. See Marghanita Laski's radio talk 'Why spend public money on art?' in *The Listener*, London 8 April 1965, pp. 507–9. Miss Laski's point is that before we spend public money on anything we should know as far as possible what we are doing and why we are doing it.

throughout Europe, brought the triumph of Realism in French art: that more truthful and down-to-earth attitude to real-life subjects, which was oddly (and so far as we know unconsciously) reflected in the rise of the Pre-Raphaelites here. Something of the same interaction of aesthetics and politics could be seen again after the First World War, in the immediate artistic impact of the German and Russian revolutions, and, by a sharp but not wholly unnatural reaction, in the disastrous Nazi and Stalinist art policies that followed in the 1930s. The Second World War too had its repercussions in the shape both of the organizational developments outlined in the last chapter and of the doctrine of 'commitment' associated with Jean-Paul Sartre. But the longest and in many ways the most interesting of these periods of narrowing of the gap between art and society was that which followed the establishment of popular education in England and the Third Republic in France. Between about 1870 and 1905 a great new movement developed for the dissemination of the arts; both the arts and crafts movement and the new approach to design preached by Morris contained an element of social philosophy, while posters, coloured reproductions, photographic block-making and the first half-tone art books sprang up as new methods of popularization. It was then that bodies like the WEA, the Universités Populaires and the Russian Proletkult were started and the European Socialist parties turned into mass organizations, and as a result the social and artistic ideas of those years are still a part of traditional left-wing and popular educational thinking. All these waves are fairly distinct. What each threw up can be clearly recognized among the strange mixture of deadwood and treasure that now lies on the beach.

The oldest and commonest social use for art, once the magic and the sanctity had gone out of it, was to symbolize and celebrate: a religious figure or idea, a ruler, a military victory or, with Jacques-Louis David after 1789, a popular revolution. This concept was extended to apply not only to the individual work of art but to everything to do with the art of a given period. Thus the artists' committee of the Paris Commune voted on 15 April 1871 to set up 'vast rooms' for teaching and to circulate reproductions of masterpieces and 'images of morality and intelligence' to town halls as a contribution 'to the splendours of the future and the universal Republic'. 'Just as one says "le style c'est l'homme",' so Courbet's uncle is supposed to have told him many years earlier, "one ought to be able to say 'l'art c'est la société".'[1] This identification of the two familiar concepts was a new idea in the nine-

[1] Quoted in Champfleury's *Souvenirs et portraits de jeunesse*. Paris 1872, p. 182.

teenth century, though it is much the same notion as underlies Roscoe's doctrine of art in a mercantile city. The people who followed Roscoe however were more concerned with the purely economic arguments for cultivating the visual arts. In France this was taken for granted: by 1836 there were eighty provincial art schools there, and the connection between artistic training and a high standard of manufacture and workmanship had been clearly seen ever since Colbert's time. The English agitation for something of the same sort was associated with Radicals like Joseph Hume, Ewart and Wyse, and particularly with the great northern cities: Haydon in 1839 was clearly thinking of Liverpool and Manchester when he mooted 'a confederation of the leading towns to join in a petition for Schools of Design and State patronage for Art'.[1] The English art schools were subsequently set up, but the problem remained. More than half a century later Conway gave one of his Slade lectures on the subject of 'The Practical Value of Art':

> The plain hard-headed man-of-business in England may some day, possibly, begin to entertain a suspicion that the question, how to improve the artistic quality of our manufactures, is a practical question of the most solid importance.[2]

During the nineteenth century the idea of art as celebration became inextricably bound up with that of art as a moral force, as Dean Farrar put it, 'to refine, to elevate, to brighten, not only the palace of the noble but the cottage of the poor'.[3] This is a concept which has caused great trouble and suffering in the wrong hands, and to some extent it is still with us. We in this country associate it above all with Ruskin, to whom the Divine, the Good and the Beautiful seemed almost interchangeable, so that a fine work of art was at once a revelation of the deity and an encouragement to the good life. Morris, Watts and other enlightened art proselytizers of the end of the century took it over from him; thus Morris in 1879:

> in my mind, it is not possible to dissociate art from morality, politics and religion. Truth in these great matters of principle is one.[4]

In France the identification was made a great deal earlier; witness Diderot's judgment of the (to us often cloyingly sentimental) pictures of Greuze – the 'Jeune fille qui pleure son oiseau mort' in the 1765 Salon, for instance. It reappears in the admonition of the French revolutionary Société Populaire et Républicaine des Arts to the artists that their job was:

[1] *Life of Benjamin Robert Haydon*. 2nd edition. Longmans, London 1853, vol. III, p. 106.

[2] In his *The Domain of Art*; John Murray, London 1901, p. 87.

[3] From his sermon to the Liverpool congress of the National Association for the Advancement of Art in 1888, printed as a preface to its *Transactions*.

[4] From his lecture 'The Art of the People' in Birmingham Town Hall, published as a pamphlet in Birmingham that year and reprinted in G. D. H. Cole's centenary volume *William Morris*, Nonesuch Press, London 1948, pp. 534–5.

> to choose subjects tending to instruct, to bring about a moral recognition, to inspire love of the country and enthusiasm for liberty.

– though this advice seems in the event to have carried little weight. And it fitted well with the strange republican utopianism that preceded and overlapped the mainly non-moralising realism of the mid-nineteenth century. Thus the left-wing Abbé Lamennais in his *Esquisse d'une philosophie* of 1841 saw art as expressing the ideology and social forms of its period and argued that it should now become the prophet of 'the religion of the future'. This part symbolic, part educative or even propagandist view of art found echoes in the great dissemination movement around 1900, just as the French Second Republic's moral-symbolic decorative projects by Chenavard found their successors in the Third Republic and Puvis de Chavannes. It underlay that early socialist mirage of the perfect society glimpsed in Morris's *News from Nowhere* and the Belgian Emile Vandervelde's references to 'la cité future': the 'cathedral of Socialism' which was the symbol of the Bauhaus in its first years. It was inherent in the arts and crafts movement, in the work of men like Walter Crane and Eric Gill, and in the readiness of Bonnard and Vuillard and the Nabis, unlike their Impressionist predecessors, to turn to decorative art. It was also the very essence of Tolstoy's artistic theories.

At the same time it was wide open to use or abuse by men whose primary interests were not artistic at all but political or religious. Under Napoleon III, for instance, the new realism in the arts was seen as subversive and immoral: 'for him,' wrote one of the Imperial cultural officials, Arsène Houssaye, 'everything was a means of governing'.[1] Although it was the emperor's policy outwardly to encourage the arts (the great exhibitions being of particular importance in speeding up European cross-fertilization) his art adviser Count Nieuwekerke was determined to stop 'eccentricity' and 'false vocations'. 'France is fertile,' he said at the opening of the 1863 Salon – the year of mass rejections and the Salon des Refusés – 'and her artists are the first in the world, just like her soldiers.'[2] Flaubert may have been acquitted of blasphemy in *Madame Bovary*, but the court that tried him took good care to denounce any idea of Realism,

> which would be the negation of the good and the beautiful and, by giving rise to works offensive to eye and mind alike, would commit continual offences against public morality and right living.[3]

The whole realist trend was subversive, and when Millet was rejected in

[1] Houssaye: *Confessions* II, p. 428.

[2] Quoted from *Le Moniteur* for 7 July 1863 in Fernand Desnoyers: *Le Salon des Refusés;* Azur Dutil, Paris 1863, p. 85.

[3] *Gazette des Tribunaux*, 9 February 1857, quoted on p. 435 of the Editions de Cluny edition of *Madame Bovary*. Paris 1936.

1863 he assumed that it was as a socialist[1], which in fact he was not. A similar but exactly contrary distortion of art in that period can be seen in the socialist philosopher Proudhon, whose *Du principe de l'art* of 1865 treats art as essentially propaganda. Where the existing state was using it as an instrument of repression, he argued, it ought rather to become the embodiment of society's aims, 'an idealist representation of ourselves and of nature, with a view to the moral and physical perfecting of our species'.[2] In both views what mattered was first the message, the subject, secondly the artist's respectful or critical approach to it.

At the end of the century Max Nordau evolved his unfortunate concept of *Entartung*[3] or 'degeneration': the notion that artistic movements could be psychologically healthy or sick. This was all that was needed to give the moral interpretation of art that final twist which we find in the reactionary doctrines of the 1930s. Both in Soviet Russia and in Nazi Germany a decade of officially-supported utopianism, experiment and flirtation with abstractionism and machine art was followed by its equally official condemnation as a symptom of social disease. Modern art was 'unhealthy'; depending on whether Zhdanov or Hitler was speaking it was seen as a symptom of Western bourgeois decadence or as 'art Bolshevism'; in other words it was identified with the regime's bogey-man, whatever colour he might be. In both cases alike it was clearly the politician's duty to stop it, to promote art with a 'content' or obviously intelligible subject and message, and to set the artists, as a disciplined task force, to glorifying what he saw as society's proper ethics and ideals. These naturally proved to be the historical forces he himself represented, the policies of which he was spokesman and, by an all too easy extension, the spokesman's own person. Duration apart, there was only one real difference between the two repressive and authoritarian aesthetic systems: the Nordic, racial, anti-semitic element which was present in Nazi but not in Soviet art. Even this was only a perversion of Proudhon's principle of representing idealized human specimens; the Nazis wanted blond heroes, and that is what the artists had to depict.

The abuses invited by the socio-ethical view of art have led at one time and another to its total rejection. Already in the 1850s Champfleury was protesting that

[1] Letter from Millet to Sensier, quoted in Moreau-Nelaton: *Millet raconté par lui-même*, Paris 1921, II, p. 129.

[2] Proudhon: *Du principe de l'art;* Garnier, Paris 1865, p. 198.

[3] *Degeneration;* Heinemann, London 1895. Nordau's principal degenerates were the Pre-Raphaelites, the French symbolists, Tolstoy, Wagner, Maeterlinck, Ibsen, Zola and Nietzsche. Since he finds symptoms of serious psychological abnormality in these and many other outstanding figures of the period it becomes difficult to see who, apart from Turgenev, he approves of.

> It's neither painting's nor music's function to expound social systems; as soon as painting turns to education it ceases to be painting. It becomes a pulpit which is depressing and disagreeable to look at, for it is a pulpit without a preacher in it.[1]

And Zola, writing a year after Proudhon's book had appeared:

> His *rational art*, his brand of realism, is really just the negation of art, the tedious illustration of philosophical clichés. My kind of art on the other hand is a negation of society, an affirmation of the individual, divorced from all rules and social obligations.[2]

Yet Zola was the outstanding social novelist of his time[3] and Champfleury was not only one of the founders of realism and the leader of the Diderot revival but also the first systematic student of the popular arts. There is an apparent inconsistency here which we find also in the position of Sir Herbert Read, who argues that art is purely autonomous; that its symbols symbolize nothing outside the artist himself; that it

> is not and never has been subordinate to moral values. Moral values are social values; aesthetic values are human values.[4]

– yet feels that it is a great social force none the less. Art in his view does lead to moral improvement, even if it is fatal to judge it by that; it does effect changes in the texture and quality of a society; and although Tolstoy is wrong in thinking that it reduces violence it could none the less fulfil humanity's needs for 'a principle of strife or rivalry which is not mutually destructive . . . but which nevertheless gives the moral equivalent, the *courageous tone* of war'.[5] Thinkers whose prime concern is with the arts, it is perhaps fair to say, will fight any moralist or politician for art's right to be independent, while admitting to themselves that it is not.

Art as a form of education for all citizens was one of the basic principles of Plato's Republic, but for the greater part of the nineteenth century the practical, economic view of the matter prevailed; indeed in 1852 art schools in this country were put under a new section of the Board of Trade called 'the Department of Practical Art'. In the art education of that time, writes Professor Quentin Bell,

[1] Champfleury: *Grandes figures d'hier et d'aujourd'hui.* Paris 1861, pp. 236–7. From the section on Courbet.

[2] Zola: *Mes Haines.* Nouvelle édition. Charpentier, Paris 1879, p. 39.

[3] Not however to the author of *Eric, or Little by Little*, who in his sermon to the Liverpool Art Congress spoke of him as having 'prostituted the gift of genius to the service of corruption'.

[4] From his essay on 'Society and Culture' (Lecture delivered at York in 1946) in *The Grass Roots of Art*, New edition, Faber, London 1955, p. 93.

[5] Ibid., p. 44.

> The curriculum had nothing to do with aesthetic feeling, nothing to do with nature or the imagination; it was established not for the benefit of the pupils but for that of their prospective employers.[1]

To those who associated art with wider human concerns, whether social or religious, this was an impossibly stunting attitude: harmful not only to the art students but to education in general. It was Ruskin above all who changed it, with his constant flow of noble prose in favour of a less mundane approach. 'Art,' wrote G. F. Watts in 1880, 'pressed into the service of general education, as once it was of religion, might again be great;' and in 1885 Ebenezer Cooke published the two articles on child art which Read sees as the first symptoms of the modern outlook.[2] This was the period of the foundation of the Roscoe Chair and the Walker Gallery, of the move of the Liverpool College of Art into its present building and of the pictures for schools scheme sponsored by T. C. Horsfall and the Manchester Museums. In 1876 the Kyrle Society was founded 'to bring beauty home to the people' by providing works of art for hospitals, workmen's clubs and parish rooms; by 1888 it had eight or nine provincial branches.[3] Nor was it all just a great educational movement in which art was, as it were, getting caught up. There was also a feeling that the arts might be 'healthful influences'[4] for the industrial proletariat (as against drink); that they might be a 'graceful source of recreation': a hope which had already been implicit in the founding of the Mechanics' Institutes half a century earlier. Views to this effect were expressed by Watts in his paper for the Edinburgh Art Congress of 1889, where he begged 'the heads of firms, often themselves men of culture, lovers and collectors of art', to start 'encouraging their workmen to be artistic.'[5]

For all his agreement with Watts, this was much what Morris at the same Congress called 'a kind of mumbo-jumbo fetishism for the working class. . . . Just the sort of tommy rot that curates talk about religion at mothers' meetings, and Oxford professors say about education at Cutlers' Feasts.'[6] Influenced more by Ruskin's social and political writings than by his ideas of art, Morris began lecturing in 1878, and from the first he spoke as a practising craftsman and in the name not of paternalism but of the working man. From

[1] Quentin Bell: *The Schools of Design;* Routledge, London 1963, p. 261.

[2] Quoted in part in Read: *Education Through Art;* Faber, London 1943, pp. 167–8, and originally published in the *Journal of Education*, December 1885, pp. 462–5, and January 1886, pp. 12–15.

[3] According to its statement in the *Transactions of the National Association for the Advancement of Art* for that year.

[4] *George Frederic Watts.* Vol. III, 'His Writings', Macmillan, London 1912, p. 264.

[5] Ibid., p. 265.

[6] Quoted from Bruce Glasier in E. P. Thompson: *William Morris Romantic to Revolutionary;* Lawrence and Wishart, London, 1955, p. 647.

Ruskin's *The Stones of Venice* he took the picture of the workman in the heyday of Gothic architecture, happily and unselfconsciously contributing his best to a great work of art, and he saw a revival of 'the decorative arts' as a means of bringing back this lost pleasure in the things we use and the things we make. Leisure, to Morris, was not so much a gap to be filled by the consumption of art as an impending stimulus to its production. What he cared about was the barrier that had grown up between artist and craftsman – a point that can be found again in Walter Gropius's original Bauhaus programme of 1919 – and the need for what he called 'intelligent popular art'.[1] By this however, he meant something a good deal more remote than had Champfleury, whose *Histoire de l'imagerie populaire*, his *Chansons populaires des provinces de France* and *Histoire de la caricature moderne* all appeared in the 1860s; for to Morris the Renaissance was 'the fruit of the five centuries of free and popular art which preceded it, and not of the rise of commercialism which was contemporaneous with it':[2] an opinion that incidentally shows how far he was from the Roscoe doctrine that had prevailed in Liverpool. 'The absence of popular art,' he told the readers of the *Manchester Examiner* in 1883

> from modern times is more disquieting and grievous to hear from this reason than for any other, that it betokens that fatal division of men into the cultivated and the degraded classes which competitive commerce has bred and fosters.[3]

Unfortunately he let his understanding of that division become swamped in his 'hatred of modern civilization',[4] thus unwittingly making a further division in the decorative arts between industry and craft. It was not really healed until the Bauhaus began its collaboration with industry in the 1920s.

'In theory', said a leading article in *The Times* of 26 November 1889, 'we all acknowledge that it is desirable to bring art home to the masses of the people'. The movement for the diffusion of art which spread out from England towards the end of the century was immense; its manifestations followed one another thick and fast. None the less it was compounded of

[1] Morris: *Selected Writings and Designs;* Pelican, London 1962, p. 93. From the lecture on 'The Lesser Arts', delivered in 1878.

[2] From 'Gothic Architecture', a lecture to the Arts and Crafts Exhibition Society. Morris: *Stories in Prose. Stories in Verse. Shorter Poems. Lectures and Essays.* Edited by G. D. H. Cole. Nonesuch Press, London 1948, p. 25.

[3] *The Letters of William Morris to his Family and Friends.* Edited by Philip Henderson, Longmans, London 1950, pp. 165–6.

[4] *Selected Writings and Designs*, p. 36. From 'How I Became a Socialist', originally published in *Justice*, 16 January, 1894. Morris's admirers today tend to play this hatred down, but I think it has to be admitted. See also the lecture on 'Gothic Architecture' quoted above.

some very contradictory elements. There is all the difference in the world between the improving effects of looking at art and the self-realization of creative work; between instruction and fun; between the charitable distribution of the arts as a good social influence (ranging from therapeutic tonic to political propaganda) and their conscious annexation by groups who have been denied them. Morris in particular treated art not as a mere social benefit but as a basic right which ought to be 'felt to be as necessary to man as his daily bread,[1] and a number of continental socialists followed him in this: Steinlen's teacher Georges Renard in Switzerland, for instance, and Emile Vandervelde, the Belgian Socialist leader.[2] In 1896 Edgar Steiger, editor of the party illustrated weekly *Neue Welt*, told the German Socialist conference at Gotha that

> We want to take all that's good and beautiful from former social systems, plus the whole capacity to enjoy it, and lay it before the working people. . . . So that we may all become complete men.[3]

Against that there was the French *Art pour Tous* society visiting London on 14 July 1904 and being received at establishments like Buckingham Palace, the Westminster Deanery, and the Association of Conservative Clubs; there were wealthy art philanthropists like Philip Rathbone and the Earl of Carlisle; there were for that matter R. A. M. Stevenson's uplifting Liverpool ladies. A very successful society was formed at the Mannheim Kunsthalle a few years later which organized lectures in the gallery (seventy-eight in the winter of 1913–14, with an average attendance of 455), bought works of art and ran an annual lottery whose winners could have them at a tenth of the price. Aimed at 'the moulding of a New Man',[4] it was called the 'Freie Bund zur Einbürgerung der Kunst': the association 'for giving citizenship to art'.

Part of this whole movement to tighten the links between art and society has always been the idea of public art, which would get out of the museums

[1] *Selected Writings and Designs*, p. 37.

[2] Renard's article 'L'Art et la vie de tous les jours' in *L'Art pour tous*, Paris, vol. II (1904), p. 343, cites Ruskin and Morris as originators of the notion of beauty as a fundamental human right. Vandervelde's lecture of the same year on 'Le Socialisme et les artistes', reprinted in his *Essais socialistes;* Alcan, Paris 1906, likewise quotes Morris and complains that 'art doesn't exist for the great mass of the workers'. Being harder-headed than Morris, he argued that it was more important to concentrate on socialized industry rather than the artist-artisan with his rich clients, and he recognized that the workers tend to like conventional and second-hand forms. (See his p. 362.)

[3] *Protokoll über die Verhandlungen des Parteitages.* Berlin 1896, first day.

[4] *Die Kunstmuseen und das deutsche Volk;* Kurt Wolff, Munich 1919, p. 31. From Fritz Wichert's essay 'Die bildende Kunst als Mittel zur Selbstgestaltung des Volkes', which describes the Mannheim system.

and make its appearance, whether independently or under the wing of architecture, in our everyday life. Thus when David was a member of the Convention he proposed a Palace of Equality, which would be decorated with frescoes and sculptures, while in England Haydon, that enthusiastic admirer of Liverpool, spent much of his time and energy in campaigning for great public decorative schemes. Listening to the Prince Regent opening parliament in the old House of Lords in November 1812, he 'conceived a grand series of designs to adorn the ample sides of the house . . . the horrors of anarchy – then the injustice of democracy – then the cruelty of despotism – the infamies of revolution – then the beauty of justice – and to conclude with the limited monarchy and its blessings'.[1] It was his barely disinterested keenness to execute this plan – first for the proposed Waterloo monument in 1815, then for the new Houses of Parliament after the fire of 1831 – that led him to lobby continually for 'moderate and judicious'[2] public art patronage of a kind previously unknown in this country, and he seized with delight on the report of the Committee for the Purchase of the Elgin Marbles as the first official admission of how the fine arts

> had contributed to the reputation, character and dignity of every Government by which they had been encouraged, and how intimately they were connected with the advancement of everything valuable in science, literature and art.[3]

He had hopes of Brougham, but Wellington in his common-sense way told him that 'No minister could go to parliament with a proposition for a vote for a picture to be painted, and there can therefore be no such encouragement here as there is in other countries. . . .'[4] Haydon of course was interested in British artists, and primarily in British historical artists (which meant himself), but the example in most men's minds at that time was Munich, where between 1819 and 1840 King Ludwig employed the Nazarene artists Schnorr and Cornelius on large-scale frescoes.[5] The Ewart Committee of 1835–6 held that the use of sculpture and painting in great public buildings was worthy of a civilized nation; a Select Committee was appointed in 1841 to 'take into consideration the promotion of the fine arts in this country in connection with the rebuilding of the Houses of Parliament',[6] and began

[1] *Life of Benjamin Robert Haydon*. Second edition. Longmans, London 1853, Vol. I, p. 207.

[2] Ibid. Vol. II, p. 60.

[3] Ibid. Vol. II, p. 57. This passage was included in Haydon's petition to the House of Commons which Brougham presented in 1823.

[4] Ibid. Vol. II, pp. 287–8. Entry for 12 October 1830.

[5] Illustrated and discussed in Keith Andrews: *The Nazarenes;* Clarendon Press, Oxford 1964. Chapter V.

[6] Samuel and Richard Redgrave: *A Century of Painters of the English School*. London 1866, Vol. II. p. 515. From Chapter XV, on 'Fresco-Painting and State Patronage.'

by flirting with the idea of using the Germans. Promoted to the status of Royal Commission, this committee pottered on for about twenty years, issuing thirteen reports and holding four public competitions; and the final results, including the suicide of the bitterly disappointed Haydon, were not happy. It is interesting that Schnorr, who felt that German artists would do the job better, was none the less in favour of restricting it to Englishmen. He argued that this would both express our particular 'artistic national culture' and at the same time have a more stimulating influence on the younger artists here.[1]

In an appendix to Haydon's posthumous memoirs Watts, one of the Westminster prize winners, commented that it would further 'public instruction and artistic training' if the State undertook to decorate all public buildings, including 'town halls, national schools and even railway stations'.[2] He suggested that art students might take Flaxman's designs and enlarge them (e.g. on the walls of Eton College) and he himself volunteered to paint the great hall at Euston; 'the architect expressed great alarm about it'.[3] This echoes a scheme which makes fleeting appearances in the history of nineteenth-century French art, for the provision of murals in stations and other non-official buildings. The originator of this is supposed to have been the utopian socialist (Fourierist) Victor Considérant who put it forward in his paper *Démocratie Pacifique* during the 1848 revolution; he also appealed to the artists to make his proposed 'phalansteries' (or pre-Corbusier communal blocks housing 2,000 people) into something finer than the cathedrals, and hoped that every man would become an artist.[4] Apparently there were actual negotiations about this time for Delacroix and Decamps to decorate the side walls of a Paris terminus.[5] Courbet and Champfleury both seem to have been aware of the idea, which from our present point of view is more interesting than either the vast symbolic projects of Chenavard or the real mural masterpiece of the period: Delacroix's frescoes in the Paris church of S. Sulpice. For Champfleury saw very early on that 'the nineteenth century has nowhere found an architectural style except in its building of market or exhibition halls and railways',[6] and pointed out that 'industry . . . has more space at its disposal than have the cathedrals, and it is waiting for an artist capable of

[1] Letter to Eastlake of 23 February, 1842, quoted in *The Nazarenes*, p. 85.

[2] *Life of Benjamin Robert Haydon*. Second edition 1853. Appendix by Watts on the public employment of artists. Vol. III, pp. 375, 372. Watts was a friend of Tom Taylor, the book's editor. Taylor was Thackeray's successor as editor of *Punch*.

[3] *George Frederick Watts*. His Writings. Macmillan, London 1912, Vol. III, pp. 120–1. From his statement to the 1863 Commission on the Royal Academy.

[4] Victor Considérant: *Destinée sociale*. Second edition, Paris 1848, pp. 318, 321.

[5] See Paul Mantz's article in the *Gazette des Beaux-Arts*. Paris 1878, Vol. I, p. 29.

[6] *Grandes figures d'hier et d'aujourd'hui*, p. 259.

covering the empty walls of its temples'.[1] Here is the same realistic attitude to the new technology as can be seen in the themes proposed by Manet in 1879 for murals in the new Paris Hôtel de Ville: 'Paris – markets, Paris – railways, Paris – bridges, Paris – underground, Paris – gardens and racing'. This scheme, alas, was not accepted, but unlike the murals painted by Morris and his friends in the Oxford Union or by Ford Madox Brown in Manchester Town Hall it did deal with the contemporary world.

The official art policy of the Third Republic favoured the commissioning of grand public art schemes, but of a celebratory and ennobling kind, as seen in the dreamlike costume pieces of Puvis de Chavannes. The Belgians had paved the way here, allotting part of their budget to murals as early as 1860; it was also in Belgium that the trimestrial review *L'Art public* (with the architect Victor Horta and the socialist deputy Jules Destrée on its committee) was started in 1907, following three international congresses on the subject (in 1898, 1900 and 1905). By then the conception of public art was broadening out, and *L'Art public* aimed to improve the standard not only of monumental art but of telegraph poles, street lamps and street furniture in general. Posters and cheap reproductions had also become relevant with the development of new printing techniques; thus the Medici Society was founded by Sir Eustace Gurney in 1908 to import old master prints for working-class homes, while an essay of 1905 by the poet Gustave Kahn described Jules Chéret, the first of the great poster artists, as more important even than Morris because he recognized the realities of industrial life:

> The pleasure palaces of future cities such as Zola conjures up in *Travail* and Morris in *News from Nowhere* are likely to find these works constructed strictly on the basis of immediate reality preferable to any other form of decoration.[2]

This was only too true. The Russian revolution of 1917 brought a short-lived wave of 'propaganda by monuments', as Lenin called it, with his visions of Campanella's ideal city – statues of revolutionary heroes, including a particularly controversial abstract Bakunin by L. Korol'ev – and there were also decorated propaganda trains, pageants and temporary decoration of whole streets before the withdrawal of the more socially-minded artists into industrial design. But generally the great monumental schemes had come to seem boringly rhetorical, and they have been out of favour with art critics ever since.

'Any *official* direction of the arts,' says an essay on 'artistic sociology' published in 1892, 'whatever the government in power, is really only a

[1] *Histoire de l'imagerie populaire*, p. 289.
[2] In Louis Lumet: *L'Art sur tous*; Edouard Cornély, Paris 1905, p. 305. Also p. 307.

charitable organization which uses everybody's money to manufacture objects that nobody wants and no-one knows what to do with.'[1] And the critic Gustave Geffroy in 1905:

> Present-day bourgeois society cannot have a good influence on public art.[2]

This was perhaps only an easy way of rationalizing in class terms what was really a much more awkward problem, but it was largely on class grounds that the social-aesthetic theorists of this period were divided. Those like Morris and Vandervelde, Franz Mehring in Germany and Plekhanov from Russia, who hoped that the working man would seize art in the same way as he was going to seize political power, were confident that he would evolve his own new styles and that the decline of 'bourgeois' art did not much matter. The Marxist interpretation of art, of which they were early exponents, could (and still can) set art movements very illuminatingly against their social background, but too few learnt from Marx himself not to identify those movements with the supposed virtues or vices of the society producing them, and in any case neither Marx's views nor theirs helped much in the choice of a constructive policy. The real difference between them and other supporters of the same social-artistic causes appeared over the question of levels of taste. Thus Watts believed that 'all great and generous reforms must originate with the upper class',[3] while Lucien Pissarro told the anarchist paper to which he used to contribute that it was better to produce for a minority than for the aesthetically backward masses.[4] It was exactly this minority that Morris, who after all did most of his work for it, claimed to mistrust; he felt that it was ineffective.

> I do not believe in the possibility of keeping art vigorously alive by the action, however energetic, of a few groups of specially gifted men and their small circle of admirers among a general public incapable of understanding and enjoying their work. I hold firmly to the opinion that all worthy schools of art must be in the future, as they have been in the past, the outcome of the aspirations of the people towards the beauty and true pleasure of life.[5]

[1] J. Maret-Leriche in *L'Art social*, Paris, March 1892, p. 114. The political tone of this paper was socialist.

[2] *L'Art pour tous*. Paris 1905, Vol. III, p. 203. Louis Lumet, the editor of this magazine and prime founder of its parent society, had two months earlier been made secretary of a committee set up by the Ministry of Education and Fine Arts to buy from the two main salons. In 1906 he was appointed to the new Conseil Supérieur des Arts Décoratifs.

[3] *George Frederic Watts*. His Writings. Macmillan, London 1912, Vol. III, p. 314.

[4] Letter to *Les Temps nouveaux*. Paris, 7 December 1895.

[5] *The Letters of William Morris to his Family and Friends*. Edited by Philip Henderson. Longmans, London 1950, pp. 355–6. Letter of 10 November 1893 to the *Daily Chronicle*.

A resounding statement, but it has two unfortunate limitations. There is no historical evidence for it, and its practical conclusion must surely be that all non-political action is a mistake.

Many of these diverse threads have reappeared in the last twenty years and in the plans and policies discussed in the previous chapter. Much of what was previously put forward as an ideal has been converted into actual administrative machinery. The underlying philosophy was summed up thus by Lord Bridges in 1958 in a lecture on 'The State and the Arts':

> First, that it is the duty of the state to provide something of the best in each of the arts as an example of inspiration to the whole country. Secondly, that the state has also a duty to see that those who can derive satisfaction from the arts have the opportunity to do so. . . .[1]

There is implicit in this system a sometimes conflicting mixture of principles: art must be good for a society and a good representative of it, yet the state must avoid imposing an aesthetic orthodoxy; art must circulate to those who need it, but without departing from a trained minority's conception of 'the best'; art helps the community, yet its public administrators speak only of helping art. Much of the recent talk about patronage indeed makes it sound as if art were an indigent old gentleman for whom a subscription were being got up.

Over on the left Morris's spirit still flickers; thus when Ralph Bond moved the famous Resolution 42 in 1960 he spoke scornfully of

> the idea that culture should be the preserve of an enlightened intelligentsia and that any old rubbish is good enough for the masses.[2]

But there are now virtually no differences between the parties in these matters; the notion of 'working-class art' has become unpopular even in Centre 42; and Arnold Wesker has recently complained to his architect that 'in the document we are forced to submit to official bodies for their help we often fall into the trap of talking about "Moral Responsibilities" and "the pattern that men's lives should take".'[3] The social mission of the movement seems in effect to have been shelved in favour of a purely artistic one, even as far to the left as that.

A good deal of the discussion about 'culture' by writers such as Raymond Williams and Richard Wollheim[4] is about culture in the sense of general

[1] Bridges: *The State and the Arts.* The Romanes Lecture, Clarendon Press, Oxford 1958, p. 16.
[2] *Report of Proceedings at the 92nd Annual Trades Union Congress;* TUC, London, 1960, p. 436.
[3] Centre 42: *Brief to René Allio.* (Duplicated.)
[4] Williams: *Culture and Society 1780–1950;* Chatto and Windus 1958. Penguin 1961. Wollheim: *Socialism and Culture;* Fabian Tract 331. London 1961.

education, based largely on the study of English literature: i.e. culture as conceived by Arnold and F. R. Leavis. But there have also in the last few years been signs of a quickening interest in the social usefulness of the arts proper. Their direct relevance to manufacture, in the form of industrial design, is more and more widely acknowledged, even in Eastern Europe; they are caught up, however ignominiously at times, in the advance of advertising and commercial television; and in England at least the treatment of art in schools as expression rather than discipline has led to a complete change in the importance attached to the subject. Admittedly an investigation conducted in 1964 with the public of twenty-one representative French art galleries led its authors to conclude that the frequenting of museums and the development of a taste for pictures are functions of a man's education, and that without wider access to certain educational levels (approximating to our 'A' levels and above) any attempt to popularize such pursuits must fail.[1] On the other hand we have recently heard a new appeal for 'embellishing public buildings with sculpture and paintings'[2] and seen new emphasis placed on the need for firms to promote amateur art as part of their welfare service, on industry's duty to support the cultural facilities of the towns where it is located, and on the practical advantages of having educated and cultivated employees.[3]

'Up-to-date corporations', wrote a reviewer in the *New York Times* at the end of 1964,

> eager to attract young executives to their outlying plants, frequently stress, and sometimes create, appropriate esthetic amenities.[4]

There is also, with the spread of automation, a much more urgent concern with the problem of leisure. This is a main theme of the book by one of the late President Kennedy's cultural advisers, which sets out from the alienation and lack of sense of direction attributed to modern American society and concludes with an appeal for 'art as a common enjoyment, a focus for the pleasures and delights of the citizenry'.[5] It proposes the carrying out of communal public works – roads, parks, fine buildings – as a means of lifting men's noses above their immediate private concerns. It calls for the improvement of street furniture, the bolder handling of space in the city and the

[1] See Pierre Bourdieu and Alain Darbel: *L'Amour de l'art*, les musées et leur public; Editions de Minuit, Paris 1966. A parallel investigation was conducted in a number of other European countries, but its results have not yet been published. England was not among them.

[2] G. R. Strauss, MP in the debate of 27 April 1965 on Government Support for the Arts.

[3] Points made by Sir W. E. Williams in *Investing in the Arts;* Institute of Directors, London 1964. See pp. 10, 13 and 21; also the article by Mr Miki Sekers in *The Director* for February 1964.

[4] Robert Lekachman, reviewing Alvin Toffler's *The Culture Consumers* in the *New York Times Book Review*, 13 December, 1964.

[5] August Heckscher: *The Public Happiness;* Hutchinson, London 1963, p. 277.

official sponsoring of art as 'the expression of order and the embodiment of inward values'.[1] Art, as the director of the York art gallery has said

> has almost been cast for the role of a substitute for faith and religion, and we expect 'Art' to satisfy all the higher aspirations of mankind.[2]

There are even now artists who are concerned above all with the idea of public art; thus Victor Vasarely's exhibition of 1963 at the Musée des Arts Décoratifs showed him to have worked out interesting and original schemes for coloured geometrical units to be incorporated in varying patterns in architecture, and he lays a fresh emphasis on the importance of teamwork and the use of mechanically-reproducible elements. But what seems largely new today is the widespread interest in popular art. Such 'sociology of the arts' as has sprung up since the 1950s in a number of Western countries – it is, as Richard Wollheim has pointed out, 'one of the most primitive reaches of the social sciences'[3] – has been mainly concerned with this. Men like Richard Hoggart and Stuart Hall at Birmingham University, where their Centre for Contemporary Cultural Studies is partly financed by a grant from Penguin Books; like Robert Escarpit at the University of Bordeaux, with his Centre de Sociologie des Faits Littéraires;[4] like the French critics Edgar Morin and Roland Barthes; like Umberto Eco in Milan and Karl Markus Michel in Frankfurt am Main: people like these are systematically investigating the ground opened up by such pioneers as Walter Benjamin and Mrs Leavis (*Fiction and the Reading Public*, 1932): that is, approaching the arts from the consumer's end and at the same time relating its production to major technological and social changes. They are not much concerned with the popular art of a remote golden age (even if Morris's images still seem to float at the back of one or two English minds), nor do they deal with the 'proletarian' culture preached by the Communists in the 1920s: art on working-class themes which somehow could earn this title without necessarily being either produced or consumed by the working class. Because it is mass consumption and mass production with which they are dealing they treat popular taste seriously, without condescension, and they have helped us all to realize that meeting it calls for more skill and organizing ability, and more artistry even, than we have in the past been prepared to allow. As a result the old barrier

[1] *The Public Happiness*, p. 267.

[2] Hans Hess: *The Artist in an Industrial Society;* Department of Adult Education, The University of Hull, n.d. 1964, p. 7. A paper read at the York conference on The Place of the Visual Arts in an Industrial Society in April 1964.

[3] *Socialism and Culture*, p. 38.

[4] His *Sociologie de la littérature* was published by the Presses Universitaires de France, Paris, in their 'Que sais-je?' series in 1958. With Nicole Robine he is the author of a report on local reading habits, *Atlas de la lecture à Bordeaux*, Faculté des Lettres et Sciences Humaines, Bordeaux, 1963. His study for UNESCO of *The Book Revolution* was published by Harrap in 1966.

between highbrow and lowbrow art is being slowly demolished: films, jazz, crime stories, comics are now quite commonly analysed by reputable critics; majority educational standards are rising, and the concept of minority culture has become eroded rather faster than its guardians think. The whole process seems unconsciously symbolized in the rise of a so-called pop art combining the use of directly accessible imagery, often drawn from our mass-produced culture, with spatial and colour conceptions that have not in the past been widely understood.

All this is more relevant to the case of Liverpool than may at first sight appear. For what we have been discussing in this sketchy tour of the vast and complex area of social-artistic interrelations is not just the background of ideas underlying the present British system of official art patronage but also the changing mental climate in which Liverpool's own tradition has been formed. The development of art teaching in the Mechanics' Institute, for instance, as encouraging useful skills and reputable habits was only part of the nation-wide campaign for art schools of which Haydon considered Liverpool to be one of the leaders. B. A. Heywood as early as 1820 saw 'the luxury and refinement of commercial employment' as replacing 'the patronage and encouragement of the arts, which were induced by the religion, patriotism and private luxury of the ancients';[1] Ewart was member for the city at the time when he inspired the Select Committee on Arts and Manufacturers whose chairman he became; even after the petering out of the Reform Age, the Liverpool Academy, by supporting the Pre-Raphaelites, was in advance both of its town and of its time. The great dissemination movement at the end of the century saw the foundation of the Walker Gallery, the 1888 Art Congress and the Art Nouveau group at the university, again as part of the new attitude to art, crafts and public enlightenment which dominated official art policies everywhere up to 1914. Philip Rathbone, like August Hecksher and Raymond Williams in our own period, hoped to strengthen social coherence, to enable the individual to realize that he is a requisite element in a living organic whole;[2] Rothenstein thought that public works and the presence of great artists might create a living school of art. Advanced German architects in the early twentieth century came to know Port Sunlight as an example of paternalist garden city-type housing; a correspondingly paternalist dissemination of art was responsible for the pictures in Johnson's Dye-

[1] Chairman's Report, 14 March 1820, p. 13, from *Resolutions, Reports and Bye-Laws of the Liverpool Royal Institution*, March 1814–March 1822.

[2] Philip H. Rathbone: *The Political Value of Art in the Municipal Life of a Nation.* A lecture delivered at the Free Library, Liverpool, Liverpool 1875.

works and in due course for the Lady Lever Gallery, though the latter arrived some twenty years too late. Almost anything that matters in Liverpool's relationship with the visual arts can be related in this way to a wider school of thought, so that the doctrines we have been discussing are doubly connected with our immediate subject. They act directly on the people who think about such matters. They shaped the institutions about which they have to think.

The ideas now floating in the Liverpool air seem to bear only an indirect relation to the old nineteenth century radioactivity. They may be summarized as follows. The Walker Gallery is perhaps fully appreciated only by a small minority, but it is worth the city's paying generously to keep it up to standard both as a great educational force[1] and as a heritage for the citizens: something they can be proud of and show off. Extreme modern art may be difficult for them and for many of the local politicians to stomach; none the less it is part of our world, and one cannot simply try to ignore it without risking spiritual stagnation. Generally speaking money spent on the visual arts is felt to be well spent; you must see it this way, a severely ill patient in the Royal Infirmary told me, 'if you've any thought at all for your city; without these things you become fourth-, fifth-, sixth-rate'. Similarly the firms who support the gallery's appeals feel that they have a stake in the city – a large one if they are large employers of labour –, that they must back anything of major civic importance, and that if the decline of the individual private patron has left a gap they must try to fill it. In doing so they are conscious that they are helping to make the city more attractive; the immediately discouraging impression which the sight of Liverpool has often made on those arriving there is present to many minds. There is a feeling among some of them that improvements and cultural amenities may help bring qualified employees and possibly even entire new firms to the area. The director of one big Aintree factory for instance was sure that better housing and a pleasant atmosphere improved the quality of the labour force, while the Engineer at Port Sunlight told me that his firm had previously found it difficult to get research staff for its old laboratories on account of the gloomy outlook from them, but that the construction of new laboratories had changed this.

The South Liverpool Festivals came about because the Domestic Mission wanted to stimulate the social forces which would raise the neighbourhood and counteract those pulling it down; art seemed to be the answer. In the university the inclusion of works of art in the new buildings was undertaken,

[1] Cotton's memorandum on the occasion of the visit of a deputation from the Sheffield conference of provincial galleries to the Chancellor of the Exchequer in 1958 spoke of the bigger galleries as the vital instruments of art education in this country.

as we saw earlier, out of a sense of obligation to students who represent the potential leaders of the nation, at a critical stage in their lives. In the new Catholic churches the visual arts are included as expressing the glory of God. One of the chief football pool promoters pointed out to me the new popularity of Coventry and its attraction for visitors. Any comparable scheme in Liverpool ought to be based on the use of the leading British artists – he instanced Moore, Nicholson, Scott and Pasmore – as an initial core. The right method was to get something started: 'give it a kick, then you've got something to talk about'; national publicity would follow. The effect would be to make Liverpool the art centre of the North West and draw people into it.

None of these arguments made a greater impression on me than the overriding principle put forward by Ben Shaw, then the chairman of the city's Arts Sub-Committee. He was talking about the success of the Van Gogh exhibition in 1955, which had led him to the conclusion that the Gallery must try to concentrate on showing really first-rate work. 'Particularly to those that don't know,' he said, 'only the best will do.' He is absolutely right. People who are not used to painting or sculpture can still be swept off their feet by the sheer force and quality of something which they do not yet 'understand'. The initiated can afford to be interested in the second- or third-rate artist; they may learn from him in all sorts of ways, and the echoes or allusions which they recognize in his work may seem quite beautiful. This escapes anybody who has no background of looking at such things and simply lacks the initial impetus to hunt for such refinements. The moral should be written out in letters of gold for all those concerned with disseminating and administering the arts.

10 : A PLAN OF CAMPAIGN

In making positive proposals for Liverpool I would like to ignore the idea of art as education, or even as a civilizing force. It is true that we judge a nation's degree of civilization partly by its art, but that is because the concept of civilization has long presupposed a condition in which the arts flourish. It would be much harder to prove that the practice or enjoyment of art makes people better individuals or even better citizens; Greek art, as Marx pointed out to those who identify art's virtues with those of society, was bound up with Greek slavery; the marvellous Roman amphitheatres were not exactly built for youth festivals; and in our own time nobody placed art on a higher pedestal than an amateur artist called Adolf Hitler.[1] No: if people need art it is not to bolster up their claim to be civilized but because it is an age-old human activity, a continual delight to practise, study or simply sit back and gape at; full of jokes, problems, explosions, sudden breath-taking beauties; something unpredictable that can be set against modern life's mechanisms and routines. 'Even when people speak of higher and lower degrees of pleasure,' wrote Brecht,

> art stares impassively back at them; for it wishes to fly high and low and to be left in peace, so long as it can give pleasure to people.[2]

Whether we take art to be a key to things beyond this world or as a marvellously refined man-made contrivance it is this that people want when they claim art as one of the basic rights of man. It is not a loud claim, though it is becoming more so. But it can easily be stifled and distorted if the art-conscious minority appears in the guise of Lady Bountiful, patronizing the artists and improving the public mind; for nobody likes being condescended to, and rightly or wrongly the suspicion is bound to arise that the guardians of art are only trying to find takers for the kind of art that they themselves enjoy.

[1] I have just read a description by a dead painter friend, whose judgments I respected, of the late Professor Klaus Schilling, a specialist in tropical diseases then (1941–2) working in Florence. He was a passionate and discriminating art lover, fascinated particularly by Giorgione: 'his conversation about painting was always fruitful and rewarding'. He was hanged for the experiments which he carried out on human beings in Dachau concentration camp. (Kurt Craemer: *Mein Panoptikum;* Hoffman und Campe, Hamburg 1965, pp. 128–34.)

[2] *Brecht on Theatre;* Methuen, London, 1964 p. 181 (Paragraph 5 of his 'Kleines Organon für das Theater'.) The last qualifying phrase could have been left out.

What the public would, on the other hand, appreciate is to see art associated with the general drive for better living: to see it as a hope rather than an implied reproach. For this reason in a city like Liverpool it should above all be linked firmly to the great schemes for replanning and redevelopment. If people are certain not to want it in that context, then it should not be forced down their throats. Morris saw further than our official patrons when he maintained that art might just as well die out as develop on a false footing. For of course art does not die; it is an indelible human habit. But if in the long run it is going to be wanted, then the corporation should make it available, and it would be wise for them to start planning for this right away.

So let us return to the city scale, and sum up the problem. Art has got itself in a false position because we have come to treat the visual arts as something set apart from other human concerns. Industrialists and business people, for instance, who are generous in their patronage of the visual arts, often have no use for them in their own works or offices. Similarly in the colleges of technology and elsewhere design seems to be treated as a dispensable extra, a luxury embellishment added to objects once the serious business of making them is over, rather than a sense of arrangement, elegance and logic that ought to guide it from the outset: something that is shared with intellectual disciplines such as mathematics, and is more fundamental than either craft or techniques. Art is accepted as a stimulating and psychologically liberating exercise for school children, particularly in lower forms, but unless he decides to make it his profession even the most gifted child finds no encouragement (and often no chance) to pursue it after he has left school. A barrier falls between it and the serious business of living; the one is shunted off into the art gallery, the other is left to get along with hideously-made goods and often with bare walls. The chance of any spontaneous visual self-expression outside the group of professonal artists is needlessly lessened.

There is another major question, and I should define my attitude to it before going further. That is the frequent incompatibility of minority judgments and the tastes of many members of the public. In a gallery that the majority hardly ever visit the problem is not really acute; sharp disputes about matters of taste are in fact likelier to arise in committee than among those who come to look at the pictures. But as soon as art gets out into the street the matter is very different, not least because it is so difficult to rectify mistakes. None the less, if Liverpool is to incorporate public works of art in its great replanning projects, then it would be wise to include some that will be outstanding in our time and bring credit to the city among the scattered but in some ways surprisingly coherent minority of art lovers throughout the world. This means works of possibly 'extreme' modern art which are bound to cause hot controversy in the city itself.

Two things are important here: first of all Shaw's Law, as we may call the principle put forward at the end of the last chapter; secondly the rapidity with which the taste for modern art is developing in this country, and its association with classes and interests far removed from the old nucleus of connoisseurs. Intolerance of the unfamiliar, as we saw earlier, is not a mark of education, and its importance is dwindling as educational benefits spread; moreover as people come to see art as fun rather than as a high Ruskinian cocktail of the Beautiful and the Good they will be less worried by the new forms it takes. Already a great work, however extreme, is likely to be accepted even if it still puzzles and occasionally irritates the older citizens. But with lesser works the situation is different. There is no point in authority's fighting aesthetic battles for the sake of inferior modern public art; the waverers will not be convinced, and if they were it would just mean a lowering of standards. Minor examples of public art ought not gratuitously to run against strong popular feelings, though whether these are aroused or not depends to some extent on how the work is presented; a high degree of abstraction may, for instance, be accepted in the guise of decoration or advertisement or some kind of superior toy, yet arouse immediate opposition if put forward as Art.

The immediate recipient of the proposals that follow is the Bluecoat Society of Arts. Much that I suggest is quite outside the society's scope, but I am putting it forward none the less in the hope that this report will also be read by others who are concerned about the future of Liverpool, its buildings and its educational system, its reputation and the general sense of life in the city. It seems to me important that the problem should be treated as a whole: that if it is to be tackled at all there must be an overall plan of campaign into which the smaller proposals fit. The plan which I outline therefore is intended to be seen as itself part of the city's plan for reconstruction and redevelopment, and to be presentable to the public as such. It should not be treated just as a string of disjointed proposals to be carried out individually; for some of them are only worth executing within the overall campaign and might otherwise do more harm than good. In short, although there are many things here that the Bluecoat Society can do on its own I would ask it first to father the whole plan, to sponsor discussion of it and to make it a Bluecoat Plan for the future of the visual arts in Liverpool. This need not prevent the society from also taking smaller steps, but it must be very certain, and be able to convince both artists and public, that they are steps towards an agreed goal.

THE GOALS I suggest are: (1) to humanize and beautify the reconstruction of the city; (2) to strengthen its identity, both to its own citizens and to outsiders; (3) to stimulate a distinctive Liverpool art, particularly among the younger generation, and to remove obstacles to visual self-expression; (4) to break down the barriers which isolate art and design as supposed inessentials; and finally (5) to create an exciting atmosphere for persons and institutions concerned with art.

Accordingly, the first thing I would propose is that a PUBLIC ART ADVISER be appointed to make a plan for the use of works of art in conjunction with any new schemes for building development, housing, street furniture and open spaces. He or she would need to have had administrative experience, to command the confidence of artists and to have a good knowledge of the best living artists both at home and abroad; he would also need a genuine understanding and appreciation of Liverpool as a place. He would have to work closely with planners, architects and private developers, and should, I think, be responsible to the Corporation rather than to the Bluecoat Society or to an outside body. He should however be much higher-powered than the corresponding municipal department in Rotterdam or the Art Commission in Hamburg; to avoid compromises with mediocrity the initiative must lie with one man. He would not be required to make proposals for each new building, but for entire areas of the city where building was going on: for the comprehensive development areas of the city centre and the 'action areas' established further out.

The works which he would commission would as a rule best be FINANCED by adding up to 2 per cent to building costs, though whether private developers would comply with this practice would depend on his powers of persuasion and on the force of the example set by the corporation. This addition would not however be automatic, and although no work would be commissioned except with a specific site in mind there would be no rigid need to apportion works to buildings. The aim rather should be to PLAN BY AREAS, corresponding broadly to areas of major development or rehabilitation within the city plan. It might also be possible to interest COLLECTIVE PATRONS (firms, the university, the nationalized industries, the trusts) in underwriting a given area. A newspaper or a television company, for instance, could do this and get an interesting story to report, from preliminary sketch projects to final public reaction.

The CHOICE OF ARTISTS would be made by the adviser, but would have to be approved by the patron and his architect, planner or engineer. It ought also to be ratified on behalf of the Corporation, preferably by a special expert committee which might contain the Director of the Walker Art Gallery, the Chief Planning Officer, a representative of the Civic Society and a representative of the Liverpool Academy, with a chairman from the majority party. In my view the important commissions should be given to the best artists for the job, irrespective of nationality; there should be no special sense of obligation to give work to English, let alone Liverpool artists, or to share the jobs out fairly; the object should rather be to create really impressive works which would stimulate the private demand for art locally and infect any artist within range. The great influence that can be wielded by an OUTSTANDING INTERNATIONAL ARTIST working in the city, if only for a few months, should not be forgotten; the example of Augustus John's brief Liverpool period should be borne in mind. Every effort should be made to attract one or more of the major figures to work in Liverpool, and if possible to make use of local collaborators. It is too late to ask Picasso, but that is the level at which Liverpool should aim.

Special measures would have to be taken to introduce each artist not only to the site(s) he is to design his work for but also to the city itself and the inhabitants for whom he is working. Any artist who is not prepared to accept this, and simply wishes to paint or sculpt as for a gallery but larger, is likely to be unsuited to public commissions. It should also be taken for granted at all levels that art, architecture and mundane matters of design such as street furniture are not independent of one another but contribute to a common scene and must be judged as a whole. One way of stressing this would be to encourage the expert committee, including the adviser, to comment on all visual aspects of the area under consideration. Another idea which might be considered is that of getting a geometrically-minded abstract sculptor at an early stage to advise on the detailing of the proposed new inner motorway and the three-dimensional shape of its junctions. This could have been a job for the late Hans Arp.

The second major proposal I would like to make is that the whole SYSTEM OF ART TEACHING in Merseyside (not Liverpool only) schools and colleges should be overhauled with a view to breaking the barrier (a) between art and adult life and (b) between design and manufacture. The first problem here is how to make it easier for the artistically gifted child who is not going on to a full-time art school to keep his hand and eye in none the less. One way of doing this would be to DIVIDE PART-TIME TRAINING in the fine arts into two categories so as to separate the younger pupils who still want to develop their techniques and their personalities from older people who simply use art schools as a cheap way of pursuing their hobby as amateurs. The smaller art schools, whose function in the new national pattern seems very unclear, might be turned over to the latter, possibly with increased fees, while part-time training under teachers from the College of Art could then be reserved for those who need to learn rather than primarily to occupy themselves.

The design barrier can only be broken by persuading teachers, especially of technical subjects, that good design is itself a discipline, where the visual sense helps to secure logical arrangement, economy and control: something that should be thought of as relating to consumer research, for instance, quite as much as to aesthetics. But it would be a great help if the university would set up a DEPARTMENT OF INDUSTRIAL DESIGN, as has been suggested, and preferably one that could serve other higher educational establishments in the city. What is needed is a small unit capable of conducting research and of supplying an element of design teaching not only to the university's own engineering faculty but to any course in the city colleges whose students are likely, by manufacture, planning, management, or simple buying and selling, to influence the appearance of our daily surroundings. Design would have to be taught not as a speciality, but as an essential component of these people's training, whether or not they themselves are ever likely to design anything. This is a field where there are many people with the missionary spirit, and some of them should be spreading it in Liverpool.

Another aid to a better-co-ordinated system of visual teaching in the city would be more exchange of information. This could be organized through some form of STANDING CONFERENCE ON ART EDUCATION, with representatives drawn from the University, the Walker Gallery, the Colleges of Art, Building and Technology, the City Libraries and the Directorate of Education, and possibly from the neighbouring boroughs too. Its function would be to advise and help art teachers in the area, and to keep itself informed about their work. It might be worth trying a preliminary meeting of such a group with a few dozen local art teachers. If it seemed to raise useful questions and even to settle a few of them, then such meetings should be made a regular institution.

There are a number of lesser measures which could be taken within the framework of a general visual arts campaign, though they might well be ineffective on their own. There is, for instance, the problem of a COMMERCIAL GALLERY FOR MODERN ART. At present this does not exist in Liverpool; the Bluecoat Society's rooms are a makeshift. In my view a lively and well-informed dealer in modern art will establish himself in the city as soon as there seems to be a stimulating artistic climate there and a keen public interest; to devise special inducements to lure one to Liverpool before then would be to put the cart before the horse. In the interval however, more might be done to advise and encourage the dealers who are already there. If the Bluecoat Society, or the Academy for that matter, were occasionally to organize an exhibition for them they might not only be pleased to show it but be able to sell the exhibits. The experience of the Medici Society with modern prints is a pointer; good modern work *can* be sold through the existing channels. The answer, in my view, is more liaison, and I would recommend an exploratory meeting at the Bluecoat Chambers with representatives of the Medici, the Boydell Gallery, Lewis's, the Academy and the Bluecoat, and if possible somebody who knows about the activities of the London dealers.

The Bluecoat Society could well sponsor a scheme for PICTURES IN HOSPITALS on the lines of that run in London. I suggest that it tries to get the support of a number of leading doctors and hospital committee members known to be interested in the visual arts, then organize an exhibition of works by local artists in a suitable hospital. Some of the artists might be willing to come and meet patients and hospital staff, and talk about the works. A report should then be prepared on the venture, with photographs, and circulated to the initial supporters, to hospital management committees and individual hospital secretaries in the area, and subsequently to the Press. Individual hospitals would be asked if they wished to come in on the scheme, whose scale would depend on the response. Up to this point the scheme would have to finance itself; it could hardly ask for outside support before it was running. The pictures would at first be borrowed from the artists, though they would be for sale (to staffs and patients as well as to institutions). The scheme could continue on this basis or could go over to the London system of itself actually buying the pictures; this is something that could be decided later.

The Society, together with the Trades Council if it were interested, could evolve a similar scheme for circulating works by local artists to FACTORY CORRIDORS, CANTEENS AND RECREATION ROOMS, and also trade union offices. Again, it should try to enlist the support of managers and directors, and start with a pilot scheme and borrowed works. Again, personal visits by some of the artists would be a help. Once the pilot scheme had been concluded and reported on, the Society and its supporters would have to choose how the use of the works was to be paid for in future; they could be hired from the artists (who might at the same time offer them for sale if they wished) or they could be purchased so as to form a central circulating collection, with the participating firms paying an annual subscription, based perhaps on the number of their employees.

Much the same principle could be applied with LOANS TO SCHOOLS. Instead of second-rate reproductions on the walls they should be encouraged to have the work of local artists, especially if these were prepared to come along and discuss it with the pupils. The Walker Gallery has already been buying works for lending, some of them by local painters. It might however be worth consulting a few interested teachers - there are some who are already members of the Academy or the Sandon Studios Society – and the TeacherTraining Department at the College. A pilot scheme with borrowed works and personal visits could be tried out at a few selected schools, and the results then reported to the Director of Education. If they seemed worth while he or the individual schools might be able to make a small annual allocation to finance hire and transport of pictures.

If a plan could then be drawn up in collaboration with the gallery all three of these projects – hospitals, industry and schools – could be run together and supplied from a single store of works of art.[1] The Society and the gallery would have to decide whether the problems of administration and storage space would permit this. The cause of Liverpool art in general would also benefit greatly from a more systematic attempt to acquaint Liverpool people with their local artists. To this end the Society should recruit a *panel of* artists and other experts who would be willing to give ILLUSTRATED TALKS ON LIVERPOOL ART, ancient and/or modern, or specifically on their own work, and should build or borrow a suitable collection of slides. They could then offer these talks to schools, factory art clubs, local art groups and any other audiences likely to be interested.

Awareness of Liverpool's own visual tradition is vitally important, especially at a time when so much reconstruction is planned. I would like to support the RECOMMENDATIONS OF THE PLANNING DEPARTMENT'S REPORT ON THE PRESERVATION OF HISTORIC BUILDINGS IN CENTRAL LIVERPOOL, which include the revision of the existing lists, the publication of a pamphlet on the subject, the fixing of plaques on outstanding buildings and the foundation of a 'history of Liverpool' museum. This report should be debated by the council; both it and the book *Seaport* by the same author deserve wide study, particularly in the context of the threat to Albert Dock. The local architectural research conducted at the University, to which some of Dr Hughes's many interesting discoveries are due, ought now to be matched

[1] Within six months of the presentation of this report, but quite independently of it, a North West Medical Arts Society had been founded by a group of doctors and their wives. Its inaugural exhibition was held at Rainhill Hospital on 12 May, 1966. Membership, entailing the right to hire pictures at a basic rate of one guinea per six months, is open not only to hospitals, but also to other entities and individuals. The Bluecoat Forum is now helping with the practical administration.

I have left my recommendation as it stood, in order to show its place in the general plan of campaign. Whether it will actually fill that place depends on Liverpool's willingness to see its problems as a whole rather than tackle them piecemeal.

by similar RESEARCHES INTO LOCAL HISTORY AND LOCAL ART. Any encouragement which can be given to these, whether in the University or at the College of Art, would be helpful in strengthening the city's identity. In Germany or Italy there would be local publishers to disseminate their results, but this is unfortunately rare in England, and even a great printing centre like Liverpool is no exception. Only poetry magazines like *Underdog* and *Phoenix* and the occasional issue of the student magazine *Sphinx* have at least tried to convey the visual character of the place; the Society should see that they continue to appear, and note their appearance and contents in its Arts Forum Bulletin. It might also be worth making contact with *Music Echo*, which could influence a large young audience by devoting an occasional column to the visual arts.

There is, however, a lack of any CENTRAL REVIEW OR NEWS SHEET for those concerned with the visual arts in the area. They need a small monthly publication, if possible illustrated, which would keep them in touch with one another and with what is going on locally. This is something that the Society could well provide, either by developing the present bulletin and giving it a less cumbersome title or by starting a new organ. Such a publication should aim in the first instance to be informative, though it might in due course become more ambitious and even solicit contributions from outside Liverpool. Its core would be news of exhibitions, projects, commissions, jobs, official purchases, gallery activities, the art schools and the various art societies, together with reports, interviews and reproductions of current work. It might delegate responsibility for certain departments to the Walker Gallery, the Civic Society and the School of Architecture, possibly also reporting the results of the type of research mentioned in the previous paragraph. It should not be over-ambitious in presentation: e.g. it could be typewriter-set.

If it is to tackle these tasks, and above all if it is to play an influential part in the suggested campaign, the BLUECOAT SOCIETY ITSELF will have to undergo some changes. At the moment it consists (trustees apart) of a committee originally instituted to manage the buildings, plus a Forum to co-ordinate the activities of tenants and other cultural societies; it has no acknowledged responsibilities outside this, and it is not really equipped for planning and new organization. In my view it ought now to be reconstituted as a buildings and finance committee, plus an arts committee, with the chairman of the Forum as a member of the latter. The arts committee would be responsible not only for the use of the society's hall and gallery but for actively furthering the arts in Liverpool, both on and off the premises. For this it would need a more or less full-time organizer, and it might well consider whether it could not meet some of the cost involved by inviting membership of the society, individual and collective. Among the inducements to members might be participation in the picture loan schemes proposed above and receipt of any publications; other benefits would transpire as soon as there was somebody systematically devoting himself to planning. They would also be supporting the campaign outlined here.

There are two other preliminary steps which ought to be taken before the main operation starts. First, it would help to arouse public interest and clarify the ideas both of the artists and of their potential patrons if there were a COMPREHENSIVE EXHIBITION DEVOTED TO PUBLIC ART at the Walker Art Gallery. Such an exhibition has not, to my knowledge, been held in this country, and many people outside Liverpool might find it a good occasion for discussing a little-understood subject; thus it would attract publicity, particularly if the Corporation could at the same time announce something like the present plan. It might be usefully be linked with a congress of experts from outside Liverpool: a revival on a more modest and less exclusively National scale of Conway's Association. The exhibits would need to include pictures, models and plans of outstanding examples throughout the world, as well as actual works of art and ideas for their siting. Some of them could be displayed in suitable places in the city, as was done in Antwerp.

Secondly, the corporation ought to mount A TRAVELLING EXHIBITION which would convey the city's particular flavour and character, above all by visual means. This should be shown not only in Liverpool itself but in London and overseas, in the many centres which have become curious about Liverpool since the rise of the Beatles. Adequately prepared, it would at the same time be a first-rate advertisement for the city, a good way of helping its citizens to discover their own assets, and a great fillip for Liverpool art. A project for a 'Look at Liverpool' exhibition on these lines which I worked out in consultation with Henri, Ballard and MacKarell is given as an appendix. We planned it to answer an objection from the Director of the Walker Gallery (at a discussion of some of the points raised in this chapter) that art with a distinctive Liverpool flavour did not exist.

To sum up this plan of campaign briefly, in rough chronological order and with indication of responsibility (in brackets), what I am proposing is:

Adoption of a plan for the visual arts.

Modification of the Bluecoat Society's committees.

Start of visual arts news sheet (Bluecoat).

Discussion of schools loan scheme with teachers (B).

Recruitment of speakers on Liverpool art and collection of slides (B).

Standing Conference on art education (Liverpool Corporation and B).

Consultation with Liverpool commercial galleries (B).

'LOOK AT LIVERPOOL' EXHIBITION (LC, with B and Liverpool Academy).

Setting-up of Department of Industrial Design (University and LC).

Reorganization of part-time art school teaching (LC and Ministry of Education).

Preliminary support for loan schemes for hospitals and factories (B, with Liverpool Trades Council).

Trial runs for loan schemes for hospitals, factories and schools, using borrowed works of art (B, with LTC).

EXHIBITION OF PUBLIC ART, possibly with conference (LC, with assistance of the Arts Council).

Appointment of Public Art adviser (LC).

Ditto expert committee on visual aspects of the city (LC).

Institution of loan schemes for hospitals (B). (See note on p. 246 above.)

Ditto factories (B, with LTC).

Ditto schools (B, with LC).

DESIGNATION OF FIRST AREAS AND ARTISTS for public works of art (LC).

Allotment of subsidiary tasks in these areas (LC).

If the operation could unfold in this way as a linked plan it would have powerful effects. It would stimulate national and international interest in Liverpool and reinforce the picture of a genuinely resurgent city. It would arouse a mixture of controversy, pride and delight in the city itself. It would help to attract lively-minded people to Liverpool, as visitors or as citizens. It would encourage the younger generation to express itself visually as well as through pop music. It would give work to Liverpool artists and strengthen their position as a distinctive school. It would breathe new life into the existing art institutions: the gallery, the College of Art, the Academy. It would also be a comprehensive operation such as had never been launched before, and it could have historic results for the visual arts.

Is this scheme a model for the development and use of art in the city? Not, I hope, on the surface. The aim has been throughout to derive the proposed measures from the specific situation of Liverpool: from a low-level look at its history, resources and tastes. They are meant to reflect the character of the place, using the experience of other cities and other theories of art as background material, but not necessarily as patterns to conform with. Nor should the scheme be used as a pattern itself. All the same I hope that the general line of approach will be found to be a helpful one, usable elsewhere under different conditions. Seen in this light it ought to serve the cause of decentralization and local cultural differentiation, as against the prevailing trend towards uniformity of methods and above all of taste, created in the name of high artistic standards and determined ultimately by a network of closely linked committees and advisory bodies, based on the capital.

For elsewhere too the need is to plan in terms of the actual situation on the ground and to take into account people's real feelings about art, rather than go only by the ideals of a minority, however admirable, or accept the largely negative public relationships that artists have come to treat as normal and even necessary. It is not that minority taste and the artist's wish for isolation should be wholly disregarded, nor is it the city's job where the arts are concerned to give the public what it says it wants. But the community's state of artistic education is a limiting factor that can only be overridden with a full knowledge of what is involved. In Germany and Russia after the First World War it was overridden too far unthinkingly, so that despite the liveliness and lasting importance of the movements that flourished then the reaction which followed did even more damage to art and (quite literally) to artists than the popular pandering of the later Victorians.

What matters for the future of art is not 'help' and 'support' so much as the straightening out of relationships and their uninhibited development in the future. It is this that has emerged as the main concern of the present enquiry. The citizens as a whole need to see that the visual arts are a source of endless fun, discovery, fascination: one of our great resources to set against aimlessness and boredom. They should learn not only to respect but to use them. The adolescent in particular must come to treat art as a natural and creditable pursuit: a potential outlet for him even if he is not making it his profession. Manufacturers and consumers – anybody who fabricates objects or uses them – must learn that art is not only decoration but the actual art of making: that there are visual means of asserting and arriving at common sense. As for the artist himself he has to feel that he is part of a community, however much he may be forced to disagree with its inexperienced criticisms and to resist its claims. None of these are new relationships. But in the modern city they have been distorted and blocked.

However local circumstances may differ, the barriers and distortions are of much the same kind whatever city we look at. The main objective for those concerned about the pattern of art there must be to clear them away and hope that the great increase in interest, understanding and activity in the visual arts will resolve many subsidiary problems. This objective is certainly being pursued in other places, but it has to be pursued locally, in terms of the local situation. In a world where communication has become so rapid and so relatively cheap, and geographical frontiers in art have been very largely swept away, this is the one hope of avoiding an ultimately cramping monotony. I hope that whether or not they accept its reasoning other cities will be moved by the present study to embark on their own. It is not just the supply of art to the city that matters. It is bringing their relationship to life.

APPENDIX A

Questionnaire: The Visual Arts in Liverpool

There were 368 replies to the questionnaire discussed on pp. 130-7. Of these fifty-four were the result of interviews in different districts of Liverpool by five students at the College of Art. In the other cases the respondents filled the forms in themselves without an interviewer. Eighty-four came from visitors to the Walker Art Gallery, thirty-one from employees (mainly clerical staff) at Littlewoods' Spinney House, 172 from pupils at Gateacre Comprehensive School and twenty-seven from the staff there.

Excluding the school children the age distribution was:

Between 15–20	58 respondents
21–35	73
35–60	52
over 60	6

There were more than ten respondents from four (variegated) Liverpool postal districts – 8, 15, 16 and 23 – and from Wallasey; the vast majority of the schoolchildren came from Liverpool 25. There were between two and nine respondents from each of the other districts apart from 1, 2, 5 and 10 (i.e., the business district, the Scotland Road area and Aintree, all of which had none), and four apiece from Birkenhead, Huyton and Formby.

Age on ending full-time education (excluding the school children):

16 or under	73
17–20	36
21 and over	33
Still at school	8
At university	20
At other colleges	13

The following shows the division of responses between the Walker Art Gallery visitors (WAG), the interviewees (Int) Littlewoods' employees (L), the Gateacre school staff (GS(s)) and the Gateacre pupils (GS). Totals in each group are shown in brackets.

Question 1

	WAG (84)	Int (54)	L (31)	GS(s) (27)	GS (172)
Are you interested in painting and sculpture?					
Yes	82	34	14	25	112
No	2	20	13	1	58

Do you ever do anything of the sort yourself?

	WAG	Int	L	GS(s)	GS
Yes	53	14	7	7	106
No	29	36	11	19	58

Do you have any of your own work hanging or showing in your house?

	WAG	Int	L	GS(s)	GS
Yes	39	7	3	6	54*
No	15	7	3	1	59

* *Of whom six had answered 'No' immediately above.*

Question 2

Do you go to public art galleries and art exhibitions?

	WAG	Int	L	GS(s)	GS
Yes	74	22	4	16	34
No	1	11	6	1	53
Sometimes	9	19	16	11	76

How long is it since you were in the Walker Art Gallery?

	WAG	Int	L	GS(s)	GS
Month or less	58	5	0	3	5
1–3 *months*	13	2	0	3	20
3–6 *months*	2	1	2	3	29
½–1 *year*	3	7	4	4	23
1–2 *years*	4	9	2	4	22
2–5 *years*	0	7	5	4	10
Over 5 *years*	1	13	5	2	7
Never	0	8	4	0	43

Name a picture you liked:

Daguerre's Holyrood Chapel	11 votes
Henry VIII (School of Holbein)	11 (including 7 GS)
The Death of Nelson (Maclise)	10 (including 9 GS)
Paul Jenkins's Phenomena Votive	7
Lowry's The Fever Van	7
Faithful unto Death (Poynter)	7 (including 5 GS)
Murillo's The Virgin and Child	5
Scott's Blue Abstract	4
The Beehive (? Zobel's To the Hive)	4
Rubens's The Virgin and Child	3
Rembrandt's Self-Portrait	3
Simone Martini	2
When did you last see your father? (Yeames)	2

There were also a number of pictures which got a single vote. One respondent said 'none', another said 'all'. Altogether there were 170 named choices, of which some were not in the gallery.

What other art gallery or exhibition do you visit?

None	43
National Gallery	26
Tate Gallery	25
Lady Lever	15
Louvre	13
Birkenhead	12
Bluecoat Manchester	11
Southport	10
Sudley Warrington Edinburgh	4
Others	36

Question 3

How long is it since you bought any sort of picture?

	WAG	Int	L	GS(s)	GS
A year or less	34	13	7	10	41
1–5 *years*	14	11	2	9	12
Over 5 *years*	2	4	2	5	2
Never	25	25	19	3	65

What was it and how much?

Thirty-four of the above were postcards. The rest fell into the following categories:
(i) Original paintings: 15 (£131 10s+); including a gouache by Peter Lanyon, Adrian Henri's *Ubu on Rhyl Sands* and a copy after Constable.
(ii) Prints and watercolours: 8 (£19 6s+); including Brangwyn, David Roberts and 'a pupil of Buffet'.
(iii) Reproductions of recognized modern artists: 17 (£15 17s+); including 5 Utrillo, 2 Picasso and one each of Marc, Monet, Renoir, Buffet, Bonnard, Cézanne, van Gogh, Modigliani, Braque and Dali.
(iv) Classical reproductions: 10 (£22+); 3 Mona Lisas, Constable's *Hay Wain*, Dürer's *Praying Hands* and pictures by Goye, Duccio, Canaletto, Vermeer and Stubbs.
(v) Popular reproductions: 45 (£57+) (may include some photographs); 4 or 5 Peter Scott, 3 Vernon Ward, 1 to 3 Tretchikoff, 9 unidentified landscapes, 6 unidentified seascape, 3 Spanish, 2 each horses, flowers and ballet.
(vi) Unidentifiable reproductions: 13 (£13 11s+).

NB Expenditure shown is below actual amounts, as about a third of respondents did not give prices.

Question 4

Have you seen films or television shows about art and artists?

	WAG	Int	L	GS(s)	GS
Yes	67	41	11	25	108
Blank	3	2	4	0	24
No	10*	12	9	2	34

**One of these commented 'They will spoil your own idea of painting.'*

Do you look out for programmes of this sort?

	WAG	Int	L	GS(s)	GS
Yes	51	21	3	12	40
Blank (or ambiguous)	7	5	4	6	35
No	12	27	11	7	81

Three of the 'no's' said they had no TV.

Question 5

Have you any friend or relative who does drawing or painting of that sort of thing?

	WAG	Int	L	GS(s)	GS
Yes	62	43	13	17	99
No	19	12	14	9	68

The GS responses are valueless here, as art is taught in the school.

Professional or amateur?

	WAG	Int	L	GS(s)	GS
Professional	27	20	2	4	10
Amateur	36	23	10	14	87

Question 6

Name a Liverpool artist

	WAG	Int	L	GS(s)	GS
No answer	35	41	23	16	117
Irrelevant (e.g. Constable, Sir G. Scott, Paul McCartney, etc.)	2	0	0	1	10
Arthur Dooley	12	8	2	5	3
Arthur Ballard	4	2	0	0	13*
Stubbs	5	0	0	1	18†
Adrian Henri	3	0	1	0	0
Edward Halliday	1	2	0	0	0
A. P. Tankard	2	0	0	0	0
Trevor Hughes	2	0	0	0	0
Will C. Penn	1	0	0	0	1

**All these are from one form (LM).*

†Sixteen of these are from one form (4Y).

The following got one mention each:

(i) By GS pupils: Peter MacKarell, Fred O'Brien. (I have disregarded four GS pupils' mentions of their own teachers).
(ii) By WAG: Mayer-Marton, Mollie Garland, Austin, Perceval, Don McKinlay, Davis, Cris Wood, Sam Walsh, Lowry, William Huggins, George Thomas, Brian Burgess, Stanley Hill, Max Eden, Stanley English, R. P. Richards, Mavis Blackburn.
(iii) By GS staff: A. Butler, Stanley Reid, E. Carter Preston.
(iv) By Littlewoods' employees: W. L. Stevenson, Sean Rice, Griffin.
(v) By interviewees: Gordon Ellis, John Heritage.

Question 7

What do you feel about the idea of seeing paintings, sculpture and so on at your place of work?

	WAG	Int	L	GS(s)	GS
Like	68*	41‡	24†	28	116
Dislike	3	9	2	0	12
No fixed place of work	10	5	2	0	43

* *Three expressed qualifications: (i) 'not sculpture'. (ii) 'except female faces.' (iii) that context, environment, etc., must be right.*

† *One 'with qualifications'. One said 'but not* too *much – consider visual art expressions are not really appreciated by majority of "passers-by".'*

‡ *One depending on quality. One 'painting only, dislike sculpture'.*

Question 8

What do you feel about the idea of seeing it *inside* public buildings - libraries, hospitals, stations and so on?

	WAG	Int	L	GS(s)	GS
Like	81*	52	29	27	141
Dislike	3	1	1	0	26

* *Four with qualifications: (i) except hospitals, (ii) except hospitals and stations, (iii) as 7 (ii) above, (iv) 'Depends on building situation, etc.'*

Question 9

What about seeing it on the *outside* of public buildings, or in squares, parks and open spaces?

	WAG	Int	L	GS(s)	GS
Like	67*	36‡	23†	25	116
Dislike	16	17	7	2	48††

* *Five qualifications: (i) sculpture only, (ii) 'but not*

paintings', (*iii*) *as* 7(*ii*) *above*, (*iv*) *as* 8(*iv*) *above*, (*v*) '*but sparingly*'.
† *One said 'but not too much', as for question* 7.
‡ *One specified 'decent architecture, not modern'. Another was impressed by Birmingham and Coventry.*
†† *It is possible that some of the younger children thought questions* 8 *and* 9 *mutually exclusive.*

Question 10

Have you any pictures in your home?

	WAG	Int	L	GS(s)	GS
Yes	71	40	14	18	90
No	10	14	16	8	76

What are they and who are the artists?

It is not worth listing the answers in detail, as they follow the pattern of those to question 3. In addition to those mentioned there the paintings included work by William Huggins, Alexander Nasmyth, S. Lamorna Birch and (of local artists) Stuart Sutcliffe, Don McKinlay, Sam Walsh and Peter MacKarell. The prints, watercolours and drawings included work by Birket Foster, Orovida, Paul Nash, Mark Gertler, Nina Hamnett, Gaudier-Brzeska, Kathleen Major (of Wigan) and Edgar Grosvenor. This was of course at one end of the scale only; at the other were calendars, photos of pop stars, paintings by the physically handicapped, and 'mural wallpaper'.

Question 11

What do you feel about the city's collection of pictures in the Walker Gallery?

	WAG	Int	L	GS(s)	GS
Proud	29*	21†	1	3	30
Should be added to	62‡	15	13††	20	47
Indifferent	5	14	10	3	25
Should stay as it is	2	3	1	0	14
Waste of money	2§	2	1	0	18

* *One says 'fairly'.*
† *One: 'A lot should be weeded out and replaced.'*
‡ *One: 'Could be greatly improved. Collection of classical Italian paintings should be diminished (could be put in museums where they belong) to make way for more progressive art of today.' Next respondent concurred.*
†† *Includes one respondent who has never been there.*
§ *Two schoolboys from Widnes.*

Question 12

Do you belong to any art society or attend any art appreciation class?

	WAG	Int	L	GS(s)	GS
Yes	25	3	0	0	—
No	52	49	30	26	—

What?

Extramural and WEA	5
Wallasey School of Art or art society	4
Bootle School of Art	2
Birkenhead School of Art	1
Southport School of Art	1
Regional College of Art	1
Liver Sketching Club	1
Chester College of Further Education	1
Warrington Art School and art group	1

The art school figures here are likely only to refer to part-time students. The Gateacre pupils have been omitted.

Question 13

Would you like to see any child of yours go to art school?

	WAG	Int	L	GS(s)	GS
Yes	45	13†	9*	14‡	81
Blank or ambiguous	16**	7	11	11	53
No	12††	13§	5	2	22

* *One says: 'if genuinely talented'.*
‡ *One: 'if so inclined'.*
† *One: 'if it wanted to', one 'if good enough', two 'would mind'.*
** *One says 'daughter yes, son no'.*
†† *One: 'unless he wanted to'.*
§ *One: 'only if exceptionally talented'. One says 'other plans'.*

Question 14

What statues are there on the Lime Street side of St George's Hall?

	WAG	Int	L	GS(s)	GS
No answer, don't know, or wrong	24	10	10	9	30
LIONS*	24	33	17	14	122

	WAG	Int	L	GS(s)	GS
(*of which Four lions*	*1*	*17*	*1*	*1*	*4*)
HORSEMEN†	16	13	7	4	70
Victoria	23	18	1	2	8
Albert	18	17	1	4	4
other royalty	7	1	4	0	16‡
DISRAELI	10§	11**	0	5	0
GENERAL EARLE††	5	2	0	0	0
WAR MEMORIAL	12‡‡	22	2	1	19
DOLPHINS (*on lamps*)	3	1	0	0	0
RELIEFS	0	4	0	1§§	0

Other suggestions include Walpole, Birkenhead, Gladstone, 'various Victorians', 'Local philanthropists', 'historic men of battle' and 'Victorian stuff'. A student at Bangor said 'I do not consider them statues'.

* *Quantities given from* 1 *to* 5. *Descriptions include 'Landseer', 'Queen's Beasts', 'Albert and the Lions'* (2–3 *times*)
† *Identified as Wellington, St George, King George IV, V or VI, etc.*
‡ *Usually named as one of the Georges.*
§ *Once identified as Shakespeare, once not at all.*
** *Twice described as 'man'.*
†† *Only once identified correctly. Also called Gordon, Kitchener and (very accurately). 'somebody brandishing a sword sunhelmeted'.*
‡‡ *Includes one mention of the sculptor, Tyson Smith. This is the only time the sculptor of any of these objects is named.*
§§ *Termed 'Greek reproductions'.*

I have omitted mentions of the Wellington monument, as its position is ambiguous in terms of the question.

Question 15

What is over the entrance to Lewis's?

	WAG	Int	L	GS(s)	GS
No answer, or don't know	10	6	8	*1*	*16*
SPIRIT OF LIVERPOOL RESURGENT *or something near**	13	6	7	15	27
EPSTEIN	27†	23	7	21‡	9
MAN, *statue or figure*	41	40	11	6	125
specifically NAKED	19	9	9	2	57

specifically on PROW	3	3	2	0	22
RELIEFS	11	7	1	1	0

* *Such as Spirit of Freedom, Spirit of Youth, The New Life of Liverpool, Upsurgence of Liverpool, Liverpool Rejuvenate.*

† *Twice identified as 'Adam', once as Apollo.*

‡ *Once identified as 'David'.*

Other suggestions included Commerce and 'Spirit of Lewis's'. There were also some ten derogatory remarks such as 'Cooo!', 'not nice', 'monstrocity' (sic) and 'vulgar looking man'.

Question 16

What is over the main Mersey Tunnel entrance?

	WAG	Int	L	GS(s)	GS
No answer, don't know, wrong or hopelessly vague	45*	23	13	13	68
KING & QUEEN†	25	24	10	10	58‡
(of which George and Mary	*20*	*19*	*8*	*8***	*34*§)
One monarch only	3	3	3	1	10
WINGED RELIEF††	8	10	5	4	25

* *'Too familiar with it to know', said a member of Crosby Borough Engineer's Department.*

† *Among monarchs suggested, in various improbable couplings, were Edward VI, Queen Anne and George IIV (sic).*

‡ *Including two descriptions just as 'man and woman' and 'two statues'.*

§ *Five of these suggest that the statues are busts or heads only.*

** *Includes one description of the pair as seated.*

†† *Only one exact description. Often described as Liverpool coat of arms.*

Question 17

Is it a good thing that the Council should spend money on works of art for:

(a) *improving the look of the city?*

(b) *the city collection in the Walker Gallery?*

		WAG	Int	L	GS(s)	GS
(a)	*Yes*	68*	39†	22	25	120
	Indifferent	3	2‡	1	0	18
	No	10§	13	3	1	16

(b) *Yes*	77	40	13	24	80
Indifferent	4	4	7**	2	39
No	3†††	10	6	1	34††

* *One: 'But not to the detriment of vital social services'.*
† *One: 'When slum clearance has been completed'.*
‡ *Includes a visitor from Solihull, who says 'No – if monuments. Yes – if like Gabriel at Coventry'.*
§ *One: 'It would be useless'.*
** *One: 'Within strict limits'.*
†† *Includes seven who under question* 11 *said that the gallery should be added to.*
††† *Includes one who under question* 11 *said that the gallery should be added to.*

Would you be willing to see an extra halfpenny rate devoted to:

(a) *works of art on new buildings or in conjunction with the new planning schemes?*
(b) *improving the city's collection?*

	WAG	Int	L	GS(s)	GS
(a) *Yes*	59	38	18	23	—
(*of whom actual Liverpool rate-payers*	*19*	*22*	*8*	*19*	—)
Indifferent	9	4	3	1	—
(*of whom actual Liverpool rate-payers*	*1*	*3*	*1*	*1*	—)
No	10	11	5	1	—
(*of whom actual Liverpool rate-payers*	*6*	*6*	*2*	*1*	—)
(b) *Yes*	70	33	10	23	—
(*of whom actual Liverpool rate-payers*	*24*	*22*	*4*	*19*	—)
Indifferent	5	6	6	2	—
(*of whom actual Liverpool rate-payers*	*1*	*3*	*4*	*2*	—)
No	3*	13	9	1	—
(*of whom actual Liverpool rate-payers*	*0*	*5*	*1*	*1*	—)
Rates included in rent	19	2	4	12	—

* *Includes one who said Walker Gallery should be added to, under* 11 *above.*

The Gateacre pupils have been omitted as not having enough experience of the rate burden.

What is the rateable value of your house or business?
Would you personally be willing to spend (½d rate on this sum) a year extra on your rates?

	WAG	Int	L	GS(s)	GS
Yes	18	20*	4	14	—
Blank	0	0	2	1	—
No	2†	7	5‡	0	—

* *Two specified 'Walker Art, not outside.'*

† *One states: 'Rates far too high already'. The other appears to be a schoolboy and not a ratepayer.*

‡ *Includes two who said Yes to* (a) *and* (b) *above.*

Question 18

Would you look through the set of cards and sort out which you definitely like, which you don't care about, and which you definitely dislike?

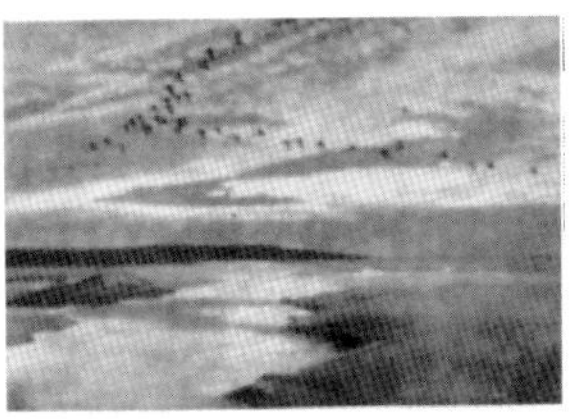

1 **Peter Scott:** Brent Geese Flighting under a Mackerel Sky. *Medici Society* PC 1213

	WAG	Int	L	GS(s)	GS
Like	24	40	24	11	124
Don't care	19	7	0	8	29
Dislike	27	6	1	8	12

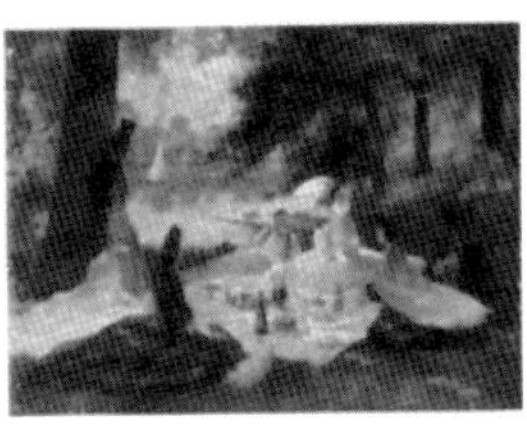

2 **Doris Zinkeisen:** The Picnic. *Medici Society* PC 1333

	WAG	Int	L	GS(s)	GS
Like	34	29	7	8	70
Don't care	18	12	15	12	57
Dislike	18	14	3	5	30

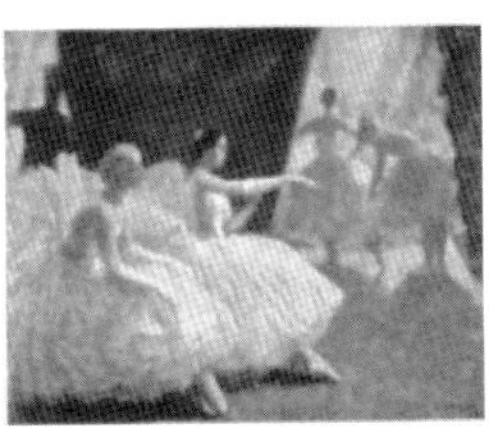

3 **Dame Laura Knight,** DBE, RA: Ballet. *In the Lady Lever Art Gallery. Medici Society* PC 957

	WAG	Int	L	GS(s)	GS
Like	18	28	13	6	99
Don't care	23	7	9	11	30
Dislike	25	18	2	8	36

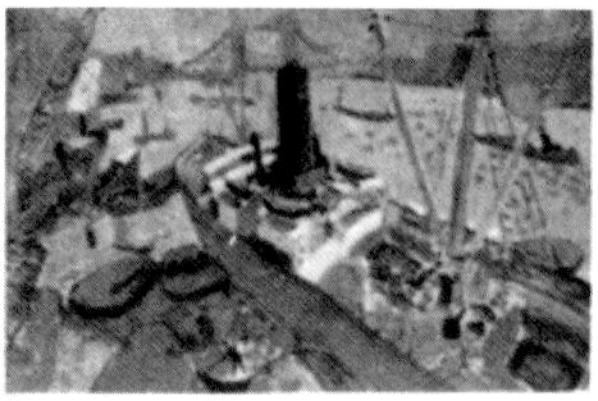

4 **André Derain**: The Pool of London 1906. *Tate Gallery* (6030)

	WAG	Int	L	GS(s)	GS
Like	24	21	7	7	33
Don't care	27	12	15	14	54
Dislike	17	21	3	6	76

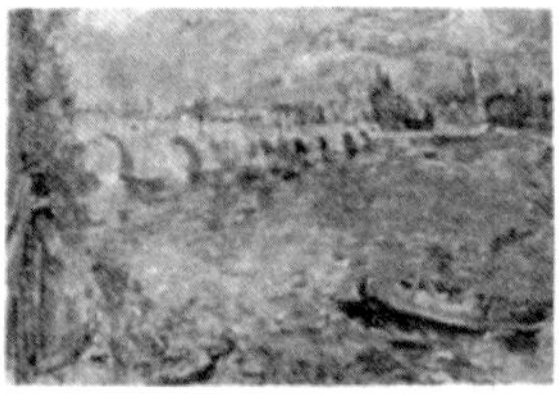

5 **Oskar Kokoschka**: The Karlsbrücke in Prague. *National Gallery, Prague. Pallas Postcard* 1251.

Like	35	31	11	11	65
Don't care	21	18	9	13	47
Dislike	8	7	5	3	45

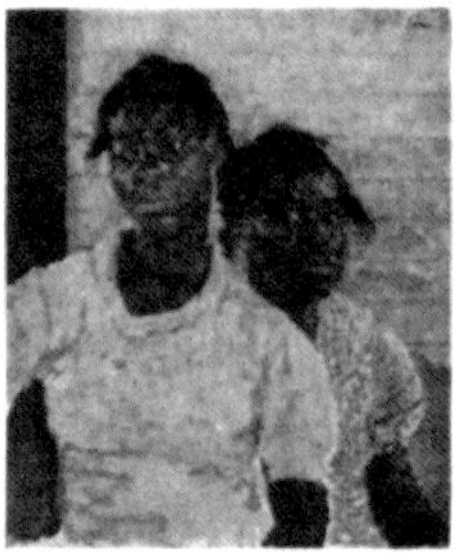

6 **Augustus John**, OM, RA: Two Jamaican Girls. *Walker Art Gallery.*

Like	38	36	8	14	57
Don't care	19	7	11	11	65
Dislike	7	10	5	0	37

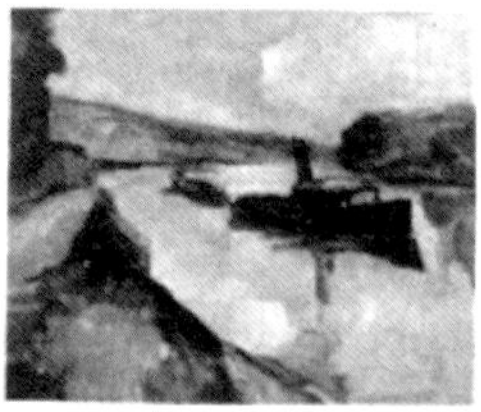

7 **Maurice de Vlaminck**: Environs de Rouen. *Walker Art Gallery.*

Like	39	34	10	14	78
Don't care	20	13	14	10	54
Dislike	8	7	1	2	28

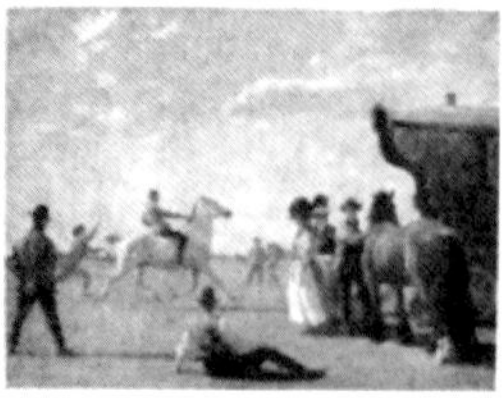

8 **Sir Alfred Munnings**, PPRA: Gipsy Life. *Aberdeen Art Gallery. Medici Society* PC 1215

Like	18	23	8	3	112
Don't care	23	20	12	15	43
Dislike	24	11	3	5	8

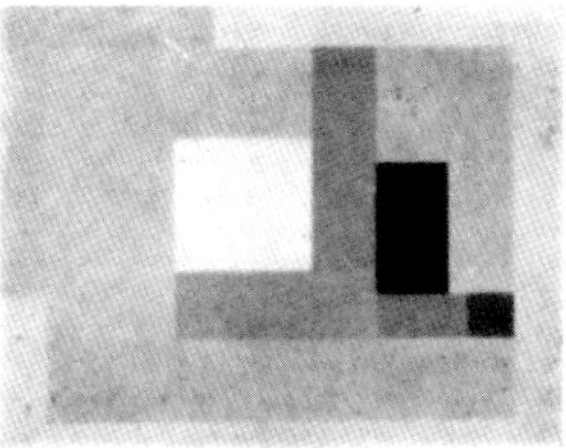

9 Ben Nicholson: Painting 1937. *Tate Gallery* (*T* 50)

	WAG	Int	L	GS(s)	GS
Like	22	6	7	9	35
Don't care	22	13	8	12	57
Dislike	25	32	11	6	71

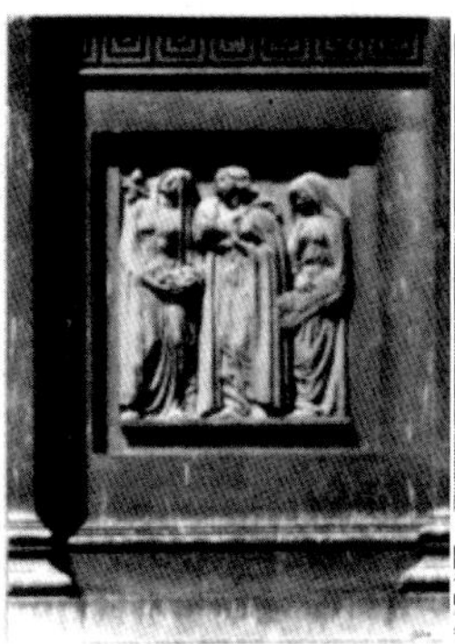

10 St George's Hall, Liverpool: Carved Panel (by Conrad Dressler). *Photograph by Eric de Maré. A Gordon Fraser Card.* BKO 2–15.

	WAG	Int	L	GS(s)	GS
Like	18	29	8	8	56
Don't care	31	12	13	14	72
Dislike	11	12	3	3	31

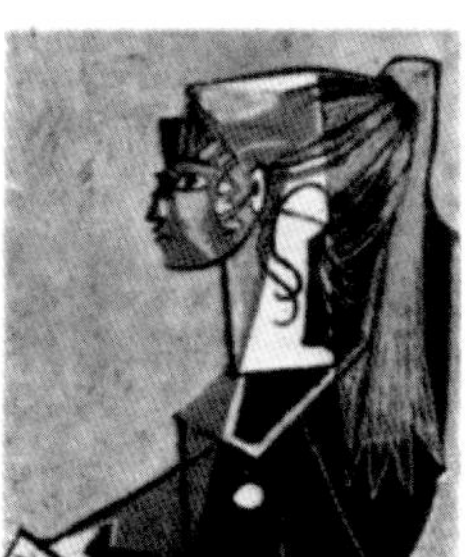

11 Pablo Picasso: Portrait of a Young Woman. Version III. *Collection of the Artist. Soho Card* 371.

	WAG	Int	L	GS(s)	GS
Like	44	20	8	16	67
Don't care	9	9	5	9	48
Dislike	16	26	13	2	45

See illustration 92 on p. 134

12 Victor Pasmore: Square Motif, Blue and Gold: The Eclipse 1950. *Tate Gallery* (5974).

	WAG	Int	L	GS(s)	GS
Like	24	3	2	5	29
Don't care	10	12	6	10	45
Dislike	34	37	18	11	92

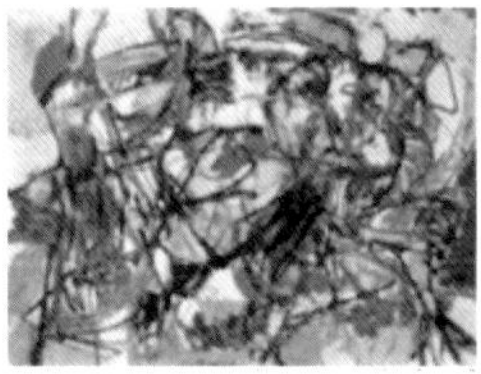

13 **Karel Appel**: Amorous Dance 1955. *Tate Gallery* (*T.* 212).

	WAG	Int	L	GS(s)	GS
Like	25	15	6	10	44
Don't care	20	5	4	8	46
Dislike	19	34	16	8	76

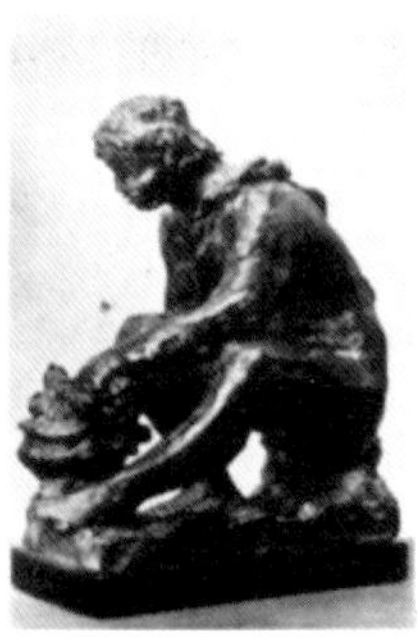

14 **Pierre Auguste Renoir**: The Little Blacksmith. *Walker Art Gallery. English Life Publications, Derby.* 6753***

	WAG	Int	L	GS(s)	GS
Like	41	27	10	11	52
Don't care	14	13	10	12	65
Dislike	6	13	4	1	39

See illustration 94 on p. 135

15 **Antoine Pevsner**: Maquette of a Monument Symbolizing the Liberation of the Spirit, 1952. *The Tate Gallery.*

	WAG	Int	L	GS(s)	GS
Like	38	19	11	5	78
Don't care	6	8	8	18	46
Dislike	19	25	8	4	39

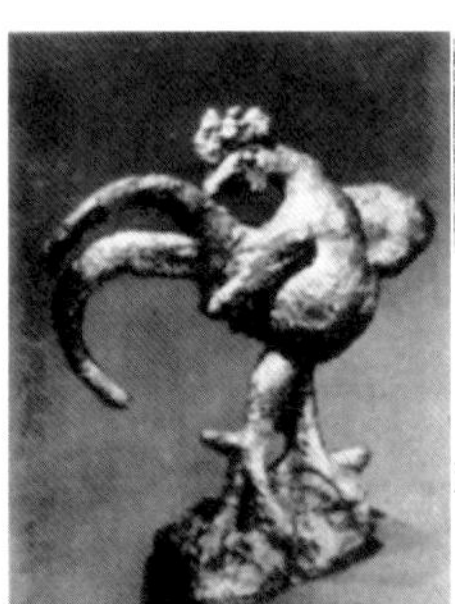

16 **Pablo Picasso**: Cock 1932. *The Tate Gallery.*

	WAG	Int	L	GS(s)	GS
Like	19	6	4	6	23
Don't care	19	7	5	10	34
Dislike	25	40	14	11	101

See illustration 91 on p. 134

17 **Germaine Richier**: Water, 1953–4. *The Tate Gallery.*

	WAG	Int	L	GS(s)	GS
Like	27	3	1	1	17
Don't care	13	6	6	4	30
Dislike	29	44	17	22	117

See illustration 93 on p. 135

18 L. S. Lowry: The Fever Van. *Walker Art Gallery.*

	WAG	Int	L	GS(s)	GS
Like	44	11	6	17	87
Don't care	22	12	12	9	51
Dislike	3	8	6	0	20

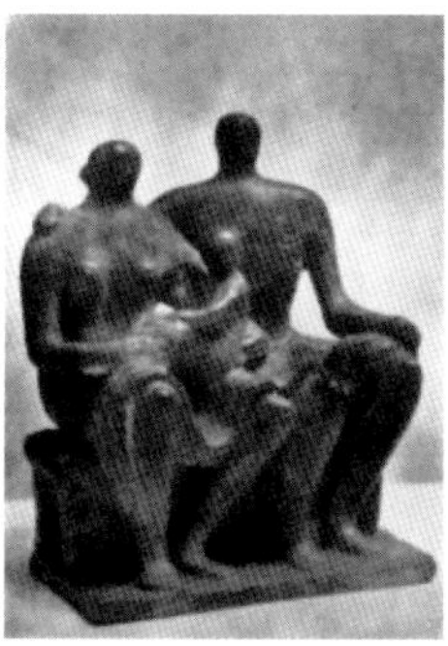

19 Henry Moore: Project for the Family, 1944. *Tate Gallery.*

Like	38	8	2	7	22
Don't care	10	5	6	11	54
Dislike	18	42	16	9	79

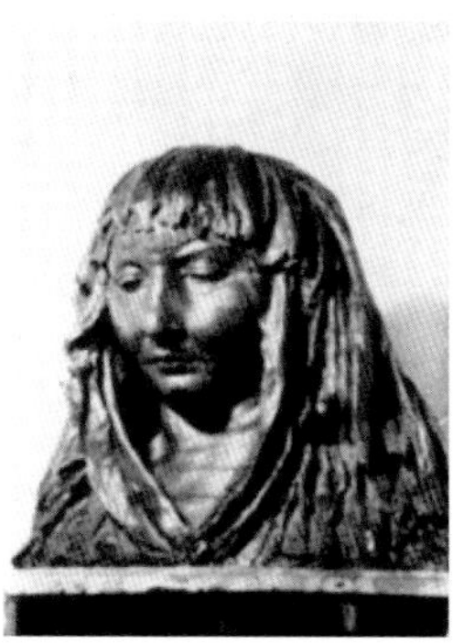

20 Sir Jacob Epstein, KBE: Mrs Epstein, 1918. *Sir Alec Martin. Photograph by Hans Wild. A Gordon Fraser card.* SKEJ–7

Like	31	27	11	12	56
Don't care	23	11	9	10	52
Dislike	8	13	3	4	47

NB The seven cards of sculpture (10, 14, 15, 16, 17, 19 and 20) were black-and-white, the remainder coloured. Special points to note are the subjects of 3 (ballet), 4 and 7 (ships), and 6 (coloured people). Also the controversial names: Munnings (8), Picasso (11 and 16) and Epstein (20). Four cards were of works in the Walker Gallery (6, 7, 14, 18), one in the Lady Lever (8) and one of a St George's Hall sculpture (10). All these represent factors affecting judgment.

APPENDIX B *Comparative data for five cities*

	Genoa	Marseilles	Antwerp	Rotterdam	Boston	Liverpool
1 *Population*	802,991 (1961)	783,738 (1962)	251,419 (1962)	731,500 (1963)	697,938 (1962)	747,490 (1961)
2 *Revenue from taxation*	£3,923,600 (1962) (6,834,934,519 lire)	£10,000,000 local taxes (137,601,038 fr.)	£2,762,000 (1962) (382,230,762 FB)	£15,800,000 from taxation and 'Municipal Fund' (fl. 158,160,000)	£54,725,000 (1962) ($152,230,470)	£12,946,508 (1962-3)
3 *Annual average tonnage through port 1958–62 (net registered tons)*	23,714,976	51,024,604	36,051,740	63,746,000 (1962)	19,642,517	28,896,996
4 *Main Public Art Galleries*	1 Palazzo Rosso 2 Palazzo Bianco 3 Galleria d' arte moderna (and seven museums)	1 Musée de Beaux-Arts 2 Musée Cantini 3 Musée Grober –Labadie	1 Royal Gallery of Fine Arts 2 Rubens's house 3 Middelheim sculpture park 4 Mayer van den Bergh museum 5 Ridder Smid van Gelder museum	Boymans/van Beuningen Musem	Museum of Fine Arts	1 Walker Art Gallery 2 Sudley Art Gallery and Museum
5 *Expenditure on principal art gallery*	£87,350 (1962) (152,159,027 lire)	£21,400 (1963 est.) (292,856 fr.)	1 £61,640 (1958) paid half by city half by state 2 £62,360 (1961)	no data	£528,600 (1961) from private sources only	£112,595 (1959–60)
6 *Amount devoted to purchase of pictures out of municipal funds*	No allocation. Decided *ad hoc*	£1,240	1 State grant of £25,300. No municipal contributions	£27,500 (1963)	(Income from private sources available: £200,000 in 1961)	£10,000

	Genoa	Marseilles	Antwerp	Rotterdam	Boston	Liverpool
			2 £16,000 of which c. £10,000 for sculpture park			
7 *Number of visitors per year at principal gallery*	121,533 (1962)	17,830 (1962) excluding free admissions and school visits	140,576 (1962)	94,000 (1962)	750,000 (1962)	125,427 (1962/3)
8 *Art schools*	Liceo artistico Nicolò Barabinò	Ecole des Beaux-Arts	Royal Academy of Arts City pays 44 per cent	Academy for Plastic Arts 30 per cent municipal	1 Massachussetts College of Art 2 Boston Museum School Both private (Also 8 others)	Regional College of Art
9 *Number of students*	452 (1962–3)	c.1000	c.1000	c.550	2 1000 including part-time	335 full-time 1,751 part-time (1962)
10 *Expenditure on art school(s)*	£35,241 (1962)	£286,000 (1963 budget)	£25,810 city contribution (1958)	no data	None from public funds	£213,575
11 *Private and commercial galleries*	7	5 plus	5	5	? 17	4
12 *University departments concerned with the visual arts*	Institute of Art history		National Higher Institute of Art	None	Boston University School of Applied and Fine Arts (also departments at Harvard, Brandeis, etc.)	School of Architecture, Department of Civic Design
13 *Expenditure on publicly commissioned murals, mosaics, sculptures, etc.*	None	£6960 from state funds (1 per cent of school building costs)	£7200 from city £36,000 from state funds	£35,000 (1962)	c. £3500 (maintenance and upkeep only)	

The cities supplying these details were also invited to name any notable painters and sculptors living in or near the city. The best known seemed to be Floris Jespers and Baron Opsomer (Antwerp), Bernard Buffet (near Marseilles), G. Romijn and L. van Roode (Rotterdam). Boston grandly claims at least 300 recognized practising artists.

They were asked if they gave preferential treatment to local artists. Rotterdam did not answer, Antwerp said not, Genoa gives a scholarship of about £300 a year to a local artist. Genoa, Antwerp, Rotterdam and Boston all said that there were no distinctions between their political parties in art matters. Asked for instances of business or trade union patronage, Antwerp said that two Zadkine sculptures had been presented by the Agence Maritime Internationale and the Banque de Paris et des Pays-Bas; Rotterdam cited the support given to art by firms who put works of art in or near their buildings or present works to the city. No city reported any case of trade union patronage.

Unfortunately it proved impossible to get comparable details from Bremen, Valencia and San Francisco. Some incomplete information came however from the Polish port of Gdansk. The estimated population there is 300,000, the port traffic (for 1962) 3,199,377 tons. The public gallery is part of the Pomeranian Museum; there is also a School of Fine Arts. There has been much reconstruction and restoration of the city's historic buildings since 1945, and the artists and the school have taken an active part in this. A report says that 'the guiding principle in decoration of the historic reconstructed buildings seems to have been the reproduction of traditional designs while using modern techniques with colouring and materials'.

APPENDIX C

Project for a 'Look at Liverpool' Exhibition

This project was worked out by me in consultation with the Liverpool painters Adrian Henri, Arthur Ballard and Peter MacKarell.

Objects are:

1 To exploit the current interest in Liverpool. To show that the city's vitality is not confined to its singers and guitarists, but that these are part of a larger pattern.
2 To convey the place's visual impact, which is like nothing else in Europe and contains much that is of unique architectural and historical interest.
3 To show off its peculiar artistic talents, both latent (in the schoolchildren, etc.) and professional; to set them tasks and to make Liverpool people as well as others more aware of them.
4 To show them in combination with the new plans and with the best of the old heritage, and in this way to suggest a possible visual climate for the future.

Scheme is for a travelling exhibition which could be sent to London, Hamburg, Paris, Rotterdam, Antwerp and anywhere else where the name of Liverpool now arouses interest. It would not be primarily an art exhibition. Pictures and sculptures would be included on the same footing as photos, models or anything else: i.e. as so many means of contributing to a total Liverpool impression.

Method of achieving this:

1 Collection of relevant photographic and documentary materials, models, poems, recordings, etc.
2 Selection of works of art from nominated artists. Further selection from certain schools and from outstanding amateurs. (All these would have been asked to put forward work and given an outline of the scheme.)
3 Writing of a script – the basis for arrangement of material and writing of captions.
4 Engagement of a first-rate professional exhibition designer, to mount the exhibition so that it can be shown in a variety of halls and spaces.
5 Artists to add further embellishments and diversions as the show takes shape.
6 Arrangement and rehearsal of any 'live' events.

Finance would have to be by the Corporation or by interested Liverpool industries, or by a combination of the two. (Industry might take advertising space on the free surfaces of the exhibition, or might care to offer prizes for participating artists.) The cost of the major project (A) might, I understand from an experienced designer, be anything from £5,000 to £15,000, plus the designer's fees which are standard at 10 per cent on £5,000, increasing 1 per cent for every £500 less. Project (B) is a much reduced version.

The absolute essential is perfection of finish in the mounting. Well-presented, the show could make a forceful and original impression, extending and consolidating the territory won for Liverpool in people's minds by the success of the music groups and the footballers. But a complicated mixed exhibition like this cannot afford the least mediocrity in mounting, captioning or lighting.

Look at Liverpool : Project A

Entrance – through a mock-up of the Lime Street cutting, showing texture of its sides.
Floor – railway lines.
In the cutting: The Gibson statue of Huskisson with material about him, the Liverpool and Manchester railway and his death, possibly models of that railway.
Ceiling: blue sky, or night sky.

Space 1 **First Impressions**
Liverpool children
St George's Hall
The Library – Walker Gallery group of buildings
Other Victorian architecture
Statesmen associated with Liverpool: Canning, Gladstone, Brougham, Creevey, etc.
Roscoe and the anti-slavers
The docks
Ships and ship models
Nineteenth-century trade (labels, advertisements, documents, etc.)
The mixed population
Paintings conveying spirit of the place
Poems

Space 2 **The churches**
Scott's cathedral
Gibberd's cathedral
Lutyens plans
Designs related to any of these (for windows, etc.)
Dooley sculptures
Orange Lodge banners
Photos of processions and of eminent clergy

Space 3 **The arts**
Liverpool paintings from Stubbs, Windus to now
Sculpture
Coloured projections of further paintings (to be changed)
Roscoe and his collection
The Moores competition: story and examples
The Royal Liverpool Philharmonic: documents and photos
Facilities for hearing its recordings

Musica Viva
Fritz Spiegl
Liverpool Theatres, actors and comedians

Space 4 **Grotto by G. W. Jardine** (if agreeable)

Space 5 **Football**
Footballers and the two teams
Football crowds
Historic moments
The pools: how they work
Historic cheques (transfer fees, pools winnings)
Nets, goalposts, etc.
Paintings relating to football and sport

Space 6 **Redevelopment**
The slums
The City Centre Plan, drawings, model etc
Plans for remainder of the city
Gordon Cullen drawings
New housing
Comparable schemes actually executed
Paintings: anything that fits the rebuilding theme or conveys the slums
Any new architecture of merit
Composite work on this theme by Maghull Grammar School pupils (if agreeable)

Space 7 **Pop Music**
A Cavern-type space. Also to be used for actual performances
Documents and other souvenirs of the Beatles
Documents and other souvenirs of other groups
Photographs from *Merseybeat* (now *Music Echo*)
Facilities for listening to records
Record sleeves
Lennon's drawings and any others by musicians
Paintings: Stuart Sutcliffe and any others relevant to the theme.

Space 8 **Natural talent**
Remarkable sequence of paintings by patient at Rainhill
Works of art by schoolchildren
Pottery and metal sculpture from Gateacre Comprehensive School
Projections from Teacher Training Departments at College of Art
Constructions from Bluecoat School
Children's poems
Photographs of school buildings, old and new
Pictures by amateurs

These spaces to be formed of adjustable units, so that they can be connected to fit the total space available, whether elongated or compact. If necessary one or more can be omitted. Projection of slides to be done by back projection; the slides to be changeable. There should be facilities for showing films (*Morning in the Streets* and other TV features on Liverpool). Recordings to be played in the spaces: Stan Kelly songs, children's songs, other Liverpool music, performances by Beatles and other groups, poetry. Individual listening to be possible too (? by earphones). Listeners to be able to pick their own records for earphone listening, as in a record shop.
Painting and sculpture. Besides what is specified above, anything else that fits in.
The ubiquitousness of children. To be conveyed by the occasional blown-up photograph.

Look at Liverpool : Project B

Section 1 **The place as it is**

Photographs of Victorian architecture (Graham Smith, etc.)
Designs for St George's Hall (Cockerell, Stevens)
The Docks. (Eric de Maré photos. Detailed drawings)
Scott's cathedral designs
Nineteenth-century trade. (Documents, bills, etc.)
The slums (Graham Smith's photos)
Walker's pubs
Liverpool children (photos)
The mixture of populations (statistics and photos)
Religious banners and processions
Stills from *Z-cars*
Paintings, etc.: Topographical
Henri's Liverpool 8 pictures
Jardine collages
Horsfield view of Mount Street
School drawings (Breckfield, St Martin's)
Music: Stan Kelly songs. Liverpool music picked by Fritz Spiegl. *Z-cars* march
Poetry: from Henri, McGough, Patten, schoolchildren, etc.

Section 2 **Sport and entertainment**

The two football teams. Photos and documents
Football crowds (Photos)
The pools. Facts and statistics
The Topham Trophy (designs and history)
Documents and souvenirs of the Beatles and other groups
Photos from *Merseybeat* (Peter Kaye)
Listening booths with earphones for hearing records
Record sleeves
Drawings by John Lennon and other musicians
Paintings: MacKarell (football)
Walsh (racing, etc.)
Sutcliffe (and his associations with Beatles)
Poems read to jazz (Patten, McGough, Gorman)

Section 3 **The arts**

The Moores show (facts, and photos of prizewinners)
The Walker Gallery (with photos of some pictures)
The Royal Liverpool Philharmonic (Documents, photos and recordings, again with listening booths)
The Liverpool Playhouse: its productions and actors
The Everyman Theatre
Paintings: (a) Historical. Windus, John, Henry Carr, Steer
(b) Present day: Artists already mentioned, plus Ballard, Sidney Bonner, Edkins, McKinlay
(c) Sequence by a patient at Rainhill
Sculpture: Dooley
Riley
School work: Gateacre Comprehensive School, Bluecoat School, examples from Teacher Training Department at College of Art

Section 4 **The future**

Model of the City Centre Plan
Exhibit from the Planning Department
New City housing (Plans, photos, etc.)
Gordon Cullen drawings
Gibberd's Catholic Cathedral (With designs for windows, etc.)
Sculpture for the Littlewoods building
New architecture of note
Paintings: Henri after Ensor
Schoolchildren's pictures on the reconstruction theme
Composite feature (pictures, paper, sculpture, figures and so on) by pupils of Maghull Grammar School on this theme
Poems
Photographs of Liverpool children

These four sections are for planning purposes only. They should not be given the titles or divided into water-tight compartments but allowed to run into each other. In this version the exhibition could be mounted on screens which could then be set up to form different flow patterns according to the varying space available, in no predetermined sequence.

At some points they could be joined together to form larger surfaces. All other elements such as lighting, loudspeaker system, floor coverings and any suspended exhibits, would then be fixed to suit the pattern chosen.

INDEX

Note: Page numbers in italic indicate proposals affecting the body in question. Bold numerals refer to illustrations. Items referring to postcard reproductions used in the questionnaire are prefaced by the letters p.c.